Core/Hardware Technology & DOS/Windows Exams

Scott Berkel
John Alumbaugh

New Riders

201 West 103rd Street, Indianapolis, Indiana 46290

A+ Fast Track

Copyright © 1999 by New Riders Publishing

All rights reserved. No part of this book shall be reproduced, stored in a retrieval system, or transmitted by any means, electronic, mechanical, photocopying, recording, or otherwise, without written permission from the publisher. No patent liability is assumed with respect to the use of the information contained herein. Although every precaution has been taken in the preparation of this book, the publisher and author(s) assume no responsibility for errors or omissions. Neither is any liability assumed for damages resulting from the use of the information contained herein.

International Standard Book Number: 0-7357-0028-1

Library of Congress Catalog Card Number: 98-89487

Printed in the United States of America

First Printing: March, 1999

01   00   99   4   3   2   1

Trademarks

All terms mentioned in this book that are known to be trademarks or service marks have been appropriately capitalized. New Riders Publishing cannot attest to the accuracy of this information. Use of a term in this book should not be regarded as affecting the validity of any trademark or service mark.

A+ Certification is a testing program sponsored by the Computing Technology Industry Association (CompTIA).

Warning and Disclaimer

Every effort has been made to make this book as complete and as accurate as possible, but no warranty or fitness is implied. The information provided is on an "as is" basis. The authors and the publisher shall have neither liability nor responsibility to any person or entity with respect to any loss or damages arising from the information contained in this book.

Executive Editor
Mary Foote

Acquisitions Editor
Steve Weiss

Development Editor
Bryan Morgan

Managing Editor
Sarah Kearns

Project Editor
Alissa Cayton

Copy Editor
Audra McFarland

Indexer
Chris Barrick

Technical Reviewers
Shawn McNutt
Michelle Poole

Proofreaders
John Rahm
Elise Walter

Layout Technician
Steve Balle-Gifford

A+ Fast Track
DOS/Windows Exam

Study with it. Learn with it. Cross-reference to other materials with it. Create your study notes with it. Review with it. Use it as your #1 supplement to studying for the DOS/Windows exam.

PART III: WHAT'S IMPORTANT TO KNOW ABOUT THE A+ DOS/WINDOWS EXAM

Five simple chapters that cover each exam objective and subobjective:

Each featuring: Easy-to-read tables   Bulleted lists
                        Unique At-A-Glance boxes   To-the-point text

Designed to let you identify what you already know and what you need to study. All from an insider's perspective: Think of this as the instructor's class notes you've always wanted to have prior to test time.

PART IV: INSIDE THE A+ DOS/WINDOWS EXAM

Features classroom-tested review strategies:

- The *Fast Facts Review* chapter is your pre-test digest of every critical point you should be ready for prior to writing the exam. **Page 465**
- The *Insider's Spin on the DOS/Windows Exam* tells you what you really need to know to be mentally prepared for the exam. **Page 497**
- *Hotlist of Exam-Critical Concepts* covers the lexicon and terminology you'll likely see used in the actual exam. **Page 509**
- *Sample Test Questions* quiz you on each key point covered in Part III. **Page 511**
- Pulled from the files of the author, *Did You Know?* offers real-world applications for the technology covered in the exam. **Page 523**

Plus: Assess your knowledge with the *Objective Review Notes* section after Part III of this book (dark-edged pages). Page 437. Work through the material in this book and in other study materials you may have, and chart your progress. Cross-reference to other materials you are using. Make notes and use them. Keep your knowledge base centralized in the *Objective Review Notes*.

Study for your exam—and pass—with the instructor-tested, classroom-proven approach designed for the advanced candidate.

Contents at a Glance

TABLE OF CONTENTS

10 Insider's Spin on the Core/Hardware Exam   253

16 Installation, Configuration, and Upgrading 345

17 Diagnosing and Troubleshooting   377

ABOUT THE AUTHORS

Scott Berkel is a Microsoft Certified Trainer and A+ Instructor and is certified on both the DOS/Windows and Macintosh A+ tracks. With more than 11 years of experience in the PC industry, Scott holds over 30 other certifications including Microsoft's MCSE, MCT, MCP, IBM PSE, two Novell CNAs, and a multitude of manufacturer-specific hardware certifications. He has authored material on multiple projects for Macmillan and New Riders Publishing, including *A+ Certification Top Score* software, a 1,000-question certification practice and review software package. Scott works as a Senior Consultant and Project Manager for Xerox Connect, Inc., a world-wide information technology services provider. Scott lives in Indianapolis, Indiana with his wife and two children.

John Alumbaugh holds the following certifications: MCSE, MCP, MCT, CNE, CNA, and CompTIA A+. The Operating Systems Team Manager for one of the largest network integrators in the Midwest, John Alumbaugh brings 9 years experience with Microsoft operating systems to *A+ Fast Track*. He is also a Microsoft Certified Trainer and trains 20–30 field engineers a month on the ins and outs of troubleshooting Microsoft Windows 95 environments.

ABOUT THE TECHNICAL REVIEWERS

Shawn McNutt has a Masters in Education from Lesley College in Cambridge, Massachusetts and is a Microsoft Certified Systems Engineer in Windows NT 4.0. He is also an A+ Certified Technician for both Macintosh and DOS/Windows environments. Since 1988, he has provided network installation, engineering, administration, computer repair, and training services to public school systems and corporations. He is currently a network engineer for Saco River Telegraph and Telephone Company and teaches for Lesley College. He also reviews training products in a monthly column for *Service News* magazine. He credits his accomplishments to the love and support of his wife Dawn.

Michelle Poole is a consultant for the Indianapolis office of Xerox Connect. She spends about half her time in the classroom and the remainder doing consulting engagements. Michelle has a Bachelor of Science degree in Management Information Systems and is certified as a Microsoft Certified Systems Engineer (MCSE) and Microsoft Certified Trainer (MCT). Her hobbies include biking, cooking, and gardening. If you want to drop her a line, her email address is `Michelle.Poole@Connect.Xerox.com`.

DEDICATION

To Ron Berkel, my dad, for teaching me to be a go-getter, and to Brenda, my wife, for putting up with the hours and the stress of going and getting.

—Scott Berkel

This book is dedicated to my wife Lesley, who reluctantly left me alone to be able to write it, and my son Isaac, who thinks it's cool that Dad works on the 'puter.

—John Alumbaugh

ACKNOWLEDGMENTS

First and foremost, I have to thank Steve Weiss for believing in me and this project. Second, I thank John Alumbaugh, who helped me through the rough spots and also wrote the portion of the book devoted to the A+ Operating Systems exam. I would also like to thank the rest of the project team for their hard work and last minute revisions. Thank you also to all those who have known me, helped me, cursed me, nurtured me, laughed at me, and befriended me. I am what I am today through influences such as these.

—Scott Berkel

Writing a book has been one of my goals for some time now. Writing *THIS* book has made completing the goal that much richer. I would like to thank the entire New Riders team for making this a good experience. Thanks, to the tech editors, Shawn McNutt and Michelle Poole, for supplying fresh eyes to my tired ones. Thanks to Steve Weiss and Bryan Morgan for providing the new guy some direction and support. Finally, thanks most of all to my longtime friend and coauthor, Scott Berkel, for convincing me that A+ is a worthwhile pursuit and for giving me this opportunity. Again, thank you all.

—John Alumbaugh

TELL US WHAT YOU THINK!

As the reader of this book, you are our most important critic and commentator. We value your opinion and want to know what we're doing right, what we could do better, what areas you'd like to see us publish in, and any other words of wisdom you're willing to pass our way.

As the Executive Editor for the Certification team at New Riders Publishing, I welcome your comments. You can fax, email, or write me directly to let me know what you did or didn't like about this book—as well as what we can do to make our books stronger.

Please note that I cannot help you with technical problems related to the topic of this book, and that due to the high volume of mail I receive, I might not be able to reply to every message.

When you write, please be sure to include this book's title and author, as well as your name and phone or fax number. I will carefully review your comments and share them with the authors and editors who worked on the book.

Fax: 317-581-4663

Email: certification@mcp.com

Mail: Mary Foote
            Executive Editor
            Certification
            New Riders Publishing
            201 West 103rd Street
            Indianapolis, IN 46290 USA

Introduction

The *A+ Fast Track* was written to be a study aid for people preparing for CompTIA A+ exams. The book is intended to help reinforce and clarify information with which the student is already familiar. This book is not intended to be a single source for student preparation, but rather a review of information and a set of practice tests to help increase the student's likelihood of success when taking the actual exam.

WHO SHOULD READ THIS BOOK

The *A+ Fast Track* is specifically intended to help students prepare for CompTIA's Core/Hardware Technology and DOS/Windows exams.

HOW THIS BOOK HELPS YOU

This book is designed to help you make the most of your study time by presenting concise summaries of information that you need to understand in order to succeed on both exams.

HOW TO USE THIS BOOK

When you think you're well prepared for either exam, use this book to test your knowledge.

After you have taken the practice tests and feel confident in the material on which you were tested, you are ready to schedule your exams. Use this book for a final quick review just before taking the tests to make sure all the important concepts are set in your mind.

PART I: WHAT'S IMPORTANT TO KNOW ABOUT THE A+ CORE/HARDWARE TECHNOLOGY EXAM

The CompTIA Core/Hardware Technology certification exam measures your ability to install, configure, support, and troubleshoot a wide variety of computer hardware and peripherals. It focuses on determining your skill in eight major categories:

- Installation, Configuration, and Upgrading
- Diagnosing and Troubleshooting
- Safety and Preventive Maintenance
- Motherboards/Processors/Memory
- Printers
- Portable Computers
- Basic Networking
- Customer Satisfaction

The CompTIA Core/Hardware Technology certification exam uses these categories to measure your ability. Before you take this exam, you should be proficient in the job skills talked about in the following sections.

INSTALLATION, CONFIGURATION, AND UPGRADING

This domain requires the knowledge and skills to identify, install, configure, and upgrade microcomputer modules and peripherals, following established basic procedures for system assembly and disassembly of field replaceable modules. Elements include ability to identify and configure IRQs, DMAs, and I/O addresses and to set switches and jumpers.

Objectives for Installation, Configuration, and Upgrading

- ◆ Identify basic terms, concepts, and functions of system modules, including how each module should work during normal operation.

- ◆ Identify basic procedures for adding and removing field replaceable modules.

- ◆ Identify available IRQs, DMAs, and I/O addresses and procedures for configuring them for device installation.

- ◆ Identify common peripheral ports, associated cabling, and their connectors.

- ◆ Identify proper procedures for installing and configuring IDE/EIDE devices.

- ◆ Identify proper procedures for installing and configuring SCSI devices.

- ◆ Identify proper procedures for installing and configuring peripheral devices.

- ◆ Identify concepts and procedures relating to BIOS.

- ◆ Identify hardware methods of system optimization and when to use them.

DIAGNOSING AND TROUBLESHOOTING

This domain requires the ability to apply knowledge relating to diagnosing and troubleshooting common module problems and system malfunctions. This includes knowledge of the symptoms related to common problems.

Objectives for Diagnosing and Troubleshooting

- ◆ Identify common symptoms and problems associated with each module and how to troubleshoot and isolate the problems.

- ◆ Identify basic troubleshooting procedures and good practices for eliciting problem symptoms from customers.

  - • Use proper troubleshooting/isolation/problem determination procedures.

  - • Determine whether a problem is hardware or software related.

  - • Gathering information using utilities and tools such as a multimeter.

  - • Evaluate the customer environment.

  - • Identify symptoms/error codes.

  - • Discover the situation in which the problem occurred.

SAFETY AND PREVENTIVE MAINTENANCE

This domain requires the knowledge of safety and preventive maintenance. With regard to safety, it includes the potential hazards to personnel and equipment when working with lasers, high voltage equipment, ESD, and items that require special disposal procedures that comply with environmental guidelines. With regard to preventive maintenance, this includes knowledge of preventive maintenance products, procedures, environmental hazards, and precautions for working on microcomputer systems.

Objectives for Safety and Preventive Maintenance

- ◆ Identify the purpose of various types of preventive maintenance products and procedures and when to use/perform them.

- ◆ Identify procedures and devices for protecting against environmental hazards.

- Identify the potential hazards and proper safety procedures relating to lasers and high-voltage equipment.

- Identify items that require special disposal procedures that comply with environmental guidelines.

- Identify ESD (electrostatic discharge) precautions and procedures, including the use of ESD protection devices.

MOTHERBOARDS/PROCESSORS/MEMORY

This domain requires knowledge of specific terminology, facts, ways and means of dealing with classifications, categories and principles of motherboards, processors, and memory in microcomputer systems.

Objectives for Motherboards/Processors/Memory

- Distinguish between the popular CPU chips in terms of their basic characteristics.

- Identify the categories of RAM (Random Access Memory) terminology, their locations, and physical characteristics.

- Identify the most popular types of motherboards, their components, and their architecture (for example, bus structures and power supplies).

- Identify the purpose of CMOS (Complementary Metal-Oxide Semiconductor), what it contains, and how to change its basic parameters.

PRINTERS

This domain requires knowledge of basic types of printers, basic concepts, printer components, how they work, how they print onto a page, paper path, care and service techniques, and common problems.

Objectives for Printers

- Identify basic concepts, printer operations, and printer components.

- Identify care and service techniques and common problems related to primary printer types.

- Identify the types of printer connections and configurations.

PORTABLE COMPUTERS

This domain requires knowledge of portable computers and their unique components and problems.

Objectives for Portable Computers

- Identify the unique components of portable systems and their unique problems. These basic components include:

  - Batteries

  - LCD panels

  - AC adapters

  - Docking stations

  - PC cards

  - Pointing devices

BASIC NETWORKING

This domain requires knowledge of basic network concepts and terminology, ability to determine whether a computer is networked, knowledge of procedures for swapping and configuring network interface cards, and knowledge of the ramifications of repairs when a computer is networked.

Objectives for Basic Networking

- Identify basic networking concepts, including how a network works.

- Identify procedures for swapping and configuring network interface cards.

- Identify the ramifications of repairs on the network.

CUSTOMER SATISFACTION

This domain requires knowledge of—and sensitivity regarding—those behaviors that contribute to satisfying customers. More specifically, these behaviors include such things as: the quality of technician-customer personal interactions; the way a technician conducts him or herself professionally within the customer's business setting; the credibility and confidence projected by the technician, which in turn engenders customer confidence; the resilience, friendliness, and efficiency that can unexpectedly delight the customer above and beyond the solving of a technical problem. This domain is *not* a test of specific company policies or procedures.

Objectives for Customer Satisfaction

- Differentiate effective from ineffective behaviors as these contribute to the maintenance or achievement of customer satisfaction. These behaviors and skills include the following:

  - Communicating and listening (face-to-face or over the phone).

  - Interpreting verbal and nonverbal cues.

  - Responding appropriately to the customer's technical level.

  - Establishing personal rapport with the customer.

  - Displaying professional conduct, for example, punctuality, accountability.

  - Helping and guiding a customer with problem descriptions.

- Responding to and closing a service call.

- Handling complaints and upset customers, conflict avoidance, and resolution.

- Showing empathy and flexibility.

- Sharing the customer's sense of urgency.

PART II: INSIDE THE A+ CORE/HARDWARE TECHNOLOGY EXAM

Part II of this book is designed to round out your Core/Hardware Technology exam preparation by providing you with the following chapters:

- "Fast Facts Review" is a digest of all the "What Is Important to Know" sections from all chapters in Part I. Use this chapter to review just before you take the exam; all the information you need is here, in an easy-to-review format.

- "Insider's Spin on the Core/Hardware Technology Exam" grounds you in the particulars of mentally preparing for this examination.

- "Sample Test Questions" provides a full-length practice exam that tests you on the actual material covered in Part I. When you have mastered the material in Part I, you should be able to pass this exam with flying colors.

- "Hotlist of Exam-Critical Concepts" is your resource for cross-checking your technical terms. Although you're probably up to speed on most of this material already, double-check yourself anytime you run across an item you're not 100% certain about; it could make a difference at exam time.

- "Did You Know?" serves as a last-day-of-class bonus chapter. It briefly touches on peripheral information designed to help and intrigue anyone using this technology to the point that they wish to be certified in its mastery.

PART III: WHAT'S IMPORTANT TO KNOW ABOUT THE A+ DOS/WINDOWS EXAM

The CompTIA DOS/Windows certification exam measures your ability to install, configure, support, and troubleshoot MS-DOS, Windows 3.x, and Windows 95 environments. It focuses on determining your skill in five major categories:

- Function, Structure, Operation, and File Management
- Memory Management
- Installation, Configuration, and Upgrading
- Diagnosing and Troubleshooting
- Networking

The CompTIA DOS/Windows certification exam uses these categories to measure your ability. Before taking this exam, you should be proficient in the job skills described in the following sections.

FUNCTION, STRUCTURE, OPERATION, AND FILE MANAGEMENT

This section addresses how the operating systems are designed, how they operate, and what is considered to be normal operation. This section also covers managing files and directories.

Objectives for Function, Structure, Operation, and File Management

- Identify the major components of DOS, Windows 3.x, and Windows 95.
- Describe the differences between DOS/Windows 3.x and Windows 95 architecture.
- Name the major system files in each OS.

- Recognize what files are needed to start the system.
- Identify the correct locations of important system files.
- Differentiate between system, configuration, and user interface files.
- Navigate the operating systems.
- Retrieve data from the operating systems using utilities.
- Know how to create, view, and manage files and directories.
- Understand the concepts of disk management.

MEMORY MANAGEMENT

This section discusses the different types of memory a computer uses and how the operating system manages it.

Objectives for Memory Management

- Know the types of memory used by DOS, Windows 3.x, and Windows 95.
- Recognize the potential for memory address conflicts.
- Understand causes of memory conflicts.
- Describe a general protection fault and an illegal operation.
- Identify and use the appropriate memory troubleshooting utilities for a given situation.
- Discuss memory management and optimization.

INSTALLATION, CONFIGURATION, AND UPGRADING

In this section, you will discover the appropriate steps for installing and upgrading the operating system.

Objectives for Installation, Configuration, and Upgrading

- Identify procedures for installing, configuring, and upgrading DOS, Windows 3.x, and Windows 95.

- Identify the boot sequence of DOS, Windows 3.x, and Windows 95.

- Bring DOS, Windows 3.x, and Windows 95 to a basic operational level.

- Select and run the appropriate setup utility for a given situation.

- Know the steps to perform before upgrading.

- Upgrade from DOS to Windows 95.

- Upgrade Windows 3.x to Windows 95.

- Identify the boot sequences.

- Identify different ways to boot the systems.

- Identify the files that are required to boot.

- Create emergency boot disks.

- Create a Windows 95 startup disk.

- Understand what Safe mode is.

- Understand what DOS mode is.

- Identify procedures for loading/adding/removing device drivers for

  - Windows 3.x

  - Windows 95

  - Plug and Play

- Identify procedures for changing options and for configuring and using the Windows printing subsystem.

- Identify procedures for installing and launching applications in

  - DOS

  - Windows 3.x

  - Windows 95

DIAGNOSING AND TROUBLESHOOTING

This section covers the proven methods of finding and fixing PC problems.

Objectives for Diagnosing and Troubleshooting

- Recognize and decipher common error codes and messages from the boot sequence and know how to correct them.
- Understand the concept of temporary and permanent swap files.
- Identify and correct common Windows-specific printing problems.
- Determine the appropriate course of action to correct common errors in a Windows environment.
- Identify and use DOS and Windows-based utilities to diagnose specific Windows/DOS behavior.

NETWORKING

This section covers the networking concepts important to the A+ exams.

Objectives for Networking

- Discuss the network capabilities of MS-DOS and Windows.
- Connect a DOS workstation to a network.
- Connect a Windows 3.x workstation to a network.
- Connect a Windows 95 workstation to a network.
- Contrast different types of network designs.
- Distinguish between different types of Network Interface Cards (NICs).
- Connect a DOS/Windows or Windows 95 workstation to the Internet.

PART IV: INSIDE THE A+ DOS/WINDOWS EXAM

Part IV of this book is designed to round out your exam preparation by providing you with the following chapters:

- "Fast Facts Review" is a digest of all the "What Is Important to Know" sections from all chapters in Part III. Use this chapter to review just before you take the exam; all the information you need is here, in an easy-to-review format.

- "Insider's Spin on the DOS/Windows Exam" grounds you in the particulars of mentally preparing for this examination.

- "Hotlist of Exam-Critical Concepts" is your resource for cross-checking your technical terms. Although you're probably up to speed on most of this material already, double-check yourself anytime you run across an item you're not 100% certain about; it could make a difference at exam time.

- "Sample Test Questions" provides a full-length practice exam that tests you on the actual material covered in Part III. When you have mastered the material in Part III, you should be able to pass this exam with flying colors.

- "Did You Know?" serves as a last-day-of-class bonus chapter. It briefly touches on peripheral information designed to help and intrigue anyone using this technology to the point that they wish to be certified in its mastery.

HARDWARE AND SOFTWARE RECOMMENDED FOR PREPARATION

The *A+ Fast Track* is meant to help you review concepts with which you already have training and hands-on experience. To make the most of the review, you need to have as much background and experience as possible. The best way to do this is to combine studying with working on real computers, printers, and networks using the products on which you will be tested. This section gives you a description of the minimum computer requirements you will need to build a solid practice environment.

Computers

The minimum computer requirements to ensure you can study everything on which you'll be tested includes one or more workstations running Windows 95 or DOS 6.x and Windows 3.x. Access to a network is a plus but not required. Specifically for the Core/Hardware Technology hardware portion of the exam, being able to build, break, and troubleshoot hardware of various types will be extremely helpful. At a bare minimum, you must be able to assemble a workstation and configure various drives and other subsystems from component parts.

Your system should meet the following requirements:

- 486DX 33MHz

- 16MB of RAM

- 200MB hard disk

- 3.5-inch 1.44MB floppy drive

- VGA video adapter

- VGA monitor

- Mouse or equivalent pointing device

- Two-speed CD-ROM drive

- Network Interface Card (NIC)

- Presence on an existing network, or use of a hub to create a test network

- Microsoft Windows 95 or Windows 3.x

You'll also need a printer in order to ensure that you are familiar with printer hardware. The exam covers dot-matrix, inkjet, and laser printers, but it focuses most on the laser printer engine.

WHAT'S IMPORTANT TO KNOW ABOUT THE A+ CORE/HARDWARE TECHNOLOGY EXAM

I

A+ Fast Track was written as a study aid for people preparing for CompTIA A+ exams. This book is intended to help reinforce and clarify information with which the student is already familiar. This book is not intended to be a single source for student preparation, but to provide a review of information and a set of practice tests to help increase your likelihood of success when taking the actual exam.

Part I of this book is designed to help you make the most of your study time by presenting concise summaries of information that you need to understand to succeed on the exam. Each chapter covers a specific exam objective area outlined by CompTIA.

1 **Installation, Configuration, and Upgrading**

2 **Diagnosing and Troubleshooting**

3 **Safety and Preventive Maintenance**

4 **Motherboards/Processors/Memory**

5 **Printers**

6 **Portable Computers**

7 **Basic Networking**

8 **Customer Satisfaction**

   Objective Review

About the Exam

Exam Number	**220-101**
Minutes	**60**
Questions	**69**
Passing Score	**65%**
Single Answer Questions	**Yes**
Multiple Answer with Correct Number Given	**Yes**
Multiple Answer without Correct Number Given	**No**
Ranking Order	**No**
Choices of A-D	**Yes**
Choices of A-E	**No**
Objective Categories	**8**

▶ Identify basic terms, concepts, and functions of system modules, including how each module should work during normal operation.

▶ Identify basic procedures for adding and removing field replaceable modules.

▶ Identify available IRQs, DMAs, and I/O addresses and know the procedures for configuring them for device installation.

▶ Identify common peripheral ports, associated cabling, and their connectors.

▶ Identify proper procedures for installing and configuring IDE/EIDE devices.

▶ Identify proper procedures for installing and configuring SCSI devices.

▶ Identify proper procedures for installing and configuring peripheral devices.

▶ Identify concepts and procedures relating to BIOS.

▶ Identify hardware methods of system optimization and when to use them.

CHAPTER 1

Installation, Configuration, and Upgrading

BASIC TERMINOLOGY AND CORE CONCEPTS

To successfully master topics covered later in this book, you must have a solid understanding of basic hardware subsystems. This understanding is necessary to the basic knowledge directly covered on approximately 30 percent of the exam. In addition, the entire certification and the knowledge that it tests is built upon this understanding of subsystems. This chapter provides the foundation of standard hardware information and progresses to the installation and configuration of these subsystems. It is also important for you to know that every computer performs four functions: input, processing, output, and storage. To understand how a computer works, you must know the various components that achieve each of these functions.

System Board

The core for any computer system is the system board. This can also be called the motherboard or planar board. Generally speaking, all components needed to start the system and begin processing are present on the system board with the notable exception of a power source. The system board is basically the "nervous system" for the computer, routing input and output to and from the "brain," or the CPU. System boards vary between manufacturers; however, commonly accepted standards place the CPU, memory, internal and external buses, firmware, and keyboard controller on the system board itself.

The system board has progressed from the simple bare-bones approach in the original IBM equipment to a fully integrated system with I/O ports, video, storage controllers, and even audio controllers built into the motherboard. The industry evolved into two design types:

- Clones
- Compatibles

The term "clone" is a throwback to the early era of the IBM PC. A clone system board was one that was virtually identical to the original IBM design. All major components and system architecture were similar, and configuration was accomplished in an almost identical fashion. Major subsystems in the computer are controlled by add-on expansion cards and are separately contained. This is why clone system boards are also known as *non-integrated*.

As new technology became available, new industry standard system boards were designed. These standards became known as the XT, AT (see Figure 1.1), baby AT, and ATX (see Figure 1.2) system boards. The XT clone has since become almost nonexistent and will not be discussed at any length in this book.

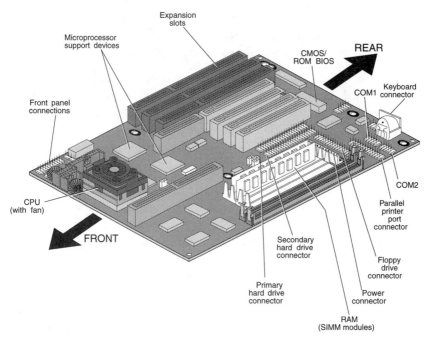

FIGURE 1.1
The AT system board.

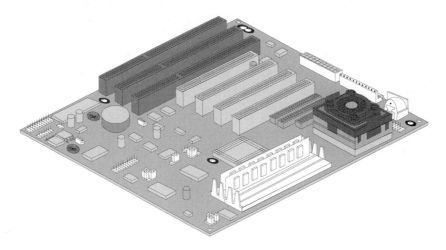

FIGURE 1.2
The ATX system board.

The term "compatible" is another early term referring to the boards manufactured with advancements and other deviations from the industry standard. Compaq, Leading Edge, Sanyo, and many others created system boards with their own technological enhancements. Often these enhancements improved performance, as in the case of Compaq's memory architecture. In other cases, they improved on the current designs by integrating video or other I/O ports into the system.

Compatible or *integrated* system boards can be split into multiple smaller boards connected through a variety of methods. These other boards include riser backplanes and daughter boards. These boards were generally cheaper and easier to produce. In addition, building systems with these boards became easier because of the integration of many devices previously available only through expansion cards.

Originally, the clones were considered the industry standard system boards, and the integrated systems were outside of these standards. These standards have shifted since the introduction of the original clone systems. The industry standards now include many of the advancements that compatibles first integrated into system boards. In fact, industry standard AT and ATX boards now include parallel and serial ports, as well as floppy disk controllers and hard disk controllers. The ATX standard system board further blurs the line between the original clones and compatibles by implementing the first major standard system board design change since the XT was replaced with the AT system board. The ATX changed the layout of the system board by relocating the processor and memory slots to allow for a cleaner, cooler, more spacious system design. In addition, the ATX standard includes integration of the floppy and hard disk controllers, parallel and serial ports, USB ports, and PS/2-style keyboard and mouse ports, as well as integrated audio support. Typically, the only additional required device lacking on these new "standard" system boards is a video adapter.

The standards are no longer based on the similarity of design to a particular manufacturer; rather, the standards are based upon de facto reasoning. New technology is developed and becomes a standard when and if the market will bear it.

The key to system board standards now can be loosely summed up with one idea: "Can this system board be replaced by a different manufacturer's system board?" If the answer is no, you most likely have a proprietary system board.

The primary components of a system board are described in the following sections.

CPU/Processor

The central processing unit, or CPU, functions as the brain of the computer. Residing on the system board, this brain has both internal and external *buses*, or pathways, for the data inside and outside the chip. This CPU contains millions of transistors on a silicon wafer the size of your thumbnail. The wafer is then encased in a ceramic square or rectangle depending on the make and model of the CPU. As technology advances and size decreases, the number of transistors on this wafer increases, and the processing power also increases proportionately. Processing power is measured in *MIPS*, or millions of instructions per second. This creates a very tightly-packed, complex electronic circuit that produces a tremendous amount of heat, limiting advancements in processing power and requiring special cooling fans and heat sinks.

The speed of the microprocessor is a function of internal and external clock speeds and bus width as well as wait-state and CPU classification. The CPU can be classified by the instruction set it contains. This *instruction set* defines the functions that it can perform on a given data set. Instruction sets are classified at a high level as *CISC* (Complex Instruction Set Computing) or *RISC* (Reduced Instruction Set Computing). These and other classifications are discussed in greater detail in Chapter 4, "Motherboards/Processors/Memory."

Math Coprocessor

In some systems, a separate coprocessor was required for greater efficiency in performing specialized math functions for programs specifically written to take advantage of this hardware. These functions are handled by an additional instruction set contained on the separate chip. These coprocessors have been integrated into the Intel CPUs since the introduction of the 80486DX.

Internal and External Buses

Buses come in different types. Primarily, the *internal data bus* is the path the data takes inside the CPU. The *external data bus* is the path the data takes from the CPU to its final destination within the system. These buses are not to be confused with the *expansion bus*, which is the physical wiring between the adapter cards and the CPU. Think of the roads on which the data rides as the expansion bus, and the route that it takes on these roads as the internal and external data buses.

Memory

Memory comes in many different forms, all of which have basically the same function. Memory is a high-speed data storage area. The many different forms provide additional features and capabilities. The two basic classifications that should readily come to mind are:

- RAM
- ROM

RAM, or Random Access Memory, provides a fast, rewritable storage area. Think of this as your short-term memory. When you're introduced to someone for the first time, you store that person's name in your short-term memory. Unless you memorize it and place it into long-term storage, the name you knew at one time becomes forgotten. RAM functions in this manner also. RAM can be broken into several different implementations, including SRAM, DRAM, EDO DRAM, and cache, to name a few. These are covered in Chapter 4.

ROM, Read Only Memory, is a storage area for a specific program. When the ROM chip is called for, this single program is run in much the same way that an executable program is started from a disk drive. Instead of being stored on a disk drive or temporarily written to a RAM chip, the program is "burned" into the chip at the manufacturing facility. Programs stored in this manner can be called long before a drive is functional and can operate at a fundamental level of the system. To change the program in ROM, you must replace the chip. ROM also has many different implementations, including EPROM, EEPROM, Flash ROM, and Shadow RAM.

BIOS

The most notable ROM program is BIOS, or Basic Input Output System. BIOS provides the initial system program and start routines when the system is turned on. The BIOS resides on a chip as *firmware*, or the program on the *ROM chip*. BIOS initiates the *POST*, Power-On Self Test, loads the operating system, and provides a translation layer between the operating system and the hardware.

CMOS

CMOS, short for Complimentary Metal Oxide Semiconductor, is the primary configuration mechanism in today's computers. Originally, settings such as video type, number of drives, and amount of RAM were configured using DIP switches. With the introduction of the 80286 chip, CMOS replaced physical switch settings with a software-driven menu used to configure options. CMOS maintains its information with a battery while the system is powered off. When the system is powered on again, the results from the POST are compared to the stored values in CMOS, and the system continues the boot process. If the values from POST and CMOS do not match, the system is halted until the error is repaired, either by changing the CMOS settings or by replacing the failed device in the system.

Input/Output Interfaces

Some I/O devices have their own proprietary interface with the CPU; others must use one of the industry standard interfaces. An interface simply provides a standardized physical connection between the expansion bus and the device in question. The most common interfaces are the *serial, parallel,* and *USB* ports.

A serial port allows a robust connection over a small number of wires. A serial device may be input, output, or a combination of both. The data is transferred one bit at a time *sequentially,* or in a series. This transfer method requires an initial breakdown of the data into single bits and a process for reassembly on the receiving end.

A parallel port provides a higher bandwidth for the data by using eight separate wires for data transfer. This allows eight bits, or one byte, of data to be transferred simultaneously. While this provides a higher rate of data throughput, distances longer than 10 feet should not be attempted. Parallel devices are generally output only; however, since the advent of bidirectional parallel ports, dual-purpose devices can make use of the higher rates of transfer on a parallel port.

The universal serial bus interface shown in Figure 1.3 is a relatively new standard that attempts to take the limitations of parallel and serial as well as some proprietary interfaces into account and replace them with a much faster and smaller connection. This will also virtually eliminate the resource conflicts inherent in existing connection schemes through an adaptive, dynamic resource allocation design. These resource conflicts are discussed in Chapter 2, "Diagnosing and Troubleshooting." This new technology has paved the way for high-bandwidth devices such as digital cameras and virtual-reality gloves and may even provide a single standard interface replacing existing storage interfaces.

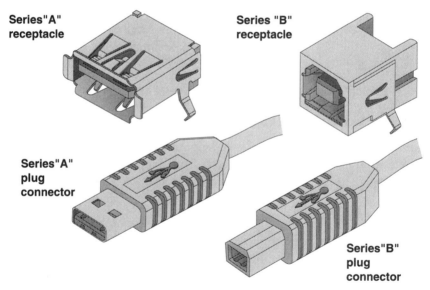

FIGURE 1.3
USB connectors.

Input/Output Devices

This section covers a wide variety of I/O devices. Some are either input or output, and some provide both of these functions. Some of the more common I/O devices are listed here:

- Keyboard
- Mouse
- Monitor
- Printer
- Modem
- Audio

Keyboard

This device is strictly for input only. Although many different keyboard styles are available, the standard "QWERTY" keyboard (named for the top row of letters) has 101 keys with additional keys possible for program-specific operations.

The keyboard is one of only two external I/O devices required during POST. A successful POST keyboard test will flash the keyboard lights on and off at least once before continuing. The keyboard is also the only I/O device that has always been controlled from the system board itself.

Mouse

The computer mouse rides at the forefront of the Windows revolution. Prior to Microsoft's product, the Apple Macintosh product was the first to popularize this Xerox innovation.

The mouse provides a more intuitive approach to computing, allowing the user to point-and-click instead of typing in commands. Mice have several different mechanisms for relaying positional data to the computer (optical, mechanical-optical, and mechanical-optical trackball, to name a few). Regardless of the method, all mice are relative positioning pointers. This means that the mouse only relays movement from a point, not from where the origination point is located spatially.

A mouse can be connected via a serial bus (do not confuse this with the buses previously discussed; in this case the term 'bus' simply means a special serial connection to the expansion bus) or proprietary port. While serial mice have been traditionally the most popular, the PS/2 mouse is a proprietary mouse that is gaining a market share and has been included in the new standards. This is due to the nature of the resources allocated for PS/2 and the smaller port size. PS/2 mice do not share their interrupts with other serial devices. Serial device resource sharing will be covered in greater detail later in this chapter.

Monitor

This output device is the only other POST-required external peripheral. This device is usually controlled by an adapter card on the expansion bus that translates the digital computer signals into readable light on the screen. This readable image of light is formed by *pixels*, or points of light arranged on a grid. Monitors are categorized by the number of pixels they can display, the number of simultaneous colors they can display, the relative distance between any two pixels, and the time between updates to a specific pixel. These measurements are called *resolution, palette, dot pitch*, and *refresh rate*, respectively. Two different types of technology are used to generate pixels in monitors today: CRT and LCD.

CRT, or cathode-ray tube, technology is a turn-of-the-century technology adapted to modern uses. CRTs display images by using magnetic fields and an electron beam energizing a phosphor coated surface in a vacuum tube. Figure 1.4 illustrates cathode-ray tube technology.

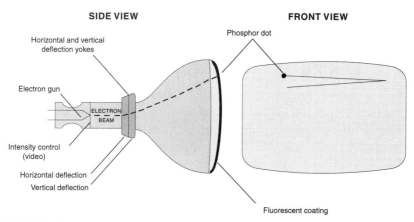

FIGURE 1.4
Diagram of a CRT.

As you can see in Figure 1.4, the signal is passed from the adapter to the electron gun in the sequential order necessary. The gun is powered on, and the electron beam passes through a magnetic directional field to strike the phosphor screen in the exact target location. Because the phosphors stay lit for only a fraction of a second, the beam must refresh the image at the *refresh rate*. Typically this refresh rate is 60Hz, or 60 cycles per second, for a VGA monitor. Because the human eye can detect pulses at lesser rates, the perceived picture quality increases in direct proportion to increasing refresh rates from 60Hz and higher.

Because of the mechanical design of a CRT, the faster refresh rates are harder to reach. To reach the faster speeds while maintaining a slower mechanical sweep, the interlaced monitor was created. This design worked to fool the human eye by refreshing every other line of pixels rather than refreshing every line in a single pass. Since the design of better mechanical technology, interlacing is not as widespread as it once was.

Most desktop computers use CRT monitors for their display units.

Liquid crystal display technology, on the other hand, is a relatively new technology for computer displays. These images are formed in a *passive matrix* LCD screen by signals sent down a vertical and a horizontal wire. Where these two lines intersect, the crystal is charged and a pixel forms. In an *active matrix* LCD panel the signal is formed much the same way, but the lines intersect at a thin-film transistor. This transistor gives a steady signal to the crystal and removes the charge when the signal ends. This enables the active matrix LCD to provide a more crisp, clean, and shadow-free display than the passive matrix.

Video Types

Monitors' capabilities vary greatly depending on their video classifications. PC video standards include Monochrome, CGA, EGA, VGA, and SVGA among others. Table 1.1 lists the different video standards.

TABLE 1.1

VIDEO STANDARDS

Video Type	Resolution	Colors/Colors Possible
Monochrome	720×350	1 (usually amber or green; text only)
Color Graphics Array	320×200 640×200	4/16 2/4
Enhanced Graphics Array	640×350	16/64
Multi-Color Graphics Array	320×200 640×480	256/256 16/256
Video Graphic Array	640×480	16/256
Super VGA	640×480 800×600	256/65,536 16/256
XGA	640×480 1024×768	65,536/16.7 million 256/65,536

Today's video adapters provide many enhancements over these standards and now reach resolutions of 1600×1280. They also include colors of over 4.2 billion for 32-bit color. These resolutions are considered enhancements to the existing standards; new official standards have not been created.

Printers

Printers are strictly output devices that enhance the ability of a computer. No other device can make the digital data inside of the computer a tangible part of the real world as easily as this. Depending on the desired output, you can choose from many different types and technologies. For more detailed information on printers, see Chapter 5.

These are the most common printer types:

- Laser
- Inkjet
- Dot-matrix
- Thermal
- Wax transfer

Laser printers are the most commonly used printers in business environments and consequently are weighted most heavily on the exam. Laser printers work more like a copier than a computer peripheral. The output is generated using the same electro-photostatic process that copiers use. This image is simply built using a digital bit-image formation process involving a laser, a light-sensitive drum surface, and electrically charged toner (which is like dry powdered ink). Laser printers print faster and at higher quality and consequently are more expensive than most other printers available.

Inkjet printers use varying technology to accomplish their tasks, but all inkjets literally spray the ink onto the page in a very controlled fashion to form characters. These bit-image characters appear to be more fully formed than their dot-matrix counterparts due to the absorption of the ink into the fiber of the paper itself. The jets in this type of printer must be cleaned regularly to prevent clogging. Most printers have a cleaning cycle that runs automatically.

Although they are older-style printers, dot-matrix printers still have a very large installation base in today's computing environment and are still covered on the exam. The image is formed one dot at a time by a series of print wires that strike the ribbon and press it against the page. This physical contact is the main reason that this obsolete technology is still necessary. No other printer method can produce multi-part forms.

People see thermal printouts almost everyday of their lives and may never realize it. Due to their low resolution and cheap, quiet function, thermal printers comprise the bulk of what's used in the retail marketplace. Most cash registers and credit card printers utilize this heat transfer device. The paper is chemically treated on one side to darken in high temperatures. When heat is focused into specific bit-images, imprecise, low-resolution characters are formed.

Many high-end photo shops utilize wax transfer printers. Due to the high cost of the device and its consumables, these are not commonly found. Colored wax can be transferred to the page in mimiographic fashion, but each page requires four separate primary color films. The other method used is more akin to that of the inkjet printer. These printers melt blocks of crayon-like wax into liquid and spray it onto the page.

Audio

Until recent years, audio devices were not considered a large enough class of I/O devices to warrant any attention. Sound capabilities are now built into some system boards, are used in business presentations, and even provide Internet conferencing with built-in applications like Microsoft's NetShow. 8-bit, 16-bit, 32-bit, and now even 64-bit sound cards are available. These bit designations indicate the different sounds a card can produce.

Because full stereo sound requires 44KHz, a 16-bit card is the minimum required to produce this stereo effect. (16 ones converted to a binary number equals 65,536, which is the smallest Base 2 number (2 to the 5th) that allows for the 44,000 discreet sound requirement.) With the addition of voice recognition and Internet conferencing to the list of audio capabilities, both the stereo speakers and microphone were made an integral part of any audio I/O system. MIDI (Musical Instrument Digital Interface), line-in, and line-out are also available ports on most standard audio cards today.

Modem

A modem is a serial device that provides both input and output. "Modem" is actually an acronym for modulator/demodulator, which to some degree describes its function. This device converts, or modulates, digital data into analog signals to be sent over standard telephone lines to another modem where the signal is again converted, or demodulated, back into digital data for the remote sharing of data.

Many standards have been developed for the negotiating of the communication acknowledgements and transmission of data through modems. Many of these standards are regulated by the International Telecommunications Union, or ITU. Table 1.2 contains a list of the most current ITU standards and their definitions.

TABLE 1.2

ITU STANDARDS

Communication Standard	Family	Enhancement
v.32	Transmission speed	Added 4800bps and 9600bps capability
v.32*bis*	Transmission speed	Added 14.4Kbps
v.34	Transmission speed	Added 28.8Kbps and 33.6Kbps capability
v.42	Link control	Added error correction standard
v.42*bis*	Link control	Added 4:1 data compression
v.90	Transmission method	Added digital 56Kbps standard

The standard configuration string for a modem contains specifications for not only transmission speed, but also the shape the data will take in terms of start, stop, and data bits, as well as parity information (see Figure 1.5).

The duplex setting is another critical concept. This communication method provides a setting for simplex, half-duplex, full-duplex, and multiplex. Simplex and multiplex are not generally used for modem communications. Half-duplex and full-duplex both allow bidirectional communication, but a setting of full-duplex allows simultaneous bidirectional communication. Full-duplex works like a phone system in that it allows both people to talk simultaneously. A half-duplex system is more like a conversation held over walkie-talkies or a CB radio; one side cannot talk while the other is talking and still be able to hear the other party.

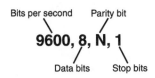

FIGURE 1.5
Transmission settings.

Storage

Throughout all three stages of computing (input, processing, and output), storage is a necessity. Storage devices can be classified in many ways: removable or fixed, optical or magnetic, read-only or writeable. The following is a list of the more common storage devices and components:

- Floppy disks
- Compact discs
- Hard disks
- Tape drives
- Interfaces

Floppy Drives

All PCs come with at least one floppy drive by default. Floppy disks are removable, magnetic, writeable storage devices. The floppy disk drive derives its name from the original 8-inch and 5 $\frac{1}{4}$-inch disks. This media was encased in a soft plastic sheath and could be bent without destroying the data. With the introduction of the Apple Macintosh, the 3 $\frac{1}{2}$-inch floppy disk became popular. Even though they are no longer "floppy," these smaller, more rigid disks are still labeled after their predecessors. Because the 3 $\frac{1}{2}$-inch disks are capable of holding more data, they naturally have become the new industry standard. Figure 1.6 shows a 5 $\frac{1}{4}$-inch disk and a 3 $\frac{1}{2}$-inch.

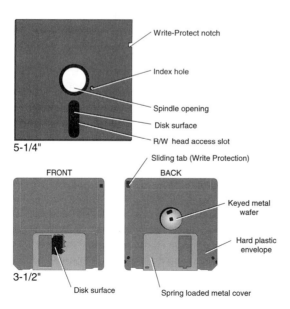

FIGURE 1.6
Floppy disks.

NOTE While the 3 $\frac{1}{2}$-inch floppy disk is often mislabeled a "hard" disk by users because of the rigid casing, the actual magnetic media inside of the disk casing is still a flexible or "floppy" disk.

Floppy drives, like hard drives, use a stepper motor to move the read/write *head*, and a spindle motor to rotate the *media*. The media is coated with a magnetic surface that accepts the polarity changes from the head to store bits of data as "on" or "off." Because of this, the disks are extremely susceptible to magnetic interference and corruption.

Data is stored on a disk's media formatted to a specific layout. This format uses *tracks, sectors,* and *heads* to provide an addressing system for the data:

- Tracks are concentric circles on the disk surface and are numbered from the inside outward starting with track 0.

- Sectors are the pie shaped wedges created by equally dividing the disk's surface into the number of tracks defined in the format.

- Heads are the mobile magnetic read/write devices that are a part of the drive itself. A single-sided drive has only one read-write head, whereas a double-sided drive has two read-write heads, one for each side of the disk.

To retrieve a particular piece of data from the disk, the computer must know which side of the disk it resides on, what track it resides on, and which sector on that track it resides in. This is generally stored in a file allocation table, or FAT.

All floppy disk drives utilize a read/write head that actually makes contact with the spinning media. This contact creates a fundamental source for wear on both drives and media, but allows for a removable and portable data storage media.

Both 5 $\frac{1}{4}$-inch and 3 $\frac{1}{2}$-inch floppy disks come in different types, which can store different amounts of data. Table 1.3 lists the various types and their distinguishing characteristics.

TABLE 1.3

FLOPPY DISK STANDARD CHARACTERISTICS

Disk Size	Type	Tracks	Sectors	Capacity
5 ¼-inch	SS SD	40	8	160KB
5 ¼-inch	SS DD	40	9	180KB
5 ¼-inch	DS SD	40	8	320KB
5 ¼-inch	DS DD	40	9	360KB
5 ¼-inch	DS HD	80	15	1.2MB
3 ½-inch	DS DD	80	9	720KB
3 ½-inch	DS HD	80	18	1.44MB
3 ½-inch	DS ED	80	36	2.88MB
3 ½-inch	LS-120	1736	variable	120MB

No current system uses single-sided drives (SS), nor do they use single or double-density drives (DD). Most of today's systems use high-density drives and LS-120 drives. (The LS-120 is thought to be a replacement for both the Zip drive and all 3 ½-inch floppy disks with one hybrid device.) All drives of the same physical media size are compatible with all preceding disk formats. In other words, a 720KB disk can be read from, written to, and even formatted in a 1.44MB disk drive, but the reverse is not true.

Hard Drives

Hard disk drives are fixed, magnetic, writeable storage devices. Hard drives are generally installed inside of the computer enclosure and connected with an *interface*. Different interfaces are available depending on the hard drive standard chosen.

Hard disk drive media generally consists of multiple, rigid, aluminum alloy platters coated with a magnetic surface contained in a vacuum-sealed container. Due to the miniscule scale on which the hard drive stores and differentiates data, even the slightest dust particle would cause a catastrophic drive failure.

Inside the sealed enclosure, you will find components similar to the floppy disk drive. The platters (disks) store the data with magnetic polarity signaling "on" or "off." The stepper motor moves the *actuator arm,* which has the read-write heads on the end of it (see Figure 1.7). The spindle motor rotates the platters at a much greater speed than is possible with floppy media—often over 5,000 RPM.

FIGURE 1.7
The workings of a hard disk drive.

The R/W heads in a hard disk drive do not physically touch the drive media as they do in a floppy drive. Rather, the head "floats" on a cushion of air generated by the fast-moving media below it. If the head were to touch the media while accessing the data, a head crash would occur. This is discussed in more detail in Chapter 2, "Diagnosing and Troubleshooting."

A major difference between the floppy disk and the hard disk is the number of media surfaces. A floppy disk has two sides, while a hard disk can have as many as 8 or even 16 sides. This brings a new factor into the addressing scheme that's not present in a floppy disk drive—a *cylinder*. A cylinder is a vertical stack of tracks in a given drive. This means that ultimately the number of cylinders matches the number of tracks on one side of one platter. The difference is that when data is written to the device, the data is spread across the different platters within the same cylinder to speed data retrieval.

The hard disk also is broken down into smaller areas called *clusters*. A cluster is a sequential grouping of sectors whose number depends on the format chosen for the hard disk drive. Because of the high number of sectors inherent in a large disk, a better addressing candidate is provided with clustering. Figure 1.8 illustrates the internal details of a hard disk.

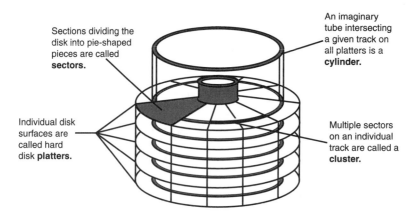

Sections dividing the disk into pie-shaped pieces are called **sectors.**

An imaginary tube intersecting a given track on all platters is a **cylinder.**

Individual disk surfaces are called hard disk **platters.**

Multiple sectors on an individual track are called a **cluster.**

FIGURE 1.8
Inside a hard disk.

Hard disk drives have many characteristics to distinguish and confuse those purchasing them. Among these are:

- Capacity
- Access time
- Interface

Capacity

A drive's capacity is described as the number of cylinders, multiplied by the number of heads, multiplied by the number of sectors per track, and multiplied by the number of bits stored in each sector. The standard formula is as follows:

(Cylinders×Heads×SPT×512 Bytes)/1,024=Capacity in Kilobytes

Access Time

The access time can further be classified as *latency time* and *seek time*. The latency time is the average amount of time it takes the actuator arm to move to the proper cylinder on the drive. The seek time is the average time that it takes for the desired sector to rotate under the read-write head. These two times can provide the average access time.

Interface

Hard disk drive interfaces provide a standards-based method for controlling the devices and transferring data between the hard drive and the external bus.

The following are examples of hard disk drive interfaces:

- ST-506
- ESDI
- IDE
- SCSI

You'll learn more about hard disk drive interfaces later in this chapter in the section, "Storage Interfaces."

Compact Disc Drives

CD technology is different from a hard disk drive, whose disk is subdivided into pie shaped sectors intersected by tracks for addressing. A CD device contains one long spiral of data. This also explains why a CD device speeds up and slows down as it is accessed. The linear speed of the data moving past the head must remain constant, causing the rotational speed to increase as the head moves to the hub, and slow down as the head moves to the edge of the disc.

CD devices come in many different standards. Depending on the technology used, the device may be read-only, write-once-read-many (WORM), or rewriteable. It may also use several different types of interfaces. Commonly IDE, SCSI, or a proprietary interface is used. In addition, the introduction of another standard, DVD or (Digital Video/Versatile Disk), has altered some performance and capacity standards. However, all CD devices use removable optical media. These devices are known as CLV, or constant linear devices. Table 1.4 outlines the various CD technologies.

TABLE 1.4

COMPACT DISC STANDARDS

CD Technology	Capacity	Pros	Cons
CD-ROM (Read-Only Memory)	650MB	Common standard	Read-only
CD-R (Recordable)	650MB	Writable; less expensive than WORM drives	Write-once; no standards
CD-RW (Read-Write)	650MB	Rewritable	Limited erases; cannot be read in CD-ROM devices
WORM (Write Once Read Many)	1GB–10GB	Writable; large storage capacity	No standards; cannot be mass-produced
DVD	4.7GB	Large storage capacity; can read CD-ROM devices	Expensive; slower devices than CD-ROM
DVD–Rewritables	2.6GB–4.7GB	Large storage capacity; rewritable	Expensive; emerging technology

Tape Drives

Tape devices are not designed for interactive storage, but rather as an offline storage device in most implementations. Tape uses a magnetic media streaming in a linear fashion. It takes much longer to retrieve data written at the end of the tape because the drive must "fast-forward" to the end to read it. Because of this limitation, interactive use is slow; however, tape devices make an excellent backup medium. Figure 1.9 shows the inner workings of a tape drive.

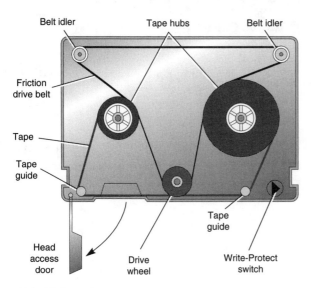

FIGURE 1.9
A streaming tape cartridge.

Tape drives can utilize the floppy disk, IDE, SCSI, or proprietary inter-faces. These interfaces will be discussed in the next section. In addition, a tape drive can use several tape standards, as described in Table 1.5.

TABLE 1.5

TAPE STANDARDS

Tape Standard	Native Capacity
QIC (Quarter-Inch Cartridge)	250MB–13GB depending on tape size and drive type
DAT (Digital Audio Tape)	2GB–12GB depending on tape size and drive type
DLT (Digital Linear Tape)	20GB–40GB depending on tape size and drive type

The tape drives listed in the following table are interactive streaming tape devices. Their increased speeds rival older hard disk drives in the 30ms range and are widely in use today. Because of this, these devices are clas-sified as removable media and compete with newer technology like the LS-120 floppy drive instead of with tape drives.

Tape Standard	Native Capacity
Iomega ZIP	100MB
Iomega JAZ	1–2GB depending on the version of the drive

Storage Interfaces

Storage interfaces provide a standards-based method for controlling the device and transferring data between the storage unit and the external bus.

The following are examples of standard storage interfaces:

- Floppy
- ST-506
- ESDI
- IDE
  - IDE
  - EIDE
  - Ultra ATA
- SCSI
  - SCSI
  - SCSI-2
  - SCSI-2 Fast
  - SCSI-2 Wide
  - SCSI-3/Ultra Wide
  - Ultra2 SCSI

Table 1.6 compares these interfaces based on several characteristics. The specific technology of IDE and SCSI will be discussed individually in later sections on those topics. ST-506 and ESDI are listed for comparison value only; they are not included on the exam.

TABLE 1.6

STORAGE INTERFACE COMPARISONS

Technology	Data Path	Speed	Encoding	# of Devices	Cabling
Floppy	8-bit	250–500Kbps	DD/HD/ED	2	1 daisy chain, 34-pin cable
ST-506	8-bit	1.2Mbps	MFM/RLL	2	1 daisy chain, 36-pin controller cable; 1 16-pin data cable for each drive
ESDI	8-bit	3Mbps	RLL	7	1 daisy chain, 36-pin controller cable; 1 16-pin data cable for each drive
IDE/ATA	16-bit	12Mbps	ARLL	2	1 40-pin daisy chain
EIDE/ATA-2	16-bit	13Mbps	ARLL	4	1 40-pin daisy chain per pair of drives
ULTRA ATA	32-bit	33Mbps	ARLL	4	1 40-pin daisy chain per pair of drives
SCSI	8-bit	5Mbps	Varies	7	50-pin daisy chain
SCSI-2	8-bit	5Mbps	Varies	7	50-pin daisy chain
SCSI-2 Fast	16-bit	10Mbps	Varies	7	50-pin daisy chain
SCSI-2 Wide	32-bit	10Mbps	Varies	7	50-pin daisy chain
SCSI-2 Fast/Wide	32-bit	20Mbps	Varies	7	50-pin daisy chain
SCSI-3 Ultra Wide	32-bit	40Mbps	Varies	15	68-pin daisy chain; can also use SCSI-2 devices with 68-to-50-pin converters
SCSI-3 Ultra2 LVD	32-bit	80Mbps	Varies	15	68-pin daisy chain or fiber optic

Power Supply

A power supply provides the proper voltage level and type of power necessary for the computer system it is in. This supply must also be capable of providing enough power without overloading, as measured in watts. Most systems require 200–300 watts of power. Standard power supplies convert 110v or 220v AC power into the four discrete DC voltages the electronic circuits need. These four voltage levels are ±5 volts for the electronic circuitry and ±12 volts for the various drive motors. Note that newer ATX power supplies add a +3.3 volt line for today's low-voltage, energy-efficient processors. All of these voltage lines are color coded with the standards outlined in Table 1.7.

TABLE 1.7

POWER SUPPLY VOLTAGE LEVELS

Color	Voltage	Amperage
Red	+5	0.0–2.0
White	–5	0.0–0.2
Yellow	+12	2.5–7.0
Blue	–12	0.0–0.3
Black	Ground	N/A

As you can see in Figure 1.10, power supplies have standardized connectors to attach to the various system components. These connectors are called Molex and Berg connectors, respectively. The connectors for the main system board also differ between the AT and ATX power supplies.

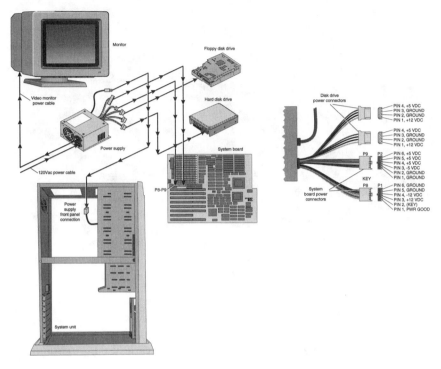

FIGURE 1.10
Power supply connections.

FIELD REPLACEMENT TECHNIQUES

This section covers the physical replacement of like equipment. Physical installation techniques may also be covered, but actual installation and configuration information appears later in this chapter.

Basic Replacement Rules

FRUs, or field replaceable units, are replaceable modules that can be swapped as a means of servicing a computer system. Generally, an FRU is not further repaired in the field; instead that component is sent to a facility that repairs increasingly lower levels of circuitry. This may be for reasons of safety, complexity, or cost. Figure 1.11 shows common replaceable units for a computer system.

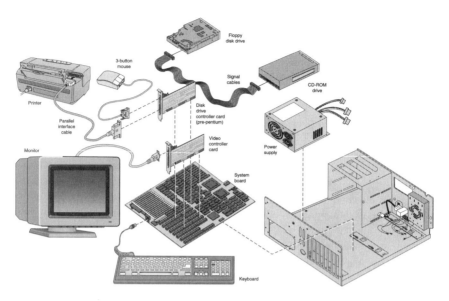

FIGURE 1.11
FRU examples.

If you decide to replace a system component with an FRU, follow these guidelines for best results:

◆ *Run a complete backup of the system.* Sometimes repairing a system destroys the data or the data storage components.

◆ *Create a clean, organized, well-lit, workspace with proper static electricity safeguards.* These safeguards will be covered in Chapter 3, "Safety and Preventive Maintenance."

◆ *Document everything.* Do not trust your memory, no matter how good it is. If necessary, draw cable diagrams as you remove components, paying special attention to the location of the striped PIN 1. Record the CMOS settings for each component, paying special attention to storage components. Record all existing jumper and switch settings on any components you intend to modify. Store all documentation in one location. This enables you to get to manuals, device drivers, and past repair reports swiftly and easily.

◆ *Exit all applications, and then shut down the system and all peripherals.* Disconnect all power cords from the system. Turning off the system is not enough to shield you from all power problems. You might also want to disconnect any data cabling from peripheral devices to ensure that nothing is providing power to the system.

◆ *Familiarize yourself with the case design and remove the case.* Typically, this is accomplished by removing the 3–6 screws at the rear of the system enclosure, although some systems use thumbscrews, plastic tabs, or slide-lock mechanisms to secure the case. Be careful not to use too much force because an internal data cable could be caught on the case.

Drive Replacement

Replacing a drive requires a few more specific steps. This section walks you through the process.

1. After recording the cable positions, disconnect the power and data cables from the drive. Disconnect the data cable from the system board and remove the cable. Note that CD-ROMs may have an additional audio cable plugged into the sound card. Record and remove this cable as well. Figure 1.12 shows a diagram of a typical disk drive arrangement.

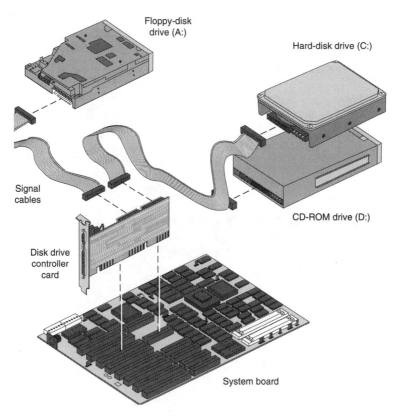

FIGURE 1.12
System disk drives.

2. Depending on the type of case, the drive may be installed in a special
drive cage (see Figure 1.13). Some systems require you to remove this
cage, but most do not. Locate the screws attaching the drive to the cage
and remove them; carefully place them together in a small container.

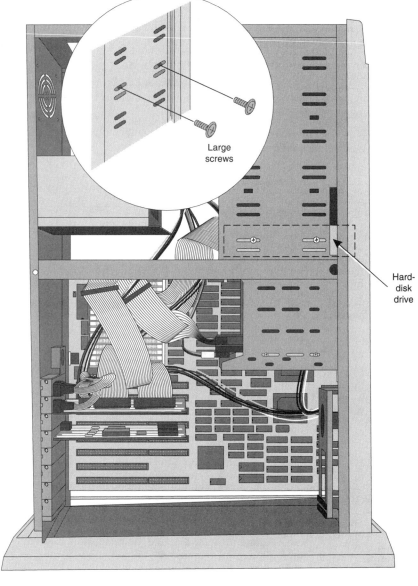

FIGURE 1.13
These screws attach the drive to the drive cage.

NOTE Most screws are standard for all drives, but it is difficult to know which systems adhere to the standards and which do not. To keep track of which screws are for what, fold a piece of tape around the screws and mark them with the device name, or label and use the individual sections in an egg carton.

3. Remove the drive and place it in a static bag.

4. To replace the drive with the replacement unit, reverse this process, paying close attention to PIN 1 on the data cable.

Newly installed drives may require you to set jumpers and switches properly. This is discussed in a later section concerning IRQ, DMA, and I/O settings, as well as hard drive-specific installation.

Power Supply Replacement

A power supply still maintains a direct line with the current even when it's turned off. For this reason, it is important to remember to remove the power cord. In addition, certain components inside of the supply may retain a potentially lethal charge even with the power cord removed. *Never* attempt to open the housing of a power supply.

When you're ready to replace a power supply, follow these steps:

1. On your diagram, mark all the power supply components. The power supply has multiple connectors attached to many different components. Although your system diagram may look like an octopus, it is necessary.

2. Carefully remove all power connectors from the various system components. The Molex connectors may be extremely stubborn. Try rocking them out of the drive connectors. Berg-style connectors may need to be lifted slightly during removal to clear the plastic lock tabs.

3. After diagramming and disconnecting all power connectors, including the system board, locate and remove only those screws necessary for removing the supply. This may vary from system to system. You'll find other screws that connect the supply housing. Do not remove those screws or attempt to remove the supply housing.

4. If the power supply itself has metal clips on the underside of the device that fit into slots in the case, remove them by sliding the supply forward and lifting gently.

NOTE

Some power supplies have an external power switch. You must often remove such switches before you replace the supply itself. Again, following the electrical precautions discussed previously, add this to your diagram and disconnect the wires. Pay close attention to the colors and the positions used.

5. To install the a replacement unit, reverse these steps.

Expansion Card Replacement

Expansion cards are generally attached vertically to the system board, although some low-profile systems employ a *riser backplane*, which allows the cards to be inserted horizontally into a specially designed adapter card that is inserted vertically into a proprietary expansion slot. Either way, the process for removing expansion cards is the same. And after you have removed all expansion cards (see Figure 1.14), you can remove the backplane card.

Follow these steps to replace expansion cards:

1. Document the location of all cables, and then remove all cabling.

2. Remove the mounting screw from the rear top edge of the case connector (see Figure 1.14). Some systems have plastic tabs or levers in place of these mounting screws. Refer to your manufacturer's documentation for the appropriate removal procedures.

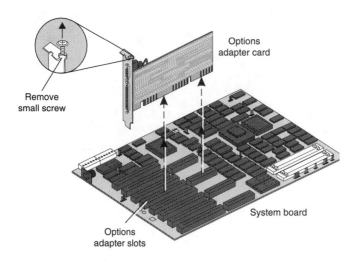

FIGURE 1.14
Removing the expansion cards.

3. Holding the card by the front and rear edges, gently rock the card back and forth to ease it out of the expansion socket. Do not rock from side to side as this could break the expansion connector off in the socket. Using force is unnecessary.

4. Place the card in a *Faraday cage* or anti-static bag.

5. To install the replacement, reverse these steps.

6. Some configuration may be necessary for newly installed equipment. Settings concerning IRQ, DMA, and I/O configuration will be discussed in a later section.

CPU Replacement

How you replace the CPU depends primarily on the type of CPU packaging you have. Some CPUs are PGA (pin grid array), some are PLCC (plastic leadless chip carrier), and others are mounted with an edge connector casing. Figure 1.15 shows several chips and their packaging.

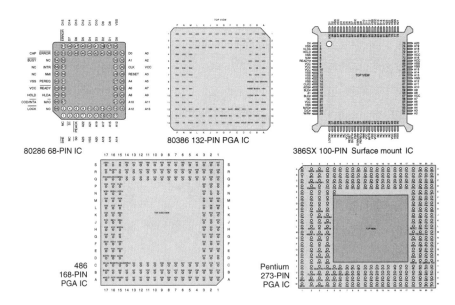

FIGURE 1.15
CPU chip packaging.

Today's CPUs are normally packaged in a PGA-style enclosure, although with the rising popularity of the Intel Pentium II processor, the edge connector may become the prevalent technology in the near future.

Because the PLCC is no longer popular and the edge connector mount is replaced in the same way as an expansion card, this section covers replacement of PGA chips and ZIF, or Zero Insertion Force, sockets. If you're replacing either of those types of CPU, follow these steps:

1. Remove the heat sink and fan assembly if necessary.

2. Gently pull the ZIF socket lever out from under the locking tab and raise it to a vertical position.

3. Adhering to all static precautions, grasp the chip and lift straight out of the socket.

4. Place the chip in a protective antistatic foam base and then in an antistatic bag.

5. Lower the ZIF lever and lock it into place with the plastic tab.

6. Gently pull the ZIF socket lever out from under the locking tab and raise it to a vertical position.

7. Align PIN 1 and place the chip into the socket. Keep in mind that there is a reason this is called "zero insertion force."

8. Give the CPU a light tap to ensure a solid seat, and then lower the lever. This will provide more pressure than raising the lever did.

9. Push the lever back under the locking tab. Then replace the heat sink and fan assembly.

In some system boards, multiple CPUs can be chosen for installation. This requires you to configure many jumper settings. Refer to the system board manufacturer's instructions for configuration.

Memory Replacement

Like the replacement procedure for the CPU, the procedure for replacing memory also depends on the type of memory packaging used. Memory can be packaged in the form of a DIPP (dual in-line pin package), SIPP (single in-line pin package), SIMM (single in-line memory module), or DIMM (dual in-line memory module) as shown in Figure 1.16.

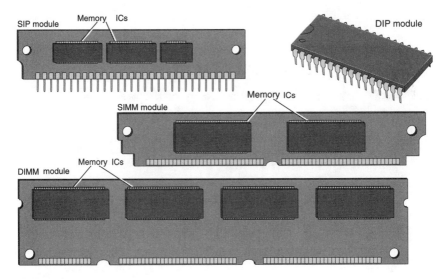

FIGURE 1.16
Memory packaging.

Because SIMM and DIMM are the primary forms of memory used today, the following steps outline the FRU replacement procedures for those memory types.

1. To remove the chip, begin by releasing the metal or plastic tab locks on either side of the chip. (Use your fingernail or a small screwdriver to pull the tabs away from the chip.) SIMM and DIMM differ slightly in the mechanisms used for this. SIMM requires a constant pressure on the tabs during removal; DIMM tabs are not spring-loaded and do not need constant pressure.

2. Removal of the DIMM chip is very straightforward. After releasing the tabs, simply pull the chip straight up. Rocking it slightly back and forth like an expansion card may help.

3. To remove a SIMM chip, rotate the chip to a 45 degree angle after releasing the tabs. From that position, pull the chip straight out. Note that you must remove SIMM chips in sequential order because one chip rotates into the space occupied by the next.

4. To replace the memory chip, reverse these steps. Note that both DIMM and SIMM must be aligned properly. They are keyed and cannot be inserted backwards.

System Board Replacement

In some systems, you must perform many of the preceding procedures before you can remove the system board. After you've removed all cabling and expansion boards (including memory), you can remove the motherboard itself. This process varies greatly based on the manufacturer, but it follows these basic steps:

1. Remove anything connected to the system board. Commonly, a system board will have a variety of LED and switch connectors. These connectors should be labeled and removed.

2. Remove the screws attaching the system board to the bottom of the case.

3. Slide the system board to the side to release the plastic tabs (see Figure 1.17) from their slots. Lift the system board up and to the left to make sure the right side of the board clears the drive cage.

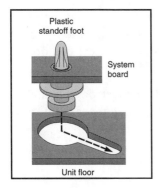

FIGURE 1.17
Release these plastic tabs for system board replacement.

4. To install the replacement component, reverse these steps, paying attention to the location of screws and whether they are ground screws or are insulated from the system board.

External Peripherals

Before you connect or disconnect a peripheral from the main system, make sure the external device is turned off and disconnected from its power source. Likewise, before you turn the power back on to the main system, you should turn on all peripherals with external power sources.

CONFIGURING RESOURCES AND DEVICES FOR INSTALLATION

This topic requires an understanding of resources and how they are used in the system architecture.

Device configuration is much like any other path in life. Follow these guidelines:

- *Know where you are.* In this case, you need to determine what resources you have allocated and what resources you have available.

- *Know where you are going.* For this section, you are going to install new hardware in the system. Knowing where you are going requires knowledge of the device you are installing. What resources can it use? What resources are commonly assigned to this type of device?

◆ *Determine how to get there from here.* This requires a plan for which resources you will use and knowledge of how to physically install the device in the system. In short, configure the new component with the settings you have chosen, and then physically install it.

◆ *When all else fails, read the map.* Have the proper documentation and software tools available to collect information that you don't already know.

Resource Allocation

What are resources? Resources are the precious commodity that all devices in any system require. The design of the system architecture imposes certain limits on the number of resources available to a device. Any system device you're configuring must be able to call the CPU using an IRQ, or interrupt request line, and must be able to communicate the data from itself to the CPU using the I/O address. In addition, a device is given a DMA, or direct memory access, number if it needs to speak directly with the system RAM.

Resource allocation is the most common problem people encounter when installing new equipment. So many possibilities are available with today's computer peripherals that often a computer will have no available hardware resources. The user's only recourse at that point is to remove something else to make room for a new device.

Some standards have evolved for resource allocation over the years. This enables many more devices to function under a variety of conditions and installation configurations.

IRQ

Interrupt request lines, or IRQs, enable devices to tap the CPU on the shoulder. This signal forces the CPU to put whatever it is doing on hold and work on data for the requesting device. A good example of this is modem communications. When a modem receives data, it has to pass it somewhere before the next packet comes in from the phone line. The CPU must pass the packet from the modem to the hard disk. If a modem has no way of forcing the CPU to listen, the CPU would happily work away on other things, and the modem would continue dropping packets because it has no place to put them.

Table 1.8 lists system IRQ settings and tells what each one is typically used for.

TABLE 1.8

IRQ SETTINGS

IRQ #	Used for	Additional Notes
0	System timer	
1	Keyboard	
2	Cascade from IRQ9	Only used when all other IRQs are full.
3	Even-numbered COM ports	Balances serial devices evenly between even and odd COM ports.
4	Odd-numbered COM ports	Balances serial devices evenly between even and odd COM ports.
5	LPT2	Usually available; often used for sound cards.
6	Floppy controller	
7	LPT1	
8	Real-time clock	
9	Redirected to IRQ2	Only used when all other IRQs are full. Often used for VGA, NIC.
10	Available	Commonly used for NIC.
11	Available	
12	Available	Often used for PS/2-style mouse.
13	Math coprocessor	
14	Hard disk controller	
15	Available	Additional hard disk controller.

On the other hand, if two devices share the same IRQ, the CPU has no way of knowing which device tapped it on the shoulder. Meanwhile, the modem is still dropping packets.

DMA

Direct memory access channels are designed to eliminate some of the CPU overhead. Because the CPU is generally the traffic cop directing all devices to handle other system functions, the CPU can become bogged down in menial tasks. This can deter system performance. To alleviate some of these problems, "smart" devices were made with controllers that could directly access the memory without the CPU becoming involved. These "smart" devices require a separate path, like an expressway, to the memory. This is precisely what a DMA channel is. Table 1.9 outlines the most common uses for each DMA channel.

TABLE 1.9

COMMON DMA CHANNEL USAGE

DMA Channel	Device	Additional Notes
0	Available	Often used for SCSI controllers.
1	Available	XT hard disk controllers use this setting; Often used for sound cards.
2	Floppy disk controller	Floppy disk controller.
3	Available	Often used for NICs.
4	Available	
5	Available	Often used for sound cards.
6	Available	
7	Available	Often used for sound cards.
8	Available	

In some newer systems, however, DMA does not provide a performance boost. It may actually degrade system efficiency due to the nature of DMA's backward compatibility and the extreme speeds of today's processors. Experiment with any devices that are capable of using DMA.

I/O Addresses

The I/O address provides a location at which the CPU can contact the device for data transfer. I/O addresses are represented in hexadecimal notation. Hexadecimal notation is easily converted to standard decimal notation using the following translation:

0=0	1=1	2=2	3=3	4=4	5=5	6=6	7=7
8=8	9=9	A=10	B=11	C=12	D=13	E=14	F=15

Table 1.10 outlines the common I/O settings.

TABLE 1.10

I/O ADDRESSES

I/O Address	Device
00-0F	DMA controller
20-21	Interrupt controller
40-43	Timer
060-06F	Keyboard
070-07F	Real-time clock
1F0-1F8	Hard disk controller
200-20F	Joystick controller
220-22F	Sound card
278-27F	LPT2
2E8-2EF	COM4
2F8-2FF	COM2
300-30F	Network card
378-37F	LPT1
3CO-3DA	VGA adapter
3E8-3EF	COM3
3F0-3F7	Floppy controller
3F8-3FF	COM1

If an I/O address is unused, the memory area can be allocated to other applications and memory managers for use. You can do this, for example, with an include argument for EMM386.EXE.

Physical Configuration

Methods for modifying any of these configuration options vary from machine to machine and component to component. Typically, you'll use jumpers, switches, and some software configuration for configuration in a non-plug-and-play system.

Jumpers are simple on/off connections. As you can see in Figure 1.18, a jumper is simply a wire connecting two pins inside of a plastic housing. When a jumper is called for, often the instructions will ask you to "short" two adjacent pins. To do so, you just slip a jumper over the two pins. There are two common non-interchangeable sizes of jumpers: standard and mini.

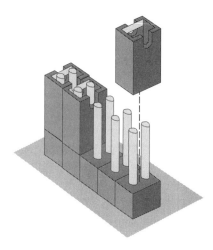

FIGURE 1.18
A jumper block.

You may find several jumpers together in a block formation, but typically this form of configuration is used for smaller, single points of change. Typically, more than five jumpers are replaced with a switch block from the manufacturer.

A switch block, like the one shown in Figure 1.19, is designed for complex configuration settings. You may find switch blocks of one or two settings, but five or more switches are more common. These switches are set by slide or rocker, depending on the switch design. In either case, a 1 or 0 will commonly be imprinted at one edge of the block to indicate the on or off position.

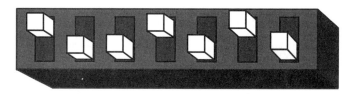

FIGURE 1.19
A switch block.

Another common configuration technique requires you to boot the system into some operating system and run a configuration utility. This utility functions much like a CMOS setup program. After you configure the device with this utility, it maintains its configuration in a powered chip. This eliminates the need to open the system enclosure and physically modify switch settings when you want to make a change.

The final step in configuring and installing devices is driver installation.

Plug and Play

If you have a Plug and Play system, sit back and relax—the Plug and Play operations will auto-configure everything for you. This type of configuration was designed to eliminate the hassle of physically changing the configuration of different components for any reason. In addition, this process eliminates the need for you to understand any resource allocation at all.

For Plug and Play operation, three components are required:

- A Plug and Play-compliant adapter card (see the card specifications)

- Plug and Play-compliant BIOS (check with the computer manufacturer)

- Plug and Play-compliant operating system (these currently include only Windows 95 and Windows 98; Windows NT will have Plug and Play functionality in version 5, also known as Windows 2000)

If any system has a single non-Plug and Play component, manual resource allocation may be your only option. As systems get more complex and more manufacturers adhere to the Plug and Play specifications, the need for manual configuration decreases—but it will never disappear. Understanding manual resource allocation and configuration is a cornerstone requirement for becoming an A+ certified technician.

PERIPHERAL PORTS, CABLES, AND THEIR CONNECTORS

So far, this chapter has covered many types of devices and peripherals. This section covers the connectors and cables used for such devices.

Often the terms "connector" and "port" are used interchangeably. This is incorrect. A *connector* is a physical specification of the shape and number of pins used in the connecting hardware itself, usually specified with a DB designation. A given connector may be used for two different ports. For example, a DB-25 female connector can be used for a parallel port or an external SCSI port. A *port* indicates the purpose and technology used to transmit the data sent over the wires in the connector and cabling, and it can use more than one type of connector. For example, a serial port can have either a DB-25 male or a DB-9 male connector.

If you're unclear about these two distinctions, the proper definition of a port should include the connector information. Through the development of the computer, certain connectors have come to be associated with certain ports as a matter of standard. This reduces the confusion and provides a common ground for the discussion of these ports.

Connectors

Connector standards define the shape of the connector and the interfacing method. Typically, a connector is designated as male (if it has pins) or female (if it does not).

Common standards include the DB connector, HP connector, Centronics connector, RJ connector, DIN connector, and USB connector. Figures 1.20 through 1.24 show each of these connector types.

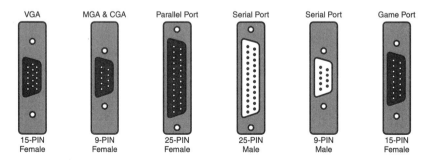

FIGURE 1.20
Various DB connectors.

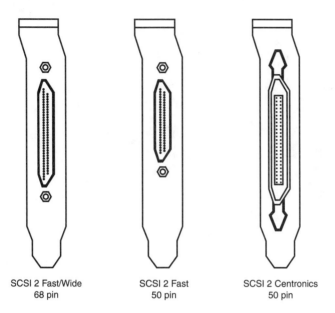

SCSI 2 Fast/Wide
68 pin

SCSI 2 Fast
50 pin

SCSI 2 Centronics
50 pin

FIGURE 1.21
SCSI HP connectors and a Centronics connector.

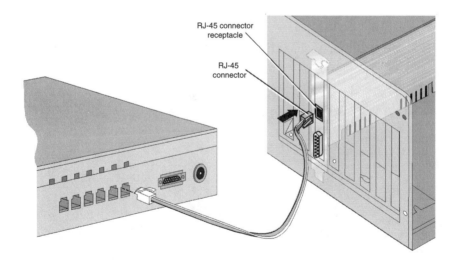

RJ-45 connector
receptacle

RJ-45
connector

FIGURE 1.22
An RJ connector.

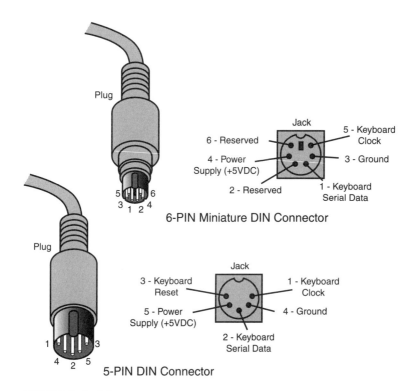

FIGURE 1.23
DIN connectors.

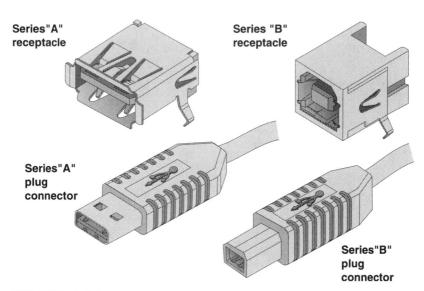

FIGURE 1.24
USB connectors.

Table 1.11 lists the various types of connectors and their distinguishing characteristics.

TABLE 1.11

CONNECTOR/PORT COMPARISONS

Interface	Pins	Connector	Port
DB-9	9	Male	Serial port
DB-9	9	Female	Mono/CGA/EGA token-ring
DB-15	15 (2 rows)	Female	MIDI, joystick, or network
DB-15	15 (3 rows)	Female	VGA
DB-25	25	Male	Serial port
DB-25	25	Female	Parallel port
DB-25	25	Female	SCSI 2 port
HP-50	50	Female	SCSI 2 port
HP-68	68	Female	SCSI 2 Fast/Wide port
RJ-11	4	Female	Internal modem
RJ-45	8	Female	Network
BNC	1	Female	Network
DIN-5	5	Female	Keyboard
DIN-6	6	Female	PS/2 mouse or keyboard
Centronics-36	36	Female	Parallel port on printer
Centronics-50	50	Female	SCSI 2 external connection

Cable

The type of cable used often depends upon the device in question. A cable is simply a set of wires designed to connect two or more devices. The shape of the connectors and the number of wires in the cable create a cable's basic structure, but the actual placement of the wires into the connector truly define what type of cable it is. Common cable for external devices is limited to parallel (see Figure 1.25), serial (see Figure 1.26), and SCSI.

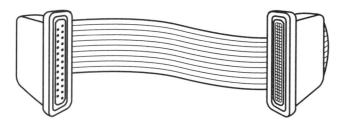

FIGURE 1.25
Parallel cable with both ends exposed.

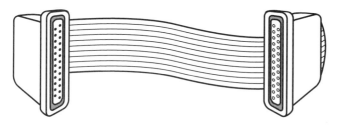

FIGURE 1.26
Serial cable with both ends exposed.

Parallel printer cables are typically limited to the standard IEEE printer cable. Serial cables, on the other hand, may have either gender on the device end. Serial cables are also "made-to-order." That is, some devices require PIN 1 on the port end to come out on PIN 12 on the device end. These are designed for specific implementations of proprietary devices. Another common serial cable is called a "null modem" cable. This cable has a specific pin configuration designed so that the output of one computer's serial port flows into the input of another computer's serial port and vice versa. Figure 1.27 shows the pin configuration for a null modem cable.

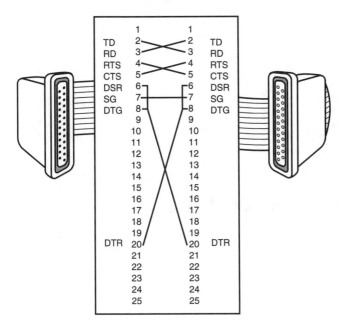

FIGURE 1.27
Pin configuration of a null modem serial cable.

SCSI external cable and connectors can vary depending on the type of SCSI controller that's used.

INSTALLATION AND CONFIGURATION OF HARD DISK SUBSYSTEMS

A hard disk subsystem is logically composed of a drive, a controller, and an expansion bus interface. However, the controller may be physically located on the drive or on the adapter card, depending on the type of drive subsystem standard. This section discusses both IDE and SCSI drive configuration.

You learned about the physical installation of a hard disk drive in the section on replacing components. After you install such a component in the system enclosure, you will have to address manufacturer- and interface-specific configuration settings such as those listed here:

- ◆ Adapter installation (previously covered)

- ◆ Drive termination and addressing

- Physical drive installation (previously covered)
- CMOS configuration
- Drive partitioning
- Drive formatting

The following sections cover the remaining topics in detail for specific interfaces.

Standard IDE Drive Configuration

Configuration of IDE hard disk drives requires you to perform the tasks described in this section.

Drive Termination and Addressing

IDE interfaces allow only two drives per *channel*. A channel is defined as a single drive bus or a direct line of communication with a chain of drives. Because IDE allows only two drives per channel, *termination* is fairly simple. Think of termination as marking the end of the bus route. Drive addressing is incorporated into the termination scheme in IDE systems. The first IDE device is known as the master or primary, and the second device is known as the slave or secondary.

These settings must be in place for an IDE system to function properly. They can typically be set using a jumper according to the drive manufacturer's documentation. Here's an overview of common settings:

Address Setting	Jumper Abbreviation	Definition
Single drive	No jumper	Only drive in the system
Master	MA	First drive in the chain; bootable
Slave	SL	Second drive in the chain; non-bootable
Cable select	CS	Assigns master and slave status based on the location of the twist in the cable

The cable select option was designed following the ST-506 formula for drive addressing. Initial IDE devices were set to cable select, and the crossover between the first and second drive defined the address scheme. While this is still possible with most IDE devices, it is rarely used.

CMOS Configuration

You must notify your system's CMOS of the type of drive you have. Techniques for doing this are listed here, from most-desirable to least-desirable:

* Automatic configuration utility
* Exact match or user-defined drive type
* Nearest match/sector translation

Today, most new systems have an "auto-configure" option in CMOS for IDE devices. This automatic configuration searches for and identifies any IDE devices present in the system and notifies CMOS accordingly. Figure 1.28 shows the CMOS configuration screen.

If the automatic function is not present and your drive does not exactly match any drives in the list, a typical CMOS configuration requires a user-defined setting. For user-defined settings, you must fill in each required drive specification, typically on drive type 40 or higher. The minimum required specifications include cylinders, heads, and sectors per track. This is the most common method for systems with pre-Plug and Play BIOS.

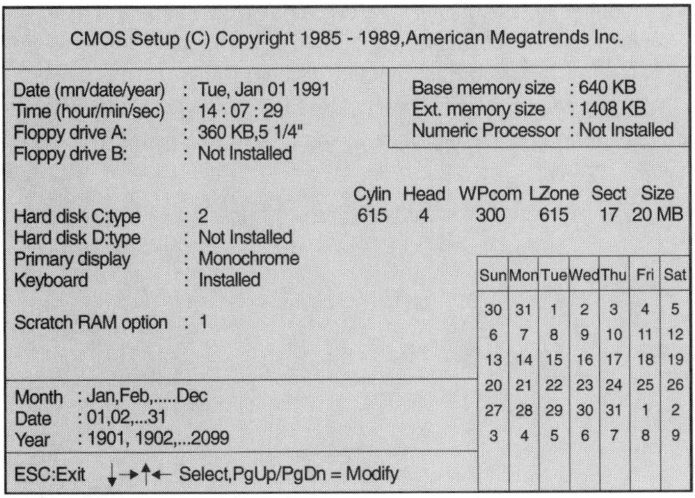

```
        CMOS Setup (C) Copyright 1985 - 1989,American Megatrends Inc.

  Date (mn/date/year)  : Tue, Jan 01 1991      Base memory size  : 640 KB
  Time (hour/min/sec)  : 14 : 07 : 29          Ext. memory size  : 1408 KB
  Floppy drive A:      : 360 KB,5 1/4"         Numeric Processor : Not Installed
  Floppy drive B:      : Not Installed

                                   Cylin Head WPcom LZone Sect  Size
  Hard disk C:type    : 2          615    4   300   615   17   20 MB
  Hard disk D:type    : Not Installed
  Primary display     : Monochrome
  Keyboard            : Installed           Sun Mon Tue Wed Thu Fri Sat

                                             30  31   1   2   3   4   5
  Scratch RAM option  : 1                     6   7   8   9  10  11  12
                                             13  14  15  16  17  18  19

                                             20  21  22  23  24  25  26
  Month  : Jan,Feb,.....Dec                  27  28  29  30  31   1   2
  Date   : 01,02,....31                        3   4   5   6   7   8   9
  Year   : 1901, 1902,...2099

  ESC:Exit  ↓→↑←  Select,PgUp/PgDn = Modify
```

FIGURE 1.28
CMOS drive parameters.

The final CMOS setting option is to simply choose the drive type that most closely matches the capacity of the new drive. With this setting, the drive controller translates the physical specifications into the drive type using sector translation. This is only recommended if all other options have been exhausted; indeed, you might even choose to upgrade your BIOS instead of choosing this option for the existing BIOS. This drive type is one choice in a pre-defined CMOS listing of common drive specifications. Drive types were commonly defined for drives manufactured prior to 1993.

> **NOTE**
>
> Another method of preparing the system for an IDE drive is available. This process involves a third-party utility like OnTrack's Disk Manager and a CMOS setting of "No Drive Defined." It is recommended you use this only as a last resort because of some incompatibilities with system and software standards.

Drive Partitioning and Drive Formatting

These topics are operating system-specific and are covered in detail in Part III of this book.

> **NOTE**
>
> Integrated Drive Electronics, or IDE, locates the controller on the drive itself and merely requires an interface to the system bus on a separate adapter card. This process eliminates a common step in earlier drive types called the low-level, or physical, format that introduces a drive to a controller. Because the controller is attached to the drive permanently, this formatting operation is performed at the factory and should never be performed in the field on an IDE drive.

Enhanced IDE (EIDE)

You configure Enhanced IDE in the same manner you do the standard IDE with one exception: EIDE interfaces allow four IDE devices. This standard was created by combining two IDE interfaces onto one adapter card. Although one channel is typically faster and allows for larger hard drives, both channels are configured in the exact same manner as the single standard IDE channel. For example, if four devices are attached to an EIDE controller, a master-slave pair is created on each channel, and the primary channel master device is bootable.

To add more devices, additional interfaces are required. The only limitation for additional interfaces is the amount of available system resources.

Basic SCSI Drive Configuration

SCSI, pronounced "scuzzy," was created from the ESDI standard. This drive standard allows seven devices to be daisy-chained in a single-cable configuration. By incorporating a complete expansion bus for these eight devices (seven drives plus one controller), you can enable simultaneous parallel communication from the controller to each device. The original SCSI implementation provided a fast, reliable, flexible drive configuration, and it is still the basis for most high-level server disk arrays today.

SCSI devices require a more complex form of addressing and termination than IDE systems due to the flexibility and sheer number of devices that can be present. Unlike IDE termination and addressing, SCSI systems define these as two distinct and separate configuration settings.

Drive Termination

Individual SCSI drives are not terminated (see Figure 1.29). However, the SCSI bus requires termination.

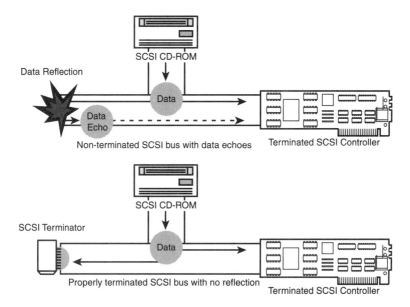

FIGURE 1.29
Electrical signal termination.

In the figure, a single wire is carrying a signal from point A to point B. Due to the nature of electrical signals, the pulse transmits to all points on the wire virtually simultaneously. At the end point, a signal is reflected back down the wire and can be received as a ghost signal, or if it is powerful enough, it may even be received as a second duplicate signal. To eliminate these ghost signals, a resistor must be used at either end of the wire to absorb the signal. This prevents the return echo. This explains the necessity for a terminating resistor on either end of the SCSI bus.

What is meant by "either end of the SCSI bus?" If a system has only internal drives or only external drives, termination is simple. The controller is on one end of the SCSI bus and is generally set to terminate from the factory. The last device on the cable (furthest from the controller) is also set to terminate. However, if a system has both internal and external devices on the same SCSI bus, the controller must *not* be terminated, and the two farthest ends of the internal/external bus *must* be terminated.

Typically, internal devices have jumpers or switches to enable termination of the last device in the chain. External SCSI devices typically require a separate terminator pack. To confuse matters further, some devices automatically terminate the bus if they determine it necessary. Consult your documentation for the proper termination settings for your SCSI device.

SCSI Addressing

Because the controller can communicate with each device individually, each device in the SCSI chain must have a unique identifier. Typically, slower devices are assigned higher identification numbers, and faster devices are assigned lower ID numbers. In addition, the boot device is usually assigned ID 0, and the controller is assigned ID 7. The SCSI ID is set using jumpers or switch blocks according to manufacturer documentation. Some generic standards do exist, as you can see in Table 1.12. However, you should consult your documentation for the final answer.

TABLE 1.12

SCSI ADDRESSING JUMPERS

Jumper Position	Drive ID
SCSI 0	**SCSI 0**
SCSI 1	**SCSI 1**
SCSI 2	**SCSI 2**
SCSI 3	**SCSI 3**
SCSI 4	**SCSI 4**
SCSI 5	**SCSI 5**
SCSI 6	**SCSI 6**
SCSI 7	**SCSI 7**

If you look at the jumpers as the first (rightmost) three binary numbering positions, SCSI ID settings become clear. Typically, the rightmost position is valued as 1, the middle position is valued at 2, and the leftmost value is 4. Therefore, a jumper, or a 1, in both the first and third positions would result in a decimal number of 5. Table 1.13 shows binary conversion, and Table 1.14 shows binary to decimal conversion.

TABLE 1.13

BINARY CONVERSION

Binary Position	Decimal Equivalent (for a 1 in the corresponding binary position)
8	128
7	64
6	32
5	16
4	8
3	4
2	2
1	1

TABLE 1.14

BINARY TO DECIMAL EXAMPLE

Decimal Conversion	128	64	32	16	8	4	2	1
Example Binary Number	1	0	1	1	1	0	0	1

$(1\times128)+(0\times64)+(1\times32)+(1\times16)+(1\times8)+(0\times4)+(0\times2)+(1\times1) = 185$

CMOS Configuration

With SCSI devices, you do not have to inform CMOS of any drive type. The SCSI bus is a completely self-contained data storage and retrieval subsystem. Only data is passed to and from the system. The proper CMOS setting is "No Drive Defined."

Drive Partitioning and Drive Formatting

These topics are operating system-specific and are covered in Part III of this book.

Other SCSI Implementations

For SCSI 2-Fast, Wide, Fast-Wide, SCSI-3, and Ultra SCSI, you follow the same basic steps as for SCSI installation. Variations in data through-put and the number of possible drives do not change these basic steps.

> **NOTE**   SCSI manufacturers have modified standards over the years to suit their individual purposes. SCSI configuration is more of an art than a science due to these non-standard modifications. Consult your documentation if anything varies from the basic standards detailed here.

PERIPHERAL DEVICE INSTALLATION AND CONFIGURATION

Peripheral devices cover a very broad category of computer components and attachments. The most common peripherals include the following:

- ◆ Monitors
- ◆ Keyboards
- ◆ Mice
- ◆ Printers
- ◆ Modems
- ◆ Scanners
- ◆ Speakers

Many of these devices were covered fairly well in the first section on basic terms and concepts. The purpose of this section is to detail the configuration of peripherals in general and specifically these individual devices.

In general, make sure you unplug a peripheral device and position it properly before attempting to connect it to the system. The computer should also be turned off when you attempt to attach external devices.

Monitors

Typically, monitors are error-proof. Because this is a required peripheral, great care has been taken to create standards for its installation and configuration. As long as your video card matches your monitor, everything else is taken care of.

> **NOTE** This does not mean that further configuration is never needed. Some video cards require you to configure additional features for increasing the refresh rates. Other cards require configuration of bus mice, parallel, or even 3D acceleration technology. Consult your manufacturer's documentation for this information.

Keyboards and Mice

Keyboards are also required devices and, therefore, usually have error-free installation. Some keyboards may have additional features that require configuration (such as programmable keys and language definitions).

Mice, on the other hand, require installation into one of three common ports: serial, PS/2, or bus. After you attach the device, you must load a driver in the operating system you choose. Mice require no additional hardware configuration aside from the adapter card configuration and installation.

Printers

Printers are covered extensively in Chapter 5. Aside from configuring a printer to match the serial port communication parameters, you do not have to perform additional configuration that is not covered in Chapter 5. Parallel printers require even less configuration.

Modems

Modems do require hardware configuration to match the communication parameters of the serial port. Modems are covered in more depth in Chapter 7, "Basic Networking."

Scanners

You install a scanner in the same manner you do any other peripheral. A scanner may be configured as a parallel device, for which there is no manual configuration, or as a SCSI device, in which case the same process for configuring drive termination and SCSI identification numbers apply.

Scanners can use a proprietary interface. If yours does, consult the manufacturer's documentation for proper installation procedures.

> **N O T E**   Be aware that the port used for SCSI devices is often confused with the parallel port. Both are DB-25 female connectors on the back of the computer system. Accidentally attaching a SCSI device to the parallel port can seriously damage, if not destroy, both the port and the device. The same is true of attaching a parallel device to the SCSI port.

Speakers

Microphones, speakers, and other audio equipment require no additional configuration. However, be aware of the magnetic fields generated by audio equipment and the damage that these fields can do to magnetic storage media and monitor display fields.

BIOS Concepts and Upgrading ROM

Many ROM and ROM BIOS concepts were covered in the first section under basic concepts. ROM BIOS is the Basic Input and Output System for your computer. It handles the most basic level of operations between the software and the CPU, and between the CPU and other hardware. If your BIOS does not support a particular function or feature you want (such as Plug and Play or an ECP parallel port), it must be upgraded.

ROM BIOS is a software program encoded into a piece of hardware. This combination is commonly known as *firmware*. In earlier systems, the only way to upgrade a ROM chip was by physically replacing the socketed chip (as you learned to do earlier in this chapter).

With today's technological advances, a new chip has been designed. This chip is called *Flash ROM* or *EEPROM*. An EEPROM is an Electrically Erasable Programmable Read-Only Memory chip. This chip is designed to allow its reprogramming through a software utility. This eliminates the previous need to open the system enclosure for an upgrade. Contact your BIOS manufacturer for an upgrade utility and updated BIOS image.

NOTE
An unsuccessful ROM BIOS upgrade can render your system absolutely worthless. Because these chips can now be upgraded via software, they are generally not socketed. If the power should fail or if the upgrade program fails, the most basic level of your system cannot function. If that happens, you must physically replace the BIOS and/or the system board to resolve the problem.

HARDWARE OPTIMIZATION TECHNIQUES

Hardware optimization topics are covered in Chapter 4, "Motherboards/ Processors/Memory."

WHAT IS IMPORTANT TO KNOW

The following list summarizes the chapter and accentuates the key concepts to memorize for the exam.

- A system board contains a CPU, RAM, expansion bus, CMOS, ROM BIOS, clock, and keyboard controller, and may have additional interfaces built into it. Know where these components are located on the system board and be able to identify them by sight.

- A CPU, or central processing unit, provides the brain functions for the entire computer.

- The expansion bus is the physical wire that the data travels on. The data bus is the specific route that the data takes to any given device. The address bus is the logical "phone book" of device addresses on the expansion bus.

- RAM is random access memory. This memory is used for the dynamic storage of information needed for processing by the CPU. RAM is erased every time the system is turned off. ROM is read-only memory. This memory is used for the long term storage of programs and data as firmware on a chip. This information is "burned" into the chip and is retained even during a power failure.

- The BIOS is the most basic input/output system. It runs the POST and interfaces with CMOS and the operating system.

- A CRT uses electrons fired at a phosphor-coated screen to display a pixel. An LCD panel uses intersecting lines of current to activate the liquid crystals at that junction.

- Modems convert digital signals into analog signals and transmit them over the phone lines. On the other end, a modem converts the analog signal back into a digital one for the computer to use.

- Full duplex is simultaneous bidirectional communication. Half duplex is bidirectional communication while taking turns.

- Floppy disk drives offer removable, rewritable, magnetic storage. Floppies come in both 5 ¼-inch and 3 ½-inch sizes and in single, double, and quadruple densities. These variations provide a range of standardized capacities from 180KB to 2.88MB.

- Hard disk drives offer non-removable, rewritable, magnetic storage. Hard disks come in many standard sizes, the most common of which are 5 ¼-inch, 3 ½-inch, and 2 ½-inch. Capacities range from 5MB to more than 18GB.

◆ CD drives are removable, read-only (depending on the specific type), optical storage technology. CD capacities range from 600+ megabytes for CD-ROM to over 4GB for DVD.

◆ A tape drive is a removable, rewritable, streaming (linear access) magnetic storage device. Standards included are DAT, QIC, and DLT.

◆ A hard disk contains several distinct parts. Tracks are concentric circles of data on a given surface. Sectors are the wedge-shaped divisions of the disk. Heads are the read/write mechanisms for each surface. Cylinders are a vertical stack of tracks on a hard disk.

◆ The IDE and SCSI standard interfaces differ greatly. SCSI supports seven devices with unique IDs and drive termination. IDE supports two drives set as master/slave pairs.

◆ Drive subsystems are installed and configured in six stages:

  • Adapter installation

  • Drive termination and addressing

  • Physical drive installation

  • CMOS configuration

  • Drive partitioning

  • Drive formatting

◆ Power supplies provide ± 12 volts or ± 5 volts, whereas ATX systems provide a 3.3 volt supply. They must be rated to handle the amount of power required by all devices it powers. This rating is expressed in watts.

◆ Follow these guidelines for working with field replacement units:

  • Run a complete backup of the system.

  • Create a clean, organized, well-lit workspace with proper static electricity safeguards.

  • Document EVERYTHING.

  • Exit all applications, and then shut down the system and all peripherals.

  • Familiarize yourself with the case design and remove the case.

  • Follow the equipment-specific FRU replacement steps necessary.

◆ Refer to Tables 1.8 and 1.9 for lists of common IRQ and DMA channel settings.

- Understand the advantages and disadvantages of manual configuration versus Plug and Play. Manual configuration can be cumbersome, but it is necessary to fall back on. Often the dynamic Plug and Play standard is not fully supported.

- Parallel communication is data being transferred over more than one separate path but that's traveling to the same location. In PCs, there are eight parallel data paths in the parallel port standard; serial communication, on the other hand, transfers data sequentially over one wire.

▶ Identify common symptoms and problems associated with each module and how to troubleshoot and isolate the problems.

▶ Identify basic troubleshooting procedures and good practices for eliciting problem symptoms from customers.

- Use proper troubleshooting/isolation/problem determination procedures.

- Determine whether a problem is hardware- or software-related.

- Gather information from the user using utilities and tools such as a mulitmeter.

- Evaluate the customer environment.

- Identify symptoms/error codes.

- Discover the situation in which the problem occurred.

CHAPTER 2

Diagnosing and Troubleshooting

DIAGNOSING GENERALITIES

The terms "diagnosing" and "troubleshooting" are used interchangeably in many texts. This is a misconception. *Diagnosis* is actually the result of successful troubleshooting steps. Diagnosis is the final step before using an FRU replacement, which was covered in the previous chapter.

Troubleshooting is as much an art form as it is a science. Yes, the technical knowledge is required, but the logical—and sometimes intuitive—leaps from one fact to another are a product of experience.

Because the process for *troubleshooting* is more a framework than a methodology and is based more on guidelines than step-by-step instruction, this chapter begins by discussing these guidelines and troubleshooting techniques. Following that is a section discussing common tools and one discussing common problems and their symptoms, causes, and resolutions. This material is tested heavily on the Core examination, not in content, but rather in the application of these principles in a set of scenarios.

TROUBLESHOOTING TECHNIQUES

The process of troubleshooting involves all of the following:

- Documentation
- Basic hardware knowledge
- Logical understanding of subsystem functions and interactions with other subsystems
- Customer interaction
- Information gathering or research

Each of these areas is required in every part of the troubleshooting process. There are three basic phases to the problem solving, or troubleshooting, process. Again, these are not carved in stone by any means. They are intended to be used as guidelines for your logical processes in repetitive iterations until the problem has been eliminated. They are

- Quantify the problem by describing it.
- Isolate the problem by removing other variables.
- Resolve the problem through repair or replacement.

Quantifying the Problem

This phase represents a series of questions you can use to begin your information gathering. Documentation of past repairs on this system should be readily available. A customer interview using open-ended questions should yield the majority of your answers.

Typically, the user will be irritated with the delay and anxious to help. These questions allow the user to express his frustration at the situation without directing it toward you. And important information may come to light while the user is venting his frustration.

These are the questions you should ask:

- *What does the computer seem to be doing?* This allows the user to express her interpretation of the system events occurring. Often, this step will lead to the next question.

- *When did you first notice the problem?* This begins your verbal isolation of time variables. If the problem began first thing this morning, you can eliminate the power surge that happened at lunchtime, for example.

- *What were you trying to do when this happened?* This establishes a baseline and provides information on what the proper responses from the system should have been. If the user was attempting to format a floppy disk and now her hard disk drive is not responding properly, it's likely that she accidentally formatted the hard disk drive instead.

- *Did you notice any error messages?* A computer gives so many messages that often the user ignores error messages until he is forced to take action. This is especially the case when a support staff is difficult to understand or is overburdened and unable to respond immediately. Often a user's own insecurities play a part in this; after all, no one likes to look ridiculous.

- *Have any changes been made to the system recently?* This leads to the majority of system problems. Often users will intentionally mislead you about system changes. If her answers seem vague or non-committal, often an unsupported system change has occurred. This is especially the case with laptop computers because they are introduced to a whole new environment—home. In these types of situations, you often find yourself supporting not only the user and company hardware and software, but also the user's family's software.

Isolating the Problem

Just like in high school algebra, to find the solution you must eliminate all variables but one. This also includes isolating any user errors that were indicated in the customer interview.

> **NOTE**
>
> If you suspect the user has made a mistake and there truly is no hardware problem, the easiest isolation tactic is to simply try the task the customer was attempting when the error was encountered. For more information on dealing with customer issues and user errors, see Chapter 8, "Customer Satisfaction."

First Things First

Start with the easy steps first. Is it plugged in? Is it on? Verify this with a complete system restart, not a system reset. A system reset will just interrupt power to the motherboard without powering down any other subsystems (as indicated in the chart below). This may overlook a soft error of some type.

Soft boot	This simply resets the CPU by setting its registers to F000.
Pressing Ctrl+Alt+Del	As you learned in Chapter 1, "Isolation, Configuration, and Upgrading," this goes to the location of BIOS.
Medium boot	This cuts power temporarily from the system board. System board components act as though a complete power-down has occurred, but drives and peripherals remain running.
Pressing a physical Reset switch on the enclosure	This completely shuts down everything on the system. Removal of the power cord or battery indicates that a complete power restart is necessary.
Hard boot	Causes a complete power-down, which may include removal of the power cord or laptop battery.

Some common errors and their resolutions are listed in the next section. If a simple resolution does not do the job, start narrowing your options.

Hardware Versus Software

Once you determine whether you're dealing with a hardware issue or a software issue, your steps for resolution change dramatically. So, how do you make that determination?

If the problem disappears after a system reboot, does not occur when you boot from a different device, or occurs in only one application, your problem is probably software. For more information on troubleshooting software, see Chapter 17, "Diagnosing and Troubleshooting."

Typically, if the problem occurs in multiple applications (and you can rule out the operating system layer), your problem could be hardware. Some type of manufacturer-specific hardware diagnostics will give you a better answer.

The remainder of this chapter deals almost exclusively with hardware malfunctions.

Hardware Isolation and Resolution

This process is very cyclical in nature. In fact, isolation is only isolation until it resolves the problem, and then it is resolution. Because these are tied so closely together, they are covered here as one phase.

Working from your understanding of hardware subsystems, define which systems are affected. For example, if you are experiencing a video failure, you would not need to bother checking out the storage subsystems. When you have identified a particular subsystem, begin your research on the components in the system. The manufacturer's documentation gathered for the system earlier will be of great importance here. If you do not find a common resolution, or if there are multiple possibilities, you must begin hardware isolation. This process is made significantly easier if you have a complete system available as a spare for replacement purposes.

If you suspect that one item could be the problem, you must remove it from the system and check to see if the problem is resolved. If it is not, simply replace that part and begin again with the next component. You may even get to a point where whole subsystems must be removed and/or replaced temporarily before you find the true problem.

If you have an integrated system board with many subsystems, you might have to replace the entire system board if one subsystem fails and cannot be overridden on it.

If All Else Fails, Read the Instructions

Contrary to the title for this section, researching the manufacturer's recommended troubleshooting should not be left for last. This material can save you a lot of time. In addition to manuals, many hardware vendors have Web sites with their most up-to-date information and software downloads.

Some common Web sites are listed below:

Apple Computer Corporation	`www.apple.com`
Compaq Computer Corporation	`www.compaq.com`
CompTIA	`www.comptia.org`
Hewlett-Packard Corporation	`www.hp.com`
IBM Corporation	`www.ibm.com`
Intel Corporation	`www.intel.com`
Microsoft Corporation	`www.microsoft.com`
Packard Bell Corporation	`www.packardbell.com`
Seagate Technology	`www.seagate.com`

To find Web addresses for other companies, use your favorite search engine.

Other documentation is available in the form of subscriptions to monthly CD updates. Some examples of this include Microsoft's *TechNet* subscription and *Compaq's Quarterly Update*. In many cases, these CDs have an entire library of available information from the manufacturer. Vendors like these because the CDs are also much cheaper to produce than the millions of pages of manuals and updates every year.

TROUBLESHOOTING COMMON ERRORS

When you begin, you may want to run through this section to eliminate simple errors before you delve into the deeper levels of troubleshooting.

User Error

The single most common error is a *user error*. These account for as many as 60 percent of service calls in many organizations. The only real way to eliminate this as a real issue is to repeat the error yourself. Generally, if an error is repeatable, it is fixable.

Software Error

The next most common problem is a software issue. Another 20–30 percent of most calls are software related or entirely software generated. The vast majority of these software and device driver errors are covered in Part III, "What's Important to Know About the A+ DOS/Windows Exam."

Hardware Error

Often errors are assumed to be hardware related when, in reality, a software remedy is called for. However, hardware errors really are the problem in about 10–20 percent of the situations in a corporate environment. Some hardware issues, such as failure of equipment power sources, are easily diagnosed. Others are random and erratic. These "disappearing" errors are the most difficult to detect and fix.

> **NOTE** Before you start learning about actual symptoms, you should think about preventive care. A clean, tidy system will prevent many hardware failures—especially heat-related failures. This will be covered in more depth in the next chapter. See Chapter 3, "Safety and Preventive Maintenance."

POST Error Codes

When ROM BIOS initiates the POST (or Power-On Self Test), a series of tests are run against various addresses in the system. These addresses represent physical devices and initiate tests on these devices, as listed here:

- ♦ When the computer is turned on, the CPU is reset to location F000h. This is the location of the POST test in BIOS.

- ♦ CPU registers are calculated against a checksum value.

- The DMA controller is checked.

- The IRQ controller is tested.

- The timer is tested for the proper speed.

- The expansion slots are tested.

- Parallel and serial ports are checked.

- The video card is tested.

- RAM is tested.

- The keyboard is tested.

- Disk drives and their controllers are tested, starting with the floppy drive.

- Drive mechanics are started.

- Adapter cards in expansion slots are polled and memorized.

- A single beep, indicating a successful test, is generated.

Often a hardware error will cause a component to fail this POST test. Table 2.1 outlines a series of highly testable, generic audio/video error codes and their indicators.

TABLE 2.1

AUDIBLE ERROR CODES

Audio Signal	Display	Possible Problem
None	None	Power failure, or system unplugged
None	Normal prompt	Defective speaker
1 short beep	Normal prompt	Improper startup
1 long beep	Error code	(Refer to visual codes)
1 short and 1 long beep	None	Monitor failure
2 short beeps	None	Monitor failure
2 short beeps	Error code	(Refer to visual codes)
Repeated short beeps	None	Power supply failure or interruption
Continuous beeps	None	Power supply failure
Continuous beeps	Normal or Error	Stuck keyboard
1 long and 1 short beep 1 long and 3 short beeps	None or Error	System board failure
1 long and 2 short beeps	None or Error	System board failure
1 long and 3 short beeps	None	System board failure

Table 2.2 lists errors that are shown during the bootstrap in coordination with an audible code of one long beep or two short beeps.

TABLE 2.2

VISUAL ERROR CODES

Error Code	Possible Error
1xx	System failure/system board error
102	ROM BIOS error
161, 162	CMOS/system options not set
163	Time/date not set
2xx	Memory failure
3xx	Keyboard failure
6xx	Floppy disk or controller failure
7xx	Math coprocessor failure
9xx	Primary parallel port failure
11xx	Primary serial port failure
17xx	Hard disk failure
1701	Drive not ready
73xx	Drive or controller failure

Beware that false errors can be generated by devices that are not fully IBM-compatible or even by static experienced during startup.

System Board

The system board is typically the most misdiagnosed replacement. Because this is the heart of the system, many times a system board will be diagnosed as the cause of the system trouble. That is not to say that it never is; however, you need to run your diagnostic tests thoroughly. The most common symptoms of a failing system board are random system lockup and long lists of POST errors.

CPU

The CPU falls into the same category as the system board in that it is often misdiagnosed. However, a failing CPU can mask itself as a faulty interrupt controller, DMA controller, or even memory. The most common cause for CPU failure is heat. Make sure your system has the manufacturer's recommended heat-dissipation mechanism, which might be a heat sink, a fan, or a combination of these.

Although not as applicable to the CPU, other socketed chips can exhibit failure if they are not properly seated. You may wonder how a chip can work itself out of a socket with no outside intervention. This phenomenon is known as *socket creep*. It occurs due to temperature shifts and the contracting and expanding of the sockets containing chips and boards. A quick application of pressure to the suspect part (as well as any other socketed devices) should remedy the situation.

Memory

Memory is checked during POST, but has been known to pass the POST test and fail in some other application. Memory can generate two types of errors: soft and hard.

A *soft memory error* is a random error or even a faulty programming event. Typically, the program or faulty memory controller command makes a request of a protected area of memory. This causes a system lockup and a Window GPF, or General Protection Fault. A reboot will eliminate the problem. For more information on GPFs, see Part III of this book.

A *hard memory error* will also lock up the computer, but it does not go away with a system reboot. This type of error is caused by a faulty chip that must be replaced. Often a corresponding error message will tell you the bank in which the memory is bad. In addition, several third-party memory testers operate on the same principle as POST, but run the RAM through a much more robust set of tests. Often, these programs will tell exactly which chip has failed.

CMOS

The single most common CMOS failure is the loss of system configuration. This is indicated by POST errors 162 and 163, but it may also show up as error 164 (memory mismatch). This error can be caused by a failed

CMOS chip, a power surge, or a BIOS failure; however, the most common cause is a CMOS battery failure. If you run system setup and save the CMOS information and the error returns on the next restart, you will need to replace the CMOS battery.

Because this battery failure can happen at any time, it is recommended that you keep a copy of all system configuration settings on disk or paper, and store them with the system's other documentation.

Sound

If you do not hear any beeps during startup but the computer starts as usual, the speaker is probably unplugged or defective. This simple part can be obtained from any computer parts store and replaced with minimum fuss.

If your Windows sound system or SoundBlaster card is failing, check the device drivers and Windows settings first. More often than not, the device just needs to be reconfigured.

Floppy Drive

Floppy disk drives are most susceptible to preventive maintenance problems (as you will learn in the next chapter). Floppy drives can become worn due to the physical contact inherent in the device. The read/write heads can also become misaligned. Typically, the remedy for these errors is drive replacement.

If your floppy disk drive LED (or hard disk LED) comes on and stays on during bootup and does not ever go off, you probably have the data cable plugged in backwards. Reattach the cable with the stripe on PIN #1 and restart the computer (see Figure 2.1).

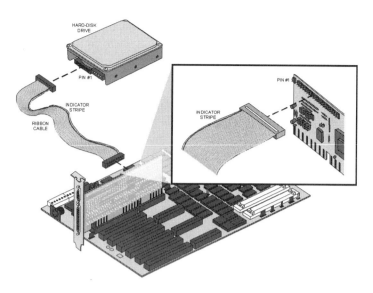

FIGURE 2.1
Aligning PIN #1.

You may have to reset the drive value in CMOS.

Hard Disk Drive

Hard disk failures are almost heart-wrenching to those who do not have regular data backups. For this purpose, it's recommended that home users back up at least once a month (more often for business users). Common hard disk failures include media shift, bearing failure, head crashes, controller failure, configuration errors, and optimization concerns.

Media Shift

Media shift is more common in older drives. Because the oxide media coats the physical platter, the media can shift over time (as shown in Figure 2.2). This is due to the extreme force created by the drive spinning at more than 3,600rpm (10,000 on some newer drives!).

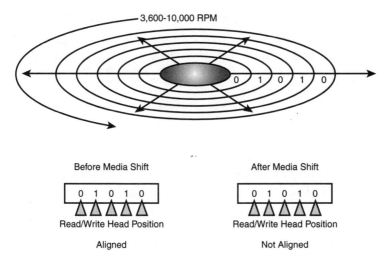

FIGURE 2.2
Oxide media shift.

If you have ever attempted to stand on the outer edge of a merry-go-round, you understand exactly what is happening. Over time the media shifts outward and, consequently, the controller cannot find the data in the tracks where it remembers putting it in. This can be remedied with a low-level format.

NOTE   As you learned in Chapter 1, IDE and SCSI drives should *never* be low-level formatted. Some utilities on the market claim to "safely" low-level format IDE and SCSI drives, but beware of them. If media shift seems to be the problem, contact the drive manufacturer to determine the best course of action.

Bearing Failure

As you'll find out in the upcoming section on the power supply, bearing failure can cause odd noises and can prevent spinning entirely. Often, this will result in sporadic failures during startup. This is a good example of when hitting the computer may temporarily fix the problem. The force from smacking the computer (which is almost therapeutic at times) actually releases the bearing's grip on the spindle and allows it to rotate as normal.

NOTE Do *not* go around hitting computers if you suspect a failure. Although doing so can sometimes fix one problem, it can cause several others. If this is necessary once, fine. But back up all data and replace the drive before a permanent freeze can occur.

Head Crashes

The most feared hard disk failure of all is the head crash (illustrated in Figure 2.3). A hard disk head crash is literally equivalent to you diving head first onto the pavement at 50mph. Due to any number of causes, the "flying" head drops from a relative height onto a thin media layer moving at up to 10,000rpm.

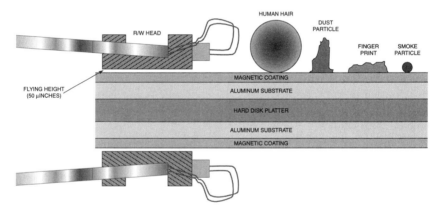

FIGURE 2.3
A hard disk crash.

This causes the head irreparable damage and literally gouges the media off the platter, taking your data with it. There is only one common method of recovering from a head crash—hard disk replacement.

NOTE There are some recovery facilities that you can ship your drive off to. These facilities will open your drive casing in a special clean room and physically move the good platters from your drive to a replacement drive. After this process is complete, they will attempt to recover the majority of the data on the drive. However, the data in the exact location of the crash cannot be recovered by any means.

Controller Failure

Typically, controller failure requires that the controller itself be replaced. On most drives, a failed controller does not automatically mean lost data. (If the controller was passing bad information to the drive over a period of time, you may experience patches of lost data.) Simply replace the controller and start the system as usual.

On IDE drives, this has a more profound effect. Because the controller is mounted on the drive, the drive must be replaced and restored from a backup. Some manufacturers will send a controller board out as a spare part to physically replace the card mounted on the bottom of the drive, but most do not.

Optimization Concerns

The DOS and Windows utilities for drive optimization are covered more thoroughly in Part III, but this section discusses it in general terms.

There are two basic types of drive optimization: media testing/recovery and disk defragmentation.

Media recovery is the process that Microsoft's ScanDisk utility performs. This utility actually scans the entire drive for bad media. When a bad sector is found, ScanDisk attempts to move the data to a new location and mark the original location with a flag. This "flag" tells the drive controller to never use this location again.

Disk defragmentation is a process more related to the type of disk format used. Typically, as a file is saved, it is written to the first empty cluster available. If the file is larger than the available space, a marker is placed at the end of the file pointing to the next free location. The balance of the file is written to this second location in the same manner. This process continues until the file is completely saved.

Because this process has the added overhead of finding additional locations for the same file during both read and write processes, it decreases drive performance. A disk optimization utility, such as Microsoft's Defrag, recombines these files in a single location (see Figure 2.4). The amount of data swapping needed depends on the condition of the drive data and the length of time since the last optimization. Consequently, the duration of the process can vary from a few minutes to several hours.

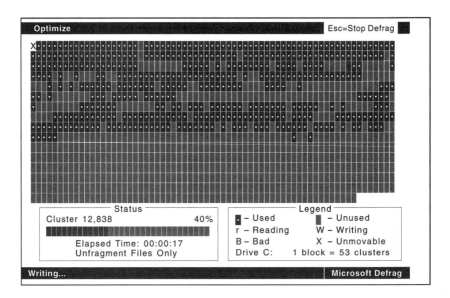

FIGURE 2.4
Disk optimization.

CD-ROM Drive

The single most common CD-ROM error is a dirty lens or scratched disc. A dirty lens can be cleaned (as indicated in the next chapter on preventive maintenance), but a scratched CD cannot be repaired.

The only other common CD-ROM failure is more disastrous. If the laser head assembly becomes misaligned, the realignment process is often more expensive than the replacement of the entire drive. A CD-ROM can become misaligned from rough handling or being dropped, or can occur gradually over time.

Power Supply

Power supply failure is usually readily seen. If the system shuts down and will not power on again, the power supply or power source are suspect. You can easily verify this by using your multimeter and testing the leads for values within the tolerances listed in Chapter 1.

Another common power supply error is overloading. The wattage rating stamped on the power supply is absolute. If this rating is exceeded, the supply can overheat or even fail more catastrophically. Power supplies have been known to smoke and catch fire in extreme circumstances.

Another less-dangerous, but still common, failure can be heard rather than seen. A steady, repetitive grinding or squeaking noise indicates a power supply fan bearing failure. Some power supplies have removable fan assemblies, but they should be opened only by a qualified electrician. Power supplies can contain dangerous levels of electricity even with the power off! This is due to the high charge levels retained in the capacitor components of a power supply. Typically, replacement of the entire supply is recommended.

Parallel and Serial Ports

The two most common problems with these ports are configuration and cabling. Port configuration occurs in CMOS, the operating system, the application using the port, and the device on the other end of the cable. No wonder it is so easy to confuse the configuration parameters. Most configuration errors are covered in the proper installation and configuration of the ports and devices (as covered in Chapter 1). Some common ones include the incorrect setting of the baud or the duplex. More of these settings will be covered in Chapter 7, "Basic Networking," under the topic of modems.

The most common cause of garbled communications from a parallel or serial port is a faulty cable. Keep in mind that both parallel and serial cables must be shielded; but even with shielding, you should not bundle a power cable and a data cable closely together due to the possibility of interference. Also, follow the device manufacturer's recommended cabling standards and length. Never exceed 10 feet for a parallel cable or 50 feet for a serial cable.

Video

Video errors can manifest themselves as a multitude of errors. Typically, the easiest troubleshooting technique is to replace the monitor. If the problem still exists on the new monitor, it is the video card. If not, it is the monitor.

NOTE

The generalization made here should not be assumed for all components. If a component is replaced and the problem goes away, you should fully eliminate the replaced part by placing the old one in another system and verifying that the problem follows the suspected bad part. Without this verification, the possibility exists that the error was caused by the combination of the suspected part and the subsystem from which it was removed. Never assume anything.

The problem in most garbled video displays is the data cable between the screen and the system. Often these cables are hard-wired into the screen and require cable splicing or complete monitor replacement. If this is the case, check to see if the problem is a bent pin. If so, you can attempt to straighten the pin with a pair of needle-nose pliers and a small straight-edge screwdriver. Many monitors today have detachable data cables for just this reason.

Table 2.3 outlines common video problems and their causes.

TABLE 2.3

COMMON VIDEO PROBLEMS

Problem	Probable Cause
Dark screen	The monitor is not plugged in or turned on. If it is, the monitor's high-voltage power supply is suspect.
White screen	The data cable is unplugged or faulty.
Distorted display	Check all horizontal and vertical controls. Verify that the monitor is of the proper type for your video card.
Bright center spot	The positioning magnets for the electron gun are failing.
Interference and distortion (snow, wavy lines, rotating horizontal bars, odd color areas)	This is often caused by electromagnetic interference because of proximity to another electrical device, including other monitors.
Random garbage characters in text mode	Bad character generator chip on the video card.
Most other problems	Faulty device drivers and software settings.

Another common monitor issue involves a distorted display. This is most commonly attributed to a magnetic field interference generated from another mechanical device. Speakers, fluorescent lights, fans, and electrical motors are the most common culprits. If the distortion changes or disappears as you move the monitor a few feet away, look for these or other devices that could be generating the field.

Mice and Keyboards

These failures typically occur due to improper cleaning. A keyboard's worst enemy is the user's beverage. More keyboards are damaged from spills than any other thing. (These topics will be covered further in Chapter 3, under preventive maintenance.)

TOOLS

Tools can be separated into two distinct categories:

◆ Hardware tools

◆ Software tools

Hardware Tools

Some of these are a subset of your average car mechanic's tool set; others are specifically designed for working with the physical components of a computer system.

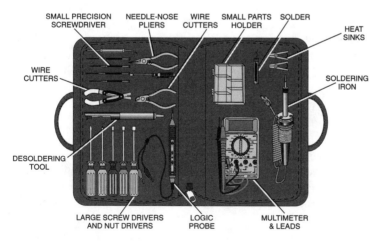

FIGURE 2.5
A common computer toolkit.

A common computer technician's toolkit may include the following tools:

- Screwdrivers (Phillips and standard)

- Torx drivers

- Pliers (standard and needle-nose)

- Nut drivers

- Tweezers or artificial fingers

- Chip extractors

- Multimeter

NOTE   ESD dissipation equipment is also included in many technician's toolkits. These items include grounding wrist straps, antistatic solutions, faraday cage static bags, and antistatic mats. ESD and ESD dissipation equipment will be covered in Chapter 3.

Screwdrivers

Both Phillips and standard (or slotted) screwdrivers are necessary. Make sure you have at least a small standard screwdriver to use for setting switch blocks. The Phillips head has two blades in an "X" formation to reduce stripping and blade slippage. The Phillips screwdriver #2 is the most common tool used for hardware repairs.

NOTE   Although they are convenient, magnetic screwdrivers often cause erratic computer behavior. The magnetic tool can damage sensitive computer IC, or integrated circuit, components without your knowledge. What's worse, these failures may not cause noticeable symptoms for an indeterminable period of time.

Torx Drivers

These unique drivers are required to work on most business-grade equipment from Compaq and Hewlett-Packard, as well as many other computers. The Torx driver takes the idea of Phillips screwdrivers one more step. Instead of two crossing blades, imagine six crossing blades that create a star-like formation. Because of this design, the Torx head is less susceptible to stripping than its Phillips counterpart.

Pliers

Both standard and needle-nose pliers make good additions to your toolkit. Needle-nose pliers are often needed to remove stubborn jumpers and various connectors.

Nut Drivers

Two standard nut sizes are used in most computers. These sizes were determined with the original IBM PC which had $1/4$-inch hex-head case screws and $3/16$-inch hex-head drive screws. The $1/4$-inch screw has become the most popular of the two, typically with a slotted or Phillips head in the inset of the hex-head.

Artificial Fingers

Regardless of what you call the small, yellow tube with the plunger, it is a lifesaver. Typically, you depress the plunger, and three metal prongs spring out to grasp any small object within reach. This device allows you to retrieve screws and other components from tight quarters without the use of potentially damaging equipment, such as magnetic retrieval tools.

Chip Extractors

A variety of chip extractors exist, as you can see in Figure 2.6.

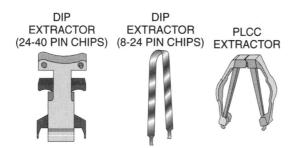

FIGURE 2.6
Chip extractors.

Many technicians use a small, flat-bladed screwdriver to remove DIP chips instead of the recommended extractor. That technique may work, but it also is more susceptible to static damage. For some chip designs such as the PLCC, the recommended extractor is the only advisable way to remove that style of chip.

Multimeter

This tool is often overlooked in today's technical world of disposable parts. This is not the case on the A+ exam. The majority of questions covering tools will discuss the proper setting and use of a multimeter to measure different values of a given circuit. The three basic settings covered here are volts, ohms, and amperes or amps.

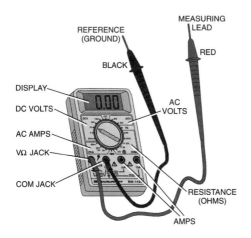

FIGURE 2.7
Digital multimeter.

Ohm's Law, a formula for calculating electrical values in a circuit, can be used to assist you in taking measurements. This mathematical formula states that in a given closed circuit, voltage (V) is equal to the current (I) multiplied by the resistance (R), or V=IR. For more information on Ohm's Law and electrical calculations, see the *A+ Training Guide* from New Riders Publishing.

The overwhelming majority of electrical measurements in computer systems are DC voltage tests. In some instances, it may be necessary to measure AC voltage, current, or resistance tolerances, but not many.

> **NOTE** It is important to remember to set the meter to a range appropriate for the expected value of the component. If the range is too small or the leads are reversed, you could damage the meter. If you are working with an unknown voltage, set the meter to the highest setting and work down from there.

Voltage

Once the meter is set to measure volts (we will deal strictly with DC voltage here) and set to the appropriate scale (a 50-volt scale is adequate for most computer system measurements), you can begin. Paying attention to the polarity of the circuit and the multimeter leads, connect the negative lead to the negative side first, and then attach the positive lead. The key to remember here is that the voltmeter must be connected to the live circuit in parallel with the component being measured. See Figure 2.8 for an illustration of a voltmeter connection.

AC voltage is handled the same way with one exception: AC voltage has a continuously cycling polarity. The positive and negative leads will not matter when measuring AC circuits.

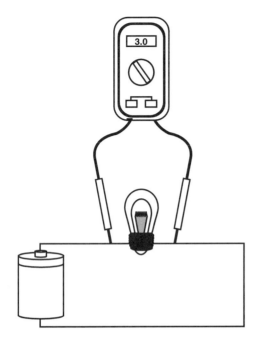

FIGURE 2.8
A voltmeter connection.

Current/Amperage

Again, after you make sure that the meter is set to the proper scale and function, you can insert the ammeter into the circuit (see Figure 2.9). This is different than the connection for a voltmeter because an ammeter measures the *current*, the amount of electricity flowing through the circuit. To accurately measure current, all of the current must flow through the meter. This requires that the circuit be broken and the multimeter be inserted into the gap in series with the circuit to be measured.

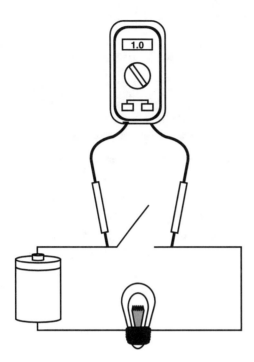

FIGURE 2.9
An ammeter connection.

Resistance/Ohms

Unlike the previous measurements, resistance must be measured without power applied to the circuit. Aside from this, the physical connection is much like that for a voltmeter. First, you set the scale and function to a high ohms scale, and then you attach the probes to the ends of the component to be tested. At this point, the meter generates a known amount of power and measures the drain of that power after it passes through the component. If the resistance is infinite, there is most likely an incomplete circuit somewhere in your test setup.

NOTE
Be aware that measuring components in a circuit may pass current to other components and (at the very least) cause your readings to be inaccurate, or (at most) damage other more sensitive components, like IC chips.

Software Tools

Software tools are split into two categories: system diagnostics and third-party utilities.

Typically, a manufacturer's system diagnostics utility will yield more detailed information about a particular system. This may be limited to a particular range of tests, or even a particular subset of systems.

To obtain a comparison to industry standards, you must use a set of third-party diagnostics. These typically cover a wider range of systems and a wider range of tests, but without the level of detail available on the system diagnostics.

Often, third-party utilities include a benchmarking utility that can provide a facility for judging performance across many manufacturers' systems. These typically run a battery of tests against your machine and compare the test results to the results of other "baseline" machines.

WHAT IS IMPORTANT TO KNOW

- There are three steps to eliminating a problem on a computer. These are to 1) quantify the problem by describing it, 2) isolate the problem by removing all other variables, and 3) resolve by repair or replacement.

- Be able to classify problems into categories.

- When all else fails, know who to ask.

- There are three different types of errors: user errors, software errors, and hardware errors.

- Know the order in which the BIOS POST checks hardware upon startup.

- A single, short beep during the boot process for your machine is completely normal and indicates that everything passed the POST examinations.

- Know the various categories of error codes. Knowledge of individual error codes is not heavily tested, so elimination of test answers by category usually works well.

- Disk optimization regroups scattered fragments of files on the drive into one contiguous location. This increases both performance and system stability.

- Know and understand the general problems that were discussed in this chapter and their resolutions.

- Voltmeters are connected to the target circuit in parallel to the load you are testing.

- An ammeter is connected to the target circuit in series because all of the electrons must flow through this meter to measure the total current.

- Voltage = Current × Amperes, or V=IR.

OBJECTIVES

▶ Identify the purpose of various types of preventive maintenance products and procedures, and when to use or perform them.

▶ Identify procedures and devices for protecting against environmental hazards.

▶ Identify the potential hazards and proper safety procedures relating to lasers and high-voltage equipment.

▶ Identify items that require special disposal procedures that comply with environmental guidelines.

▶ Identify ESD (Electrostatic Discharge) precautions and procedures, including the use of ESD protection devices.

CHAPTER 3

Safety and Preventive Maintenance

PREVENTIVE MAINTENANCE BASICS

The topics of preventive maintenance and safety comprise approximately 10 percent of the exam. But what is preventive maintenance? What does it actually prevent? Is it really necessary? These are all very good questions, but ultimately the choice comes down to performing preventive maintenance of equipment or replacing equipment. It is that simple. Preventive maintenance is one of the most overlooked necessities of maintaining a system. If an effective preventive maintenance program is not on your list of priorities, add money to your repair and replacement budget.

Preventive maintenance takes many different forms for each piece of equipment, but one underlying procedure exists for every single component in the system: cleaning. We will take a look at the cleaners involved and the steps you should take to clean each unique component.

The need to clean arises primarily from dust and dirt causing heat-related, and sometimes mechanical, failures. In addition to a clean system, clear and open designs as well as unobstructed ventilation pathways are extremely important. The most common solution for cleaning dust is a vacuum cleaner; however, this is not the recommended method in the PC arena. A low-powered vacuum may be used, but the preferred method is to use a can of compressed air to blow the dust out of the system. The primary concern with vacuums is the risk of vacuuming components off the board, or removing jumpers in the same way.

Another cleaning material to use is a lint-free cloth, which limits the amount of stray fabric and fuzz added to the computer. This cloth can be used to clean many system surfaces, but most commonly it is used for the outside case. In addition, a non-abrasive household cleanser may be used. Test this solvent on an inconspicuous area of the plastic to ensure that the solvent will not cause discoloration.

EXTERNAL PREVENTIVE MAINTENANCE PROCEDURES

For external cleaning, ordinary household cleaners should suffice. Some of the methods and materials necessary are listed in the following sections.

Enclosures and Peripheral Devices

For the system enclosure, or case, you can use a damp, lint-free cloth.

N O T E When using any liquid solution to clean electronic equipment, be sure to apply a small amount of the solution to the cloth only. This will prevent the liquid from seeping into ventilation holes and protective bezels.

If the computer case has your two-year old daughter's peanut-butter-and-jelly sandwich stuck to it, the use of household solvents may be necessary. Trust me. Test the solvent on the casing prior to use as mentioned previously.

Monitor

Ordinary household glass cleaner applied to the cloth will suffice for cleaning a dirty screen. For the monitor housing, adhere to the guidelines listed above for enclosures.

Monitors require a lot of ventilation for heat dissipation of their high-voltage power supplies. Do not lay any papers or other objects on top of a monitor.

Keyboard

Keyboards are best cleaned with bursts of compressed air from a can. You can buy cans of compressed air at most computer parts stores. Do not use any solvents on computer keys, as the letters have a tendency to be removed along with the dirt.

As a last resort for cleaning up a spilled soda or coffee, you can remove all the keys from the keyboard and soak it in the bathtub or dishwasher with no soap. Make sure that you allow enough time for the keyboard to dry thoroughly before you reattach it to the PC.

Mouse

The mouse picks up lint and dirt very easily. The rubber roller ball is designed to grip the mouse pad for traction and has a tendency to grip any debris on the mouse pad as well. After a while, it tends to display jerky or erratic mouse movement.

In order to properly clean a mouse, remove the mouse ball and clean it with water or a rubber restorative solution. In addition, tracks of grit can develop on the plastic wheels the roller contacts. With the ball removed, you can clean these rollers using a pencil eraser and a little elbow grease (see Figure 3.1).

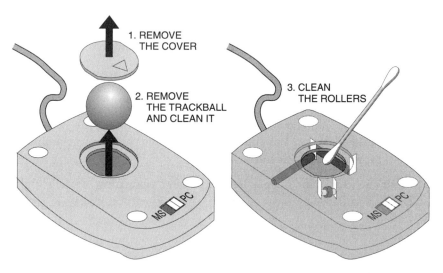

FIGURE 3.1
Cleaning the mouse.

Printers

To clean the external casing of a printer, follow the same instructions as for the system enclosure. To clean the printer more thoroughly, follow the manufacturer's specifications. A few common techniques are listed here.

Dot-Matrix Printers

After cleaning the outside casing, remove the covers and vacuum or blow out the paper dust, paper punch-outs, and other debris. You can clean the *platens*, or paper rollers, using a damp cloth or rubber restoration solution. To clean the print head and metal components, use a cotton pad with denatured alcohol applied (see Figure 3.2).

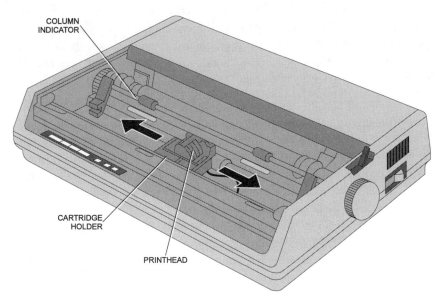

FIGURE 3.2
Dot-matrix printer carriage.

N O T E   Many texts advise the use of cotton swabs or Q-tips to clean components. Avoid this if possible because the swab can leave cotton fibers behind on the equipment.

Inkjet Printers

Inkjet printers are the easiest printers on which to perform preventive maintenance. The majority of these printers need nothing more than the built-in cleaning cycle. This cycle cleans the ink jets by sliding the print head off to the side and alternately forcing ink through the jets.

Laser Printers

Laser printers typically require the most maintenance. Because of their design, most preventive maintenance is taken care of by replacing the toner cartridge. On most models, all disposable components of the electrophotographic process, or EP process, are contained within the single disposable EP or toner cartridge. For more information on the EP process, see Chapter 5, "Printers."

> **NOTE** Do not use remanufactured or recycled toner cartridges. I cannot emphasize this enough. When cartridges are remanufactured, typically, the toner supply is refilled, but other consumable parts are not modified. This will cause toner leaks, streaks, and other image formation errors. Likewise, you should avoid recycled dot-matrix printer ribbons. Worn, plastic gears in the mechanisms are not replaced during recycling, and often the proper ribbon lubricant is not added for the print wires in the printhead. This is a leading cause of printhead failure.

In addition to changing the toner cartridge, you might need to clean other components. You should vacuum excess toner from the inside of the printer, but beware! A special vacuum filter is required for this step. 3M makes a special laser printer vacuum for exactly this purpose.

If you get toner on your hands or clothing, use *cold* water to remove it. Hot water can melt the toner into your clothing permanently.

The corona wires should be cleaned with a special tool, which is often mounted inside the printer casing somewhere. A cotton swab, either dry or dipped in alcohol, can be used in a pinch.

Be careful not to touch the drum or transfer roller assemblies during this process, and *never* attempt to clean those components with anything. This can lead to repetitive image defects from the contact. When you finish the preventive maintenance process, run multiple printer test pages to remove any additional toner that has been knocked loose along the way.

INTERNAL PREVENTIVE MAINTENANCE PROCEDURES

For internal cleaning procedures, especially for circuit boards, a can of compressed air is often your only tool. However, low-power vacuums and even electronic contact cleaning solutions, such as Blue Shower, can be used in extreme cases.

Floppy Disk Drive

Because floppy disk drives open to the outside environment, they collect more dirt and dust than most other internal devices. These devices require periodic cleaning with a special kit (see Figure 3.3) that includes a cloth diskette and an alcohol-based solution. For further information, follow the directions of the kit you intend to use.

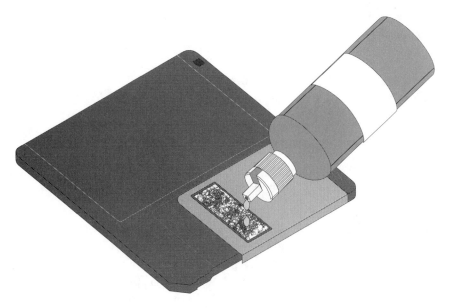

FIGURE 3.3
A floppy disk cleaning kit.

NOTE Use these cleaning kits only if the drive is already having problems. These floppy cleaning kits are not recommended for preventive maintenance schedules because of their abrasive nature. Because floppy heads have direct contact with the media, over-cleaning can wear out the read/write head in the drive.

Hard Disk Drive

Because the hard disk drive is in a sealed case, no real preventive maintenance tasks are necessary for the physical device. You can perform certain software-based preventive tasks on a regular basis, however. These tasks include sector scanning (using the MS-DOS ScanDisk utility) and file defragmentation (using the MS-DOS Defrag utility); both topics were discussed in Chapter 2, "Diagnosing and Troubleshooting."

Power Supply

Power supplies are relatively simple devices because there is not much the average technician should do to a power supply. Aside from using a can of compressed air to blow out the dust that might clog the ventilation paths, the best preventive measure is to place the system on a surge protector of some kind. Also, be aware of the noise coming from the fan bearings; as these bearings fail, the noise will increase. If a fan is failing, replace it as soon as you notice. The heat buildup that results from a damaged fan can wear out and even set fire to some power supplies.

CD-ROMs

CD-ROMs require maintenance procedures similar to those for floppy disks. You clean the CD-ROM with a special kit designed to clean the lens of the laser head. These kits may or may not contain contact cleaners, but again, you should assume the worst and avoid cleaning the drive unless errors arise. You can also buy kits for cleaning the CD-ROM media itself. Typically, these kits include a lint-free cloth and an alcohol-based cleaner. Be sure to stroke radially outward from the hub (instead of spiraling out) to avoid scratching the media surface.

ENVIRONMENTAL HAZARDS AND PREVENTIVE TECHNIQUES

Table 3.1 outlines the eight basic categories of environmental hazards for electronic computer equipment.

TABLE 3.1

ENVIRONMENTAL HAZARDS THAT CAN AFFECT COMPUTERS

Hazard	*Additional Notes*
Heat	Acceptable range: 50–80 degrees Fahrenheit. Heat is a cause of failure in several of these environmental concerns. Dirt and dust are the primary causes of overheating, although power issues can cause some overheating as well.
	Avoid room temperatures above 80 degrees at all costs.
Humidity	Extremes are not acceptable and may cause other environmental concerns. High humidity (above 70 percent) can cause condensation (water). Low humidity (below 30 percent) can cause excessive static.
Water	Use halon-based fire extinguishers instead of sprinkler systems. Sprinklers can cause electrical damage even if the fire doesn't reach the computer. **Note:** Halon extinguisher systems must be installed by a professional because of their hazardous nature.
	Also, see the environmental concern regarding food and drink in this table.
Power	Surge protectors and SPS/UPS systems will reduce the danger of surges, spikes, brownouts, and blackouts. This is covered in more detail later in this chapter.
Magnetic fields	Magnetic fields, particularly moving or pulsing magnetic fields, can cause electrical damage by inducing a harmful level of current in a closed circuit. In addition, magnetic media can be destroyed if it is placed near a magnetic field.
Food and drink	Food and drink are potential problems for those who eat like *Sesame Street*'s Cookie Monster. If you can keep your area neat and tidy, these are not harmful concerns by themselves.
Smoke	Smoke from any source, but specifically cigarettes, will clog the ventilation passageways for computer systems. In addition, it can deposit conductive material that will cause heat-related and intermittent failures.
Static	Static is the number one PC killer. Static is extremely hard to avoid in some conditions. Anti-static mats, bands, and sprays are all viable solutions. These will be discussed in more detail later in this chapter.

SAFETY

This topic deals mostly with the dangers of working with electricity. Here are some basic guidelines to follow:

- Wear shoes with non-conductive soles to maintain insulation from the ground.

- Always unplug the device you're preparing to work on and discharge any capacitors (if necessary) using the proper tools and techniques.

- Do not wear any jewelry or neckties.

Commonly, a technician will not be exposed to high voltages or currents when working on standard PCs; however, dangerous voltages and currents do exist in power supplies, monitors, and some printers. Both AC and DC can harm mostly, and even kill you. If you are unsure about the proper way to proceed, please seek assistance.

High Voltage and Current

As a general rule, high current is more dangerous than high voltage. High voltage can harm you, but what's even more dangerous is the deception that low voltage cannot. A current rating of 0.3 amps is enough to kill a person, even at a low voltage. When working with high voltage circuits, it is imperative that you not be grounded with your ESD wrist strap or conductive flooring. Maintain a level of respect and distance from the device.

When you believe that the power has been cut and the device is safe, as the very last verification of a circuit, test it with the back of your right hand. You use the back of your hand because electricity will make muscles contract. If you use the palm of your hand, the charge could well make you grab onto the live wire and not let go. Also, using your right hand is not prejudiced against left-handed people; rather, the human heart is closer to the left side of the body. This adds a little more insulation for your vital organs in case a shock does pass through your right side.

How to Properly Discharge a CRT

Capacitors maintain their charge even when the power is off and the system is unplugged. Beware of large capacitors inside of power supplies and monitors if you should need to remove the casing. The procedures for discharging a monitor are listed below for testing purposes, but leave the actual tasks to someone who has experience with the procedure.

- Obtain a high voltage probe rated at 40,000 volts or higher.

- Turn off the monitor and unplug it. Let it cool for a few minutes.

- Remove *all* jewelry, especially rings and watches.

- Remove the enclosure from the monitor.

- Attach the ground lead to a common electrical ground point.

- Slide the tip of the high-voltage probe under the rubber suction cup on the top of the vacuum tube (see Figure 3.4). You may hear a slight pop as the probe begins to discharge. The meter will gradually decrease to zero.

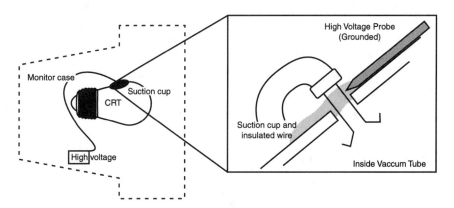

FIGURE 3.4
High-voltage probe and anode connection.

- Repeat these steps at least twice, at 5–10 minute intervals. Charges from the lesser capacitors in the monitor can be drawn into the tube, requiring the tube to be drained again.

Lasers

The laser devices, often called laser scanner assemblies, in laser printers can cause significant damage to the retina of your eye or even blindness. Fortunately, there are safety switches that prevent the printer from being powered on while the case is open. Do not disable these switches; they are there to protect you.

ESD AND POWER CONCERNS

Both electrostatic discharge and power fluctuations are environmental concerns and have been mentioned previously. However, because they are probably the two most important environmental concerns, they will be covered in more detail here.

Power

Electricity from the local power company can fluctuate within specified tolerances, and even outside of these tolerances on occasion. Obviously, interruptions in electricity can cause the computer to fail. Unfortunately, the power company can be well within its tolerances and be far outside the range that is acceptable to computers. Table 3.2 lists four events that fall outside of tolerance ranges.

TABLE 3.2

POWER FLUCTUATIONS

Event	Explanation	Protective Device
Spikes	Electricity jumps to a high level for a fraction of a second. (Imagine a spark on the wire.)	Surge/spike protectors, UPSs, and line conditioners
Surges	Electricity levels rise above tolerances for extended periods of time. (Imagine someone turning up the volume temporarily.)	Surge/spike protectors, UPSs, and line conditioners
Brownouts	Electricity levels dip below tolerances for extended periods of time. (Imagine someone turning down the volume temporarily.)	UPSs and line conditioners
Blackouts	Electricityis interrupted completely for any amount of time.	UPSs and SPSs

As the table shows, there are four types of power protection devices. The most common of these devices operate off of two variables: clamping voltage and clamping speed.

Clamping voltage is the level the electricity must reach before protective measures are engaged. A good analogy would be the rating for a circuit breaker. *Clamping speed* is the time it takes the protective measures to take effect once they're activated.

Another factor to consider is the total wattage supported by the device. This is especially important for devices that contain backup batteries.

Surge/Spike Protectors

Using the clamping voltage and speed measurements, these devices can lower the voltage levels coming into the power supply. All of these devices are different and can be rated at higher and lower levels of protection, as well as by their clamping ratings.

Beware of old surge and spike protectors. The clamping mechanisms can wear out over time, but you will see no indication of failure until your computer is hit by a spike.

Standby Power Supplies (SPSs)

SPS devices use the same clamping measurements that surge/spike protectors do with one significant change. The SPS device only protects against blackouts with a battery backup. (Note that today's SPS devices can also be combined with surge/spike protectors to add additional protection.)

SPS devices use the clamping voltage to determine when the power has failed. If clamping speeds remain under 10 milliseconds, the computer never knows the power was interrupted. Unfortunately, SPSs are also susceptible to the clamping issues discussed with surge and spike protectors.

Uninterruptible Power Supplies (UPSs)

No, UPSs are not the trucks that deliver your computer. This device takes an SPS one step further. Instead of using a clamping mechanism to switch the power over in time of need, the UPS always provides power from its battery. The battery is charged by the line power, and through a separate circuit, the battery provides power to the PC (see Figure 3.5). Because the power comes straight from the battery and not the power company, there are absolutely no surges, spikes, brownouts, or blackouts unless the battery fails. However, UPS batteries notify the user of battery faults before failure occurs, so you can replace the battery at your leisure (typically, once every five years).

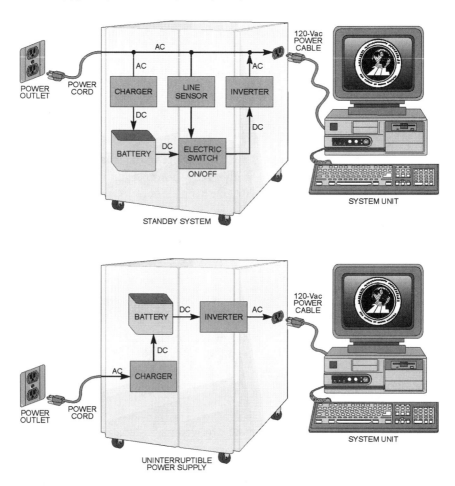

FIGURE 3.5
SPS and UPS design.

Different UPS devices can produce output in the form of square or sine waves. Sine wave output is the better choice.

N O T E Never plug a laser printer into a UPS or SPS device. As the heating lamp in the printer powers up, it will cause the battery to drain in a matter of minutes because of the high wattage needed.

Line Conditioners

These devices are rarely made for individual PCs. Instead, they are often implemented as whole-building solutions. They also may not be necessary except in extreme cases where the local company experiences many power problems.

A line conditioner works in a similar fashion to a UPS device, but without the ability to provide a battery backup in the case of a complete power failure. They actually condition the power to meet the more demanding tolerances for a particular building.

Electrostatic Discharge (ESD)

ESD is an event that occurs when two materials physically contact one another. This can include air brushing against a computer component, or even your hair coming into contact with the component. During this contact, electrons are transferred from one material to the other. This transfer of electrons causes one component to be negatively charged, because it has a surplus of electrons, and the other component to be positively charged, because it has a shortage of electrons. Because electricity seeks a balance in a given medium, the next time either of the components touches anything else, the charges attempt to equalize. This often creates disastrous results.

You can easily build static electricity of well over 30,000 volts simply by walking across the carpet in a dry room. You can feel a spark when you touch a doorknob at about 5,000 volts. Unfortunately, computers work at about 5 volts and can be damaged by as little as 30 volts. This means you can damage components without ever knowing it. ESD is often ignored, and ESD-damaged equipment is often misdiagnosed as defective equipment.

There are two ways to eliminate static electricity: charge equalization and charge neutralization. *Charge neutralization* is generally difficult to accomplish in the field and is used mainly in highly controlled manufacturing facilities.

Charge equalization is simply the ability to maintain a constant common ground between you and the device you are working on. This is most often accomplished with an ESD wrist strap and mat (see Figure 3.6). You attach the wire to the computer case, your wrist, and the workspace mat. For added protection, you can then attach the wire to the ground screw in a household electrical outlet.

You can also use antistatic sprays, but they may be expensive and cannot be used on the equipment itself. A homemade solution of 20 parts water to 1 part liquid fabric softener can be sprayed onto the work area and wiped dry and will work just as well.

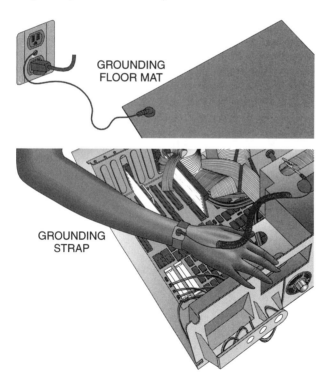

GROUNDING
FLOOR MAT

GROUNDING
STRAP

FIGURE 3.6
An ESD wrist strap and alligator clip.

For additional component protection, use a static bag or faraday cage. These items protect the device inside by forcing all static charges to remain on the outside of the bag. Make sure you wear your ESD wrist strap when inserting or removing a device from one of these bags.

DISPOSAL

Disposal techniques range from just tossing parts into the dumpster to delivering your equipment to a recovery specialist, depending on local ordinances. These specialists may take all of the equipment and reclaim the gold from the contacts. This is a very time-consuming process and is not profitable for the average person.

Environmentally friendly laws are just around the corner for computers as well. Approximately one-fourth of the lead in solid waste depositories is estimated to come from consumer electronics. Batteries and toner top the list for target items in the near future.

WHAT IS IMPORTANT TO KNOW

- Preventive maintenance is often overlooked because it is difficult to convince people to spend money on problems they haven't had yet. Nevertheless, it is extremely important.

- Cleaning is the biggest part of preventive maintenance for many reasons. Heat dissipation is the primary cause of problems. Dirt and dust insulate devices, preventing them from dissipating all the heat they generate.

- Household cleaners, lint-free cloths, and canisters of compressed air are often the best preventive maintenance tools.

- Specialized cleaning kits for floppy drives are abrasive and can damage the read/write head over time. Only clean floppies when you are experiencing problems.

- The eight environmental hazards to computer systems are heat, humidity (or lack thereof), water, inadequate power, magnetic fields, food and drink, smoke, and static.

- Safety often is simply common sense (which isn't always common).

- Don't wear jewelry, ties, watches, and so on when you're working on components. These can cause circuits to short out some components while you're trying to repair other components.

- Know the steps for discharging a CRT, as indicated in this chapter.

- ESD can damage circuits even if you cannot feel it. ESD can cause damage at 30–50 volts, even though the average person cannot feel a shock below 5,000 volts.

- Clamping voltage is the voltage level that power must reach before a safety device is enabled. Clamping speed is the speed at which the device is enabled after the clamping voltage is met.

▶ Distinguish between the popular CPU chips in terms of their basic characteristics.

▶ Identify the categories of RAM (Random Access Memory) terminology, their locations, and physical characteristics.

▶ Identify the most popular type of motherboards, their components, and their architecture (for example, bus structures).

▶ Identify the purpose of CMOS (Complementary Metal-Oxide Semiconductor), what it contains, and how to change its basic parameters.

CHAPTER 4

Motherboards/Processors/ Memory

CENTRAL PROCESSING UNIT (CPU)

At A Glance: Intel CPU Comparison

Model	Speed	Clock Multiplier	Data Bus Width	Internal RAM Cache	Math Coprocessor
Intel 8086	4.77–7.16MHz	1x	16-bit	No	8087
Intel 8088	4.77–12MHz	1x	8-bit	No	8087
Intel 80286	6–25MHz	1x	16-bit	No	80287
Intel 80386SX	16–33MHz	1x	16-bit*	No	80387SX
Intel 80386SX	16–40MHz	1x	32-bit	No	80387DX
Intel	25–33MHz	1x	32-bit	8KB	80487SX** 80486SX
Intel 80486DX	25–50MHz	1x	32-bit	8KB	Built-in
Intel 80486 DX2	50–66MHz	2x	32-bit	8KB	Built-in
Intel 80486 DX4	75–100MHz***	3x	32-bit	8KB	Built-in
Intel Pentium	60MHz–150MHz	Varies	64-bit	16KB	Built-in
Intel Pentium MMX	150–233MHz	Varies	64-bit	16KB	Built-in
Intel Pentium Pro****	150–200MHz	Varies	64-bit	256KB– 512KB	Built-in
Intel Pentium II	233–450MHz and up	Varies	64-bit	512KB at half bus width	Built-in

* The 80386 has a 16-bit external data bus, but a 32-bit internal data bus. This allows the chip to be retrofitted to many 80286-style system boards.

** The 80486SX is really an 80486DX that failed the math coprocessor test. Due to a very high number of these failures, Intel decided to remarket the failed chips as a new model line, without the coprocessor. The 80487SX is simply a working 80486DX chip with a pin configuration that fits into the coprocessor slot.

*** The DX4 chip is truly only a 3x speed multiplier. The DX4-100MHz is really a 99MHz machine. In addition, much like the data bus issues with the 80386SX, the DX2 and DX4 chips need a properly optimized hardware setting to function properly. And even then, clock multiplied chips tend to work at only 80–90 percent of their rated speeds.

**** The Intel Pentium Pro is optimized for 32-bit operation systems and programming. Although 16-bit applications will run, they may suffer in performance.

The central processing unit, or CPU, functions as the brain of the computer, as you learned in Chapter 1. This section goes into more detail on the various types of CPUs and their characteristics. The majority of the information covered here will be characteristic of Intel chips (as they are de facto PC industry standards) and their major competitors.

First you need to know some of the categories of characteristics. CPUs can be classified by any of the following:

- Size/socket type

- Speed (internal and external)

- Instruction set

- Data bus width (internal and external)

- Integrated floating point math coprocessor

- Internal cache

Size/Socket Type

CPUs can vary in size and in the shape of the physical chip itself. As chip technology progressed, the CPU never settled on a standard socket type, and even with the advent of the Pentium II chip, this has not changed. The socket size has been changed with every newly released chip design from Intel.

Speed

Chip speed is a measure of how many cycles per second a chip can run at. In some computers, the speed inside the chip is 2–3 times faster than the rest of the motherboard. These are known as clock doubling or tripling chips. Clock doubling and tripling chips have an elaborate buffer scheme to prevent the CPU from spinning its wheels while it waits for information from the rest of the system.

NOTE

Beware of clock multiplying technology. DX2 and DX4 chips may say they run at 66 or even 100MHz, but the rest of the system runs at half or one-third of that same speed. This implies that a poorly tuned 486 DX2 66MHz CPU can run slower than a regular 486 DX 50MHz.

Instruction Set

The instruction set is also known as the microcode. This is the set of commands the CPU understands and executes. The two primary types are CISC (Complex Instruction Set Computing) and RISC (Reduced Instruction Set Computing).

CISC Versus RISC

CISC is capable of processing more instructions, but it runs them at a slower speed. RISC, on the other hand, runs fewer possible instructions at a higher speed. A good example of this is a mathematical calculation: Hypothetically, a CISC chip would understand both addition and multiplication, whereas a RISC chip would understand only addition. Given the equation 2×4=?, a CISC chip would look through its many instructions and come back with 2×4=8. Given the same equation, a RISC chip would have to break down the equation into smaller, more manageable parts to calculate. A RISC chip would have to look into its instructions and determine that the proper equation to solve is 2+2+2+2=?. RISC would then be able to perform the calculation and determine that the answer is also 8.

NOTE

This is an example only. This example does not reflect the actual instruction sets in either chip set.

All of the Intel chips in this chapter are CISC type CPUs.

MMX Technology

MMX is the first major instruction set change for the Intel 80x86 chip line since the advent of the 80386 chip. This enhancement includes 57 new instructions for multimedia operations. In addition, MMX incorporates a new process called SIMD, or Single Instruction-Multiple Data. SIMD allows the processor to perform the same instruction on multiple data pieces simultaneously. This eliminates the one-on-one approach to handling data for processing. Additionally, the L1 cache size was increased for more information in the queue.

Data Bus Width

The data bus can be thought of as a highway. The number of cars that can fit side-by-side onto the highway is determined by the number of lanes. The number of lanes determines the width of the road. In addition, the speed at which the cars travel corresponds to the MHz, or millions of cycles per second.

In this analogy, each car represents a single bit of information traveling in a string of data bits. The more data strings that can be transmitted simultaneously, the more data that can be passed between the CPU and the system.

There are other factors involved, but at a simple level, this implies that a 16-bit CPU running at 40MHz can pass the same amount of data as a 32-bit processor running at 20MHz. To further use our highway analogy, the number of cars using any given stretch of road in a given amount of time is the same whether it is broken down into 16 cars traveling at 40 miles per hour or 32 cars traveling at 20 miles per hour.

N O T E   At least one Intel processor was designed to have a 32-bit internal data bus and a 16-bit external data bus. This processor was the 386SX, which was designed with the smaller external data bus to take advantage of the surplus of 80286-compatible motherboards on the market at the time.

Math Coprocessor

The math coprocessor simply adds a mathematically intensive instruction set on a separate floating point processor. In most CPUs since the 486DX, this coprocessor is built into the CPU itself.

Internal Cache

The internal cache is a memory buffer zone. Due to the extreme speeds of today's processors, a queue of instructions must be present to take full advantage of that speed. Otherwise the CPU would just sit idle. This buffer zone is built into the chip itself and stores the most recently used data or the data anticipated for the next instruction. There is a point of diminishing returns, but in general, the more cache in a CPU, the faster it can operate.

RAM

Memory comes in many different forms, but basically it all has the same function. Memory is a high-speed data storage area. There are many different terms for the varying forms and classifications. These terms include the following:

- Physical forms
    - DIP
    - SIP
    - SIMM
    - DIMM
    - Parity
    - Banks

- Logical classifications
    - DRAM
    - EDO DRAM
    - SRAM
    - VRAM
    - WRAM

Physical Forms

Table 4.1 lists the physical forms of memory, which are depicted in Figure 4.1.

TABLE 4.1

PHYSICAL FORMS OF **RAM**

Form	Description	Data Width	Additional Notes
DIP (Dual In-line Package)	Small single chip; nine chips are required to make a bank (eight if there is no parity).	8-bit.	DIP banks were popular with the 8088, the 80286, and even some 80386 computers. These are not used for most RAM purposes today.
SIP (Single In-line Package)	Typically three, eight, or nine chips make a bank. The three-chip combination uses two quad-density chips and a single density chip for parity.	Natively 8-bit; in banks of 2 or 4, 16-bit; readily available in 32-bit.	SIP chips never seemed to catch on because of the fragile connection to the system board. The SIMM standard that came shortly after was more physically sturdy and easier to install and remove safely.
SIMM (Single In-line Memory Module)	30-pin and 72-pin versions. Similar to SIP in design except that the memory module uses an edge connector instead of a row of fragile pins.	30-pin SIMMs were natively 8-bit and required four identical chips to make a 32-bit bank. 72-pin SIMMs are natively 32-bit, although some implementations were originally 16-bit.	The locking mechanism made installation and removal easier. The chips are typically installed at a 45-degree angle and lock into a vertical position.
DIMM (Dual In-line Memory Module)	168-pin boards with edge connectors similar to those of the. SIMM.	168-pin DIMMs are natively 64-bit. This makes them perfect for most higher-end computer server implementations.	DIMM chips are installed into a locking slot mechanism similar to that of a SIMM, but installation occurs vertically instead of at a 45-degree angle.

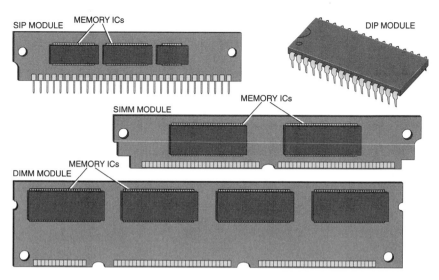

FIGURE 4.1

DIP, SIP, SIMM, and DIMM memory modules.

Memory Banks

A *memory bank* is a group of memory chips that work as a single unit. If you recall that various processors have 8-bit, 16-bit, 32-bit, and even 64-bit data paths, this becomes clear. Because the CPU requires information across the entire width of its data path to be efficient, memory chips must "drive" the data side-by-side along the data path. Using the highway example again, the "cars" must be driven side-by-side. This is accomplished by assigning each individual chip a "lane" on the highway, as illustrated in Figure 4.2.

A memory bank is also the smallest complete memory unit the CPU can address. If a bank is incomplete, the CPU will be unable to address it. This can cause the CPU to ignore this memory, or it can even cause the CPU to malfunction because it cannot see the missing memory in the bank.

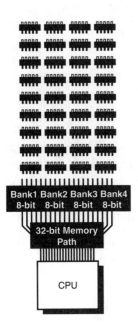

FIGURE 4.2
The logical need for memory banks.

Parity

Often there will be an extra bit of memory for every eight used bits. This extra bit is used for parity functions. Parity is an error-detection scheme used by many processes. Parity is created like this:

1	0	1	1	0	1	0	1

In the example of a memory bank, each chip can hold only one bit. By adding a ninth bit to the memory bank, you can use it for error checking on the other eight bits.

1	0	1	1	0	1	0	1 ?

This is done by mathematically ANDing the data bits in single-digit binary mathematics to create the ninth bit. The following chart shows the mathematical keys for calculating parity:

0 AND 0 = 0   0 AND 1 = 1   1 AND 0 = 1   1 AND 1 = 0

> **NOTE** In the real world, a chip can hold more than one bit. Typically, a single chip can hold as many as 1 million bits, all in the logical position to which the chip is assigned.

There are two different types of parity, odd and even. These are better described as guarantees. If the parity scheme that's used is odd, the parity bit must be set to a value to make the entire bank (including the parity bit) odd. Even parity must accomplish the same task, but force the entire bank to be even instead. This is outlined in the chart below:

If the parity scheme is...	and the first eight bits are...	the parity bit should be:
Even	Even	Even
Even	Odd	Odd
Odd	Even	Odd
Odd	Odd	Even

Assuming an even parity scheme, an example byte looks like this:

1   0   1   1   0   1   0   1   1   = Even

What happens when a bit is sent incorrectly? In this byte, the third bit has failed and produced a 0 instead of a 1:

1   0   1   1   0   1   0   1   1   ≠ Even

The parity bit no longer sets the entire byte to even parity. It is now odd parity and does not match. As a result, the entire byte must be discarded and retransmitted. Often this will lock up the computer with a Parity Check error. (You'll learn more about this error in Part III.)

> **NOTE** Programmers often use other checksum methods because of the inherent failure of parity. Parity cannot detect an error if two errors occur in the same byte. If the two errant bits reverse, the byte is incorrect, but the parity is still correct.

Logical Classifications

This section explains some of the differences between memory types. The most basic difference is DRAM versus SRAM. The other types of memory are subclasses of these two.

DRAM

DRAM, or dynamic RAM, is the most common memory type available. All DRAM implementations require that data be refreshed at specific intervals, much like a CRT display screen. This refresh circuit simply reads the data in the chip and writes it back to the same chip every 2 milliseconds. This may seem like a very short amount of time, but remember: Memory is accessed at speeds measured in nanoseconds (over 2,000 times between refresh times).

Because DRAM is measured at speeds of 60–80 nanoseconds (historically, DRAM has been as slow as 300 nanoseconds!) whereas SRAM runs at 15–20 nanoseconds, methods of speeding up DRAM have been invented. The following sections discuss some of these methods.

EDO RAM

EDO RAM is a fast page mode enhancement for DRAM. Memory inside of a chip is arranged in rows. This enhancement allows the chip, once read, to remain in the "row" where it found the last bit of data. If the next incoming request is for data in the same row, the data is returned much faster.

> **NOTE** Imagine you're using a phone book. If the name you are looking for is on the page you are already turned to, you can find that name almost immediately. If finding the second name requires you to turn several pages, your "access time" slows down accordingly.

SDRAM

SDRAM, or synchronous DRAM, allows the memory to synchronize with the system clock and transmit data on the pulses. In this manner, the memory controller can anticipate when a request will be received and act accordingly. Another advancement of SDRAM allows the memory to "burst" a data stream out before it is requested. Typically, the next bit of information requested is in sequential order. Anticipating this and sending the extra information out before it is needed is an attempt to play the averages. On most occasions, this works as intended.

VRAM

VRAM is another form of DRAM, but instead of being used for system RAM, it is typically used for video controllers. Video controllers are unique in that the data flows in only one direction—that is, to the monitor. Video RAM allows the data to flow through it on a FIFO (First-In-First-Out) basis. This is accomplished by having two separate "doors," or ports, for the data, one for monitor refresh commands and one for data (as opposed to the single two-way "door" on DRAM).

WRAM

Windows RAM is much like VRAM in that it also uses dual data ports. Unlike VRAM, WRAM has a smaller designated video port and supports fast-page mode features like EDO DRAM.

SRAM

SRAM, or static RAM, is faster than DRAM and consequently more expensive. Contrary to what most people think, SRAM does not use static electricity. The term static in this case refers to the fact that the RAM does not need the refreshing circuitry that DRAM does. Once data is written to an SRAM chip, it remains there until system board power is interrupted or the data is overwritten.

SRAM operates in the range of 10–20 nanoseconds and is 3–8 times faster than comparable DRAM. Because of this great speed and expensive price tag, SRAM is most commonly used for cache RAM.

Cache

Cache RAM is an interesting design for system efficiency. Typically, the bottleneck in data flow is the delay from RAM to the CPU. To increase efficiency, manufacturers are adding L2 cache to operate in much the same manner as the L1 cache Intel added to its processors, as was discussed earlier in this chapter.

Cache RAM works on the concept that during use, one area of memory and its closest neighbors are repeatedly accessed. If this data is loaded from the DRAM in main system memory into the SRAM in cache memory, future requests for this data can be handled at a much higher speed from SRAM. If the data request is intercepted and fulfilled from cache, it is called a *hit*. Figure 4.3 depicts the data path between caching memory devices.

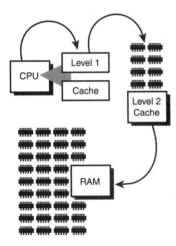

FIGURE 4.3
Cache RAM.

MOTHERBOARD ARCHITECTURE

System boards were covered fairly well in Chapter 1, "Installation, Configuration, and Upgrading." This chapter includes a few figures and diagrams of various system boards and their components; however, the majority of this discussion will pertain to bus structures—primarily the expansion bus.

In Chapter 1, you learned that buses come in different types. Primarily, the *internal data bus* is the path the data takes inside the CPU. The *external data bus* is the path the data takes from the CPU to the final destination within the system. These buses are not to be confused with the *expansion bus*, which is the physical wiring between the adapter cards and the CPU. Think of the road the data rides on as the expansion bus and the route it takes on this road as the internal and external data buses.

NOTE There is another bus in the system board. This bus is called the *address bus*. It is the bus the CPU utilizes to contact and communicate with the various devices on the expansion bus and attached to the various ports. The address bus can fit into our "highway" analogy as the map or phone book in which you look up the numbers and addresses for where you want to go.

Expansion Bus

At A Glance: Expansion Bus Types

Bus Type	*Bus Width*	*Bus Speed*	*Physical Characteristics*
PC-bus/ISA 8	8-bit	8MHz	Edge connector, about 3.5 inches long.
ISA bus	16-bit	8MHz	Edge connector, about 5.5 inches long. The remaining 16 bits are crammed into the additional 2 inches to maintain backward compatibility.
MCA	32-bit	10MHz	Edge connector, about 4 inches long. MCA boards are easily identified by the blue plastic release tabs on the cards.
EISA	32-bit	10MHz	Edge connector, about 5.5 inches long, but twice as tall. EISA maintains backward compatibility with ISA by allowing the card to be plugged into the top half of the slot. The additional lines are in the lower half of the connector.
VESA	32-bit	40MHz	Edge connector, about 9 inches long.
PCI	64-bit	CPU speed	Edge connector, about 3.5 inches long. Card faces opposite of all other expansion cards.
PCMCIA	16-bit	33MHz	Pin connector, about 2 inches wide.
CardBus	32-bit	33MHz	Pin connector, about 2 inches wide. CardBus cards are not backward compatible and can use only CardBus slots. This is why CardBus cards have a series of small bumps on the top of the pin connector.

The expansion bus provides a shared (or direct, depending on the bus) line of communication between the CPU and the adapter cards.

With the exception of Apple's NewBus architecture and PCMCIA cards, all expansion bus slots use an edge connection slot. This slot is the same style, though not the same form, as the edge connector used for the Pentium II CPU and SIMM memory. Some of the copper connectors in the slot provide power; others transmit data.

Many standards of the expansion bus have developed over the years. To give you an accurate perspective, the following sections compare the various buses and discuss them in more detail.

Expansion buses can be compared based on the following characteristics:

- Bus speed, in megahertz.
- Bus width, in bits.
- Physical characteristics (size, shape, and number of connectors).
- Bus mastering. (Can the bus be mastered or not? Bus mastering is the ability of an adapter on the bus to take control from the CPU and provide device arbitration.)
- Configuration of the adapter cards. (What is used? Software, Jumpers, etc.?)
- Local bus or shared bus. (Is there a direct line from each slot to the PC, or are the data paths shared across all devices?)

PC Bus

The PC bus was the original IBM implementation of an expansion bus. The bus speed was 4.77–8MHz, and it had only eight interrupt lines and four DMA channels available. This bus was only 8-bits wide.

ISA Bus

The Industry Standard Architecture bus, ISA for short, was the next logical advancement of the PC bus. IBM was also the primary developer of this bus, but others became more involved with the tremendous PC explosion due to the clone market. As a result, IBM was forced to release the ISA standards to the public.

The ISA bus added eight interrupt lines and four more DMA channels to the PC bus. The PC bus connector was also modified to support the new 16-bit bus. All of these changes were accomplished while maintaining backward compatibility. The interrupt and DMA lines were supported by "piggy-backing" the new lines onto a single line from the PC bus. This is where the cascade between interrupts 2 and 9 originated. The PC bus connector was supported by adding a second connector at the end of the original 8-bit connector for the full 16-bit path. This comparison is illustrated in Figure 4.4.

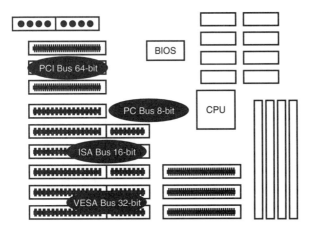

FIGURE 4.4
ISA bus connector.

Micro-Channel Bus

MCA, or Micro-Channel Architecture, was the subsequent development by IBM following the introduction of ISA. The design was very advanced for its time, but the marketing of it seemed to fail. Even though the ISA design was running into some limitations, MCA was developed as a backlash against the industry standards and the clone manufacturers in general. IBM created a licensing standard that required major manufacturers of MCA cards to pay IBM a premium to use their design. As a result, these cards were more expensive than any others. MCA never caught on, and even IBM has stopped manufacturing MCA systems.

MCA was the first 32-bit bus. In addition, the bus speed was marginally faster, and multiple bus mastering devices were available. The primary benefit of MCA was in the process for configuring adapter cards.

Whereas the ISA cards required jumpers and switch settings, their MCA counterparts were software configurable using IBM utilities called a *Reference Diskette* and an *Options Diskette.*

EISA Bus

The Extended Industry Standard Architecture bus was developed by several competitors of IBM. Designed as a standards-based alternative to IBM's MCA design, EISA is a 32-bit bus that is fully backward-compatible with ISA and PC bus devices. The designers accomplished this by making the adapter slot deeper than the ISA slot and offsetting the connections in the slot. This allowed the standard ISA cards to use only the top row of connections, while the deeper EISA cards reached the 32-bit row of connections in the bottom of the slot. Because of this, it is often difficult to differentiate between an ISA slot and an EISA slot.

EISA offers more available I/O addresses than ISA does, and it imitates IBM's software-based setup design for MCA. EISA uses an EISA card identification and configuration utility much like the MCA reference utility. And, like MCA, EISA also allows multiple bus mastering devices. EISA bus speeds are also 50 percent faster than MCA speeds.

VESA Local Bus

Until the time the VESA local bus appeared, all adapters shared the same lines to the CPU. This occasionally caused communication collisions and conflicts. To circumvent this, the Video and Electronics Standards Association (VESA) developed a bus in which each adapter had its own individual channels to the processor. Another benefit to this design was that the adapters ran at the same external speed as the processor. This eliminated bus-driven bottlenecks. VESA was also backward compatible with the ISA bus because its connector was added to the end of the ISA adapter slot (refer back to Figure 4.4).

VLB, which stands for VESA Local Bus, was primarily used for video and some I/O controllers. VLB has a three-card limitation and consequently must be used in conjunction with a standard ISA bus for more expandability.

PCI Bus

PCI, or Peripheral Component Interconnect, is a 64-bit version of a local bus. This design has become the most popular local bus design in existence and far outsells the VLB version of local bus. With added features like 32-bit and 64-bit data paths, up to 264Mbps throughput, a more compact and efficient connector, Plug and Play capability, and bus mastering support, it is no wonder PCI is fast becoming the de facto standard.

PCI slots typically are in sets of three closest to the CPU. PCI is a mezzanine bus, or a super bus, contained on a different layer of the system board from the standard ISA bus, and it uses an intermediate bus controller instead of relying on the CPU. For every three PCI slots, a PCI controller must be used. To accommodate more PCI slots, one of the existing three slots must be allocated to another on-board PCI controller, which in turn controls three PCI slots. This gives a total of five slots.

Because PCI is not backward compatible with ISA bus adapter cards, an ISA bus is generally used in conjunction with the PCI bus.

> **NOTE**
>
> PCI is not limited to the Intel line of processors. In fact, it is completely processor-independent and is the design standard for all new Apple Macintosh systems.

PC Card

The PC Card is composed of four types of PC card standards. The first three are all 16-bit implementations of PCMCIA, or *Personal Computer Memory Card Industry Association*. The fourth is the new 32-bit CardBus specification. The first three are backward compatible with one another; that means that all older cards will fit in and function in each larger slot. The most common PCMCIA card today is the Type 2. Type 1 devices were primarily memory cards, and Type 3 are primarily 2-inch notebook hard disk drives. Type 2 cards vary from memory to SCSI controllers to sound cards, modems, network cards, and even cellular communications (see Figure 4.5 for an illustration of PCMCIA card types).

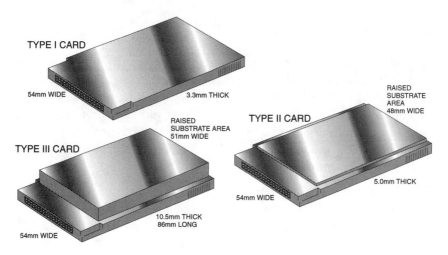

FIGURE 4.5
PCMCIA card types.

CardBus slots are also backward compatible and support all previous designs of PCMCIA. However, CardBus adapters will not function in PCMCIA slots. To avoid the problems of a duplicate form factor, the CardBus cards have a small row of bumps on the metal housing for the connector, which prevent them from fitting into PCMCIA sockets of any type (see Figure 4.6).

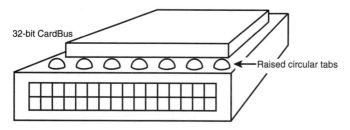

FIGURE 4.6
CardBus comparison to a PCMCIA Type 2 card.

Prior to the advent of Plug and Play operating systems, PC cards required a hot-plug slot driver and an online recognition system. This was accomplished using the 16-bit utilities known as Card and Socket Services.

CMOS

Originally, PC computers were configured by switch settings. These were fairly simple to configure, especially when the options were limited. Video settings could be determined by switches 5 and 6, memory by switches 3 and 4, and disk drives by switches 7 and 8. As more and more options became available, however, this system became impossible to use. When IBM introduced the IBM AT, an 80286-based machine, CMOS came into the picture.

CMOS allows you to configure the system information with software settings. This information is checked during startup until either it is determined to be correct or a POST error code is generated. CMOS handles the addition and removal of any and all devices attached to the system.

Because CMOS stores this information on an erasable chip, the data must be retained with constant power to the CMOS chip. If this battery fails, all system settings will have to be re-entered after the failed battery is replaced. For this reason, it is recommended that all users record their CMOS settings and store them in a safe place. Often, you can use the Print Scrn key on most printers to print a copy of the BIOS setup screen as a means of recording these values.

Typically, the following settings can be modified:

- Display
- Memory
- Hard disk drive
- Boot device
- Built-in I/O ports
- Date/time

WHAT IS IMPORTANT TO KNOW

- ◆ The Intel CPU families vary in voltages, sizes, and special design features. Know the information in the "At A Glance" table at the beginning of this chapter.

- ◆ CISC is the instruction set on the CPU. CISC can operate more complex functions, but they are significantly slower.

- ◆ RISC is another CPU instruction set. RISC operates on fewer and smaller functions but processes them very quickly. Only applications written for the RISC instruction set can take advantage of this feature.

- ◆ Megahertz is the number of cycles per second. There can be differences between the speeds internal and external to the CPU. Clock doubling or tripling technology speeds up the processor by increasing the clock speed internal to the chip.

- ◆ RAM is random access memory. This memory is used for the dynamic storage of information needed for processing by the CPU. RAM is erased every time the system is turned off.

- ◆ ROM is read-only memory. This memory is used for the long-term storage of programs and data as firmware on a chip. This information is "burned" into the chip and is retained even during a power failure.

- ◆ DRAM is cheaper and more often used as base, or main, memory.

- ◆ SRAM is static RAM and does not have to be refreshed almost continuously.

- ◆ Parity is a binary calculation used as a checksum to verify a single byte of information. This parity bit is stored in the ninth bit position of the byte being checked.

- ◆ Bus structures are the heart of the data communication process. These structures include ISA, MCA, VESA Local Bus, EISA, PCI, and PCMCIA (or PC Card/CardBus).

- ◆ AT-class system board designs are more common.

- ◆ ATX computer system boards have an updated design and require an additional 3.3v line on the power supply. In addition, the case must allow for the redesigned peripheral port connections.

- ◆ All 8-bit PC Bus cards will function in any ISA slot. All ISA adapters will function in a VESA slot. Also, all ISA adapters will function in an EISA computer. PCI and MCA are not compatible with any other standard.

- ◆ A local bus provides a direct, exclusive expansion bus for cards that are local bus compatible. Local bus standards include VESA Local Bus and PCI buses.

- ▶ Identify basic concepts, printer operations, and printer components.

- ▶ Identify care and service techniques and common problems associated with primary printer types.

- ▶ Identify the types of printer connections and configurations.

CHAPTER 5

Printers

In Chapter 1, you learned the four stages of computing: input, processing, output, and storage. Printing is the main form of the third stage of computing: output. In fact, printing is the only form of common tangible output. Printers are also the most common peripheral. This chapter looks at the basic concepts and differences between printer categories and their most common problems.

BASIC PRINTING CONCEPTS

Characters are formed on the page through one of several types of technology. This varies from one printer make and model to another.

At A Glance: Printer Types and Facts

Printer Type	Character Type	Line versus Page	Feeder Type	Consumables
Daisywheel	Fully formed	Line	Friction or tractor	Print wheel, print head, ribbon, paper
Dot-matrix	Bit image	Line	Friction or tractor	Print head, ribbon, paper
Inkjet	Bit image	Line/page	ASF	Ink cartridge, paper
Laser	Bit image formation, fully formed transfer	Page	ASF	EP cartridge, paper
Thermal	Bit image	Line	ASF or friction	Print head, paper
Hot wax	Bit image, fully formed transfer	Page	ASF	Wax, paper

Bit Image Versus Full Character

Characters are formed in one of two ways. Either the character is premade on a die of some type, or it is created by a series of consecutive printed dots.

A typewriter character is a classic example of a fully formed character. The letters are set into tabs on a wheel or on individual strikers. The strikers are forced into the ink ribbon and then to the paper to form the character. In the computer printing industry, this is the process used by a daisywheel printer. The fully formed characters are on tabs on a wheel, which strike the ribbon and press it into the page as on a typewriter. This method produces the highest-quality character, but it is incapable of graphic printouts. Figure 5.1 gives an example of a bit-image character in contrast to a fully formed character.

The other method, bit-image formation, is the method most common in the computer industry. In this method, a processor in the printer turns a letter into several consecutive dots, which are re-created on the page by the printer mechanism. If you look at a newspaper image, you can see this method quite clearly. The closer you get to the page, the more apparent the dots are. This is known as the *resolution*, or print density. This method can produce stunning graphics as well as a high-quality print, depending on the implementation of the bit-formation process.

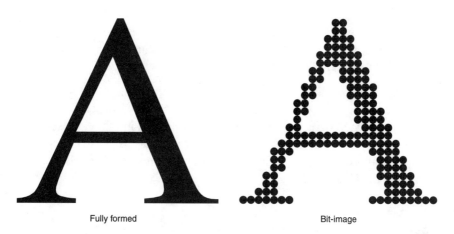

Fully formed   Bit-image

FIGURE 5.1
A bit-image versus a fully formed character.

Line Printers Versus Page Printers

The distinction here is usually fairly obvious. If you can send a print command to the printer and read output while the page is still able to be printed on, this is a line printer. Another way to look at it is if the print command for a single letter uses only a partial page, or even only one line, this is a line printer. On a page printer, printing one letter requires feeding an entire sheet of paper through the print process before that one letter can be read by the user.

Impact Printers Versus Non-Impact Printers

Impact printers are so called because of the force used to drive the pin into the ribbon and then into the page. Examples of impact printers include dot-matrix and daisywheel printers. A non-impact printer uses more gentle methods of ink transfer. This can be found in all inkjet and laser printers. This comparison becomes critical when dealing with two issues: noise and multi-part forms.

Typically, an impact printer creates a great deal of noise when striking the paper, while a non-impact printer creates only the mechanical noise of the small motors moving paper.

Impact printers do have one advantage over their silent counterparts: the ability to print multi-part forms. The "carbon-copy" process relies on the force of the character creation to push the ink into the subsequent layers of the form. Non-impact printers do not have this capability. The best you can do using a non-impact printer for multiple forms is to print the form multiple times.

Feed Mechanisms

There are several feed mechanisms. The most basic feed method is friction. In a friction feeder, a single sheet of paper is passed through a set of rollers that push it along. This method of paper movement has an inherent flaw: Unless the paper is perfectly lined up before printing, the paper will become skewed and can cause a paper jam.

The next feeder type is the tractor feed, or continuous feed. This works in a fashion similar to the friction feed, but the paper stays aligned because pins fit into the holes in the tractor paper feed (see Figure 5.2).

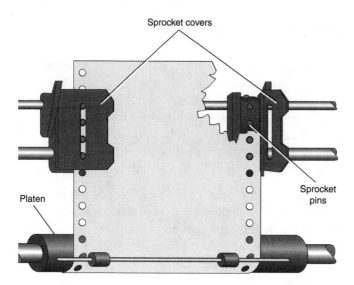

FIGURE 5.2
A standard tractor feeder.

Typically, this method is used for dot-matrix printers. Because of the perforations and tractor feed holes cut into the paper, this type of paper tends to be very dusty and can cause problems if the dust buildup is not removed during regular preventive maintenance.

Our final feeder type is the ASF, or automatic sheet feeder. This works like the feed mechanism for a copy machine. Similar to the friction feed, the automatic sheet feeder has an additional part called a separation pad that keeps multiple sheets from being fed simultaneously. In addition to the potential problem of multiple sheets, the paper itself can cause many problems if it is outside the manufacturer's tolerances. Made popular by the laser printer, the sheet feeder is the most commonly used feeder type today in inkjet printers and laser printers.

Consumables

Consumables are those parts of the printer that regularly wear, or get used. In all printers, paper and ink are the most common consumables. The remainder of the consumables are printer specific and are listed in the At A Glance table at the beginning of this section.

DOT-MATRIX PRINTERS

Pin printers, or *dot-matrix printers*, form their characters by using 9, 18, or 24 pins (depending on print resolution) in vertical rows that strike the ribbon against the paper. Historically, this has been the most common type of PC printer. These printers are falling out of favor due to the newer technology of inkjet and laser printers, but dot-matrix printers are still the least expensive graphics printers available. As one of the few impact printers, a primary use for these is to print multiple-part forms.

Some dot-matrix printers have a near-letter-quality mode to improve print quality. This mode makes two passes for every line, printing half of the character on the first pass, and then shifting the paper up one-half the distance between pin-strikes and printing the other half of the character. This significantly slows the printer but provides a higher-quality output, especially for those printers that have fewer pins in the first place.

Another print mode common to dot-matrix printers is bidirectional printing. This mode allows the print head to travel both left-to-right and right-to-left while printing. After printing one line from left to right, instead of returning to the starting point to continue printing left-to-right, it prints the next line from right to left. While this mode can increase print speed, quality can be sacrificed if the printer is even the slightest bit out of alignment.

The Printing Mechanism

The print head in a dot-matrix printer is the driving force behind the print wires striking the paper. This force is generated through the use of a high-powered spring, a static magnet, and an electromagnetic wire. As you can see in Figure 5.3, the print wire is in line with a standard magnet and is wrapped by a spring.

The print wire is also wrapped by a standard wire coil. The standard magnet draws the wire to it, compressing the spring. When a charge is applied to the coil, the print wire itself becomes an electromagnet in opposition to the standard magnet. The combined force of the electromagnetic print wire and the spring is enough to forcefully break away from the print head magnet, causing the print head to strike the ribbon and paper.

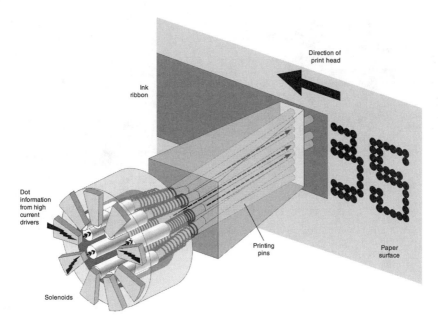

FIGURE 5.3
Dot-matrix printing.

INKJET PRINTERS

Inkjet printers, like their dot-matrix counterparts, are bit-image line printers. The primary differences between the two are the paper feed mechanisms and the ink transfer mechanism.

The inkjet printer made the automatic sheet feeder a cost-effective solution, replacing the tractor paper feed mechanisms favored by the dot-matrix printer.

The ink is transferred to the page when ultra-fine droplets are "squirted" onto the paper in a specific pattern (see Figure 5.4). While this method may seem much more primitive than the print wire method, the resolution and speed capabilities of the inkjet far exceed those of pin printers. The ink may be sprayed onto the page in several methods; either the ink it subjected to a pressure from a small vibrating electric crystal, or the ink is boiled using a tiny heating element. Either way, this printer provides output that rivals some laser printers at a fraction of the cost, but without the noise or lack of speed associated with dot-matrix printers.

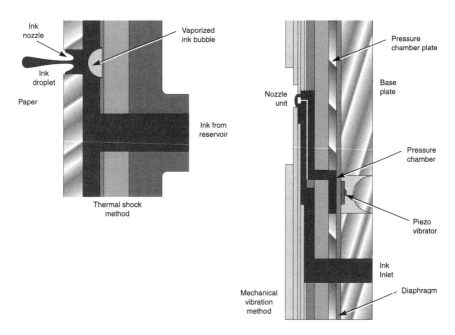

FIGURE 5.4
Inkjet mechanisms.

LASER PRINTERS

Laser printers are the highest-quality printers. These printers provide high-speed, high-quality, high-durability output. For most users, the cost of a laser printer is a limiting factor. These printers can run from $500 to in excess of $5,000. However, the quality is often well worth the cost of the printer. These printers provide quiet, high-resolution bit-image page printing using an electro-photostatic process similar to that of a copier machine.

Laser Printer Components

Before you can begin to understand how a laser printer functions, you need to know about several individual components and what they do. The following sections outline these components.

Paper-Handling Components

The *pickup roller* initially grabs the paper from the feed tray and moves it past the separation pad and along to the registration rollers.

The *separation pad* allows only one page to pass it at a time, preventing paper jams by keeping multiple sheets of paper from feeding at once.

The *registration rollers* stop the forward advancement of the paper until the drum is lined up and ready to proceed.

The *fusing roller* pulls the paper from the registration rollers and passes it to the output rollers, while performing the final stage of the EP process. (This is covered in greater detail in the section titled "The EP Process," later in this chapter.)

The *output rollers* pass the paper out of the printer, where it waits in the *output bin* until the user retrieves it.

EP Cartridge Components

The *EP cartridge* is actually composed of several other components. It contains most of the printer's consumables in one easy-to-use component that houses four-and-a-half of the six stages of the EP process (as defined later in this chapter).

The *photosensitive drum* is an aluminum cylinder that has been coated with an organic coating that can hold a charge in the dark. When exposed to any form of light, the surface charge is dissipated to the grounded aluminum center of the drum.

Toner is a fine black powder made from plastic. This powder can hold a static charge and is used as ink in this process.

The *cleaning blade* is a small blade that runs the length of the drum and is used to scrape excess toner into an internal waste bin.

The *charging corona wire* or *charging roller* is a device that transfers a charge to whatever runs past it. The *transfer corona* or *transfer roller* performs the same function.

Signal Components

The *DC controller* controls all the motors and sensors in the printer and synchronizes the entire process.

The *formatter board* translates the computer signals into pulses to pass to the laser.

The *laser scanning assembly* takes the pulse from the formatter board and shines it across the scanning mirror to the drum in order to create an image.

Fusing Components

The *fusing assembly* performs several functions. Portions of this were explained in the section on paper-handling components. Additionally, the fusing assembly has a *fusing roller*, which is Teflon coated and contains a heat lamp that heats the roller to over 350 degrees in order to melt toner.

The *pressure roller* is below the fusing roller and presses the paper against the fusing roller as the toner melts to ensure adhesion.

The EP Process

The electro-photostatic process, or EP process, is the technology and method that is used in a laser printer to produce an image. This process is broken down into six distinct, logical phases. Most of these stages or phases revolve around a photosensitive drum and its electrical properties. Figure 5.5 outlines each of these stages and their relative positioning in a laser printer.

The purpose of each of these stages will be explained, but together the stages form the toner into an image on the drum, move it to the paper, and then melt it onto the page. The six stages are

- Cleaning
- Conditioning
- Writing
- Developing
- Transferring
- Fusing

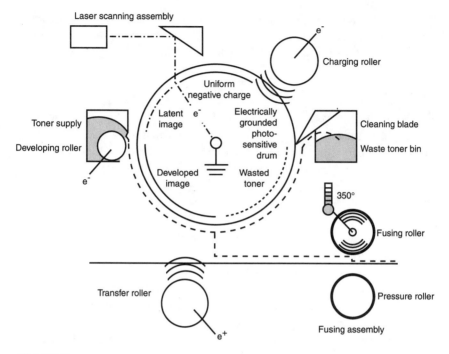

FIGURE 5.5
The electro-photostatic process.

Cleaning

The cleaning stage, illustrated in Figure 5.6, can be at the beginning or the end of the process, depending on how you look at the cycle. Most manufacturers place it at the beginning of the process to start fresh on the first cycle. A cycle is defined as a single revolution of the drum.

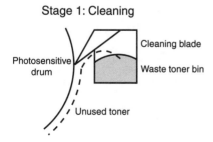

FIGURE 5.6
Stage one: Cleaning.

In the cleaning stage, the cleaning blade scrapes any residual toner off the photosensitive drum. This used toner is stored in a waste container usually located inside the toner cartridge itself.

Conditioning

The conditioning stage, illustrated in Figure 5.7, uses high voltage generated from the power supply and passes it through a corona wire or transfer roller to apply a solid negative charge to the surface of the drum. The chemical coating on the drum is unique in that it can maintain this charge only in the dark, which makes it photosensitive.

Writing

After the charge is applied to the drum, a signal is sent to the DC controller notifying the printer that the drum is ready. The writing stage (see Figure 5.8) is only partially completed inside the EP cartridge. It begins as the formatter board sends a signal to the laser, which pulses the signal in bursts of laser light reflecting off the rotating scanning mirror. The scanning mirror, in effect, moves the laser beam across the drum very rapidly. This creates a latent image on the drum by pulsing onto the photosensitive surface. If you cannot picture this, imagine a high-speed, single-pin, dot-matrix printer creating letters using a pin made out of reflected laser light. The latent image is formed because the drum cannot hold the negative charge on its surface where the light strikes it, so the charge dissipates to the grounded aluminum center of the drum. At the completion of this stage, the latent image areas on the drum have no charge, whereas the nonprintable areas of the drum have a strong negative charge.

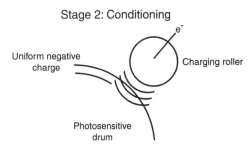

FIGURE 5.7
Stage two: Conditioning.

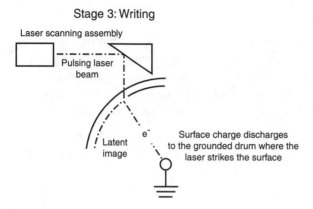

FIGURE 5.8
Stage three: Writing.

Developing

In this stage (see Figure 5.9), before the latent image can be transferred to paper, the drum must roll through a supply of toner particles. The negatively charged toner particles are repulsed by the negatively charged areas on the drum, but they adhere to the areas of the latent image where the charge has been dissipated.

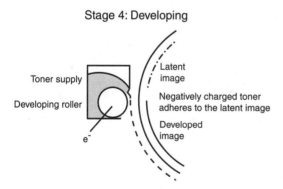

FIGURE 5.9
Stage four: Developing.

Transferring

In the transferring stage (see Figure 5.10), a strong positive charge is applied to the paper by another corona wire or transfer roller assembly before it is rolled under the drum. The developed, negatively charged toner forming a reverse image on the drum jumps to the paper because the paper has a stronger positive attraction than the latent areas on the drum.

At this point, the drum rotates back around to the first stage and is cleaned for the next cycle. The paper and the image on it then progress to the final stage.

Fusing

This final stage, fusing (see Figure 5.11), is usually the only complete stage that occurs outside the toner cartridge, or EP cartridge. In this stage, the transferred image is heated to the point of melting by the heat lamp inside the fusing roller, and the toner is pressed into the fibers of the page by the pressure roller. This permanently attaches the image to the page and passes the paper out of the printer.

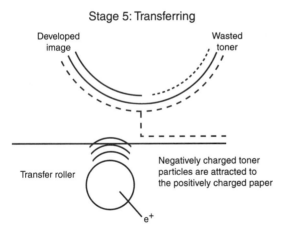

Stage 5: Transferring

Developed image

Wasted toner

Transfer roller

Negatively charged toner particles are attracted to the positively charged paper

e^+

FIGURE 5.10
Stage five: Transferring.

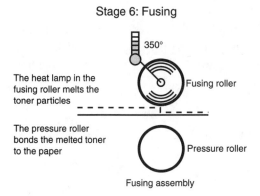

Stage 6: Fusing

350°

The heat lamp in the fusing roller melts the toner particles

Fusing roller

The pressure roller bonds the melted toner to the paper

Pressure roller

Fusing assembly

FIGURE 5.11
Stage six: Fusing.

THERMAL PRINTERS

Thermal printers are generally special-application printers. These printers are not covered in the same depth as dot-matrix, inkjet, and laser printers on the test or in this book, but they will be discussed briefly.

These are generally inexpensive printers with poor quality—often 75dpi or less. These printers use no ink; instead, they use heating elements in the print head to heat the special chemically treated paper to form characters. This paper is generally thin and fragile and must be stored in a cool area.

The benefits of using these printers are twofold. They are relatively inexpensive, and there is no ink cartridge or ribbon to replace. This makes them excellent for low-volume, low-maintenance printing. The most common applications for these printers are for older fax machines, cash registers, ATMs, and other similar point-of-sale devices.

HOT WAX PRINTERS

These printers occupy the higher end of the printing scale, providing full-color magazine-slick type output. The printing quality is extremely good and can be used as an alternative to professional color-separation techniques. These printers are not covered on the exam but are covered here so you can get a better grasp of the range of printing available today.

The mechanism used to create the characters is a hybrid of laser printer and inkjet technology. To form a character, the proper color-wax (imagine a big crayon) is melted and sprayed onto the page in inkjet fashion. However, the printer shape and size and its paper-handling processes are more reminiscent of a laser printer.

PREVENTIVE MAINTENANCE

Preventive maintenance is the best way to eliminate printer problems before they occur.

General Practices

In general, the first step in any printer's preventive maintenance procedure is to replace the consumables. Begin with the paper, then the ink source, and then any mechanical consumables. Only if these preliminary steps fail should you proceed with replacing FRUs. (As you learned in Chapter 2, "Diagnosing and Troubleshooting," an FRU is a field replaceable unit, or more commonly, a replacement part.)

Often the paper can be the source of many problems that have been misdiagnosed, especially if you're dealing with many paper jams. Paper curl, finish, cut edge, and basis weight are all factors you must consider when selecting the proper paper for your printer. Refer to your manufacturer's documentation to determine the proper paper for your printer.

NOTE | Many people don't realize that there is a "right side up" for paper you're loading into a printer. If you are called to fix a printer that constantly jams, check the paper. Even if it adheres to the manufacturer's specifications, the paper may have been inserted upside-down. The proper orientation of the paper should be marked on every ream.

Print-quality defects are most often caused by the ink source, but they can also be caused by both out-of-spec paper and mechanical issues. If the ink source has not been replaced in a while (or refilled/refurbished), check it first. It's not recommended that you use refurbished cartridges for any printer because they are outside of the design tolerances for any print cartridge. Gears, lubricant, and jets wear out, but they are not replaced in most refurbished ink cartridges.

TROUBLESHOOTING

Table 5.1 outlines printing problems that are common to all printer types. The following sections then break down troubleshooting information as it applies to the most common printer types: dot-matrix, inkjet, and laser printers.

TABLE 5.1

COMMON PRINTING ISSUES

Symptom	Probable Cause	Possible Solution
Print job is sent, but no visible reaction from the printer occurs.	Printer is turned off or is offline, or the data cable is disconnected.	Check all connections and make sure that the printer is on and is online. Try restarting the computer. You should hear the printer reset during POST.
Printer is printing garbage in Windows.	Incorrect driver, cable, or connection.	Try printing from DOS. If there is no garbage, it is the Windows driver. If DOS printing does not work either, check the connections and then replace the cable.
Network printer is not responding.	Need more information.	Have another user try to print. If this works, check your permissions or the printer queue you are using.
Paper continually jams.	Paper does not meet specifications.	Improper cut edge, grain curl, or paper finish could cause this.

Dot-Matrix Printers

Table 5.2 outlines printing problems specific to dot-matrix printers.

TABLE 5.2

DOT-MATRIX PRINTER PROBLEMS

Symptom	Probable Cause	Possible Solution
Printer sounds like it is printing, but no print appears.	Printer ribbon isn't installed properly.	Reinstall or replace printer ribbon.
Print is too light.	Paper thickness lever is set incorrectly.	Move lever closer to paper to allow for single thickness again.
Print is too light.	Ribbon is worn or refurbished.	Replace printer ribbon with a new ribbon cartridge.
Print is too dark.	Paper thickness lever is set incorrectly.	Adjust the lever to allow for thicker paper.
Paper does not advance.	Paper is installed incorrectly.	Install paper properly into tractor feeder. Set paper selector to tractor-feed paper. If paper is installed properly, the problem could be a bad stepper motor.
Letters are not fully formed.	Ribbon is worn.	Install new printer ribbon.
Letters are not fully formed.	Print head has worn or missing pins.	Replace print head.
Printer keeps jamming print-head pins.	Refurbished printer ribbon was used.	Replace the ribbon with a new one from the printer manufacturer. Often a refurbished ribbon does not have the specified lubricant in the ink, which causes excessive print-head wear.

InkJet Printers

Table 5.3 outlines printing problems specific to inkjet printers.

TABLE 5.3

INKJET PRINTER PROBLEMS

Symptom	Probable Cause	Possible Solution
Printer sounds like it is printing, but no print appears.	Printer cartridge is not installed properly or is out of ink.	Reinstall or replace printer cartridge.
Print is too light.	Cartridge needs to be cleaned.	Start the printer's cleaning cycle. *Never* attempt to clean the jets manually.
Print is too light.	Cartridge needs to be replaced.	Replace printer cartridge with a *new* cartridge (*not* refurbished).
Solid black lines of ink appear across the page.	Cartridge needs to be cleaned because of banding, or it needs to be replaced because of leaks.	Start the printer's cleaning cycle, or replace the printer cartridge with a new cartridge.
Paper does not advance.	Paper is installed incorrectly.	Install paper properly into feeder. Set paper selector to the proper size. If paper is installed properly, the problem could be a bad stepper motor.
Letters are not fully formed.	Cartridge needs to be cleaned or replaced.	Start the printer's cleaning cycle, or replace the printer cartridge with a new cartridge.

Laser Printers

Ten percent of the Core exam covers printers, and 80–90 percent of that coverage focuses on laser printers and the EP process. This is the reason the EP process was so heavily stressed earlier in this chapter. The three self tests described here can give you a window into the EP process itself. This is an invaluable tool for troubleshooting printers.

Three types of self tests can be run on most laser printers. The first is simply an engine test to see if all the mechanics and related sensors are working. This generates a page of solid vertical lines in most cases. Refer to your printer's manual to determine how to initiate this test. The second is the test more commonly known as a "printer self test." This test generates alphanumeric data and prints the characters. This test verifies that the formatter board is working properly and is communicating with the DC controller. If both of these tests work, typically your problem is in the cabling, the driver, or even the network interface, but not the printer itself.

The third test is called the "printer half-self-test." This test is simply a standard self-test that you abort by raising the printer cover.

By running this self test, you can verify whether print is making it to the page, in which case the first five stages are functioning properly. If there is no print on the paper, you can open the drum shutter and verify that the first four stages are functioning if there are characters on the drum. If there are no characters on the drum, you can sprinkle a little toner on the drum and verify that the first three stages are working. In this way, you can isolate the stage that is not functioning properly.

Table 5.4 outlines other common printing problems specific to laser printers.

TABLE 5.4

LASER PRINTER PROBLEMS

Symptom	Probable Cause	Possible Solution
Blank pages.	Printer cartridge is not installed properly or is out of toner.	Remove the sealing tape and reinstall the printer cartridge. If this fails to resolve the problem, replace the printer cartridge.
Blank pages.	High voltage power supply is not functioning.	Perform a half-self-test. If there is text on the drum, the HVPS is working, but the transfer roller may not be receiving the charge properly. If there is no text on the drum, the HVPS may not be working.
Image smears.	Fuser is not functioning.	Check the AC voltage supply. This provides the power to the heating lamp. If the voltages and current check out, replace the fuser.
Poor image quality.	The toner cartridge is old or refurbished.	Replace the toner cartridge with a new one.
Repetitive defects occur on the page.	A roller surface has been scratched.	Align the page with the manufacturer's printer defect ruler. The repeating defect will provide the measurement of the circumference of the defective roller. Different roller sizes are used to facilitate this troubleshooting technique.

Symptom	Probable Cause	Possible Solution
Black pages.	Bad HVPS or charging roller.	The charging roller is not transferring a uniform negative charge to the drum; therefore, the toner is attracted to the entire surface of the drum during the developing stage.
Vertical lines.	Scratched/grooved drum or other roller.	Troubleshoot the printer for the defective part. Replace the defective part.
Horizontal lines.	Defect on the surface of one of the rollers.	Using the manufacturer's image defect ruler, you can determine which part is defective by placing the paper on the ruler and measuring out of where the next mark came from. The distance between defects is the circumference of the defective roller.
Splotched page edges.	Dirty corona wire.	Clean the corona wire using the tool provided or a clean Q-tip.
Ghost images.	Bad cleaning blade.	This is extremely common with refurbished cartridges. Replace the toner cartridge with a new one.
Garbage characters.	Bad formatter board.	Attempt a self-test. If the characters do not form properly, the formatter board should be replaced.
Garbage characters.	Bad printer driver.	If the self-test works, use the common troubleshooting techniques above to determine if it is the driver or the cable/connection.

Safety

Most of the topics on safety were mentioned in Chapter 3, "Safety and Preventive Maintenance." However, this section briefly discusses safety again as it applies to printers.

You should follow certain obvious safety precautions when dealing with any electronic equipment. Regarding printers in particular, laser printers are usually the only ones with safety issues. Laser printers, by their very name, project a need for precaution. No, the laser in these printers cannot cut through metal or defeat Darth Vader, but it is extremely dangerous to the human eye. Many safety interlocks in most laser printers prevent you from opening the housing without powering down the printer. However, these locks can be defeated and can malfunction. Exercise caution when looking into a laser printer.

Also, although it's not as dangerous as the laser, toner from an EP cartridge can be hazardous to your clothing. If you get this substance on your hands or clothes, be sure to wash it off with *cold* water. Hot water can melt the toner and make it impossible to remove from skin and clothes alike. Toner spills can present another hazard. Because of toner's electrically chargeable nature and extremely fine granularity, cleaning with a common household vacuum cleaner is not recommended. Toner can pass right through the filters and back into the air. Toner can also get into the engine and short the electrical components of the vacuum cleaner, melting into them in the process. 3M makes a special toner vacuum for this explicit purpose.

PRINTER CONNECTIONS

Possible printer connections include infrared and SCSI connections. The three most common connection methods will be discussed here:

- Serial
- Parallel
- Network

For more information on these and other I/O ports, refer to Chapters 1 and 4.

Serial

Serial connections are no longer as common as they once were for printer communications. The longer distances supported by serial connections have been replaced by network connections, and the slower speeds of serial communications are no longer viable for today's high-speed printers.

The manual configuration of multiple parameters and proprietary cabling are a thing of the past. Most serial connections today are for legacy systems or newer handheld palmtop computers and PDAs. That being said, serial printer communication was once the method of choice and still is for older, legacy, or special-application systems.

Parallel

Parallel printers provide the most common local printer connection method. Parallel communication allows for Plug and Play-style setup, making connection as easy as possible. This may require replacing your parallel printer cable with a bidirectional substitute (see Figure 5.12). This would allow the printer to "talk" to the computer, and the computer to "talk" to the printer.

Network

Network printing and shared workgroup printing are the designs of the future. Already in many corporations, network printing has allowed tremendous cost savings over having a printer on every desk. A single high-speed network printer can service multiple workgroups of users with more efficiency and features than a number of desktop printers would allow. Network printers as network resources will be covered in more detail in Chapter 7, "Basic Networking." Suffice it to say that the network provides a higher speed, higher bandwidth connection than any previous communication method has.

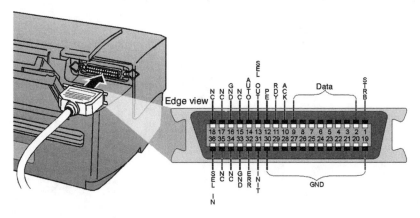

FIGURE 5.12
Parallel printer connection.

Printer Languages

Straight text can be printed to most printers using the ASCII character standards. This standard involves a set of escape sequences or data strings starting with the escape character (ASCII 27) followed by the data to be printed. For more graphics-intensive printing, additional controls must be used. There are two main printer languages in use today that can do this: Postscript and PCL.

Postscript is a page-definition language created by Adobe Systems that actually accepts the data from the printer and then lays out the entire page prior to printing. Postscript is generally more memory intensive, but it can deliver some stunning output using vector graphics and other advanced features.

PCL, or Printer Command Language, was developed by Hewlett-Packard. Many manufacturers outside of HP also use this standard, and many printers can support both PCL and Postscript.

With the advancement of the PCL language and the power of today's MS Windows printer drivers, few differences between PCL and PostScript can be seen by the average user. For production environments, however, the added cost of Postscript is worth it.

WHAT IS IMPORTANT TO KNOW

- Bit-image printers form the characters using a series of dots. Fully formed character printers strike the page once for each letter, creating a whole character at a time.

- Line printers are generally limited to dot-matrix and daisywheel printers. A page printer must print an entire page and eject it from the printer before you can read the text.

- Impact printers do exactly that. They impact the page when creating a character. Non-impacts, inkjets, and lasers never actually touch the page.

- Know the popular feed mechanisms including tractor feed and automatic sheet feed.

- Review the chart on consumables. Remember which printers relate to which consumables.

- Review the chart on troubleshooting. Remember which printers relate to which techniques.

- Review and understand the components of dot-matrix, laser, and inkjet printers.

- Know the six stages of the EP process and their functions. They are cleaning, conditioning, writing, developing, transferring, and fusing.

- Understand the differences and the uses of the three self tests: engine test, self-test, and half-self-test.

▶ Identify the unique components of portable systems and their unique problems. These basic components include:

- Batteries
- LCD panels
- AC adapters
- Docking stations
- PC cards
- Pointing devices

CHAPTER 6

Portable Computers

PORTABLE COMPUTING BASICS

The portable computer industry has made great strides in recent years. This is due to advancements in the miniaturization of technology. Whereas one of the first computers was the size of a mobile home, now computers the size of this book have hundreds of times the processing power of that first computer. Portable technology in the PC industry progressed from the first "luggables" from Compaq, through "laptops" from IBM and Zenith, to the current "notebook" systems available from many manufacturers today. Portable computers from a sub-notebook class, called "palm computing," are also available.

Portable computers are typically the tools of the upper levels of management, although many users can justify the need for a portable computer through most business-related travel. Generally, today's laptop can provide almost everything a desktop system might. However, there are some limitations and a few differences to discuss.

COMPONENTS

The following sections discuss several laptop-specific components.

Batteries

The key use for a portable system is realized when a power outlet is not available. Most portables today have batteries in one of three types:

- Nickel cadmium (NiCd)
- Nickel metal hydride (NiMH)
- Lithium ion

The NiCd, or nicad, rechargeable battery is the most common type of portable computer battery and the least expensive. One problem with NiCd batteries is the phenomenon known as a *memory effect*. The memory effect is inevitable. It is a gradual lessening of the charge that can be held, which results from the charging process itself. After a varying period of regular use, the length of available battery time will gradually decrease to zero. This memory effect can be reduced by fully discharging the battery every time before recharging. Unfortunately, even this will not prevent or eliminate the memory effect.

NiMH batteries surpass their NiCd counterparts by eliminating the memory effect completely. This makes the battery somewhat more expensive than the NiCd, but most users believe that it makes up for the cost in functionality. At their individual peaks, NiCd and NiMH batteries last for approximately the same length of time.

The lithium ion portable battery provides a longer window for use between chargings. Containing no lithium metal, Li-Ion technology simply uses the ions of lithium and shuttles them back and forth on the charge and discharge cycles. This is rapidly becoming the battery of choice in many new portable systems, but extreme measures must be taken by the manufacturer to rigidly control the charging and discharging cycles. This is because these batteries have a tendency to vent and cause fires or explosions under adverse conditions.

LCD Panels

Liquid Crystal Display panels were discussed briefly in Chapter 1, "Installation, Configuration, and Upgrading." These color laptop displays are the latest generation of flat-screen displays. Other types have been gas plasma and monochrome LCD panels. LCD panels can be broken into two separate technologies for image creation: passive matrix and active matrix.

In a *passive matrix* LCD screen, the images are formed by sending a signal down a vertical and a horizontal wire. Where these two lines intersect, the crystal is charged, and a pixel forms. Unfortunately, there is no active discharge circuitry built into a passive matrix (hence, the name). The image passively removes itself by fading out gradually after the charge is withdrawn from the intersection. This causes bleeding and ghosting images in motion on a passive matrix LCD panel.

In an *active matrix* LCD panel, the signal is formed in much the same way as in a passive matrix, but the lines intersect at a *thin-film transistor*, or *TFT*. This transistor gives an instantaneous and steady signal to the crystal, forming a clear, sharp pixel. When the video card gives the signal to remove that pixel from the image, the TFT reverses and completely removes the charge from the crystal. This provides a more crisp, clean, shadow-free display. Unfortunately, these displays are more expensive and cause a heavier drain on the battery.

AC Adapters

Because most portable systems do not have the space for an exhaust/cooling fan, and power supplies generate a great deal of heat as well as take up valuable space, most laptop power supplies are located outside the case as a separate unit called a "brick." This is much like the transformer power packs used for other small, direct current devices, such as modems and video game units.

> **NOTE**
>
> AC adapters are *not* interchangeable. Laptops from the same manufacturer, and even the same family from within that manufacturer, have been known to have different power requirements. Always match up the output voltage and current from an AC adapter to the input requirements on the portable device.

Docking Stations

As laptop computers become more powerful and more reliable, users want more from their portable solutions. External ports on the laptop itself are fine, but a more flexible solution is sometimes required. The docking station permits the laptop to double as a full-function desktop. With permanent ports for an external keyboard, monitor, mouse, and various other I/O devices, the laptop can be removed or inserted at will, while the remainder of the "desktop" system remains intact. Often docking stations provide additional expandability not normally available in portable systems. This expandability may include additional hard drives, tape backup units, and expansion bus adapter cards.

Potential problems may arise from the use of a docking station. Because all the devices on the docking station do not exist when the laptop is used by itself, anything short of a plug-and-play operating system is problematic at best.

PC Cards

PC cards were covered extensively in Chapter 4, "Motherboards/ Processors/Memory," in the section on bus structures. This section provide supplemental information to that chapter.

PC cards are designed to be hot-swappable. As with anything else of this nature, if you have the ability to shut down or stop the PCMCIA services before removing a card, it is recommended that you do so.

If the card must be hot-swapped, it can be, but you should do that only as an alternative and not the primary method of removal.

Pointing Devices

Mice and other pointing devices were covered in Chapter 1. However, some alternative methods for controlling pointing devices may cause system incompatibilities or issues and should be touched on here as well.

The trackball, touchpad, and button mouse are all examples of portable versions of pointing devices. They all use the mouse drivers in the same fashion a normal mouse would.

The trackball, much like an upside-down mouse, is the most popular built-in pointing device among many laptop manufacturers. Due to the space required and the constant need for cleaning, the trackball has fallen out of favor with most users.

Many laptops today have touchpad, or glidepoint, devices. These devices have a small, flat pad that looks like a digitizer. As the user moves a finger across the pad, the heat sensors (or pressure sensors in some devices) pick up the movement and translate it into pointer motion. Most of these devices are relative positioning systems, rather than the absolute positioning used in a digitizer. One point worth mentioning: The majority of these devices are impossible to use a stylus with and are difficult to use with extremely cold hands. The heat sensors cannot pick up either of these pointing methods.

Also called a pin mouse or fingertip mouse, a button mouse is basically a small, extremely sensitive joystick located in the middle of the laptop keyboard, usually between the letters "G," "H," and "B." These mice may take a while for the user to become proficient in maneuvering, and are somewhat more difficult to use for small movements.

WHAT IS IMPORTANT TO KNOW

- Laptop computers have advanced to the level that they can replace desktop computers in many situations. These portable computers can approach a similar level of expandability using both external ports and additional docking station features.

- Batteries are the blessing and the bane of many laptop computers. Batteries come in three different "flavors": NiCD, NiMH, and Li-Ion. NiCD batteries are the most prevalent because of their relatively low cost. NiCD batteries have a memory effect that reduces charging to full capacity over time.

- LCD panels on laptop computers are either passive or active. Active displays utilize TFT-based display technologies and are the brighter and more robust of the two displays. The trade-off is in the power consumption.

- PC cards are a mainstay of laptop peripherals. The PCMCIA card has enabled the previously proprietary laptop industry to standardize. These standards are based on PCMCIA type I, II, and III cards.

- Pointing devices for laptops are somewhat different than their desktop counterparts. The miniature trackball, touchpad, and button mouse are three of the most popular designs.

OBJECTIVES

▶ Identify basic networking concepts, including how a network works.

▶ Identify procedures for swapping and configuring network interface cards.

▶ Identify the ramifications of repairs on the network.

CHAPTER 7

Basic Networking

Why do we need networks? Why have they become so popular within the last decade? The answer is simple. Computers are all about information: inputting, processing, outputting, and storing data. Because of the increasing number of computers—and more importantly the increasing amount of information on these computers—it is necessary that these computers can communicate to facilitate the sharing of this information. That is the primary goal of a network: to share information (see Figure 7.1). Therefore, a *network* is any method of sharing data between two or more computers over some form of transmission media, such as a wire.

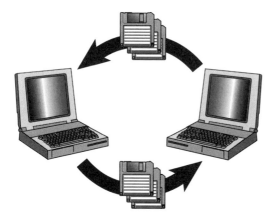

FIGURE 7.1
A basic communication network.

BRIEF HISTORY

Networks are not a new concept. Networks were prevalent with the mainframe style of computing in the 1970s.

NOTE Mainframes were the basic style of network; however, there are no references to mainframe technologies on the A+ examination. The networking technologies covered on the exam are related primarily to LANs, or local area networks, and WANs, or wide area networks.

With the introduction of PCs, users finally had control over their own data. This was not necessarily a good thing. Data was easily lost or destroyed, and it was hard to share information with co-workers. The only method of sharing data was the "sneaker-net." (Picture someone saving data to a floppy disk, putting on his tennis shoes, and running the disk over to his friend's computer to share the data, as depicted in Figure 7.2.)

FIGURE 7.2
Sneaker net in action.

Networks came about out of sheer necessity for the information age to continue.

COMPONENTS OF A NETWORK

A network is all about communication. You could say that when two people hold a verbal conversation, they are networking using audible signals on the transmission media of air. Society and courtesy dictate the protocols used. One person contacts another by calling out the other's name. The second person answers and asks why the first called. The first person explains the nature of the call and requests some information. The second person decides whether he wants to answer, and then does or doesn't do so. Either party can break the communication at any time. When the conversation is at an end, both people go on about their business.

In a similar fashion, a computer network is made up of two computers (or more), a transmission media, and an accepted mode of communication. One computer must request the data, and the other must provide the data requested. Both computers must be speaking the same language over a common connection.

Servers

The *server* is the computer that provides the data or services to computers that request it. This server may provide services in the form of data from storage, data from processing, or access to another resource (like printing).

Clients

The *client* is the computer doing the requesting. This client must be able to initiate communication with the server, speak the server's "language," and formulate a request.

> **NOTE**
>
> Do not confuse this client computer with the client software installed in MS Windows Networking. Although the client software allows the client computer to function, this chapter is currently talking about abstract concepts and components. For more information about the network client software, see Chapter 18, "Networking."

Media

The common connection and transmission media is determined by the type and classification of the network. This communication is typically an electronic signal sent over a conducting wire or other media of some form. Other types of media include glass tubing for fiber optics and even air for microwave transmissions. These will be discussed in greater detail at a later point in this chapter.

Security

Security is the most often overlooked basic component of a network. When you allow computers to communicate, you invite disaster. Because a network is a synergetic entity, no individual network component can be totally secure against all other network components. This would defeat the purpose of opening up for communication.

Security can be handled in many fashions, but the most common form of network security is a list of keys. Usually, one must have two keys (a user identifier and a password) to access any network resource. Each computer that acts as a server must have access to the database where these security keys are stored. Where this database is located is one of the criteria for determining what type of network you have.

TYPES OF NETWORKS

Networks can be broken down into two primary types: centralized and decentralized. These concepts can be applied to security, resources, and processing, as outlined here.

Type of LAN	Security	Resources	Processing
Terminal	Centralized	Centralized	Centralized
Server	Centralized	Centralized	Decentralized
Client/server	Centralized	Shared	Shared
Peer-to-peer	Decentralized	Decentralized	Decentralized

As centralization increases, administration of security and network services is made significantly easier, but flexibility (as perceived by the user) decreases. With increased decentralization, the reverse is true. A hybrid is created in the client/server environment. This hybrid entails that part of the processing be completed on the server and part on the workstation. The function of data storage may also be shared between the two components.

Terminal/Mainframe Networks

Mainframe systems were the original networks. All of the underlying network hardware existed. They used network cards and cabling and all of the requisite connection materials. Multiple clients were connected to a centralized system that provided basic services to the users on the system. Looking at it from another point of view, however, the mainframe/terminal network was a single entity. The users could not function unless they were logged on to the mainframe. The terminals were simply extensions of the central computer system. On these systems, although the information is shared between users, there really is only one computer processor on the entire network. Everything is centralized into one machine.

Server-Based Networking

Server-based networking is the easiest to understand. This is the first true LAN design to be discussed that uses intelligent PCs. This design allows for centralized storage of data and shared resources (such as printers) with a centralized security database. All applications are stored on the local PC, and all processing occurs on the user's individual PC as well.

Client/Server-Based Networking

Client/server is a hybrid technology that came about as a combination of the benefits of server-based technology with the increased processing horsepower of today's PC. Data can be centralized, printing can be centralized, and security is centralized, but the processing and applications can be shared between the server and the client. Almost all network servers today are of this type at some level. Different applications may be classified as either client/server or just plain server depending on their design, but both can coexist on the same network server.

Peer-to-Peer Networking

Peer-to-peer, or workgroup, computing provides the most flexible but hardest environment to administer. Each member can act as both server and client, and each system has its own security database (as shown in Figure 7.3). Although individual users have control over what data they would like to share, they also must maintain the security accounts. The inherent problem with this is that a user may have a password on one system and an entirely different password on another system. This can lead to confusion and prevent network access for even the rightful users.

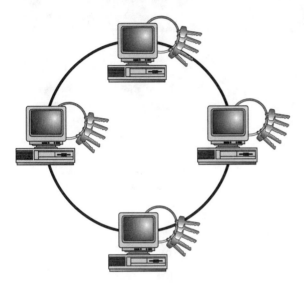

FIGURE 7.3
Peer-to-peer workgroup security.

TOPOLOGIES

Network topologies, like topographical maps, present a graphical representation of the network layout. However, whereas a map would indicate physical features only, a network topology can be expressed logically or physically.

Figure 7.4 illustrates three common network topologies: bus, ring, and star. These three topologies are covered in detail in the following sections.

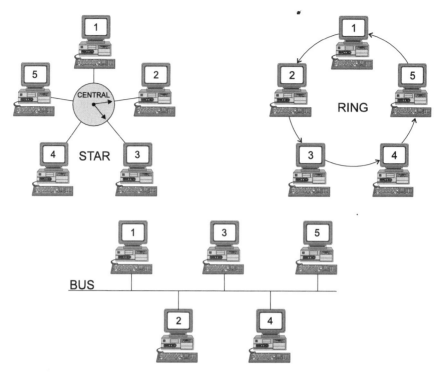

FIGURE 7.4
Network topologies: star, ring, and bus.

Bus

Originally implemented with coaxial cabling, a physical bus topology is simply a single cable line that connects all workstations in a design similar to a daisy chain. All the computers on the network share this cable, but they can use it only one at a time. The cable must be terminated on either end to eliminate signal reflection (in the same fashion as a SCSI bus). If a break occurs in the cabling, the entire network may go down because neither side is terminated. This makes it extremely difficult to determine where the break in the cabling occurred.

Often a logical bus topology is implemented in a physical star configuration using a hub and 10BASE-T cabling. This configuration keeps the entire network from crashing when one computer fails or is removed. (You'll see the internal design of a hub up close in a later section.) The Ethernet network protocol is most often used for this style of topology.

Ring

Ring topologies were also created with coaxial cable in the earlier days of networking. Using this medium, the ring was very much like a bus topology in which the terminators were removed and the two ends were connected.

Unfortunately, this yields the same flaws as the bus topology: A single cable break would bring the entire network down. In addition, it is difficult to determine where the break occurred. To eliminate this, a ring topology is most often forced into a star configuration using an MAU as the central point of contact. For further clarification of the internal design of an MAU, see Figure 7.5. In this configuration, with either 10BASE-T cabling or IBM cabling, a ring topology and a bus topology are physically similar but are logically and electrically different. IBM's Token Ring network protocol is most often associated with this topology.

Star

Star topologies rarely exist in logical form. The only applicable example is a mainframe system, in which all individual terminals can connect directly to the server. In the PC networking field, the star topology has become the single most widespread physical network topology housing other logical topologies.

In a star topology, all computers and devices on the network connect to a central device. Because of this, a failed node will not bring down the rest of the network, which indeed makes determining the location of the failure much easier. A star network is modular in design, most often using 10BASE-T cabling and either a hub (logical bus) or an MAU (logical ring). To see the differences, one must look at the circuitry inside a hub and MAU.

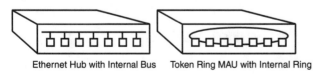

Ethernet Hub with Internal Bus   Token Ring MAU with Internal Ring

FIGURE 7.5
Internal wiring: hub versus MAU.

Star topologies can provide the most architectural flexibility combined with ease of administration, but they require more cabling than the original bus and ring physical topologies.

Mesh

Mesh topology can be summarized in one word: redundancy. Mesh networks are typically designed to provide a high availability, fully fault-tolerant network. Every node is directly connected to every other node. If a direct connection fails, the two nodes attempting communication can route the data through another node using its direct connections to the original nodes. This design is extremely expensive and difficult to administer. Because of this, it is typically used for WANs more than for LANs.

CLASSIFICATIONS OF NETWORKS

It's called a local area network. But how far is local? What differentiates between local and wide? Below are some definitions that should clarify this issue. Keep in mind that these are general guidelines; there are no definite points where one leaves off and the next begins.

Local Area Networks (LANs)

Local area networks are generally defined as being within a single building. There may be discreet networks on each floor, but a vertical backbone, called a *riser,* can connect the different floors. LAN speed is generally 10Mbps to 100Mbps and can be used to determine if your network is a LAN, WAN, CAN, or MAN. Typically in a LAN, the cabling and connecting devices are owned by the company that owns the LAN.

Campus Area Networks (CANs)

Campus area networks typically are LANs that have expanded to several geographically contiguous buildings. A dissimilar network topology or technology, like FDDI, might connect two buildings, or the CAN may be split into separate LANs that have individual administrators. CANs typically operate at speeds close to those of a LAN, and the cabling is generally owned by the company that owns the network.

Metropolitan Area Networks (MANs)

Metropolitan area networks are very similar to CANs, but the most prevalent difference is the owner of the cabling. Generally, a local telephone/telecom company leases the cabling service to the company that owns the network. MANs can also operate at speeds close to those of a LAN, but they may operate as slowly as an ISDN line.

Wide Area Networks (WANs)

Wide area networks provide a link that crosses local telephone company boundaries and may require a third-party nationwide or worldwide connection service. WANs can operate as slowly as ISDN speeds, or as fast as what your company is willing to pay for.

NETWORK COMMUNICATIONS

Network communications are all about connectivity and compatibility. Originally, each network required a canned and proprietary solution. As more manufacturers joined the network industry, standards for intercommunication were developed. These standards are simply rules for communication to which the manufacturers adhere. The manufacturers are free to implement these rules in any fashion, but deviating from the rules will quickly lead them right out of the industry.

The rules, or protocols, for network communication are defined by the OSI model. The OSI, or Open Systems Interconnect, protocols are further defined by IEEE, the Institute for Electrical and Electronics Engineers.

OSI

The OSI model is broken into seven layers:

- *Application*. Provides the interface between the user application and the network APIs. The network redirector exists here and intercepts application calls to the local machine for network resources and passes them to the network for access to the proper location.

◆ *Presentation*. This provides a translator for dissimilar character generation codes. For example, this layer will translate EBCDIC into ASCII for proper communication.

◆ *Session*. This layer is responsible for initiating, maintaining, and completing the communication session between computers. The network client exists here to provide a common communication to compatible networks.

◆ *Transport*. This layer is responsible for ensuring that the data packets arrive intact at the end of the route. It contains error correction, flow control, and fragmentation/reassembly rules.

◆ *Network*. This layer is responsible for plotting the route for packets to take to other subnetworks and networks. To provide for this routability, the Network layer is also responsible for providing a common method of addressing other network nodes; for example, IP addresses.

◆ *Data Link*. This layer defines how the computer formats the data into packets and accesses the network cabling to transmit data. It is responsible for providing error-free data to the layers above it. Every NIC contains a unique MAC address that works with this level.

◆ *Physical*. This defines the specific pin positions, shielding, and maximum transmission lengths for physical cabling. The NIC also partially resides here.

With the exception of the Physical layer, each layer can physically communicate with only the layer above or below it. Logically, however, the layers communicate with their counterparts in the OSI stack on other computers. This modular approach allows a manufacturer of network cards to create a card that can work with any Network Operating System (NOS). The NOS operates at a higher level and can work with any Network Interface Card, or NIC, because the network card need only work at the Physical layer, interfacing with the Physical layer cabling and the Data Link layer protocols.

Protocols

What is a protocol? Protocols are defined in the real world as procedures or rules. Network protocols are essentially the same thing. Any given network protocol contains a list of rules and procedures for moving data between OSI layers. This section discusses only the protocols of the first four layers. Table 7.1 contains that information.

TABLE 7.1

PROTOCOLS IN THE FIRST FOUR LAYERS OF THE OSI MODEL

OSI Layer	*Protocol Examples*	*Description*
Transport	TCP, SPX	These protocols are responsible for ensuring that the data packets arrive intact at the end of the route.
Network	IP, IPX, NetBEUI*	These protocols determine the route that the data must take through connection devices to get to other networks. These are the protocols most commonly talked about in regard to a network. They provide the addressing scheme for contacting other computers.
Data Link	Ethernet, token-ring, FDDI standards; IEEE 802.2, 802.3 802.5, and so on	These define how the network formats the data into packets and accesses the network cabling to transmit data. Ethernet and token-ring are standards based on these protocols.
Physical	IEEE 802.2, 802.3, 802.5; 10BASE-T and 10BASE-2 cabling are designated in these IEEE standards	These define the specific pin positions, shielding, and maximum transmission lengths for physical cabling. Most of these protocols partially cross into the Data Link layer as well.

* NetBEUI is not a routable protocol and does not take full advantage of the Network layer.

Ethernet Versus Token-Ring

The two most common Data Link layer protocols are often misnamed as network "types." These provide another level of rules for communication as defined in the OSI model. However, they are the most common network "types" in existence today, so we will discuss these Data Link layer protocols and their method for transmitting the data onto the wire, or *access method*, in more detail here.

Ethernet

Ethernet, originally developed by Xerox in the 1970s, has become the de facto standard for networking today. The IEEE standards 802.2 and 802.3 define its characteristics. Ethernet uses 10BASE-5 (thicknet), 10BASE-2 (thinnet), or 10BASE-T (unshielded twisted pair) cabling. Ethernet is also capable of 10Mbps throughput and uses the Carrier Sense-Multiple Access with Collision Detection, CSMA/CD, access method.

NOTE
> The Fast Ethernet standard specified by 100BASE-X is capable of 100Mbps on Category 5 unshielded twisted pair cabling.

Carrier Sense Multiple Access with Collision Detection (CSMA/CD) can be better defined by breaking up the pieces. Carrier Sense is readily understood; this simply means that the NIC listens to the network and waits for a "dial-tone." Multiple Access is exactly that: Multiple computers can access the network simultaneously. Collision Detection requires a little more explanation. A collision is an event that occurs when two computers try to "talk" at the same time. They both hear the dial tone, they both can access the network, but they do not realize that the other is attempting to talk. When their electrical signals collide on the wire between them, a collision occurs. Generally, each will wait a random (and hopefully different) amount of time and then attempt to resend the original data.

Token-Ring

Token-ring was originally created by IBM, although the complete specifications were shared with IEEE to create the 802.5 standard. This competitor to Ethernet uses a logical ring usually inside of a physical star configuration with a 4Mbps (or 16Mbps after 1990) throughput. Initially, this specification called for shielded twisted pair cabling, but it has been relaxed somewhat with the advent of 10BASE-T cabling. Token-ring technology avoids the collisions inherent in Ethernet and provides a more reliable network under load by using a token passing access method.

The token passing access method allows only one person to talk at a time, taking turns as the "token" is passed around the ring. Determining which node gets the token next is based on 1) length of time since the node last had it and 2) network priority. This token passing method prevents collisions, so no collision detection is necessary.

NETWORK CONNECTIVITY

Network connectivity is the basis for network communication. This is the foundation for the OSI Physical layer. The connectivity of a network relies on two parts: transmission media and connection devices, or hardware.

Media

Transmission media is classified based on several characteristics. These can include bandwidth, minimum and maximum segment lengths, and susceptibility to interference in the form of EMI. Table 7.2 breaks down the characteristics for each type of cable.

TABLE 7.2

CHARACTERISTICS OF TRANSMISSION MEDIA

Cable	Cost	Installation	Capacity	Range	EMI	Connectors
Thinnet/ 10BASE-2	Less than STP but more than UTP	Not as easy as STP	10Mbps	185 meters	Less susceptible than UTP	Bayonet nut Connectors (BNC)
Thicknet/ 10BASE-5	More than STP and less than fiber	Not as easy as thinnet	10Mbps	500 meters	Less susceptible than UTP	AUI
Shielded twisted pair (STP)	More than UTP and less than thicknet	Easy	16Mbps to 500Mbps	100 meters	Less susceptible than UTP	RJ-45
Unshielded twisted pair (UTP)/ 10BASE-T	Cheapest	Easiest	10Mbps to 100Mbps	100 meters	Most susceptible of all	RJ-45
Fiber optic	Most expensive	Hard	100Mbps	Kilometers	Not susceptible to EMI	Similar to BNC

Hardware

Connection devices are designed to connect not only nodes on the LAN (as in the case of a Hub or MAU), but also to interconnect different networks.

Repeater

Repeaters function at the Physical layer of the OSI model. They simply repeat a degrading signal by amplifying it to full strength to defeat signal strength loss, or *attenuation*, caused by some of the transmission length limitations inherent in cabling. Beware: A repeater has no intelligence and repeats absolutely everything it hears, including bad packets.

Hub/MAU

Both an active hub and an MAU generally have repeaters built into them, while a passive hub does not. A hub is the center of an Ethernet star configuration, whereas an MAU is the center of a token-ring star configuration. As you could see in the earlier diagram of the hub versus the MAU, the hub has a bus built into it, and the ports in the hub simply act as connection points to that central bus. The MAU has an internal ring into which the ports are connection points. Both hubs and MAUs can be daisy-chained to create a longer bus or ring (respectively) with more ports. MAUs must maintain the ring; therefore, dual connections must be made with any additional MAUs to maintain a "ring-in" and a "ring-out" configuration.

> **NOTE**
> There is a limitation to this method of extending a bus. Generally, after five levels deep, these devices become a detriment to network performance, and the network should be split into separate physical segments.

Bridge

Bridges connect similar LANs. They operate on the Data Link layer of the OSI model and improve network performance by keeping traffic contained within segments. Unfortunately, bridges cannot stop broadcast traffic, or broadcast storms, from occurring. Bridges can connect LANs with similar layer 2 or data link protocols using homogenous bridging or dissimilar layer 2 protocols using heterogeneous bridging. Bridges need very little configuring and operate transparent to the user.

Router

Routers perform similar functions to a bridge, except that the routing occurs on the Network layer of the OSI model. Unlike a bridge, a router does not typically pass broadcasts. The router is intelligent and works more like a traffic cop than a bridge. Often, the router must choose from among several routes based on cost, time, and load criteria. The router determines where your data packet needs to go and sends you there (and only there). Routers provide a good measure of security as well.

Brouter

A brouter is exactly what it sounds like. It is a hybrid combination of a bridge and a router. Often, a network will have multiple protocols in use on the Network and Data Link layers. If a broadcast-based protocol (such as NetBEUI) and a routable protocol (such as TCP/IP) were both in use, the bridge portion of the brouter would pass the broadcast protocol, and the router portion of the brouter would route the routable protocol to the proper place.

Gateway

A gateway translates your data into the proper form for diverse and different remote networks. Often, an SNA gateway will be used to allow PCs to communicate with a mainframe. Gateways actually read and reform all data sent through them. Because of this, gateways typically operate much more slowly than other connection devices discussed here.

CONFIGURING NETWORK INTERFACE CARDS

Configuring a network interface card is exactly like configuring any other expansion card, as discussed in Chapters 1 and 2. The adapter requires a unique IRQ, I/O address, and DMA channel (if the card supports it), and a ROM address. As previously discussed, the Plug and Play standards alleviate the need to configure any of this manually, instead allowing the computer to arbitrate the settings with the card itself.

Some additional considerations do need to be made for a network interface card, or NIC. Because any one segment of the network operates as a single entity, all NICs must be compatible and use, or be bound to, the same protocols. In addition, all NICs on that segment must be able to connect to the same cabling type. After the card has been properly installed and the cabling has been attached, a network client must be configured on the PC. For further information on this process, consult Chapter 18, "Networking."

MAC Address

A unique identifier is hard-coded into all NICs from the manufacturer. This is known as a Media Access Control, or MAC, address. The MAC address must be unique on the network to enable communication. This address is used at the Data Link layer for distinctive communication between network nodes.

NETWORK REPAIRS

Because of the all-encompassing nature of a large network, many hundreds of users can become upset and extremely agitated when the network fails. In addition, because these users cannot get their work done, management is assigning dollar values to the loss of production. This can cause a very tense and volatile situation that needs to be remedied swiftly and expertly.

The basics of network repairs require a fast, logical mind. Using all the basic troubleshooting steps discussed in Chapter 2, you must be able to use your expertise combined with a little common sense. Ask questions that isolate a group of users. Remember, networks are all about communication. Determine the common failure and who the failure is affecting. This will go a long way toward narrowing down the prospective issues. Some of the more common issues include bandwidth, interruptions, and interference.

Bandwidth

Bandwidth is a representation of the limit of data that you can cram into the cable. Just how much is too much? Understand the nature of the applications with which the users are working. Graphics tend to grab more than their fair share of the bandwidth. If you do find that bandwidth is an issue, try scheduling some network access or large jobs for off-hours. If the network's slow speeds become unbearable, you can always purchase more bandwidth.

This is a particularly nasty issue with Ethernet networks because the more bandwidth you are using, the heavier the traffic gets. When the traffic gets heavy, more collisions occur. This may compound your speed problems.

Interruptions

Interruptions may occur for several reasons:

- The network may be scheduled for maintenance at that time.
- A connection device or cable may fail.
- A network node or server may fail.

All of these issues can cause network interruptions, but the best option is to schedule your servers for preventive maintenance down time. This can eliminate many other issues that could cause a network interruption.

NOTE

For the best administration, plan at least 6–8 hours of down time every night after backups. This will allow a window of opportunity for any future failure to be corrected during expected down times. Overall, this will increase customer satisfaction by properly setting the customer expectation.

WHAT IS IMPORTANT TO KNOW

- A transmission medium is a physical pathway that connects systems.

- Protocols are rules for network communication.

- Commit the OSI model to memory. The following mnemonic device should help you remember the layers, in order from top to bottom: All People Seem To Need Data Processing.

- Centralized computing gathers all network security into one location. Additionally, processing and storage can be centralized to varying degrees.

- In decentralized computing, the security, processing, or data storage (or some combination of all three) resides away from the central server location.

- The four basic networking topologies are bus, ring, star, and mesh.

- Logical and physical topologies differ in many ways. The physical topology is a description of what you can see; the logical topology is a description of how it actually works.

- LANs and CANs are smaller area networks in which the cable is owned by the company using the network.

- MANs and WANs are wider area networks in which the cable is owned by the connection provider.

- Ethernet is a logical bus topology that's often implemented in a physical star configuration on a CSMA/CD network.

- Token-ring is a ring topology that's often implemented in a physical star configuration on a collision avoidance network.

- The five media types (thinnet, thicknet, STP, UTP, and fiber) vary in terms of cost, installation, and other characteristics (as outlined in Table 7.2).

- Repeaters repeat the signal being transmitted on the wire in cases of signal attenuation.

- Hubs and MAUs provide a central location to connect logical bus and ring topologies (respectively) into physical star topologies.

- Bridges connect two similar networks with dissimilar networking protocols at OSI layer 2 to transmit traffic.

- Routers connect similar subnetworks, functioning as traffic cops that can limit excessive traffic. These operate at layer 3.

◆ Gateways connect dissimilar networks as translators.

◆ To configure a NIC, the cabling protocol and network protocol must match those of the network it will join.

◆ A network is a synergetic entity. If network repairs interfere with its operation, you are affecting many more users than if you were repairing only a single computer.

OBJECTIVES

▶ Differentiate effective from ineffective behaviors as they contribute to the maintenance or achievement of customer satisfaction. These behaviors and skills include the following:

- Communication and listening.

- Interpreting verbal and nonverbal cues.

- Responding appropriately to the customer's technical level.

- Establishing personal rapport with the customer.

- Displaying professional conduct.

- Helping and guiding a customer with problem descriptions.

- Responding to and closing a service call.

- Handling complaints and upset customers, conflicts, conflict avoidance, and resolution.

- Showing empathy and flexibility.

- Sharing the customer's sense of urgency.

CHAPTER 8

Customer Satisfaction

CUSTOMER SATISFACTION AND THE CTIA A+ EXAM

Customer satisfaction is an interesting part of the exam. While this topic covers 10 percent of the examination questions, the results of these questions are not used in the calculation of the final exam score. Customer satisfaction is much more an art form than a hard science. Indeed, these skills are often called "soft" skills or "people" skills. For this reason, the customer satisfaction topic will be covered here, but should not concern you greatly for the exam. However, these are extremely necessary skills for your success in the real world.

Customer satisfaction is valuable on many levels. It is far easier and more cost effective to keep an existing customer satisfied than it is to acquire a new customer. In addition, many studies have proven that a dissatisfied customer will tell more than five times as many people about how bad you are than a satisfied customer will tell people how good you are. In both of these situations, it is far preferable to keep your existing customers and keep them satisfied.

There are three key points to maintaining customer satisfaction:

◆ Communication

◆ Professional conduct

◆ Technical skills

You will notice that technical skills are at the bottom of this list. The rest of this book covers technical skills, and indeed you would not be in a position to try to satisfy a customer if you could not provide a solution to their technical problems. For these reasons, the appropriate technical skills will be assumed as a given. This chapter will be devoted to the first two points: communication and professional conduct.

Communication

To be sure, technical skills are necessary for resolving the problem that is causing the customer's concern. However, the customer's concern is often more important than the technical cause of the problem. The customer's perception is often a fickle and flexible thing that requires you to have a firm understanding but a delicate hand on the situation. Nothing can make this easier than good communication.

NOTE The best book I have ever encountered for increasing customer satisfaction and especially communication skills is *How to Win Friends and Influence People* by Dale Carnegie. I highly recommend this book for anyone who is truly trying to improve his or her communication skills.

Good communication revolves around the customer. The following five items are primary aspects of good communication for customer support:

- Listening
- Questioning
- Handling difficult situations
- Setting expectations
- Following up

Listening

- *Put yourself in the customer's shoes.* If you can see the problem from his point of view, his explanations will begin to make more sense.

- *Don't interrupt the user if it can be avoided.* Not only is this rude, but an agitated customer can calm himself by letting his irritation play itself out in his words.

- *Avoid talking down to the customer.* Do not use patronizing tones and terms. Also, do not use highly technical terminology. Try to find the customer's true level of understanding and talk to him on that level.

- *Use positive body language.* Look the customer in the eye when you talk with her. Be attentive.

- *Take thorough notes.* The first note you should take is a mental one. Commit the customer's name to memory. Nothing pleases a human being so much as to be remembered and recognized. After this, take written notes so that the customer can see you are listening and hearing what he or she has to say.

◆ *Paraphrase.* After the customer finishes an explanation, repeat the explanation back to him in your own words and ask him if you understand correctly in order to verify a common understanding.

Questioning

◆ *Ask more questions and give fewer statements.* This will make the customer feel part of the solution. After all, the customer most likely caused the situation, and no one likes to feel helpless.

◆ *Understand the difference between open-ended questions and closed-ended questions and when to use them.* Open-ended questions cannot be answered with a yes/no answer. These questions are used to draw information out of the customer. Closed-ended questions can be answered with a yes/no answer and are used for confirmation of facts previously gathered. These will limit the customer's responses to a set pattern. Progressing from mostly open-ended to mostly closed-ended questions is a natural part of the isolation process of troubleshooting.

NOTE | Never make the customer feel like the problem is his fault. He may have caused the worst computer problem in the world, but no one likes to be accused of making a mistake.

Handling Difficult Situations

Obviously, all service technicians have experienced difficult situations. This is part of the nature of the service industry. We are usually called when something is broken and tension is high. This tense atmosphere can lead to some pretty difficult situations.

◆ To defuse the situation, the best thing you can do is to simply listen. Often the customer can blow off steam by talking about it.

◆ Never argue. Just nod your head and empathize. Be sincere! Be careful that you avoid seeming patronizing because this can often be worse than arguing. Instead, if you provide a calm demeanor, the customer will naturally calm himself down.

- Be understanding. The customer may have an easily resolved, relatively insignificant problem, but to her it is a big deal. Acknowledge that she has a problem, but reassure her that it can be resolved.

- Show the customer some appreciation. Thank him for working with you and answering your questions. Thank him for his time and apologize for taking so long, even if it took only a few minutes. Thank him for providing you with business and assure him that if he has any more problems you will be happy to help.

Setting Expectations

By setting the proper expectations as early as possible, you can avoid some difficult situations. Often the actual problem or its solution is not the key element in customer satisfaction. The best way to satisfy the customer is to set expectations and then follow through with them or finish early.

- *Set realistic time frames.* People are basically optimistic creatures. Be careful that you do not become overzealous when committing to a time frame. Only bet on a sure thing. If you cannot guarantee a certain solution at a certain time, do not promise it. Make the customer aware of your intentions, but clarify the difference between promises and intentions. The customer can be an optimistic creature also. She will hear the earliest date you mention and assume the entire solution will be ready then.

- *Never offer an unrealistic solution.* If you are not sure that a particular solution is even technically or logistically possible, do not even mention it. Research it at a later time. If you determine that you can use that solution to save time, you can mention it then, or you can simply finish the project ahead of schedule.

- *Document your commitments.* Do not leave anything to memory; write down your commitments. An honest mistake on your part can often be perceived by the customer as deliberate misconduct. Good intentions aside, if you cannot remember a commitment, how can you honor it?

NOTE

Use the Scotty rule. Did you ever notice that the ship's engineer on the Starship Enterprise seemed to complete projects ahead of schedule in some of the most amazing situations? (Okay, so it was written into the script that way, right?) The point is this: The psychology of setting low expectations works. Set the customer expectations lower than you expect, and then when you finish ahead of schedule, the customer is even more satisfied. Don't be obvious though; you only get one take at real life, and there is no script.

Follow-Up

Aside from the obvious follow-ups of verifying the solution, follow-up communication is very important. In follow-up communication, the problem has been resolved and tensions have been relieved. At that point, the customer will be the most honest and forthcoming with you.

There may be a time when the customer will not be satisfied with your work, but giving him the chance to express that dissatisfaction directly to you eliminates his need to express it to other potential customers. In short, soliciting suggestions gives the customer a chance to review your performance and almost challenges his dissatisfaction. Many customers will not be able to express this dissatisfaction directly to you, face-to-face. Later, however, when they have the opportunity to complain to another potential customer, they will most likely refrain because they did not express their dissatisfaction directly to you when they had the chance.

Professional Conduct

Much of this was covered in the previous section on communication skills; however, there are a few points to make here.

- ◆ *Know your customer.* Look at it from a different perspective by viewing the situation from your manager's role. Your manager really doesn't care that Joe in Accounting can't access the network. What she cares about is that Joe cannot complete his work. Your job is to enable Joe to complete his work, and your immediate task may be to get Joe access to the network. Sometimes it helps to know a customer's background. Detailed records of past customer service calls can be very helpful. Have other technicians had trouble understanding or solving this customer's problems? Sometimes having background on a customer can prevent embarrassing mistakes. Even if you cannot enable Joe to access the network, at least try to work around this by thinking outside of the box. This will satisfy your apparent customer (Joe) and your real customer (your manager).

◆ *First impressions are priceless.* Dress appropriately. Nothing will improve your image so much as dressing one step above the accepted norms for your position. Greet the customer with a firm handshake and a sincere smile.

◆ *Attitude is everything.* When you're asked the question "How are you?", your answer should be "Great!" or some other positive affirmation—even if it's not true. This positive attitude is infectious and will brighten the mood in an otherwise tense situation.

◆ *Be prepared.* Professional conduct means planning ahead. Professional conduct should also incorporate a healthy sense of business ethics.

WHAT IS IMPORTANT TO KNOW

- Customer satisfaction is the best way to keep a customer loyal and gain others like him. It is harder to get a new customer than to maintain a current one.

- The two keys to customer satisfaction (outside of technical skills) are good communication and professional conduct.

- Customer satisfaction is not only about what you know, but how you impart that knowledge.

- Communication revolves around the customer. The five keys to good communication are listening, questioning, handling difficult situations, setting expectations, and follow-up/follow-through.

- Ask open-ended questions to elicit explanation. Use closed-ended questions to confirm acquired information.

- Handle difficult situations by not losing your own temper and by truly listening to the customer's complaint.

- Be honest. If you make a mistake, own up to it, correct it, and move on. Be thorough when investigating and do not jump to conclusions, but when it is time to make a decision, be decisive. Nothing ventured is nothing gained.

- Be prepared. Nothing imparts competency like being prepared for any given situation.

- Attitude is everything. What you believe is what you perceive. A healthy, positive attitude will rub off on the customer and brighten a bad situation.

Think of this as your personal study diary—your documentation of how you beat this exam.

The following section of Objective Review Notes is provided so you can personalize this book for maximum effect. This is your workbook, study sheet, notes section, whatever you want to call it. *You* will ultimately decide exactly what information you'll need, but there's no reason this information should be written down somewhere else. As the author has learned from his teaching experiences, there's absolutely no substitute for taking copious notes and using them *throughout* the study process.

This section lists all the A+ Core/Hardware Technology objectives. Each objective section falls under the main exam category, just as you'd expect to find it. It is strongly suggested that you review each objective and immediately make note of your knowledge level. Then flip to the Objective Review Notes section repeatedly and document your progress. Your ultimate goal should be to be able to review this section alone and know if you are ready for the exam.

OBJECTIVE REVIEW NOTES

Suggested use:

1. Read the objective. Refer to the part of the book where it's covered. Then ask yourself the following questions and act accordingly:

   - *Do you already know this material?* Then check "Got it" and make a note of the date.

   - *Do you need to brush up on this objective area?* Check "Review it" and make a note of the date. While you're at it, write down the page numbers you just looked at because you'll need to return to that section soon.

   - *Is this material something you're largely unfamiliar with?* Check the "Help!" box and write down the date. Now you can get to work.

2. You get the idea. Keep working through the material in this book and in the other study material you probably have. The better you understand the material, the quicker you can update and upgrade each objective notes section from "Help!" to "Review it" to "Got it."

3. Cross reference the materials you are using. Most people who take certification exams use more than one resource at a time. Write down the page numbers where this material is covered in other books you're using, which software program and file this material is covered on, which video tape (and counter number) it's on, or whatever you need that works for you.

Installation, Configuration, and Upgrading

► Objective: Identify basic terms, concepts, and functions of system modules, including how each module should work during normal operation.

☐ Got it
Date:_____

☐ Review it
Date:_____

☐ Help!
Date:_____

Notes:

_____
_____
_____
_____

Fast Track cross reference, see pages:

_____
_____

Other resources cross reference, see pages:

_____
_____
_____

► Objective: Identify basic procedures for adding and removing field replaceable modules.

☐ Got it
Date:_____

☐ Review it
Date:_____

☐ Help!
Date:_____

Notes:

_____
_____
_____
_____

Fast Track cross reference, see pages:

_____
_____

Other resources cross reference, see pages:

_____
_____
_____

OBJECTIVE REVIEW NOTES

►Objective: Identify available IRQs, DMAs, and I/O addresses and procedures for configuring them for device installation.

☐ Got it
Date:_____

☐ Review it
Date:_____

☐ Help!
Date:_____

Notes:

_____

_____

_____

_____

_____

Fast Track cross reference, see pages:

_____

_____

Other resources cross reference, see pages:

_____

_____

_____

_____

►Objective: Identify common peripheral ports, associated cabling, and their connectors.

☐ Got it
Date:_____

☐ Review it
Date:_____

☐ Help!
Date:_____

Notes:

_____

_____

_____

_____

_____

Fast Track cross reference, see pages:

_____

_____

Other resources cross reference, see pages:

_____

_____

_____

_____

OBJECTIVE REVIEW NOTES

► Objective: Identify proper procedures for installing and configuring IDE/EIDE devices.

☐ Got it   ☐ Review it   ☐ Help!
    Date: *Date:*   *Date:*

Notes:

_____
_____
_____
_____

Fast Track cross reference, see pages:

_____
_____

Other resources cross reference, see pages:

_____
_____
_____
_____

► Objective: Identify proper procedures for installing and configuring SCSI devices.

☐ Got it   ☐ Review it   ☐ Help!
    Date: *Date:*   *Date:*

Notes:

_____
_____
_____
_____
_____

Fast Track cross reference, see pages:

_____
_____

Other resources cross reference, see pages:

_____
_____
_____
_____

OBJECTIVE REVIEW NOTES

►Objective: Identify proper procedures for installing and configuring peripheral devices.

☐ **Got it** / ☐ **Review it** / ☐ **Help!**
    *Date:*_____ /   *Date:*_____ /   *Date:*_____

Notes:

_____
_____
_____
_____
_____

Fast Track cross reference, see pages:

_____
_____

Other resources cross reference, see pages:

_____
_____
_____
_____

►Objective: Identify concepts and procedures relating to BIOS.

☐ **Got it** / ☐ **Review it** / ☐ **Help!**
    *Date:*_____ /   *Date:*_____ /   *Date:*_____

Notes:

_____
_____
_____
_____
_____

Fast Track cross reference, see pages:

_____
_____

Other resources cross reference, see pages:

_____
_____
_____
_____

OBJECTIVE REVIEW NOTES

► Objective: Identify hardware methods of system optimization and
when to use them.

☐ Got it	☐ Review it	☐ Help!
*Date:*_____	*Date:*_____	*Date:*_____

Notes:

_____

_____

_____

_____

_____

_____

Fast Track cross reference, see pages:

_____

_____

Other resources cross reference, see pages:

_____

_____

_____

_____

OBJECTIVE REVIEW NOTES

Diagnosing and Troubleshooting

►Objective: Identify common symptoms and problems associated with each module and how to troubleshoot and isolate the problems.

☐ **Got it**　　☐ **Review it**　　☐ **Help!**
*Date:*_____　　*Date:*_____　　*Date:*_____

Notes:
_____
_____
_____

Fast Track cross reference, see pages:
_____

Other resources cross reference, see pages:
_____
_____

►Objective: Identify basic troubleshooting procedures and good practices for eliciting problem symptoms from customers.

♦ Use proper troubleshooting/isolation/problem determination procedures.

♦ Determine whether a problem is hardware- or software-related.

♦ Gather information from the user by using utilities and tools such as a multimeter.

♦ Evaluate the customer environment.

♦ Identify symptoms/error codes.

♦ Discover the situation in which the problem occurred.

☐ **Got it**　　☐ **Review it**　　☐ **Help!**
*Date:*_____　　*Date:*_____　　*Date:*_____

Notes:
_____
_____
_____

Fast Track cross reference, see pages:
_____

Other resources cross reference, see pages:
_____
_____

OBJECTIVE REVIEW NOTES

Safety and Preventive Maintenance

► Objective: Identify the purposes of various types of preventive maintenance products and procedures and when to use or perform them.

☐ Got it   ☐ Review it   ☐ Help!
Date:_____   Date:_____   Date:_____

Notes:

_____
_____
_____
_____
_____

Fast Track cross reference, see pages:

_____
_____

Other resources cross reference, see pages:

_____
_____
_____
_____

► Objective: Identify procedures and devices for protecting against environmental hazards.

☐ Got it   ☐ Review it   ☐ Help!
Date:_____   Date:_____   Date:_____

Notes:

_____
_____
_____
_____
_____

Fast Track cross reference, see pages:

_____
_____

Other resources cross reference, see pages:

_____
_____
_____
_____

OBJECTIVE REVIEW NOTES

►Objective: Identify the potential hazards and proper safety procedures relating to lasers and high-voltage equipment.

☐ Got it   ☐ Review it   ☐ Help!
*Date:*_____   *Date:*_____   *Date:*_____

Notes:
_____
_____
_____
_____
_____

Fast Track cross reference, see pages:
_____
_____

Other resources cross reference, see pages:
_____
_____
_____
_____

►Objective: Identify items that require special disposal procedures that comply with environmental guidelines.

☐ Got it   ☐ Review it   ☐ Help!
*Date:*_____   *Date:*_____   *Date:*_____

Notes:
_____
_____
_____
_____
_____

Fast Track cross reference, see pages:
_____
_____

Other resources cross reference, see pages:
_____
_____
_____
_____

OBJECTIVE REVIEW NOTES

► Objective: Identify ESD (Electrostatic Discharge) precautions and procedures, including the use of ESD protection devices.

☐ Got it	☐ Review it	☐ Help!
Date:___	Date:_____	Date:___

Notes:

_____
_____
_____
_____
_____
_____

Fast Track cross reference, see pages:

_____
_____

Other resources cross reference, see pages:

_____
_____
_____
_____

OBJECTIVE REVIEW NOTES

Motherboards/Processors/Memory

► Objective: Distinguish between the popular CPU chips in terms of their basic characteristics.

☐ Got it   ☐ Review it   ☐ Help!
   *Date:*____   *Date:*____   *Date:*____

Notes:
_____
_____
_____
_____
_____

Fast Track cross reference, see pages:
_____
_____

Other resources cross reference, see pages:
_____
_____
_____
_____

► Objective: Identify the categories of RAM (Random Access Memory) terminology, their locations, and physical characteristics.

☐ Got it   ☐ Review it   ☐ Help!
   *Date:*____   *Date:*____   *Date:*____

Notes:
_____
_____
_____
_____
_____

Fast Track cross reference, see pages:
_____
_____

Other resources cross reference, see pages:
_____
_____
_____
_____

OBJECTIVE REVIEW NOTES

► Objective: Identify the most popular types of motherboards, their components, and their architecture (for example, bus structures and power supplies).

☐ Got it
Date:_____

☐ Review it
Date:_____

☐ Help!
Date:_____

Notes:

_____
_____
_____
_____
_____

Fast Track cross reference, see pages:

_____
_____

Other resources cross reference, see pages:

_____
_____

► Objective: Identify the purpose of CMOS (Complementary Metal-Oxide Semiconductor), what it contains, and how to change its basic parameters.

☐ Got it
Date:_____

☐ Review it
Date:_____

☐ Help!
Date:_____

Notes:

_____
_____
_____
_____
_____

Fast Track cross reference, see pages:

_____
_____

Other resources cross reference, see pages:

_____
_____
_____

OBJECTIVE REVIEW NOTES

Printers

▶ Objective: Identify basic concepts, printer operations, and printer components.

☐ **Got it**   ☐ **Review it**   ☐ **Help!**
Date:_____   Date:_____   Date:_____

Notes:
_____
_____
_____
_____
_____

Fast Track cross reference, see pages:
_____
_____

Other resources cross reference, see pages:
_____
_____
_____
_____

▶ Objective: Identify care and service techniques and common problems associated with primary printer types.

☐ **Got it**   ☐ **Review it**   ☐ **Help!**
Date:_____   Date:_____   Date:_____

Notes:
_____
_____
_____
_____
_____

Fast Track cross reference, see pages:
_____
_____

Other resources cross reference, see pages:
_____
_____
_____
_____

OBJECTIVE REVIEW NOTES

► Objective: Identify the types of printer connections and configurations.

☐ Got it	☐ Review it	☐ Help!
Date:	*Date:*	*Date:*

Notes:

_____
_____
_____
_____
_____

Fast Track cross reference, see pages:

_____

Other resources cross reference, see pages:

_____
_____
_____
_____

OBJECTIVE REVIEW NOTES

Portable Computers

▶ Identify the unique components of portable systems and their unique problems. These basic components include

- ◆ Batteries
- ◆ LCD panels
- ◆ AC adapters
- ◆ Docking stations
- ◆ PC cards
- ◆ Pointing devices

☐ **Got it**
Date:_____

☐ **Review it**
Date:_____

☐ **Help!**
Date:_____

Notes:
_____
_____
_____
_____
_____
_____

Fast Track cross reference, see pages:
_____
_____

Other resources cross reference, see pages:
_____
_____
_____
_____

OBJECTIVE REVIEW NOTES

Basic Networking

▶ Objective: Identify basic networking concepts, including how a network works.

☐ Got it   ☐ Review it   ☐ Help!
   Date:_____   Date:_____   Date:_____

Notes:

_____

_____

_____

_____

_____

Fast Track cross reference, see pages:

_____

_____

Other resources cross reference, see pages:

_____

_____

_____

▶ Objective: Identify procedures for swapping and configuring network interface cards.

☐ Got it   ☐ Review it   ☐ Help!
   Date:_____   Date:_____   Date:_____

Notes:

_____

_____

_____

_____

_____

Fast Track cross reference, see pages:

_____

_____

Other resources cross reference, see pages:

_____

_____

_____

OBJECTIVE REVIEW NOTES

Objective: Identify the ramifications of repairs on the network.

☐ **Got it**　　　☐ **Review it**　　　☐ **Help!**
　 Date:＿＿＿　　 *Date:*＿＿＿＿　　 *Date:*＿＿＿

Notes:

＿＿＿＿＿＿＿＿＿＿＿＿＿＿＿＿＿＿＿＿＿＿＿＿＿＿
＿＿＿＿＿＿＿＿＿＿＿＿＿＿＿＿＿＿＿＿＿＿＿＿＿＿
＿＿＿＿＿＿＿＿＿＿＿＿＿＿＿＿＿＿＿＿＿＿＿＿＿＿
＿＿＿＿＿＿＿＿＿＿＿＿＿＿＿＿＿＿＿＿＿＿＿＿＿＿
＿＿＿＿＿＿＿＿＿＿＿＿＿＿＿＿＿＿＿＿＿＿＿＿＿＿

Fast Track cross reference, see pages:

＿＿＿＿＿＿＿＿＿＿＿＿＿＿＿＿＿＿＿＿＿＿＿＿＿＿
＿＿＿＿＿＿＿＿＿＿＿＿＿＿＿＿＿＿＿＿＿＿＿＿＿＿

Other resources cross reference, see pages:

＿＿＿＿＿＿＿＿＿＿＿＿＿＿＿＿＿＿＿＿＿＿＿＿＿＿
＿＿＿＿＿＿＿＿＿＿＿＿＿＿＿＿＿＿＿＿＿＿＿＿＿＿
＿＿＿＿＿＿＿＿＿＿＿＿＿＿＿＿＿＿＿＿＿＿＿＿＿＿
＿＿＿＿＿＿＿＿＿＿＿＿＿＿＿＿＿＿＿＿＿＿＿＿＿＿

OBJECTIVE REVIEW NOTES

Customer Satisfaction

► Objective: Differentiate effective from ineffective behaviors as they contribute to the maintenance or achievement of customer satisfaction.

- ◆ Communicating and listening (face-to-face or over the phone).

- ◆ Interpreting verbal and nonverbal cues.

- ◆ Responding appropriately to the customer's technical level.

- ◆ Establishing personal rapport with the customer.

- ◆ Displaying professional conduct; for example, punctuality, accountability.

- ◆ Helping and guiding a customer with problem descriptions.

- ◆ Responding to and closing a service call.

- ◆ Handling complaints and upset customers, conflict avoidance, and resolution.

- ◆ Showing empathy and flexibility.

- ◆ Sharing the customer's sense of urgency.

☐ Got it
  Date:_____

☐ Review it
  Date:_____

☐ Help!
  Date:_____

Notes:
_____
_____
_____
_____
_____

Fast Track cross reference, see pages:
_____
_____

Other resources cross reference, see pages:
_____
_____
_____
_____

OBJECTIVE REVIEW NOTES

II

INSIDE THE A+ CORE/ HARDWARE TECHNOLOGY EXAM

Part II of this book is designed to round out your exam preparation by providing you with the following chapters:

OBJECTIVES

This exam is divided into eight objective categories:

▶ **Installation, Configuration, and Upgrading**

▶ **Diagnosing and Troubleshooting**

▶ **Safety and Preventive Maintenance**

▶ **Motherboards/Processors/Memory**

▶ **Printers**

▶ **Portable Computers**

▶ **Basic Networking**

▶ **Customer Satisfaction**

CHAPTER 9

Fast Facts Review

WHAT TO STUDY

This chapter highlights the concepts needed for each section of the A+ Core/Hardware exam. Use it as a review on the day of the exam.

INSTALLATION, CONFIGURATION, AND UPGRADING

A system board contains a CPU, RAM, expansion bus, CMOS, ROM BIOS, clock, and keyboard controller, and may have additional interfaces built into it. Know where these components are located on the system board and be able to identify them by sight.

A CPU, or central processing unit, provides the brain functions for the entire computer.

The expansion bus is the physical wire that the data travels on.

The data bus is the specific route that the data takes to any given device.

The address bus is the logical "phone book" of device addresses on the expansion bus.

RAM is random access memory. This memory is used for the dynamic storage of information needed for processing by the CPU. RAM is erased every time the system is turned off.

ROM is read-only memory. This memory is used for the long term storage of programs and data as firmware on a chip. This information is "burned" into the chip and is retained even during a power failure.

The BIOS is the most basic input/output system. It runs the POST and interfaces with CMOS and the operating system.

A CRT uses electrons fired at a phosphor-coated screen to display a pixel. An LCD panel uses intersecting lines of current to activate the liquid crystals at that junction.

Modems convert digital signals into analog signals and transmit them over the phone lines. On the other end, a modem converts the analog signal back into a digital one for the computer to use.

Full duplex is simultaneous bidirectional communication. Half duplex is bidirectional communication while taking turns.

Floppy disk drives offer removable, rewritable, magnetic storage. Floppies come in both 5.25-inch and 3.5-inch sizes and in single, double, and quadruple densities. These variations provide a range of standardized capacities from 180KB to 2.88MB.

Hard disk drives offer non-removable, rewritable, magnetic storage. Hard disks come in many standard sizes, the most common of which are 5.25-inch, 3.5-inch, and 2.5-inch. Capacities range from 5MB to more than 18GB.

CD drives are removable, read-only (depending on the specific type), optical storage technology. CD capacities range from 600+MB for CD-ROM to over 4GB for DVD.

A tape drive is a removable, rewritable, streaming (linear access) magnetic storage device. Standards included are DAT, QIC, and DLT.

A hard disk contains several distinct parts. Tracks are concentric circles of data on a given surface. Sectors are the wedge shaped divisions of the disk. Heads are the read/write mechanisms for each surface. Cylinders are a vertical stack of tracks on a hard disk.

The IDE and SCSI standard interfaces differ greatly. SCSI supports seven devices with unique IDs and drive termination. IDE supports two drives set as master/slave pairs.

Drive subsystems are installed and configured in six stages:

- Adapter installation
- Drive termination and addressing
- Physical drive installation
- CMOS configuration
- Drive partitioning
- Drive formatting

Power supplies provide + and − 12 volts or + and − 5 volts, whereas ATX systems provide a 3.3 volt supply. They must be rated to handle the amount of power required by all devices it powers. This rating is expressed in watts.

Follow these guidelines for working with field replacement units:

- Run a complete backup of the system.
- Create a clean, organized, well-lit workspace with proper static electricity safeguards.
- Document *everything*.
- Exit all applications, and then shut down the system and all peripherals.
- Familiarize yourself with the case design and remove the case.
- Follow the equipment-specific FRU replacement steps necessary.

Tables 9.1 and 9.2 list the IRQ and DMA channel tables.

TABLE 9.1

IRQ SETTINGS

IRQ #	Used for	Additional Notes
0	System TIMER	
1	Keyboard	
2	Cascade from IRQ9	Use only when all other IRQs are full.
3	Even numbered COM ports	Balance serial devices evenly between even and odd COM ports.
4	Odd numbered COM ports	Balance serial devices evenly between even and odd COM ports.
5	LPT2	Usually available; often used for sound cards.
6	Floppy controller	
7	LPT1	
8	Real-time clock	
9	Redirected to IRQ2	Use only when all other IRQs are full. Often used for VGA, NIC.
10	Available	Commonly used for NIC.
11	Available	
12	Available	Often used for PS/2-style mouse.
13	Math coprocessor	
14	Hard disk controller	
15	Available	Additional hard disk controller.

TABLE 9.2

COMMON DMA CHANNEL USAGE

DMA Channel	Device	Additional Notes
0	Available	Often used for SCSI controllers.
1	Available	XT hard disk controllers use this setting; often used for sound cards.
2	Floppy disk controller	Floppy disk controller.
3	Available	Often used for NICs.

continues

TABLE 9.2 continued

4	Available	
5	Available	Often used for sound cards.
6	Available	
7	Available	Often used for sound cards.
8	Available	

Understand the advantages and disadvantages of manual configuration versus Plug and Play. Manual configuration can be cumbersome, but it is necessary to fall back on. Often the dynamic Plug and Play standard is not fully supported.

Parallel communication is data being transferred over more than one separate path but that's traveling to the same location. In PCs, there are eight parallel data paths in the parallel port standard; serial communication, on the other hand, transfers data sequentially over one wire.

DIAGNOSING AND TROUBLESHOOTING

There are three steps to eliminating a problem on a computer. These are to 1) quantify the problem by describing it, 2) isolate the problem by removing all other variables, and 3) resolve the repair or replacement.

Be able to classify problems into the categories mentioned above.

When all else fails, know who to ask.

There are three different types of errors: user errors, software errors, and hardware errors.

The Power-On-Self-Test begins when the computer is powered on and the CPU is reset to location F000h. Various hardware and controllers are checked by POST in the following order: CPU, DMA, IRQ, timer, expansion slots, I/O ports, video, RAM, keyboard, disk drives.

A single short beep during the boot process for your machine is completely normal and indicates that everything passed the POST examinations.

Know the various categories of error codes. Individual error codes are not heavily tested, so elimination of test answers by category usually works well (see Table 9.3).

TABLE 9.3

POST ERROR CODES

Error Code	Possible Error
1xx	System failure/system board error
102	ROM BIOS error
161, 162	CMOS/system options not set
163	Time/date not set
2xx	Memory failure
3xx	Keyboard failure
6xx	Floppy disk or controller failure
7xx	Math coprocessor failure
9xx	Primary parallel port
11xx	Primary serial port failure
17xx	Hard disk failure
1701	Drive not ready
73xx	Drive or controller failure

Disk optimization regroups scattered fragments of files on the drive into one contiguous location. This increases both performance and system stability.

Voltmeters are connected to the target circuit in parallel to the load you are testing. This is because all of the moving electrons have the same potential.

An ammeter is connected to the target circuit in series because all of the electrons must flow through this meter to measure the total current.

Voltage=Current × Amperes, or V=IR. Another mathematical expression is I=V/R or R=V/I.

SAFETY AND PREVENTIVE MAINTENANCE

Preventive maintenance is often overlooked because it is difficult to convince people to spend money on problems they haven't had yet. Nevertheless, it is extremely important.

Cleaning is the biggest part of preventive maintenance for many reasons. Heat dissipation is the primary cause of problems. Dirt and dust insulate devices, preventing them from dissipating all the heat they generate.

Household cleaners, lint-free cloths, and canisters of compressed air are often the best preventive maintenance tools.

Specialized cleaning kits for floppy drives are abrasive and can damage the read/write head over time. Only clean floppies when you are experiencing problems.

The eight environmental hazards to computer systems are heat, humidity (or lack thereof), water, inadequate power, magnetic fields, food and drink, smoke, and static.

Safety often is simply common sense (which isn't always common).

Don't wear jewelry, ties, watches, and so on when you're working on components. These can cause circuits to short out some components while you're trying to repair other components.

The following list outlines the proper steps for discharging a CRT:

- Obtain a high voltage probe rated at 40,000 volts or higher.

- Turn off the monitor and unplug it. Let it cool for a few minutes.

- Remove *all* jewelry, especially rings and watches.

- Remove the enclosure from the monitor.

- Attach the ground lead to a common electrical ground point.

- Slide the tip of the high voltage probe under the rubber "suction cup" on the top of the vacuum tube. You may hear a slight pop as the probe begins to discharge. The meter will gradually decrease to zero.

- Repeat these steps at least twice, at 5–10 minute intervals. Charges from the lesser capacitors in the monitor can be drawn into the tube, requiring that the tube be drained again.

ESD can damage circuits even if you cannot feel it. ESD can cause damage at 30–50 volts, even though the average person cannot feel a shock below 5,000 volts.

Clamping voltage is the voltage level that power must reach before a safety device is enabled. Clamping speed is the speed at which the device is enabled after the clamping voltage is met.

MOTHERBOARDS/PROCESSORS/MEMORY

The Intel CPU families vary in voltages, sizes, and special design features. Table 9.4 outlines the distinguishing characteristics of the CPU families.

TABLE 9.4

CPU COMPARISONS

Model	Speed	Clock Multiplier	Data Bus Width	Internal RAM Cache	Math Coprocessor
Intel 8086	4.77–7.16MHz	1x	16-bit	No	8087
Intel 8088	4.77–12MHz	1x	8-bit	No	8087
Intel 80286	6–25MHz	1x	16-bit	No	80287
Intel 80386SX	16–33MHz	1x	16-bit*	No	80387SX
Intel 80386SX	16–40MHz	1x	32-bit	No	80387DX
Intel 80487SX** 80486SX	25–33MHz	1x	32-bit	8KB	
Intel 80486DX	25–50MHz	1x	32-bit	8KB	Built-in
Intel 80486 DX2	50–66MHz	2x	32-bit	8KB	Built-in
Intel 80486 DX4	75–100MHz***	3x	32-bit	8KB	Built-in
Intel Pentium	60MHz–150MHz	Varies	64-bit	16KB	Built-in
Intel Pentium MMX	150–233MHz	Varies	64-bit	16KB	Built-in
Intel Pentium Pro****	150–200MHz	Varies	64-bit	256KB–512KB	Built-in
Intel Pentium II	233–450MHz and up	Varies	64-bit	512KB at half bus width	Built-in

* The 80386 has a 16-bit external data bus, but a 32-bit internal data bus. This allows the chip to be retrofitted to many 80286-style system boards.

** The 80486SX is really an 80486DX that failed the math coprocessor test. Due to a very high number of these failures, Intel decided to remarket the failed chips as a new model line, without the coprocessor. The 80487SX is simply a working 80486DX chip with a pin configuration that fits into the coprocessor slot.

*** The DX4 chip is truly only a 3x speed multiplier. The DX4-100MHz is really a 99MHz machine. In addition, much like the data bus issues with the 80386SX, the DX2 and DX4 chips need a properly optimized hardware setting to function properly. And even then, clock multiplied chips tend to work at only 80–90 percent of their rated speeds.

**** The Intel Pentium Pro is optimized for 32-bit operation systems and programming. Although 16-bit applications will run, they may suffer in performance.

CISC is the instruction set on the CPU. CISC can operate more complex functions, but they are significantly slower.

RISC is another CPU instruction set. RISC operates on fewer and smaller functions but processes them very quickly. Only applications written for the RISC instruction set can take advantage of this feature.

Megahertz is the number of cycles per second. There can be differences between the speeds internal and external to the CPU. Clock doubling or tripling technology speeds up the processor by increasing the clock speed internal to the chip.

DRAM is cheaper and more often used as base, or main, memory.

SRAM is static RAM and does not need to be refreshed almost continuously.

Tables 9.5 and 9.6 outline the basics of parity and binary mathematics.

TABLE 9.5

BOOLEAN AND'ING

0 AND 0 = 0	0 AND 1 = 1	1 AND 0 = 1	1 AND 1 = 0

TABLE 9.6

PARITY CALCULATION

If the parity scheme is...	*and the first eight bits are...*	*the parity bit should be:*
Even	Even	Even
Even	Odd	Odd
Odd	Even	Odd
Odd	Odd	Even

Bus structures are the heart of the data communication process. These structures include ISA, MCA, VESA Local Bus, EISA, PCI, and PCMCIA (or PC Card/CardBus). Table 9.7 lists the characteristics of each.

TABLE 9.7

EXPANSION BUS SPECIFICATIONS

Bus Type	*Bus Width*	*Bus Speed*	*Physical Characteristics*
PC-bus/ISA 8	8-bit	8MHz	Edge connector, about 3.5 inches long.
ISA bus	16-bit	8MHz	Edge connector, about 5.5 inches long. The remaining 16 bits are crammed into the additional 2 inches to maintain backward compatibility.
MCA	32-bit	10MHz	Edge connector, about 4 inches long. MCA boards are easily identified by the blue plastic release tabs on the cards.
EISA	32-bit	10MHz	Edge connector, about 5.5 inches long, but twice as tall. EISA maintains backward compatibility with ISA by allowing the card to be plugged into the top half of the slot. The additional lines are in the lower half of the connector.
VESA	32-bit	40MHz	Edge connector, about 9 inches long.
PCI	64-bit	CPU speed	Edge connector, about 3.5 inches long. Card faces opposite of all other expansion cards.
PCMCIA	16-bit	33MHz	Pin connector, about 2 inches wide.
CardBus	32-bit	33MHz	Pin connector, about 2 inches wide. CardBus cards are not backward compatible and can use only CardBus slots. This is why CardBus cards have a series of small bumps on the top of the pin connector.

AT-class system board designs are more common.

ATX computer system boards have an updated design and require an additional 3.3v line on the power supply. In addition, the case must allow for the redesigned peripheral port connections.

All 8-bit PC Bus cards will function in any ISA slot. All ISA adapters will function in a VESA slot. Also, all ISA adapters will function in an EISA computer. PCI and MCA are completely not compatible with any other standard in place now.

A local bus provides a direct, exclusive expansion bus for cards that are local bus compatible. Local bus standards include VESA Local Bus and PCI buses.

PRINTERS

Bit-image printers form the characters using a series of dots. Fully formed character printers strike the page once for each letter, creating one whole character at a time.

Line printers are generally limited to dot-matrix and daisywheel printers. A page printer must print an entire page and eject it from the printer before you can read the text.

Impact printers do exactly that. They impact the page when creating a character. Non-impact, inkjets, and lasers never actually touch the page.

Popular feed mechanisms include tractor feed, automatic sheet feed, and single-sheet feed.

Table 9.8 lists the types of consumables associated with each type of printer. Remember what printers relate to which consumable.

TABLE 9.8

PRINTER COMPARISONS

Printer Type	Character Type	Line versus Page	Feeder Type	Consumables
Daisywheel	Fully formed	Line	Friction or tractor	Print wheel, print head, ribbon, paper
Dot-matrix	Bit image	Line	Friction or tractor	Print head, ribbon, paper
Inkjet	Bit image	Line/page	ASF	Ink cartridge, paper
Laser	Bit image formation, fully formed transfer	Page	ASF	EP cartridge, paper
Thermal	Bit image	Line	ASF or friction	Print head, paper
Hot wax	Bit image, fully formed transfer	Page	ASF	Wax, paper

The six stages of the EP process and their functions are cleaning, conditioning, writing, developing, transferring, fusing.

The three user-based printer self tests are the engine test, self-test, and half-self-test.

PORTABLE COMPUTERS

Laptop computers have advanced to the level that they can replace desktop computers in many situations. These portable computers can approach a similar level of expandability using both external ports and additional docking station features.

Batteries are the blessing and the bane of many laptop computers. Batteries come in three different "flavors": NiCD, NiMH, and Li-Ion. NiCD batteries are the most prevalent because of their relatively low cost. NiCD batteries have a memory effect that affects charging to full capacity over time.

LCD panels on laptop computers come as either passive or active. Active displays utilize TFT-based display technologies and are the brighter and more robust of the two displays. The trade-off is in the power consumption.

PC cards are a mainstay of laptop peripherals. The PCMCIA card has enabled the previously proprietary laptop industry to standardize. These standards are based on PCMCIA type I, II, and III cards.

Pointing devices for laptops are somewhat different than their desktop counterparts. The miniature trackball, touchpad, and button mouse are three of the most popular designs.

Basic Networking

A transmission medium is a physical pathway that connects systems.

Protocols are rules for network communication.

Table 9.9 lists the seven layers of the OSI model. The following mnemonic device should help you remember the layers in the proper order, from top to bottom: All People Seem To Need Data Processing.

TABLE 9.9

OSI Model

OSI Layer	Description
Application	Provides the interface between the user application and the network APIs. The network redirector exists here and intercepts application calls to the local machine for network resources and passes them to the network for access to the proper location.

continues

TABLE 9.9 continued

OSI Layer	Description
Presentation	This provides a translator for dissimilar character generation codes. For example, this layer will translate EBCDIC into ASCII for proper communication.
Session	This layer is responsible for initiating, maintaining, and completing the communication session between computers. The network client exists here to provide a common communication to compatible networks.
Transport	This layer is responsible for ensuring that the data packets arrive intact at the end of the route. It contains error correction, flow control, and fragmentation/reassembly rules.
Network	This layer is responsible for plotting the route for packets to take to other subnetworks and networks. To provide for this routability, the Network layer is also responsible for providing a common method of addressing other network nodes, for example, IP addresses.
Data Link	This layer defines how the computer formats the data into packets and accesses the network cabling to transmit data. It is responsible for providing error-free data to the layers above it. Every NIC contains a unique MAC address that works with this level.
Physical	These define the specific pin positions, shielding, and maximum transmission lengths for physical cabling. The NIC also partially resides here.

Centralized computing gathers all network security into one location. Additionally, processing and storage can be centralized to varying degrees.

In decentralized computing, the security, processing, or data storage (or some combination of all three) resides away from the central server location.

The four basic networking topologies are bus, ring, star, and mesh.

Logical and a physical topologies differ in many ways. The physical topology is a description of what you can see; the logical topology is a description of how it actually works.

LANs and CANs are smaller area networks in which the cable is owned by the company using the network.

MANs and WANs are wider area networks in which the cable is owned by the connection provider.

Ethernet is a logical bus topology that's often implemented in a physical star configuration on a CSMA/CD network.

Token-ring is a ring topology that's often implemented in a physical star configuration on a collision avoidance network.

Table 9.10 outlines the differences between the five media types (thinnet, thicknet, STP, UTP, and fiber).

TABLE 9.10

MEDIA COMPARISONS

Cable	Cost	Installation	Capacity	Range	EMI	Connectors
Thinnet/ 10BASE-2	Less than STP but more than UTP	Not as easy as STP	10Mbps	185 meters	Less susceptible than UTP	Bayonet nut Connectors (BNC)
Thicknet/ 10BASE-5	More than STP and less than fiber	Not as easy as thinnet	10Mbps	500 meters	Less susceptible than UTP	AUI
Shielded twisted pair (STP)	More than UTP and less than thicknet	Easy	16Mbps to 500Mbps	100 meters	Less susceptible than UTP	RJ-45
Unshielded twisted pair (UTP) /10BASE-T	Cheapest	Easiest	10Mbps to 100Mbps	100 meters	Most susceptible of all	RJ-45
Fiber optic	Most expensive	Hard	100Mbps	Kilometers	Not susceptible to EMI	Similar to BNC

Repeaters repeat the signal being transmitted on the wire in cases of signal attenuation.

Hubs and MAUs provide a central location to connect logical bus and ring topologies (respectively) into physical star topologies.

Bridges connect to dissimilar networking protocols at OSI layer 2 to transmit traffic.

Routers connect similar subnetworks, functioning as traffic cops that can limit excessive traffic. These operate at layer 3.

Gateways connect dissimilar networks as translators.

To configure a NIC, the cabling protocol and network protocol must match those of the network it will join.

A network is a synergetic entity. If network repairs interfere with its operation, you are affecting many more users than if you were repairing only a single computer.

CUSTOMER SATISFACTION

Customer satisfaction is the best way to keep a customer loyal and gain others like him. It is harder to get a new customer than to maintain a current one.

The two keys to customer satisfaction (outside of technical skills) are good communication and professional conduct.

Customer satisfaction is not necessarily only about what you know, but how you impart that knowledge.

Communication revolves around the customer. The five keys to good communication are listening, questioning, handling difficult situations, setting expectations, and follow-up/follow-through.

Ask open-ended questions to elicit explanation. Use closed-ended questions to confirm acquired information.

Handling difficult situations is attained by not losing your own temper and by truly listening to the customer's complaint.

Be honest. If you make a mistake, own up to it, correct it, and move on. Be thorough when investigating and do not jump to conclusions, but when it is time to make a decision, be decisive. Nothing ventured is nothing gained.

Be prepared. Nothing imparts competency like being prepared for any given situation.

Attitude is everything. What you believe is what you perceive. A healthy, positive attitude will rub off on the customer and brighten a bad situation.

CHAPTER **10**

Insider's Spin on the Core/Hardware Exam

At A Glance: Exam Information

Exam number	220-101
Minutes to complete	60
Questions	69
Passing score	65
Single-answer questions	No
Multiple-answer with correct number given	Yes
Multiple-answer without correct number given	No
Ranking order	No
Choices of A–D	Yes
Choices of A–E	No
Objective categories	8 (7 tested and 1 on customer service)

The A+ Core/Hardware Exam consists of 69 multiple-choice questions aimed at determining the test takers' skill level with microcomputer hardware. CompTIA states that this exam is designed so that a technician with six-months experience with these products should be able to pass the exam. The exam must be completed in one hour. The multiple-choice questions are not misleading and mostly ask for specifics that require little thought for the experienced candidate. Experience with all seven testing categories prior to taking this exam greatly increases your odds of passing. You could be given one of several possible exams. When this exam was in its beta cycle, there were literally a couple hundred questions in the exam pool.

Once CompTIA decided which questions were valid, a few versions of the exam were created. Although there are different versions, all the major categories are tested in each version.

GET INTO THE COMPTIA MINDFRAME

Unlike many vendor-specific exams, the A+ Core/Hardware Exam is as vendor-nonspecific as it can be. One example would be the following: In questions about processor architecture in the motherboards/processors/memory section of the exam, the questions maintain a vague nature.

Intel, AMD, and Cyrix manufacture the majority of PC microprocessors, but all adhere to common architecture standards. The questions already assume you are talking about these standards, so a typical question would read similar to the following:

1. Which of the following is not a valid processor slot architecture?

    A. System 7

    B. Socket 7

    C. Slot 1

    D. Socket 6

Answer: A. System 7 is not a processor slot architecture.

As this example shows, the exam focuses more on concepts than on vendor specifics.

UNDERSTAND THE TIMEFRAME OF THE EXAM

This exam has been live since July, 1998, and replaced the previous A+ Exam, which focused primarily on 80386 hardware standards. The new exam is based on hardware technology that includes current standards, such as Universal Serial Bus. Obviously, any components or standards that have been introduced since July, 1998 (such as Riva TNT-based AGP video cards and 128-bit PCI sound cards) are not likely to be tested.

All previous hardware technologies are still tested, but the majority of the test is geared toward more modern hardware and general concepts. The more you know about the exam, the better. Knowing what you will face is one of the most important factors in exam preparation. Many candidates fail exams because they are caught off-guard by the concepts on which they're being tested. This exam is only the second version of the A+ Core test, and because it is very new, it will probably not be replaced soon.

GET USED TO ANSWERING QUESTIONS QUICKLY

The exam is one hour long, which gives you less than one minute per question. This is no cause for concern; the nature of this exam is very short, multiple-choice questions. Knowing the concepts being tested and reading the questions carefully usually helps you identify the correct answer quickly. Do not be rushed; one hour is plenty of time for this test. However, if you are running out of time, note that all unanswered questions are automatically counted wrong. At least attempt to answer all the questions before time runs out.

BECOME ACQUAINTED WITH ALL AVAILABLE SERVICES

Begin by registering for the A+ Certification exam by calling 1-800-77-MICRO (1-800-776-4276). Tests are given at Sylvan Prometric™ Authorized Test Centers. The A+ test is given throughout the world in English.

When you call, please have the following information available:

- ◆ Social Security number or Sylvan Prometric™ ID number (provided by Sylvan Prometric™)

- ◆ Mailing address and telephone number

- ◆ Employer or organization

- ◆ Date you wish to take the test

- ◆ Method of payment (credit card, check, or purchase order; call CompTIA Certification Department at 630-268-1818, extension 305 or 359, for further clarification)

The test is available to anyone who wants to take it. There are no prerequisites. Candidates may retake the test as often as they like, but the Core/Hardware and the DOS/Windows exams must be passed within 90 calendar days of one another in order for the user to become certified.

Visit the CompTIA Web site at www.CompTIA.org and familiarize yourself with the exam process and the objectives. Read the objectives and try to identify any areas in which you may be weak. Once you have made yourself familiar with all aspects of the exam, you may opt to try a practice exam. Practice exams are available from a number of third-party software developers.

WHERE THE QUESTIONS COME FROM

As stated before, the more you know about the testing process, the better your odds of passing are. Try to understand what types of questions you will be presented with and understand how they are created.

When this exam went through its beta phase, hundreds of questions were submitted by the exam writers. Up to the release of the beta exam, these writers reviewed the questions and removed the ones that were deemed too vague, too specific, too leading, and so forth. Once the beta pool was decided upon, it was released to the public. Hundreds of beta test takers challenged the exam. The beta results were reviewed, and again, the questions that were determined to be bad were removed from the pool. From this point, the final exams were compiled into the various A+ Core exams that you will encounter at testing time.

DIFFERENT FLAVORS OF QUESTIONS

Unlike many vendor-specific certification exams, there are currently no variations of CompTIA A+ exam questions. Multiple-choice with answers from A–D are all that you will see. In addition, you will see mainboard diagrams and be asked to identify various components.

IN THE FUTURE

In the future, you may see more exam questions geared toward new hardware technology such as the Accelerated Graphics Ports (AGP) and 3D video technology. Windows NT Workstation and Windows 98 will certainly make their way into the DOS/Windows exam pool in addition to the existing Windows 95 questions. Obviously, as the industry evolves, the A+ exams must follow suit.

Another popular testing innovation in use by other vendors is that of the adaptive exam. The adaptive exam asks weighted questions. A question is asked that is considered to be of medium difficulty. If the candidate answers correctly, a more-difficult question is asked. If the candidate answers incorrectly, a less-difficult question is asked. This type of test asks fewer questions and takes the difficulty level of each question into account when calculating the final score.

Exam writers see the adaptive exam as a better testing tool because performance-based questions actually ask the test taker to demonstrate a skill. In addition, because the exams are shorter in length, they give the exam taker a smaller sample of the questions at random from the question pool, making it more difficult for the candidate to get by on strict memorization. Less memorization equates to a more valid test because the candidate will not have had his peers tell him all the answers prior to the test.

CONCEPTS YOU MUST KNOW

This section outlines the concepts you must know for the various objective categories covered on the exam.

Installation, Configuration, and Upgrading

Absolute must-have concepts for this section:

1. Know the terminology of microcomputers. The PC world is full of TLAs (three-letter acronyms). Not understanding these abbreviations leaves you at a grave disadvantage.

2. Know how each component works and its dependencies on system resources.

3. Know the steps to take when replacing hardware.

4. Know how to tell when hardware is not functioning correctly.

5. Understand system resources including IRQs and their corresponding devices.

6. Know major modem AT commands.

7. Know what cables attach to what ports.

8. Know what different cable types are used for.

9. Understand how to configure IDE/EIDE devices.

10. Know the appropriate ways to configure SCSI devices.

11. Know the proper procedures for adding and removing expansion cards.

12. Know the procedures for upgrading system BIOS.

13. Know which topics system component to optimize for a given situation.

Diagnosing and Troubleshooting

Absolute must-have concepts for this section:

1. Beyond the shadow of a doubt, be able to differentiate between a hardware and a software problem.

2. Know different troubleshooting procedures.

3. Interpret diagnostic equipment measurements (such as a multimeter's output.)

4. Know common system error codes and be able to interpret them.

Safety and Preventive Maintenance

Absolute must-have concepts for this section:

1. Know the hazards of ESD and how to avoid them.

2. Know common PC cleaning products and what devices to use them on.

3. Know what devices prevent system disasters caused by power surges and power spikes.

4. Know what devices are potential shock hazards.

5. Know the dangers associated with laser devices (CD-ROMs, DVDs, and laser printers).

6. Know which devices require special disposal (batteries, toner, and so on).

Motherboards/Processors/Memory

Absolute must-have concepts for this section:

1. Know the difference between various CPU chips in terms of speed, voltage, number of pins, and so on.

2. Know the different memory architectures (such as SIMMs and DIMMs).

3. Know RAM types (EDO, SDRAM, and so on).

4. Understand the difference between AT and ATX motherboards and the components of each.

5. Understand different bus architectures and be able to visually identify them.

6. Know the appropriate CMOS settings for any given situation.

Printers

Absolute must-have concepts for this section:

1. Understand the difference between dot-matrix, laser, and inkjet printers.

2. Recognize common printing problems.

3. Know how to set up and connect printers to a PC or network.

4. Know major printer components.

Portable Computers

Absolute must-have concepts for this section:

1. Know your PCMCIA slots and sizes.

2. Recognize problems specific to laptops.

Basic Networking

Absolute must-have concepts for this section:

1. Understand what a network is and its benefits.

2. Understand what protocols do.

3. Know different network cabling types.

Customer Satisfaction

First and foremost, note that this section does not impact your score. However, without proper customer service skills, your success in this highly customer service–based industry may not be smooth. CompTIA wants to ensure that A+-certified people are courteous.

Use common sense and select answers based on how you would want to be treated.

Finally...

All in all, this is not a difficult test for those candidates who have a few months' experience and know the objectives. The concepts are the testable portion of what you have studied. You do not have to have worked with every type of hardware available, but you must know what most types do, their basic designs, and common configuration problems.

CompTIA Web Site Frequently Asked Questions

The CompTIA Web site is located at www.CompTIA.org and has a great wealth of information. The following list of frequently asked questions can be obtained from the Web site. (I added them to this section to save you valuable preparation time.)

Retaking the Test

I took the old version of the A+ test, and my score report says I have 90 days to retake the test. Didn't the old test close on July 30, 1998?

On any score report dated on or before July 30, the 90-day stipulation is incorrect. You were right that you had to pass both tests by close of business day July 30. This message was given out when you called Sylvan Prometric to register as part of the forced message. Furthermore, this has been posted on our Web site. The old test was no longer available after close of day on July 30, 1998.

Who Can Take the Test

What qualifications are needed to take the exams?

A+ Certification is open to anyone who wants to take the tests. The A+ exam is targeted for entry-level computer service technicians with at least six months on-the-job experience. No specific requirements are necessary, except payment of the fee.

How Many Questions

How many questions are on the new A+ tests?

There are 69 questions on the Core/Hardware portion. There are 70 questions on the DOS/Windows portion.

Percentage Needed to Pass

What do I need to score to pass the A+ exams?

To pass the Core/Hardware exam, a score of at least 65 percent is required. To pass the DOS/Windows exam, a score of at least 66 percent is required. Candidates are given one hour to complete the

Core/Hardware portion, and candidates are given 1 hour and 15 minutes to complete the DOS/Windows portion.

90 Calendar Days

What is the 90-calendar-days rule?

The 90-calendar-days rule states that a candidate must take the Core/Hardware and DOS/Windows portions within 90 calendar days of one another. If the two parts are taken outside of the 90 calendar day window, the candidate must re-take both sections in order to receive the A+ designation. It is the responsibility of the candidate to count the days and to take the portion of the exam that is needed by the 90th calendar day. It is for this reason that we strongly encourage candidates to take the Core/Hardware and DOS/Windows portions at the same time.

> **NOTE**
>
> If you took the Core/Hardware or DOS/Windows module prior to July 31, 1998, and did not earn your A+ Certification, you will need to re-take both portions to become A+ certified. This is required because the new exam does not reflect any of the materials covered on the previous version.

Mixing and Matching Tests

Can I take part of the earlier version of the A+ exam and part of the exam released on July 31, 1998, to earn my certification?

The earlier version of the A+ exam is no longer available. If a candidate did not receive the A+ designation prior to July 31, 1998, both the Core/Hardwate and DOS/Windows portions of the revised exam must be taken, regardless if one part of the A+ was previously passed.

Macintosh Questions

Are there going to be Macintosh questions on the Core/Hardware exam?

Due to the discontinuation of the Macintosh OS module, there will be no Macintosh questions on the A+ Certification exam.

Customer Service Questions

Are customer service questions included?

There are customer service questions on the Core/Hardware exam. Your answers to these questions are not counted toward the final score. The score from this section is reported at the bottom of the score report so that employers and clients know how the candidate performed on this section.

Seeing the Answers

If I failed, can I see my answers?

As an internationally recognized entry-level professional certification for service technicians, the test must remain secure at all times. Thus, no test questions or answers are ever released. In order to maintain the high quality of the exam, no exceptions are made.

Failing Part of the Test

If I failed a portion of the test, will I have to pay to retake that portion?

Yes, each time you take the test, you must pay a fee. Call Sylvan Prometric at 1-800-776-4276 to re-register.

Unhappy with a Test Question

What if I am unhappy with a test question?

If you are unhappy with the wording of a test question, you may comment on these issues at the time you take the exam. Furthermore, we invite your comments in writing. Please fax them to 630-268-1384 to the attention of the Certifications Department.

Test Vouchers

How long is my test voucher good for?

The vouchers are valid for one calendar year and expire after that period.

Taking the Modules Separately

Can I take the Core/Hardware and the DOS/Windows modules at different times?

Although it is possible to take them separately, we strongly recommend that you take both parts of the exam at the same time.

Lost Certificate or ID

What do I do if I lose my A+ Certificate or ID card?

Please call Sylvan Prometric at 1-800-776-4276 and request a replacement.

How Long Is Certification Good For

How long is the A+ Certification good for?

Once you are A+ certified, you are certified for life.

New Exam Codes

What are the new exam codes for the new A+ tests?

The new exam code for the Core/Hardware test is 220-101. The new exam code for the DOS/Windows test is 220-102.

Getting a Reprint of Certificate

If you need a new certificate within three months of the original printing, the first copy is free. Each subsequent printing carries a $15 charge. This charge is also instituted for any reprint requested six months after certification.

I took the Macintosh OS module to earn my A+ Certification, and I know that you are no longer offering this module. However, I lost my certificate. Can I get a reprint?

Yes, A+ certificates with the Macintosh OS Specialty will continue to be printed indefinitely. However, you will receive a certificate and logo sheet (with the new A+ logo) only. Pins and ID cards will not be provided. Please call Sylvan Prometric at 1-800-776-4276 to request a reprint.

I earned my certification under the previous version of the exam. All the other techs have certified under the test version used as of July 31, and our certificates do not look the same. Can I get my certificate reprinted on the new certificate paper?

Yes, this option is available to you. There will be a $15 charge for this printing because this is considered a request for a duplicate. Please call Sylvan Prometric at 1-800-776-4276 to request a copy.

CHAPTER 11

Sample Test Questions

QUESTIONS

1. **What is the first thing you should do before removing an expansion card from a computer?**

   A. Unplug the computer.
   B. Unscrew the card anchor screw.
   C. Unplug the monitor.
   D. Plug in the computer.

2. **A PS2 mouse uses which IRQ?**

   A. 11
   B. 13
   C. 7
   D. 12

3. **You installed a second hard drive, and now the system will not boot. What is the most likely problem?**

   A. The floppy cable is installed backwards.
   B. The original IDE drive is not jumpered to be a master drive with a slave present.
   C. The drive is too large for the PC to recognize.
   D. The floppy drive is jumpered incorrectly.

4. **Which of the following is not a valid SCSI ID for a single-channel controller?**

   A. 2
   B. 3
   C. 4
   D. 9

5. **Your monitor is flickering. Which of the following could be the cause?**

   A. A weak video card signal
   B. A strong video card signal
   C. A wrong refresh rate
   D. A bad monitor

6. **The BIOS on a 386SX 20MHz PC does not detect your new 18GB hard drive. What is the problem?**

   A. Operator error.
   B. The PC BIOS is too old to recognize drives larger than 540MB.
   C. The drive is not formatted.
   D. The drive does not have defined partitions.

7. *You just replaced an old dot-matrix printer with a new HP inkjet printer, and the PC is having trouble communicating with the printer. What is the most likely problem?*
   A. The driver is not compatible with the computer.
   B. The printer cable does not support bidirectional communication.
   C. The software is installed incorrectly.
   D. The printer is broken.

8. *Your modem has no dial tone. Which of the following is* **not** *the problem?*
   A. Your modem has an IRQ conflict.
   B. The modem is not plugged into the phone line.
   C. The modem is installed improperly.
   D. The computer has only one expansion slot available.

9. *You have a computer that is connected to a UPS. After a thunderstorm, the PC stops working. What could be the problem?*
   A. The modem was not plugged into a surge suppressor.
   B. The UPS failed.
   C. Coincidental massive system failure.
   D. User error.

10. *A user complains of distortion on her monitor. Which of the following could be the problem?*
    A. The monitor is sitting too close to an oscillating fan.
    B. The monitor display is configured for a very high resolution.
    C. The OS has the wrong monitor type selected in Display Properties.
    D. The video card is damaged.

11. *When booting your system, you notice that your SCSI controller displays the message* `BIOS not installed`. *What is the problem?*
    A. The SCSI controller has lost its CMOS settings.
    B. The system has lost its CMOS settings.
    C. There is nothing wrong; this is normal for a SCSI controller that is not using SCSI BIOS.
    D. The SCSI device ID is incorrect.

12. *Your PC monitor is black upon startup. What should you check?*
    A. Brightness and contrast knobs on the monitor
    B. Printer cable
    C. Keyboard
    D. CMOS settings

13. *What should you be aware of when servicing PCs in a carpeted environment?*
    A. Lighting
    B. Lightning
    C. Carpet fuzz getting stuck in the PC intake vents
    D. Static electricity

14. *What does a UPS do?*
    A. Protects the PC from static electricity.
    B. Allows enough time to power down your PC in the event of a power failure.
    C. Allows your PC to operate without being plugged in.
    D. Protects your modem from lightning.

15. *Which of the following devices can cause serious eye injury?*
    A. The laser from your CD-ROM
    B. The mouse
    C. Your computer RAM chips
    D. The keyboard connector

16. *Which of the following does not have to be disposed of in accordance with EPA regulations?*
    A. Monitor CRT
    B. Toner cartridge
    C. CMOS battery
    D. Packing material

17. *On what device should you use a head cleaner to maintain optimal performance?*
    A. Hard disk drive
    B. Headphones
    C. Microphone
    D. Tape backup drive

18. *What does the notched corner of a socket 7 CPU indicate?*

    A. PIN #1
    B. Faulty manufacturing
    C. Manufacturer's trademark
    D. PIN #128

19. *SLOT 1 is used for which processor?*

    A. 8088
    B. NextGen
    C. Pentium Pro
    D. Pentium II

20. *Which RAM modules are faster?*

    A. EDO
    B. Interleaved banks
    C. Synch DRAM
    D. Norwegian

21. *What key sequence will* **not** *access CMOS setup on any system?*

    A. Ctrl+Alt+S
    B. Ctrl+Alt+Esc
    C. Ctrl+Alt+Del
    D. F1

22. *What type of slot is* **not** *used for expansion cards?*

    A. MCA
    B. PCI
    C. EISA
    D. Socket 6

23. *What function does the pickup roller serve?*

    A. Picks up toner from the toner cartridge
    B. Picks up paper from the paper tray
    C. Picks up dust left over from the burn process
    D. Picks up the corona wire, allowing the fuser to operate

24. *What printer mechanism presents a burn hazard?*

    A. Hot ink from an inkjet printer
    B. The power supply of a LaserJet printer
    C. The pins from a plotter
    D. The print head on a dot-matrix printer

25. **What is the effect of using paper that is too thin in an inkjet printer?**
    A. The printer will feed too many sheets at once.
    B. Nothing; the printer will operate normally.
    C. The print will not be sharp.
    D. The printer will overheat.

26. **Which of the following is not a valid printer interface?**
    A. Parallel
    B. Serial
    C. Network
    D. ISA

27. **A laptop computer with a PCMCIA network card cannot connect to the network from a DOS boot disk even though the boot disk has the appropriate network card drivers. What is the probable cause?**
    A. The boot disk is missing drivers for the PCMCIA card sockets.
    B. The network card is bad.
    C. The network is down.
    D. PCMCIA network cards do not work in DOS.

28. **Over time, a customer discovers that his laptop's nickel cadmium battery does not last as long between charges as it did when it was new. What is the most likely cause?**
    A. The laptop uses more power than it used to.
    B. The battery was not completely drained between charges, causing the battery to have a "memory" of how long to charge.
    C. The battery was overcharged and damaged.
    D. The leads in the laptop case are dirty.

29. **You plug a PC into the network and notice that the link light on the NIC is not on. Which of the following is not a possible cause?**
    A. Bad network cable.
    B. The network is down.
    C. The computer is off.
    D. The monitor is off.

30. **You recently replaced a PCI NIC with an ISA NIC, and now the user complains of slower performance. What is the cause?**

A. The LAN is just experiencing increased traffic; the NIC is not the problem.

B. The NIC is not plugged into the LAN.

C. PCI NICs are slower than ISA NICs.

D. ISA NICs are slower than PCI NICs.

31. **A user moved a PC from one segment to another segment on the network and is complaining that he cannot log on. What is the likely cause?**

A. The PC is configured for another LAN segment.

B. The user is not logging in correctly.

C. The PC has a bad network software installation.

D. There is a LAN hardware failure.

32. **A customer calls and complains that every time he is put on hold, he gets cut off before talking to a technician. What should you do for this customer to keep him calm and confident?**

A. Put him on hold.

B. Keep him on the line and take notes about his problem. Then hang up.

C. Keep him on the line and help resolve the problem.

D. Transfer the call to someone else.

33. **A user calls you with a problem that you have repeatedly fixed and shown the user how to avoid. What should you do this time?**

A. Tell the customer off.

B. Take care of the problem again and patiently show the user how to avoid it again.

C. Take care of the problem and be mean to the customer.

D. Hang up.

Answers and Explanations

1. **A**   Never touch the inside of a computer that is still plugged in.

2. **D**   IRQ 12 is reserved for the PS2 mouse.

3. **B**   The most common cause of trouble when adding a second hard drive is that it is jumpered incorrectly.

4. **D**   Valid SCSI IDs for a single-channel controller are 0–7, where 7 is usually the controller.

5. **C**   An incorrect refresh rate causes flickering.

6. **B**   Older BIOS did not recognize drives greater that 540MB.

7. **B**   Many HP inkjet printers require a bidirectional printer cable to communicate with the PC. Older printer cables were unidirectional.

8. **D**   Having an expansion slot available does *not* cause modem trouble.

9. **A**   Many UPS systems do not have a plug for your modem. If the phone line is directly connected to the PC, a surge can enter your system through the phone line.

10. **A**   An oscillating fan creates a magnetic field that will distort video display.

11. **C**   This message is normal for a SCSI controller that is not using its onboard BIOS to manage its devices.

12. **A**   Brightness and contrast settings are easily changed by accident. Check this before trying more elaborate troubleshooting.

13. **D**   Static electricity can cause damage to sensitive electronic equipment like computer components. Wear a static discharge wrist band or shoe strip when working in a carpeted environment.

14. **B**   A UPS allows enough time for a computer to shut down successfully in the event of a power failure.

15. **A**   All of these devices *could* cause a serious eye injury, but the one to be aware of is the laser from your CD-ROM. Lasers cannot be seen and can damage the eye quickly.

16. **D**   Packing materials are not an environmental hazard. All other answers are subject to disposal regulations by the EPA.

17. **D**   Like a VCR, a tape drive has heads that need to be cleaned.

18. **A**   The notch designates PIN #1 on a socket 7 processor.

19. **D**   Intel's Pentium II processor uses the SLOT 1 connection on P II motherboards.

20. **C**   SDRAM is the fastest RAM available, operating at only 10 nanoseconds.

21. **C**   The Ctrl+Alt+Del key sequence is reserved by software manufacturers as an action key sequence. In Windows 3.x, it can reboot the computer system. In Windows 95, it activates the Task Manager.

22. **D**   Socket 6 is not an expansion slot.

23. **B**   The pickup roller picks up paper from the paper tray.

24. **D**   The print head on a dot-matrix printer gets extremely hot.

25. **A**   Using paper that is too thin for an inkjet printer will cause multiple sheets to feed at once.

26. **D**   ISA is an expansion slot, not a printer interface.

27. **A**   Laptop computers using PC card modems have Card and Socket Services drivers that enable the OS to recognize the PC cards. If a boot disk is missing the Card and Socket Services drivers, it will not find the PC card (in this case, the network card).

28. **B**   Not draining a nickel cadmium battery between charges will significantly decrease the battery's ability to stay charged.

29. **D**   The monitor has no bearing whatsoever on the network link light.

30. **D**   An ISA NIC transfers data 16 bits at a time, whereas a PCI NIC can transfer 32 bits at a time and utilize the full motherboard bus speed while doing so. The ISA NIC is noticeably slower.

31. **A** The PC is likely to be configured to use another segment of the LAN.

32. **C** Communication with the customer is the key to keeping him satisfied with your service. All other options can add fuel to the fire.

33. **B** Take care of the customer in a courteous way. All other options simply make the user angry and make the situation more stressful.

This list of terms applies to the computing industry in general. This list is meant as a reference in case you run across a term you do not know while studying for this exam. The terms themselves are not likely to be test material for the A+ Core/Hardware exam.

CHAPTER 12

Hotlist of
Exam-Critical Concepts

Term	*Definition*
alias	A short name that represents a more complicated one. Often used for mail addresses or host domain names.
analog	A form of electronic communication that uses a continuous electromagnetic wave, such as television or radio. Any continuous wave form as opposed to digital on/off transmissions.
ANSI	American National Standards Institute. This is the membership organization responsible for defining U.S. standards in the information technology industry.
ASCII	American Standard Code for Information Interchange. A code in which each alphanumeric character is represented as a number from 0 to 127, translated into a 7-bit binary code for the computer. ASCII is used by most microcomputers and printers and, because of this, text-only files can be transferred easily between different kinds of computers. ASCII code also includes characters to indicate backspace, carriage return, etc., but does not include accents and special letters not used in English. Extended ASCII has additional characters (128-255).
AT	Advanced Technology. An IBM PC introduced in 1984 that was the most advanced PC at that time; it had an Intel 80286 processor, 16-bit bus, and 1.2MB floppy drive.
attribute	A form of a command-line switch as applied to tags in the HTML language. HTML commands or tags can be more specific when attributes are used. For example, in <BODY BGCOLOR="#FFFFFF">, BGCOLOR is the attribute. Not all HTML tags use attributes. Also, file properties are known as attributes. The most common are System, Hidden, Read-Only, and Volume.

Term	*Definition*
backbone	Generally very high-speed T3 telephone lines that connect remote ends of networks to one another. Can also be the main network segment that connects the network nodes.
baseband	A network technology that requires all nodes attached to the network to participate in every transmission. Ethernet, for example, is a baseband network.
binary	A system of numbers having 2 as its base and using 0s and 1s for its notation. Binary code is used by computers because it works well with digital electronics and Boolean algebra.
BinHex	A program that encodes binary files as ASCII so they can be sent through email.
BIOS	Basic Input/Output System. A set of instructions stored on a ROM chip inside IBM PCs and PC-compatibles, which handles all input-output functions.
BNC	British Naval Connector, or barrel nut connector. A coaxial cable connector.
Boolean logic	Logic dealing with true/false values. (The operators AND, OR, and NOT are Boolean operators.)
Bootstrap	The process of computer startup or boot.
BPS	Bits per second. The rate of data transfer over a communication line. The data rate of a modem is measured in kilobits per second. A measurement that expresses the speed at which data is transferred between computers.
bridge	A device that operates at the Data Link layer of the OSI model, connecting one physical section of a network to another and often providing isolation.
broadband	A network technology that multiplexes multiple network carriers into a single cable.

Term	*Definition*
broadcast	A packet destined for all hosts on the network.
brouter	A computer device that works as both a bridge and a router. Some network traffic may be bridged, and other traffic is routed depending on need.
browser	A utility that enables you to look through collections of items. A file browser, for example, enables you to look through a file system. Applications that enable you to access the World Wide Web are called browsers.
buffer	A storage area used to hold input or output data.
cache	A temporary storage area for frequently accessed or recently accessed data. Having certain data stored in cache speeds up the operation of the computer. There are two kinds of cache: internal (or memory cache) and external (or disk cache). Internal cache is built into the CPU, and external cache is on the motherboard. All cache contents are written to disk when the computer is idle.
checksumming	A service performed by UDP that checks to see whether packets were changed during transmission. Another term for CRC.
client	User of a service. Also often refers to a piece of software that gets information from a server. Additionally, *client* refers to an application that makes a request of a service on a (sometimes) remote computer; the request can be, for example, a function call.
CMOS	Complementary Metal Oxide Semiconductor. A kind of integrated circuit used in processors and memories.
compress	A program that compacts a file so that it fits into a smaller space. Also can refer to the technique of reducing the amount of space a file takes. PKZIP for PC and Stuffit for Macintosh are data compression programs.

Term	*Definition*
connection	A logical path between two protocol modules that provides a reliable delivery service.
context	Many functions return either array values or scalar values depending on the context. That is, whether it returns an array or a scalar value is appropriate for the place where the call was made.
cooperative multitasking	Multitasking model where the process using processor time maintains processor control until it is finished.
CRC	Cyclic Redundancy Check. A number derived from a block of data and stored or transmitted with the data in order to detect any errors in transmission. It is similar to a checksum, but more complicated. A cyclic redundancy check is often calculated by adding words or bytes of the data. The receiving computer recalculates the CRC from the data received and compares it to the value originally transmitted; if the values are not the same, it indicates a transmission error.
CRT	Cathode Ray Tube. The main component in computer monitors.
CSMA	Carrier Sense Multiple Access. A simple media access control protocol that enables multiple stations to contend for access to the medium. If no traffic is detected on the medium, the station can send a transmission.
CSMA/CD	Carrier Sense Multiple Access with Collision Detection. Networking media access process that detects when two stations transmit simultaneously. If that happens, both stop signaling and retry the transmission after a random time period has elapsed.
cyberspace	Refers to the entire collection of sites accessible electronically. If your computer is attached to the Internet or another large network, it exists in cyberspace.
daemon	A program that runs automatically on a computer to perform a service for the operating system or for clients on the network. One example of a daemon is a network printer service.

Term	*Definition*
database	A structured way of storing that's often described in terms of a number of tables; each table is made up of a series of records, and each record contains a number of fields.
DB-9	A 9-pin serial cable connector.
DB-25	A 25-pin serial cable connector.
defragment	The process of re-aligning data in a computer file allocation table so that it resides in consecutive blocks.
DES	Data Encryption Standard. A private key encryption algorithm developed by the U.S. government to provide security for data transmitted over a network.
device driver	A software program written to instruct an operating system about how to handle a specific piece of computer hardware.
DHCP	Dynamic Host Configuration Protocol. A protocol that provides dynamic address allocation and automatic TCP/IP configuration.
dial-up connection	A connection to the Internet through dial-up. Or, a modem and telephone line allowing email and running processes to occur on a remote computer.
digital	A type of communication used by computers, consisting of individual on and off pulses. *See also* analog.
DIP switch	One means of opening or closing circuit board circuits. Replaced primarily today by jumpers.
direct connection	A connection to the Internet through a dedicated line, such as ISDN, ADSL, or Frame Relay.
DMA	Direct Memory Access/Addressing. A method of transferring data from one memory area to another without having to go through the central processing unit.

Term	*Definition*
domain	Highest subdivision of the Internet, for the most part by country (except in the United States, where it's by type of organization, such as educational, commercial, and government). Usually the last part of a hostname; for example, the domain part of ibm.com is .com, which represents the domain of commercial sites in the United States.
download	To move a file from a remote computer to your local computer.
EDO RAM	Extended Data Out Random Access Memory. Same as Extended Data Out Dynamic Random Access Memory. A memory chip used mostly with Pentium processors, which accesses data faster by overlapping cycles of data output.
EIDE	Enhanced Integrated Drive Electronics. A hardware interface that is faster than IDE and can connect up to four devices (such as hard drives, tape drives, and CD-ROM drives) to the computer.
EISA	Extended Industry Standard Architecture. A PC bus that extends the ISA bus from 16 bits to 32 bits but can still hold ISA expansion cards.
email	An electronic mail message delivered from one computer user to another. Short for electronic mail.
email address	An address used to send email to a user on the Internet. It consists of the username and hostname (and any other necessary information, such as a gateway machine). An Internet email address usually takes the form of *username@domainname*.
encryption	The process of scrambling a message so it can be read only by someone who knows how to unscramble it.
ESD	Electrostatic Discharge. Static electricity. ESD is damaging to circuit boards and can degrade their performance.

Term	Definition
Ethernet	A type of local area network hardware. Many TCP/IP networks are Ethernet-based.
FAQ	Frequently Asked Question(s). A document that contains frequently asked questions and typical answers. Most Usenet newsgroups have an FAQ to introduce new readers to popular topics in the newsgroup.
FCS	Frame Check Sequence. A computation about the bits in a frame; the result is appended to the end of the frame and recalculated within the frame it is received. If the results differ from the appended value, the frame has presumably been corrupted and is therefore discarded. It is used to detect errors in transmission. Another method of error checking in addition to CRC.
FDDI	Fiber Distributed Data Interface. The formal name for fiber-optic wiring, which enables high-speed data transfers.
FDISK	Utility for partitioning hard disk drives.
FIFO	First-In First-Out. A queue in which the first item placed in the queue is the first item processed when the queue is processed. The opposite of LIFO.
file	Basic unit of storage of computer data; files can normally be binary or text only (ASCII).
file system	An operating system's catalog of items stored on the hard disk.
firewall	A device placed on a network to prevent unauthorized traffic from entering the network. Can also be used to restrict outbound flow.
firmware	Software stored in ROM or PROM; essential programs that remain even when the system is turned off. Firmware is easier to change than hardware but is more permanent than software stored on disk.

Term	*Definition*
flow control	A mechanism that controls the rate at which hosts may transmit at any time. It is used to avoid congestion on the network, which may exhaust memory buffers.
format	The process of putting a file system on a hard disk.
FQDN	Fully Qualified Domain Name. A combination of the hostname and the domain name.
fragment	A piece that results when a datagram is partitioned into smaller pieces. It is used to facilitate datagrams too large for the network technology in use.
frame	A set of packets as transmitted across a medium. Differing frame types have unique characteristics.
frame relay	A type of digital data communications protocol.
freeware	Software that the author makes available at no cost to anyone who wants it (although the author retains rights to the software).
FTP	File Transfer Protocol. A popular Internet communications protocol that enables the transfer of files between hosts on the Internet.
gateway	A device that connects two networks that use different protocols.
GIF	Graphics Interchange Format. A computer image format.
gigabit	A very high-speed data communication that transmits at 1 billion bps.
gigabyte	A unit of data storage approximately equal to 1 billion bytes of data.
GPF	General Protection Fault. An error that occurs when another program or device tries to address memory in use by another program or device.

Term	*Definition*
Greenwich Mean Time	An international time standard reference, also known as Universal Time.
GUI	Graphical User Interface. A computer interface based on graphic symbols rather than text. Windows environments and Macintosh environments are GUIs.
hacking	Originally referred to playing around with computer systems; now often used to indicate destructive computer activity.
hardware address	The physical hardware address of a host used by the Media Access Control sub-layer of the Data Link layer in the OSI model.
home page	The document that serves as the entry for all the information contained in a company's WWW service. Your World Wide Web browser loads this page when it starts.
host address	A unique number assigned to identify a host on the network (also called an IP address or a dot address). This address is usually represented as four numbers between 1 and 254 and separated by periods (for example, 192.58.107.230).
host ID	The portion of an IP address that identifies the host in a particular network. It is used with network IDs to form a complete IP address.
hostname	A unique name for a host that corresponds to the host address.
hosts	Individual computers connected to the network. Can also include printers and routers.
HOSTS file	A text file containing mappings of IP addresses to hostnames. HOSTS files are still used today but were originally developed before DNS existed.
HTML	Hypertext Markup Language. The formatting language/protocol used to define various text styles in a hypertext document, including emphasis and bulleted lists.

Term	*Definition*
HTTP	Hypertext Transfer Protocol. The communications protocol used by WWW services to retrieve documents quickly.
hyperlinks	The areas (words or graphics) in an HTML document that cause another document to be loaded when the user clicks them. *See also* links.
hypertext	An online document that has words or graphics containing links to other documents. Usually, selecting the link area onscreen (with a mouse or keyboard command) activates the link.
IDE	Integrated Drive Electronics. An interface for connecting additional hard drives to a computer.
IEEE	Institute of Electrical and Electronics Engineers. The professional society for electrical and computer engineers.
input device	Any device used to put information into a computer system. Examples include the keyboard, mouse, and scanner.
Internet	The term used to describe all the worldwide-interconnected TCP/IP networks.
InterNIC	The NSFNet Manager sites on the Internet that provide information about the Internet.
I/O	Input/output.
IP	Internet protocol. The communications protocol used by computers connected to the Internet.
IP address	*See* host address. A unique number assigned to identify a host on the network (also called an IP address or a dot address). This address is usually represented as four numbers between 1 and 254 and separated by periods (for example, 192.58.107.230).
IPv4	Internet Protocol, version 4. This is the current version of TCP/IP in use today.

Term	*Definition*
IPv6	Internet Protocol, version 6. IPv6 is a 128bit HEX IP addressing scheme that is in development for future use. It has a greater flexibility of Address class assignments and number of possible networks.
IRQ	Interrupt Request. Designations of hardware interrupt in a PC. A PC has either 8 or 16 lines that accept interrupts from attached devices (such as a keyboard, SCSI card, scanner, sound card, or mouse). Different devices competing for the same IRQ cause conflicts.
ISA	Industry Standard Architecture. A PC expansion bus used for modems, video displays, speakers, and other peripherals. PCs with ISA commonly have some 8-bit and some 16-bit expansion slots.
ISDN	Integrated Services Digital Network. A dedicated telephone-line connection that transmits digital data at rates of 64kbps and 128kbps. In reality, because of the overhead, the data transfers are approximately 56/122.
ISO	International Standards Organization. An organization responsible for setting worldwide standards in many different areas.
ISP	Internet Service Provider. A provider of Internet services, including connectivity, for individuals and companies.
Java	A programming language developed by Sun Microsystems that is platform independent.
JPEG	Joint Photographic Expert Group. A computer graphics compression standard.
jumper	A connector used on a circuit board to either close or open a circuit. Used primarily for setting options like voltage and clock speed.

Term	*Definition*
LAN	Local Area Network. A network of computers that is usually limited to a small physical area, like a building.
LIFO	Last-In First-Out. A queue in which the last item placed in the queue is the first item processed when the queue is processed. Opposite of FIFO.
link	The area (word or graphic) in an HTML document that causes another document to be loaded when the user clicks it.
LLC	Logical Link Control. A protocol that provides a common interface point to the Media Access Control (MAC) layers.
local host	The computer currently in use.
log on	The process of entering your user ID and password at a prompt to gain access to a service.
LPT	Line printer port.
MAC	Media Access Control. A protocol that governs the access method a station has to the network.
MAC address	*See* hardware address.
MAN	Metropolitan Area Network. A physical communications network that operates across a metropolitan area.
master	The term used to designate the primary drive on an IDE/EIDE chain.
MBR	Master Boot Record. The first track on the active hard drive partition.
memory	RAM. The working space used by the computer to hold the program that is currently running. The main memory is built from RAM chips. The amount of memory available determines the size of programs that can be run and whether more than one program can be run at once. RAM is dynamic; its contents are lost when the computer is turned off.

Term	Definition
memory map	A graphical representation for what addressable memory area(s) are being used. The memory map can be viewed with the DOS utility MSD.EXE.
MIB	Management Information Base. A database made up of a set of objects that represent various types of information about devices. It is used by SNMP to manage devices.
MMX	Multimedia Extensions. An instruction set telling the processor how to execute multimedia code.
modem	Modulator/demodulator. An electronic device that allows digital computer data to be transmitted via analog phone lines.
monitor	The video output device of a personal computer.
Multihomed host	A TCP/IP host that is attached to two or more networks, requiring multiple IP addresses.
multimeter	PC hardware troubleshooting tool that combines a voltmeter and ohmmeter.
name resolution	The process of mapping a computer name to an IP address. WINS and LMHOSTS are two ways of resolving names.
NetBIOS name	The unique name assigned to a computer in Windows networking. Usually its computer name from the Identification tab in Windows 95.
Netscape	A popular commercial World Wide Web browser manufacturer.
network	A number of computers physically connected to enable communication with one another.
network ID	The portion of an IP address that identifies the network. It is used with host IDs to form a complete address.

Term	*Definition*
NIC	Network Information Center. A service that provides administrative information about a network.
NIC	Network interface card. An add-on card to allow a machine to access a LAN.
nodes	Individual computers connected to a network.
non-parity memory	RAM that does not contain a parity chip. Used in PCs that do not use parity checking for their memory banks.
NOS	Network Operating System.
null character	A character with the value 0.
null list	An empty list represented as empty parentheses [ ] or ( ).
OSI	Open Systems Interconnection. A set of ISO standards that define the framework for implementing protocols in seven layers.
parallel	Means of communication in which digital data is sent multiple bits at a time, with each simultaneous bit being sent over a separate line.
parallel port	A connector on a computer for transmitting data in parallel, meaning more than one bit at a time. There might be 8, 16, or 36 channels; each channel carries one bit of information, so eight channels would be used to transmit one eight-bit byte at a time. Not all the channels are used for data; some are used for control signals. A parallel port, also called a female connector, has 25 holes, and the cable that plugs into it has 25 pins. It is the kind of port used to connect tape drives, CD-ROMs, extra hard disks, and most printers. A parallel port transmits faster than a serial port but cannot reliably send data more than 20 feet.
parameter	An argument.

Term	*Definition*
parity	An integer's property of being odd or even. Parity checking is used to detect errors in binary-coded data.
parity memory	RAM that uses a parity chip for data checking.
partition	A logical portion of a hard disk drive that has been formatted for use.
PCI	Peripheral Component Interconnect. A personal computer local bus designed by Intel, which runs at 33MHz and supports Plug and Play. It provides a high-speed connection with peripherals and allows connection of seven peripheral devices. It is mostly used with Pentium computers but is processor independent and, therefore, able to work with other processors. Can be used with an ISA or EISA bus.
peer-to-peer	Internet or network services that can be offered and accessed by anyone, without a special server.
PID	Process Identifier. The number assigned to a process by the operating system.
PING	Packet Internet Groper. A utility included in the TCP/IP Protocol Suite that sends out a packet to a network host and waits for a response. If the intended recipient is online and has TCP/IP bound correctly to his or her network card, it will respond. (This is often used to check TCP/IP functionality.)
pipe	The concept in an operating system where the output of one program is fed into the input of another.
Plug and Play	The process of hardware auto-detection and configuration used by Windows 95.
polymorphic	The term applied to a virus that is able to hide itself from a detection program once it has been used for the first time.
POP	Point of Presence. Indicates availability of a local access number to a public data network.

Term	*Definition*
POP	Post Office Protocol. An email protocol specifying how email is stored on a server and retrieved by a client.
port (hardware)	A physical channel on a computer that enables you to communicate with other devices (printers, modems, disk drives, and so on).
port (network)	An address to which incoming data is sent. Special ports can be assigned to send the data directly to a server (FTP, Gopher, WWW, Telnet, or email) or to another specific program.
port ID	The method used by TCP and UDP to specify which port the application is using to send or receive data.
PPP	Point-to-Point Protocol. A driver that enables network communications protocols over a phone line; used with TCP/IP to enable you to have a dial-in Internet host.
PPTP	Point-to-Point Tunneling Protocol. A revision to PPP that's used mostly to create Virtual Private Networks (VPNs), which allow the encapsulation on another protocol inside of TCP/IP and transported by means of PPP.
power supply	The device that regulates power to the motherboard.
preemptive multitasking	Multitasking process in which the processor maintains control and schedules time with all processes needing processor time.
process	In operating systems such as UNIX, many programs can be run at once, and each one running is called a process.
protocol	The standard that defines how computers on a network communicate with one another.

Term	*Definition*
proxy	A connection through a modem and telephone line to the Internet that enables clients to access. Can also be used in a LAN or WAN environment. Allows companies to use non-registered IP addresses internally and a registered IP address for the proxy server. When requests are sent from the client computer to the destination host, the proxy server intercepts the packets. It wraps the packet with its own IP address first so the packet will appear to "belong" to a registered host, and then it transmits the packet to the proper destination. When packets return, they are sent to the proxy first. It removes the wrapping, determines the proper host IP address (internal), and sends the packet to the originating client.
PS/2 mini-din	A round 6-pin connector used for PS/2 mice and keyboards.
remote host	A host on the network other than the computer you currently are using.
repeater	Device that enables you to extend the length of your network by amplifying and repeating the information it receives.
RFC	Request For Comments. A document submitted to the Internet governing board to propose Internet standards or to document information about the Internet.
RJ-11	The standard telephone jack used in the United States to plug a telephone or modem into the wall.
RJ-45	The standard network cable jack used in the United States. Used for 10BASE-T and 100BASE-T networks.
route	The path that network traffic takes between its source and its destination.
router	Equipment that receives a packet and sends it to the next machine in the destination path.

Term	*Definition*
RPC	Remote Procedure Call. An interface that allows an application to call a routine that executes on another machine in a remote location.
ScanDisk	Utility used to verify the integrity of the file system and physical surface of a hard disk.
script	An interpreted set of instructions in a text file.
segment	A protocol data unit consisting of part of a stream of bytes being sent between two machines. It also includes information about the current position in the stream and a checksum value.
serial	Means of communication in which digital data is sent one bit at a time over a single physical wire.
serial port	A connector on a computer that is usually used to connect a modem, mouse, scanner, or serial printer. Sometimes two computers are connected by their serial ports to send data between them. A serial port, also called a male connector, has 9 or 25 pins. A serial port sends information through a cable one bit at a time, and a serial port is reliable for transmission over a longer distance (maximum transfer is 50 feet).
server	A provider of a service; a computer that runs services. It also often refers to a piece of hardware or software that provides access to information requested by clients.
service	An application that processes requests by client applications (for example, storing data or executing an algorithm).
share	A directory or resource (like a printer) that has been made available for use on a network.
shareware	Software that is made available by the author to anyone who wants it, with a request to send the author a nominal fee if the software is used on a regular basis.

Term	*Definition*
site	A group of computers under a single administrative control.
slave	The term used to designate the secondary drive on an IDE/EIDE drive chain.
SLIP	Serial Line Internet Protocol. A way of running TCP/IP via the phone lines to enable you to have a dial-up Internet host.
Slot 1	The slot used by Pentium II style processors.
SMTP	Simple Mail Transport Protocol. The accepted communications protocol standard for exchange of email between Internet hosts.
SNMP	Simple Network Management Protocol. A communications protocol used to control and monitor devices on a network.
socket	A means of network communications via special entities. Also a connection socket on a motherboard.
Socket 7	The Zero Insertion Force (ZIF) socket used by Pentium-style processors.
spike	A sudden pulse of extra voltage, lasting a fraction of a second, which can cause the computer to crash and can damage files or computer components if there is no surge protector on the line.
SRAM	Static Random Access Memory. A kind of random access memory that requires a constant supply of power in order to hold its content, but does not require refresh circuitry as Dynamic Random Access Memory (DRAM) does. Unlike Read-Only Memory (ROM), SRAM will lose its content when the power is switched off. Static RAM is usually faster than Dynamic RAM, but it takes up more space and uses more power. It is used for the parts of a computer that require highest speed, such as cache memory.

Term	*Definition*
storage device	A hard drive or floppy drive. Any media capable of holding electronic data.
string	A sequence of characters.
subnet	Any lower network that is part of the logical network; identified by the subnet ID.
subnet mask	A 32-bit value that distinguishes the network ID from the host ID in an IP address.
surge	A large power spike of extra voltage that lasts longer than several seconds.
syntax	A statement that contains programming code. Also refers to the correct usage of commands.
system board	The motherboard; the main printed circuit board that contains the central processing unit for the computer, memory, and sometimes printer ports or other devices.
T1	A dedicated telephone line that transfers data at the rate of 1.544Mbps.
T3	A dedicated telephone line that transfers data at the rate of 45Mbps.
Task Manager	A Windows 95 utility that allows you to see what processes are running at any given time. It is accessed by pressing Ctrl+Alt+Del simultaneously. Task Manager allows you to recover the processor from a stalled program.
TCP	Transmission Control Protocol. The connection-oriented transport layer protocol.
TCP/IP	Transmission Control Protocol/Internet Protocol. A communications protocol suite that allows computers of any make to communicate when running TCP/IP software.

Term	*Definition*
Telnet	A program that allows remote logon to another computer.
terminal emulation	Running an application that enables you to use your computer to interface with a command-line account on a remote computer as if you were connected to the computer with a terminal.
thread	All messages in a newsgroup or mailing list pertaining to a particular topic or message. Also is the smallest form of executable code. Many threads make up a process.
token-ring	A Physical layer protocol for LAN, based on a token-passing access method.
Traceroute	A utility that enables you to find how many routers are between your host and another host.
traffic	The packets flowing through a network.
transceiver	Transmitter/receiver. A device that connects a host interface to a network. It is used to apply signals to the cable and to sense collisions.
trap	A block of data that indicates some request failed to authenticate. An SNMP agent will issue a trap when a specified event has occurred. For example, the SNMP service sends a trap when it receives a request for information from a host with a community name different than its own.
TTL	Time To Live. A measurement of time, usually defined by a number of hops, that a datagram can exist on a network before it is discarded. It prevents endlessly looping packets.
UDP	User Datagram Protocol. A connectionless transport layer protocol that enables an application program on one machine to send a datagram to an application program on another machine. Delivery is not guaranteed; there is also no guarantee that the datagrams will be delivered in the proper order.

Term	*Definition*
UMB	Upper Memory Blocks.
UNC	Universal Naming Convention used by Windows networking. Distinguished by this syntax: *computer_(host_ name)*\\(*share_name*)
Universal Time	An international time standard reference also known as Greenwich Mean Time.
upload	To move a file from your local computer to a remote computer.
UPS	Uninterruptible Power Supply. A backup power supply that supplies battery power when electrical power to the computer is interrupted.
URL	Universal Resource Locator. A means of specifying the location of information on the Internet for WWW clients. Also known as Uniform Resource Locator.
USB	Universal Serial Bus. A personal computer bus that can support up to 127 peripheral devices in a daisy chain configuration and has a total bandwidth of 1.5 megabytes per second. It uses inexpensive cable, which can be up to five meters long.
Usenet	An online news and bulletin board system accommodating more than 7,000 interest groups.
username	The ID used to log on to a computer.
VESA Local Bus	(VL-Bus). A local bus defined by the Video Electronics Standards Association, which provides a high-speed connection between the CPU and peripherals. It allows video cards to communicate faster with the CPU. Computers with VESA Local Bus have two or three VL-Bus slots on the motherboard, along with several ISA or EISA slots, so VESA Local Bus can be used alone or in combination with these other buses.

Term	*Definition*
viewers	Applications used to display non-text files, such as graphics, sound, and animation.
virus	A computer program that covertly enters a system by means of a legitimate program, usually doing damage to the system; compare to worm.
VPN	Virtual Private Network. Technology that allows companies to use public access points and PPP to establish a secure channel from one site to another.
WAN	Wide Area Network. A network of computers that are geographically dispersed.
Web	Short for World Wide Web (WWW).
World Wide Web	WWW (World Wide Web). Hypertext-based system that allows browsing of available Internet resources.
wrist strap	A device worn by computer service techs as a ground to prevent ESD.
X-modem	A communication protocol that enables you to transfer files over a serial line. *See also* Y-modem and Z-modem.
Y-modem	A communication protocol that enables you to transfer files over a serial line. *See also* X-modem and Z-modem.
Z-modem	A communication protocol that enables you to transfer files over a serial line. By design, the fastest modem transfer protocol.

CHAPTER 13

Did You Know?

Installation, Configuration, and Upgrading

◆ New technology called "FireWire" (developed jointly by Texas Instruments and Apple Computers) is similar to the Universal Serial Bus and allows for up to 255 devices on a single wire to be added or removed from a system on-the-fly.

◆ Advances in expansion board technology allow for modems and sound cards to be built with and to take advantage of PCI interfaces. This allows for much faster performance by these devices in comparison to their ISA counterparts.

◆ PCI sound cards enable many new games and programs to use the new 3D sound. 3D sound is an excellent complement to 3D AGP video.

◆ Advanced computer graphics were the predecessor to the new high definition televisions (HDTVs).

Diagnosing and Troubleshooting

◆ Numerous troubleshooting tools are available on the market that make your life easier when it comes to dealing with error messages. Microsoft publishes *TechNet* on a monthly basis. *TechNet* is a list of common problems found with all Microsoft products and their appropriate fixes. A free trial subscription to *TechNet* is available at http://204.118.129.122/giftsub/Clt1Form.asp. Another example of a good troubleshooting tool is the *PC Mechanic*, available on CD-ROM.

◆ Third-party utilities like Norton Utilities and Nuts and Bolts can perform deeper troubleshooting functions than the operating system utilities can alone.

◆ After you've done a cursory check to make sure the software is configured properly, *always* suspect hardware as being the problem. It's quite irritating to spend hours troubleshooting software only to find out you have bad hardware.

Safety and Preventive Maintenance

- A warm, dry environment is a breeding ground for electrostatic discharge (ESD).
- Fluorescent lighting can cause signal degradation on a network, if cabling is placed too close to the lights.

Motherboards/Processors/and Memory

- Major processor manufacturers predict the development of the first 1,000MHz processors by the year 2001.
- New motherboards utilizing AGP, Pentium II technology, and Synch DRAM have a bus speed of 100MHz.

Portable Computers

- The typical portable computer stays in manufacturing without a configuration change for less than six months.

Basic Networking

- CompTIA has plans to release a vendor-nonspecific networking certification to accompany A+. It will be called Network+.
- A cable modem gives you Internet access that can equal speeds of a 10MB network and does not tie up your phone line or cable television. A cable modem does display your computer to all other users in your workgroup, so it is important that you do *not* share directories with the Full Control option.
- Many satellite companies provide Internet access through a satellite that has greater download speeds than traditional modems do. Satellite Internet access has increased download rates up to 600KB per second, but it still requires a modem for uploading.

Customer Satisfaction

- You know this to be true: The customer is always right.

What's Important to Know About the A+ DOS/Windows Exam

The A+ DOS/Windows certification exam measures your ability to install, configure, support, and troubleshoot MS-DOS, Windows 3.x, and Windows 95 environments. Part III of the book is intended to help reinforce and clarify information with which the student is already familiar.

Part III of this book is designed to help you make the most of your study time by presenting concise summaries of information that you need to understand to succeed on the exam. Each chapter covers a specific exam objective area outlined by CompTIA.

14   Function, Structure, Operation, and File Management

15   Memory Management

16   Installation, Configuration, and Upgrading

17   Diagnosing and Troubleshooting

18   Networking

     Objective Review Notes

ABOUT THE EXAM

Exam Number	**220-102**
Minutes	**75**
Questions	70
Passing Score	**66%**
Single Answer Questions	Yes
Multiple Answer with Correct Number Given	**Yes**
Multiple Answer without Correct Number Given	No
Ranking Order	**No**
Choices of A-D	Yes
Choices of A-E	**No**
Objective Categories	5

OBJECTIVES

▶ Identify the major components of DOS, Windows 3.x, and Windows 95.

▶ Describe the differences between DOS/Windows 3.x and Windows 95 architecture.

▶ Name the major system files of each OS.

▶ Recognize what files are needed to boot a system.

▶ Identify the correct locations of important system files.

▶ Differentiate between a system file, a configuration file, and a user interface file.

▶ Navigate the operating systems.

▶ Retrieve data from the operating systems using system utilities.

▶ Know how to create, view, and manage files and directories.

▶ Understand the concepts of disk management.

CHAPTER 14

Function, Structure, Operation, and File Management

COMPARING DOS, WINDOWS 3.X, AND WINDOWS 95

As you prepare to take this exam, it is imperative that you understand the major differences between DOS, Windows 3.x, and Windows 95. At even the slightest glance, these products do not look alike. Taking advantage of the visible differences is only the beginning: You must be able to differentiate between the way the systems are constructed, how they behave, and how they react to the programs running within them. Each system represented state-of-the-art technology at the time of its release.

The following table outlines some of the major differences of each system.

At A Glance: Comparison of Microsoft Operating Systems

System and Release Dates	Function	Architecture	Ability to Multitask	User Interface	Memory Usage
DOS 1981–1994	Operating system	16-bit	None	Text	Conventional at first; XMS/EMS later
Windows 3.x 1990	Runs in on top of DOS (shell)	16-bit with 32-bit disk and software access	Cooperative	Program Manager	Temp or perm swap file
Windows 95 August, 1995	Operating system	32-bit	Preemptive	Explorer	Virtual memory

The concepts of structure, architecture, multitasking, memory usage, and user interface will continue to be important throughout this book and on the exam. The structure of DOS has remained relatively constant during its many revisions.

The primary analogy to describe the structure of DOS has been that of a file cabinet where drawers represent disks drives, folders represent directories and subdirectories, and individual pieces of paper equal computer files. This is also the basic organizational structure of Windows 95 today. Windows 3.x gave the text-based structure of DOS a graphical representation or *shell*. You will learn more about these facts as you explore further the major components of all three systems.

MAJOR COMPONENTS

Part of understanding the operating systems involves knowing what the major components are and what they do. The following sections discuss the major components of each operating system.

DOS

As you dissect each product, you begin to see certain constants. DOS, Windows 3.x, and Windows 95 function by relying on several kinds of files. The first kind of file is a *system file*. A system file is required for the system to operate properly. The next file type is the *configuration file*. The configuration file contains instructions for the system regarding how to handle one task or multiple tasks. Configuration files are not required to boot the system, but they are needed to allow the system to perform certain functions such as memory management and defining the paths to commonly used files. The third file type is a user interface file. The user interface file controls what the user sees and how the user does things. Examples include the keyboard layout file in DOS and the Program Manager (PROGMAN.EXE) in Windows 3.x.

The following sections outline the major components of DOS.

IO.SYS

IO.SYS is required for the system to boot. Known as IBMBIO.COM in previous versions of IBM PC-DOS, this file is classified as a system file and resides at the root of the boot drive (usually C:). IO.SYS is responsible for loading real-mode drivers and terminate-and-stay resident programs (TSRs) specified in the CONFIG.SYS and AUTOEXEC.BAT files (in other words, input and output devices; thus the name IO.SYS). It retains the file attributes of system, hidden, and read-only. IO.SYS is copied to the root of the boot drive when the drive is formatted with the /s switch, or when the DOS command sys.com is used.

MSDOS.SYS

MSDOS.SYS is also classified as a system file that's required to boot the system. Also known as IBMDOS.COM in previous DOS versions, MSDOS.SYS is the program responsible for communication between internal computer components. It is located at the root of the boot drive. It retains the file attributes of system, hidden, and read-only. MSDOS.SYS is copied to the root of the boot drive when the drive is formatted with the /s switch, or when the DOS SYS.COM command is used.

COMMAND.COM

COMMAND.COM also is a system file required to boot the system. COMMAND.COM is the command interpreter that actually interprets commands from the keyboard and decides how they should be executed. COMMAND.COM is the main boot file that differentiates between whether MSDOS.SYS or IO.SYS handles a request. It is also located at the root of the boot drive and retains the file attribute of system. COMMAND.COM is not a hidden file. Like MSDOS.SYS and IO.SYS, COMMAND.COM is also copied to the root of the boot drive during a format with the /s switch, or when the DOS sys.com command is issued.

These three system files at the root of a disk constitute a bootable partition (if the partition is marked as active). In MS-DOS version 6.0, DBLSPACE.BIN is also copied to the root of a drive during a system format. In MS-DOS versions 6.1 to 6.22, the filename is DRV-SPACE.BIN. Neither file is required in order to boot unless compression is being used on the volumes you are trying to access.

CONFIG.SYS

CONFIG.SYS is classified as a configuration file. It resides at the root of the boot drive and retains the system file attribute. CONFIG.SYS is loaded automatically during the second phase of the boot process and is responsible for telling DOS how to handle system hardware. CONFIG.SYS is where memory management begins as well.

Some common commands in CONFIG.SYS are FILES=, BUFFERS=, DEVICE=, and LASTDRIVE=. The FILES= command controls how many files DOS will allow to be open simultaneously. The BUFFERS= command tells DOS how much memory to set aside for disk buffers. This buffer reserves the memory area that is directly available to the processor for disk access. Each buffer sets aside 512KB. The DEVICE= command gives the system specific configuration information for a particular hardware device. The LASTDRIVE= command tells the system what the last available drive letter is that can be used for local drives. This statement is most important in networked environments because the system needs to know what drive letters will be available for network drives.

AUTOEXEC.BAT

Also found at the root of the boot volume, AUTOEXEC.BAT is a configuration file that works in conjunction with CONFIG.SYS to complete the DOS system configuration. AUTOEXEC.BAT (short for "automatically execute") has the system file attribute. AUTOEXEC.BAT contains commands and final configuration settings in a DOS system. Common statements in AUTOEXEC.BAT are *prompt*, which is used to configure how the command prompt appears; *Echo*, which is used to either show or hide text on the screen during the AUTOEXEC sequence; and most commonly, *path*, which tells DOS and Windows where to look for files.

Internal DOS Commands (Part of COMMAND.COM)

Several common DOS commands are not found on the disk at all but are actually part of COMMAND.COM. These are known as *internal* DOS commands. These commands are used for file and directory maintenance. The most common internal DOS commands are listed here:

- ◆ CD is the command issued to change directories.
- ◆ CLS clears the display.

- COPY is used to copy files.

- DEL is the delete files command.

- DIR lists the contents of the directory.

- MD creates a directory.

- MORE pauses a large display of text one page at a time, making it possible to see what scrolls by on the screen.

- PATH (as discussed in the previous section) tells DOS where to look for files.

- PROMPT allows the user to display the DOS prompt in a certain way (for example prompt=$t changes the prompt to display the system time).

- REN is the rename command.

- TYPE displays the contents of a text file to the screen (and is commonly used with the MORE command).

- VER displays the version of DOS being used.

EMM386.EXE

EMM386 is the DOS memory manager. It is a system configuration file and is located in the DOS directory. (Windows has a version as well that resides in the Windows directory. Either can be used in CONFIG.SYS. The newest version should be used.) EMM386.EXE enables the system to recognize memory above 640KB. EMM386.EXE is marked with the system file attribute.

HIMEM.SYS

HIMEM.SYS is the device driver that enables DOS to use the High Memory Area (memory above 640KB). HIMEM.SYS is a system configuration file that is located in the DOS directory. (Like EMM386.EXE, HIMEM.SYS has a Windows counterpart located in the Windows directory that can also be used.) HIMEM.SYS is marked with the system file attribute. HIMEM.SYS must be used with a memory manager (usually EMM386.EXE) to enable full use of high memory in a DOS/Windows 3.x environment. Windows 95 has upper memory management built in, so a HIMEM.SYS entry in CONFIG.SYS is not necessary unless a legacy application requires it.

ANSI.SYS

ANSI.SYS is a configuration file loaded as a device driver in CONFIG.SYS to enable the system to recognize the ANSI character set. It is located in the DOS directory and is marked with the system file attribute. A common example of a need for ANSI.SYS would be to display colors associated with BBS screens.

Windows 3.x

The following section covers the major Windows 3.x components.

KRNLxxx.EXE

The KRNLxxx.EXE (krnl386.exe in Windows 3.x and Windows 95) file controls the PC's memory and I/O resources and loads Windows. This file is required in order for Windows to manage memory and I/O resources; it is not a replacement for IO.SYS and MSDOS.SYS. KRNL386.EXE is also known as the Windows kernel. It is located in the Windows system directory, has the system file attribute, and is required to start Windows.

USER.EXE

USER.EXE is the Windows user interface file and is required to start Windows. It is responsible for interpreting commands from the mouse, the keyboard, and the I/O ports or serial/parallel ports. It is located in the Windows system directory and has the system file attribute.

GDI.EXE

GDI.EXE controls all the graphics display functions of Windows. It is a user interface file and is located in the Windows system directory. It has the system file attribute and is required to start Windows.

WIN.COM

WIN.COM is the command file that launches Windows. It coordinates the efforts of KRNL386.EXE, USER.EXE, and GDI.EXE into the Windows interface familiar to most computer users. WIN.COM is a system file and is required to start Windows. It is located in the Windows directory and has the system file attribute.

WIN.INI

WIN.INI is the configuration file that allows the system to initialize Windows with the proper environment settings, such as printer settings and desktop wallpaper choices. WIN.INI is located in the Windows directory and has the system file attribute.

SYSTEM.INI

SYSTEM.INI is located in the Windows directory and is marked with the system file attribute. It is a system configuration file and is required to start Windows. It contains device-specific information Windows needs to use those devices.

PROGMAN.EXE

PROGMAN.EXE is the Windows 3.x Program Manager program. It is located in the Windows directory and has the system file attribute. It is required to use Windows 3.x.

PROGMAN.INI

PROGMAN.INI is located in the Windows directory and is marked with the system file attribute. PROGMAN.INI is a configuration file and is used to initialize Windows. It contains information about program groups and their locations on the desktop.

Windows 95

The major components of Windows 95 are covered in the following section.

IO.SYS

IO.SYS in Windows 95 (like the IO.SYS in DOS) is a system file that is required for the system to boot. As a system file, it resides at the root of the boot drive (usually C:). IO.SYS is responsible for loading real-mode drivers and terminate-and-stay resident programs (TSRs) specified in the CONFIG.SYS and AUTOEXEC.BAT files. It retains the file attributes of system, hidden, and read-only. IO.SYS is copied to the root of the boot drive when the drive is formatted with the /s switch or when the DOS command sys.com is used.

MSDOS.SYS

MSDOS.SYS in Windows 95 is virtually the same as its DOS predecessor. It is also classified as a system file that is required to boot the system. It is located at the root of the boot drive, and it retains the file attributes of system, hidden, and read-only. MSDOS.SYS is copied to the root of the boot drive when the drive is formatted with the /s switch, or when the DOS command sys.com is used. In Windows 95, MSDOS.SYS can be edited and manipulated to allow for various menu options. One difference from the previous version of MSDOS.SYS is the addition of all the *X*'s at the end of the file. The *X*'s are there to make the file at least 1,024 bytes so that MSDOS.SYS can be easily identified by some antivirus programs. MSDOS.SYS is required to boot Windows 95.

COMMAND.COM

COMMAND.COM in Windows 95 is simply an updated version of the DOS COMMAND.COM. The ver command issued from a Windows 95 command prompt would return the version as DOS 7.0. It is still classified as a system file that is required to boot the system. Just as in DOS, COMMAND.COM is the command interpreter that actually interprets commands from the keyboard and decides how they should be executed. COMMAND.COM is the main boot file that differentiates whether MSDOS.SYS or IO.SYS handles a request. It is also located at the root of the boot drive and retains the file attribute of system. COMMAND.COM is not a hidden file. Like MSDOS.SYS and IO.SYS, COMMAND.COM is also copied to the root of the boot drive during a format with the /s switch or when the DOS command sys.com is issued.

REGEDIT.EXE

Windows 95 stores its entire 32-bit system configuration in what is known as the Registry instead of relying on 16-bit .INI files. REGEDIT is the Windows 95 Registry editor. It is located in the Windows directory and has the file attribute of system.

USER.DAT

USER.DAT is located in the Windows directory and has the file attributes of system, hidden, and read-only. USER.DAT is the file that stores Windows 95 user information from the Registry. USER.DAT corresponds directly to the Registry key HKEY\Current User. USER.DAT is loaded when a user logs on to Windows 95 and is updated when the user exits.

SYSTEM.DAT

SYSTEM.DAT is located in the Windows directory and has the file
attributes of system, hidden, and read only. SYSTEM.DAT is the file that
contains the Registry information about the system hardware configuration. It directly corresponds with the HKEY\Local Machine Registry
key. SYSTEM.DAT is updated every time the system boots and initializes Windows 95.

At A Glance: PC Operating System Major Components

File	System	Type	Location	File Attributes
AUTOEXEC.BAT	DOS	config	root	S
CONFIG.SYS	DOS	config	root	S
IO.SYS	DOS, Win95	system	root	S, H, R
COMMAND.COM	DOS, Win95	system	root	S
MSDOS.SYS	DOS, Win95	system	root	S, H, R
EMM386.EXE	DOS	config	C:\DOS C:\WINDOWS	S
HIMEM.SYS	DOS	config	C:\DOS C:\WINDOWS	S
ANSI.SYS	DOS	config	C:\DOS C:\WINDOWS	S
KRNL386.EXE	Win3. x	system	C:\WINDOWS	S
WIN.COM	Win3.x, Win95	system	C:\WINDOWS	S
WIN.INI	Win3.x, Win95	config	C:\WINDOWS	S
SYSTEM.INI	Win3.x, Win95	config	C:\WINDOWS	S
USER.EXE	Win3.x, Win95	user	C:\WINDOWS\ SYSTEM	S
GDI.EXE	Win3.x, Win95	user	C:\WINDOWS\ SYSTEM	S
PROGMAN.INI	Win3.x	config	C:\WINDOWS	S
PROGMAN.EXE	Win3. x	user	C:\WINDOWS	S
REGEDIT.EXE	Win95	config	C:\WINDOWS	S
USER.DAT	Win95	config	C:\WINDOWS	S, H, R
SYSTEM.DAT	Win95	config	C:\WINDOWS	S, H, R

FILE SYSTEMS

Now that you have an understanding of the major files involved with each system, you should look at the available file systems that can be used in a DOS/Windows computer system.

Two major file systems are available to a DOS/Windows system: FAT (file allocation tables), which is sometimes referred to as FAT16, and FAT32, a file system based on FAT that allows for large disk support (larger that 2GB). There is also some confusion about a third kind of available file system known as VFAT. VFAT is sometimes mistaken for FAT32. It is actually a software file system driver that allows for 32-bit disk access and is controlled by the operating system. Both FAT and FAT32 are disk file systems that can be installed to a disk partition prior to the loading of the operating system. FAT has been the file system standard since DOS became DOS.

In Windows 95, the 32-bit virtual File Allocation Table file system is the primary file system and cannot be disabled. VFAT can use 32-bit protected-mode drivers or 16-bit real-mode drivers. Actual allocation on disk is still 12-bit or 16-bit (depending on the size of the volume), so FAT16 on the disk uses the same structure as previous versions of this file system. VFAT handles all hard disk drive requests, using 32-bit code for all file access for hard-disk volumes. FAT32 first shipped with Windows 95 version OSR2. OSR2 does not require FAT32, but a Windows start disk from OSR2 allows FDISK.EXE to enable large disk support and format a drive for FAT32.

At A Glance: Operating System Feature Comparison

Feature	*FAT*	*VFAT*	*FAT32*
Filename length	8.3	255	255
8.3 Compatibility	NATIVE	Yes	Yes
Maximum files in root directory	512	512	No limit
Maximum files in nonroot directory	65,535	No limit	No limit
Partition size	2GB	4GB	2048GB
Accessible from DOS	Yes	Yes	Yes
Accessible from OS/2	Yes	Yes	No
Accessible from Windows NT	Yes	NA	No
Case-sensitive	No	No	No
Case preserving	No	Yes	Yes
Supports compression	Yes	Yes	No

NAVIGATING THE OS AND RETRIEVING INFORMATION

Navigating the operating system refers to the user's ability to use the operating system to retrieve information, manage files, and generally find your way around the computer. The following sections discuss the common ways of navigating.

Navigating DOS

The primary means of getting around in a DOS environment is through the command line. Simply knowing what directory you are in and where you want to go are tremendous aids in navigating DOS, and in fact, that is what you should know first. Look at your command prompt. It will be your first clue to help you identify your location. In DOS 5 and higher, the prompt tells you which directory you are in. For instance, C:\windows\desktop> indicates that you are in the Desktop subdirectory of the Windows directory, which is a root-level directory of the C: drive. To move up a single directory, you would issue the cd.. (Change Directory) command. To move to the root of drive C:, you would type cd\.

The DIR (Directory) command is also key in navigating the system because it displays what files and subdirectories are in the current directory. The DIR command has several useful switches. All are available in versions of DOS greater than 5.0.

The MKDIR or MD (Make Directory) command allows you to create a directory, and the RMDIR or RD (Remove Directory) command allows you to remove one. (RMDIR only works if a directory is empty.) The DOS TYPE command enables you to display the contents of text-based files to the monitor screen. Files such as CONFIG.SYS and AUTOEXEC.BAT can be displayed in this manner because they are comprised of ASCII text.

There are a few shortcuts built into DOS that allow a user to navigate DOS more efficiently. The most used are the F1 and F3 function keys. F1 causes the last command typed to be retrieved from the command buffer one character at a time. F3 retrieves the entire last command. Wildcard characters are also an important feature built into DOS. You can use the * (asterisk) when you know part of a filename but are unsure of multiple remaining characters or the location. You can use the ? in place of a single character.

Navigating Windows

For many users, navigating within a Windows environment is easier because of the many graphical tools at your disposal. For the most part, navigating within Windows is still a matter of knowing where you are located and knowing where you want to be. The difference is that inside the Windows interface, the use of the mouse supplements many normal keyboard commands.

The main means of navigating within Windows 3.x is the Program Manager. Program Manager initializes when Windows starts, and it displays groups of programs that you can select by double-clicking the mouse pointer on the desired icon. If you select File Manager from the Tools program group, you can manage files and directories just like you did in DOS, but with a graphical front end (see Figure 14.1).

In Windows 95, the primary means of navigation is not the Program Manager, but the Windows desktop. The Windows desktop is the gateway to a number of ways to do anything. For example, in DOS, you could execute commands only from the command line. In Windows 3.x, you could still use the command prompt to issue commands, or you could use the File Manager to select and launch executable files directly or via an icon. With Windows 95, there are multiple ways to perform any task. The command prompt is still available, but now you also can use the My Computer icon, the Start menu, or the Windows Explorer (see Figure 14.2).

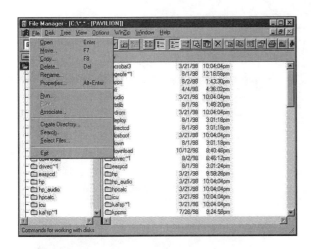

FIGURE 14.1
The File Manager's File menu contains the most common DOS commands.

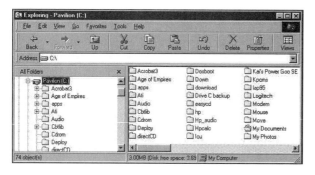

FIGURE 14.2
Windows 95 Explorer.

The Windows Explorer program is associated with virtually all objects inside of Windows 95, which makes it very simple for a user to manage files and directories and to obtain information. Selecting My Computer, for instance, links the user to the Windows Explorer.

The mouse also has a great impact on Windows 95 users. In Windows 3.x, only a single mouse button was effective. In Windows 95, the primary mouse button evokes the same kind of action it did in Windows 3.x, but the alternate mouse button brings up a context menu of shortcuts to common user functions, as shown in Figure 14.3.

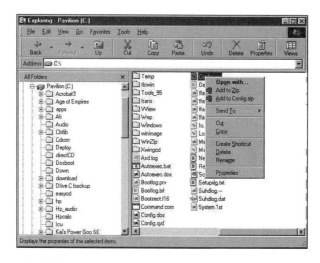

FIGURE 14.3
Windows 95 context menu.

From inside Windows 3.x and Windows 95, you now have the ability to find, copy, delete, rename, move, and perform any other needed function on a file or directory simply by accessing menus or using drag-and-drop functionality.

CREATING, VIEWING, AND MANAGING FILES

One way to manage files in all operating systems is by managing file attributes. Upon creation, all files have attributes already set. The four main file attributes are system, hidden, read-only, and archive.

The system file attribute is assigned to files used by the operating system. The system file attribute denotes that the system requires this file for normal operation.

The OS or the user can assign the hidden file attribute. Files that retain the hidden attribute are just that—hidden—which means they do not appear in a DOS directory list. The user can set Windows or Windows 95 to show hidden files in the File Manager and Explorer views. In the Windows 3.x File Manager, a red exclamation point denotes hidden files when they are displayed in the directory containing the file. In Windows 95, the hidden files appear as opaque icons.

The Archive file attribute denotes the file's backup status.

The Read-Only attribute designates files as read-only, which means users cannot make changes to the files.

The At A Glance table shows you how to view file attributes in each system.

At A Glance: Viewing File Attributes

Operating System	How to View File Attributes	How the Attributes Are Displayed
DOS	Use the DOS ATTRIB.EXE command.	-s –h –r -a.
Windows 3.x	Select the file and select Properties from the File pull-down menu.	A Properties dialog box appears.
Windows 95	Select the file and select Properties from the context menu.	Attributes are part of the Properties window.

The following DOS syntax enables you to view a file's attributes:

```
C:\>attrib IO.SYS
      SHR     IO.SYS          C:\IO.SYS

C:\>
```

Figure 14.4 shows how file attributes are displayed in the Windows 3.1 File Manager.

Windows 95 attributes are displayed on the properties sheet for each file. Figure 14.5 shows the properties of IO.SYS.

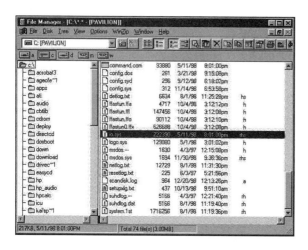

FIGURE 14.4
File attributes as displayed in Windows 3.x File Manager.

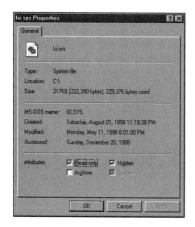

FIGURE 14.5
The IO.SYS properties sheet.

File Naming Conventions

To dig a little deeper into files, you should examine naming conventions. You must follow these file naming rules:

◆ All files must have a name.

◆ All names must be unique within their directory.

NOTE   If you have files of the same name in different directories and you decide to move one of them to the same location as the other, you will be prompted to overwrite the file in the destination folder.

◆ Filenames (in DOS and Windows 3.x) can be up to eight characters long with a three-character extension. Windows 95 supports long filenames of up to 255 characters, but Windows Explorer accepts only 250 characters.

◆ When using a filename in a command, you must use its extension.

◆ Some characters are not allowed in filenames. In DOS and Windows 3.x, these include the brackets, colon, semicolon, plus sign, equal sign, backslash, forward slash, and comma ([ ] : ; + = \ / ,). In Windows 95, you can use the comma, plus sign, brackets, and equal sign. However, Windows 95 does not allow the use of the backslash, forward slash, colon, asterisk, question mark, quotation marks, greater than sign, less than sign, and pipe. Figure 14.6 displays the Windows 95 error message listing the illegal filename characters.

FIGURE 14.6
The Windows 95 illegal filename characters.

◆ When telling DOS to carry out a command, you must specify the command, the location (if it does not exist in a directory in the path), and the drive on which to execute the command (depending on the type of command).

♦ To indicate a specific file, you must specify the drive, filename, and
extension, as in the following example:

```
(A:\filename.txt)
```

Disk Management

At the very ground level of disk management is the concept of partitioning. Hard disk drives generally need to be set up to accept an operating system. If you look at the file systems available to MS-DOS,
Windows 3.x, and Windows 95, you have a better idea of how disks must
be set up. MS-DOS (and more importantly, FAT16) cannot recognize
partitions larger than 2GB. Thus for a DOS formatted system, you must
make a partition smaller than 2GB. If you want to use FAT32, you can
create a partition up to 2,048GB.

You prepare hard disks for formatting by creating partitions with a DOS
utility called FDISK. From a bootable floppy disk with the FDISK.EXE
command, you can boot the system with COMMAND.COM on the floppy drive
and partition your hard disk (see Figure 14.7).

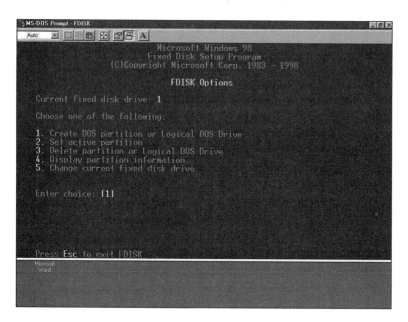

FIGURE 14.7
FDISK utility options.

The first time the system starts with its new partition, the operating system assigns the partition a drive letter. (The first drive usually becomes C:\.) If the partition is to be used as a bootable drive, it must be marked as active and formatted with the /s switch. (Remember that /s copies COMMAND.COM, IO.SYS, and MSDOS.SYS to the drive, making the drive bootable, but it does not copy program files.) After formatting a drive, you can install an operating system. You will learn more about operating system installation issues in Chapter 16.

Other utilities are available for keeping your system running at peak performance. The first of these is the ScanDisk utility.

ScanDisk is a disk maintenance utility that scans the disk's file allocation tables and checks the physical disk to see if the entries are correct. It gives you the option of correcting any errors that it finds. Common errors that it finds are FAT entry errors, cross-linked files, and physically bad sectors of the hard disk. Making sure that the disk is in good operating order is a great way to keep the system running at peak performance. All of the errors ScanDisk identifies have a significant impact on system performance. Figure 14.8 shows ScanDisk running under Windows 95.

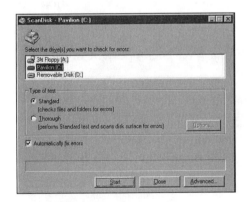

FIGURE 14.8
The ScanDisk utility.

Another way to maintain peak performance is to regularly defragment the hard drive. To do this, you use the DOS utility called Defrag. Defrag has gone through several interface changes from DOS, Windows 3.x, and Windows 95, but the functionality has remained the same.

When information is written to the hard drive, it is originally written to consecutive blocks on the disk. As files are deleted, this leaves open blocks on the hard drive. When a file is added to the disk, it is written to the first available free block and every free block following until the file is completely copied to the disk. If the file that was deleted was smaller than the file being copied to that space, the new file is fragmented and written to hard drive blocks that are not continuous. After a while, this slows programs down because added disk seek time is required to find where all the program file fragments reside. The defrag utility fixes this by reorganizing the files so they are located in continuous blocks.

There are occasions when preventive maintenance does not prevent disaster. This is when backup and restore utilities become invaluable. MS-DOS 6.x and higher shipped with a backup utility called MSBackup. Windows 3.x supported both MSBackup and a new backup utility that had a graphical Windows interface. Following suit, Windows 95 had a completely rewritten backup program. However, all iterations of MSBackup have one thing in common: They all provide an effective means of using tape media (or floppies) to keep copies of the information on your hard disk. The following are some important notes about MSBackup:

- Backup sets created in the various versions of MSBackup are recognizable only in the particular version in which they were created.

- Windows 95 Backup gives the option of backing up the system Registry. A restore of the Registry merges the current Registry and the backed up one.

Types of backups available to the system are outlined in the At A Glance box.

At A Glance: Comparison of Valid Backup Types

Backup Type	*What It Backs Up*	*How to Restore It*
Full	All selected files. Click this option to back up all the files that you have selected. If you want to back up only those files that are new or have changed since your last full backup, click New and Changed Files. This option backs up every file, regardless of the file's archive bit status. When the backup is complete, the archive bits are turned off.	Restore using the last full backup tape.
Differential	Backs up all the selected files that have changed since the last full backup. All files for which the archive bit is turned on are backed up. When the backup is complete, the archive bit(s) are left on.	Restore using the last full backup tape plus each differential up to the point of failure.
Incremental	Backs up all selected files that have changed since the most recent full or incremental backup. All files for which the archive bit is turned on are backed up. When the backup is complete, the archive bit(s) are turned off.	Restore using the last full backup plus each incremental since the point of failure.

WHAT IS IMPORTANT TO KNOW

♦ The function of DOS is to be the disk operating system. DOS is the interface between the computer hardware and the user.

♦ Windows 3.x is a shell that runs on top of DOS. Its function is to provide a graphical user interface and to better manage program resource management.

♦ Windows 95 is a combination of DOS and Windows 3.x. It functions as both the operating system and the graphical user interface. Windows 95 provides better program control and system stability.

♦ The major components of DOS are IO.SYS, MSDOS.SYS, and COMMAND.COM. These files are required to boot the system. CONFIG.SYS and AUTOEXEC.BAT are system configuration files. EMM386.EXE and HIMEM.SYS are DOS memory configuration files. ANSI.SYS and KEYBOARD.SYS are user interface configuration files. Common internal commands that are part of COMMAND.COM are VER, CLS, DIR, CD, COPY, DEL, MD, MORE, PATH, PROMPT, REN, and TYPE.

♦ Windows 3.x runs on top of DOS, so Windows 3.x also needs all files that are needed to run DOS. Some files, such as EMM386.EXE and HIMEM.SYS, have been updated since the initial DOS release and have Windows counterparts. Using the Windows counterparts makes the system more efficient. The major components of Windows 3.x are KRNLxxx.EXE, USER.EXE, GDI.EXE, WIN.COM, and PROGMAN.EXE. These files are required to launch Windows. Windows needs WIN.INI, SYSTEM.INI, and PROGMAN.INI, which are the Windows configuration files.

♦ Windows 95 requires its own version of MSDOS.SYS, IO.SYS, and COMMAND.COM. As in DOS, these files are required to boot the system. Windows 95 does not require CONFIG.SYS and AUTOEXEC.BAT, but it does use them for backward compatibility with older DOS/Windows 3.x programs.

♦ Windows 95 has its own versions of WIN.COM, USER.EXE, and GDI.EXE. The Windows 95 operating system uses the system Registry instead of INI files for configuration. You can access the Registry with the Regedit utility. USER.DAT and SYSTEM.DAT are the user- and system-specific Registry files.

♦ Windows 3.x is a 16-bit shell that runs on top of DOS. Windows 3.x uses cooperative multitasking. The primary user interface is Program Manager. Windows 3.x uses the DOS memory management model based on conventional memory and a swap file. Pressing Ctrl+Alt+Del reboots the system.

◆ Windows 95 is a 32-bit operating system. The primary user interface is Windows Explorer. Windows 95 utilizes preemptive multitasking for all programs but emulates cooperative multitasking for 16-bit programs. Windows 95 utilizes a more efficient swap file than its Windows 3.x predecessor. Pressing Ctrl+Alt+Del accesses the Task Manager and allows you to shut down non-responsive programs.

NOTE

For greater clarification of the use of Ctrl+Alt+Del, see the Fast Facts Review under system lockup.

◆ IO.SYS is responsible for loading real-mode drivers and terminate-and-stay resident programs (TSRs) specified in the CONFIG.SYS and AUTOEXEC.BAT files. (In other words, it loads input and output devices—thus the name IO.SYS.)

◆ MSDOS.SYS is responsible for communication between internal computer components.

◆ COMMAND.COM is the command interpreter that actually interprets commands from the keyboard and decides how they should be executed.

◆ CONFIG.SYS is responsible for providing DOS with system hardware configuration information. CONFIG.SYS is where memory management begins as well.

◆ AUTOEXEC.BAT contains commands and final configuration settings in a DOS system.

◆ ANSI.SYS is a device driver in CONFIG.SYS that enables the system to recognize the ANSI character set.

◆ EMM386.EXE enables the system to recognize memory above 640KB.

◆ HIMEM.SYS is the device driver that enables DOS to use the high memory area (memory above 640KB).

◆ KRNLxxx.EXE controls the PC's memory and I/O resources and loads Windows. It is also known as the Windows kernel.

◆ WIN.COM launches Windows. It coordinates the efforts of KRNL386.EXE, USER.EXE, and GDI.EXE into the Windows interface familiar to most computer users.

◆ WIN.INI is the initialization file containing the information on the appearance and behavior of Windows.

- SYSTEM.INI contains configuration information about the available devices.

- PROGMAN.INI contains configuration information about the appearance and behavior of Program Manager.

- PROGMAN.EXE is the Windows 3.x Program Manager program.

- USER.EXE controls the user interface in Windows. It is responsible for interpreting commands from the mouse, keyboard, and COM ports.

- GDI.EXE controls all the graphics display functions of Windows.

- IO.SYS is the same as IO.SYS for DOS, only for Windows 95.

- MSDOS.SYS for Windows 95 is virtually the same as its DOS predecessor. In Windows 95, you can edit and manipulate MSDOS.SYS to allow for various menu options.

- COMMAND.COM in Windows 95 is simply an updated version of the DOS COMMAND.COM. Issuing the VER command from a Windows 95 command prompt would return the version number of DOS as 7.0. Newer versions of Windows 95 return the version number as Windows 95. You can use REGEDIT.EXE to edit the Windows 95 Registry.

- SYSTEM.DAT is the hidden system file that contains system information from the Registry.

- USER.DAT is the hidden system file that contains user information from the Registry.

- DOS navigation consists primarily of command line executables like CD, DIR, MD, COPY, and DEL.

- In Windows 3.x, navigation is performed with Program Manager and File Manager. The File Manager interface offers all major DOS commands from the pull-down menus. File Manager is a graphical representation of the computer's file system hierarchy.

- The main means of navigating Windows 95 is the Windows Explorer interface. Explorer is a blend of Windows 3.x Program Manager and File Manager. All DOS commands are available from both pull-down menus and context menus. For those users who are uncomfortable with the graphical interface, navigating through a DOS window is possible. Although this type of navigation was not covered in this book or on the exam, keyboard commands are available for navigating Windows 95 as well. For more information on using keyboard commands, refer to the Windows 95 user manual.

- You can view file attributes of Windows 95 objects by selecting the object in Explorer, right-clicking, and selecting Properties (or by simply selecting Properties from the pull-down menu). This displays the file attributes and allows you to modify them if desired. Explorer allows you to create folders and populate them by selecting objects in Explorer and dragging them to the folders.

♦ Filenames in DOS and Windows 3.x can be eight characters long with a three-character extension. Windows 95 supports long filenames of up to 255 characters, but Windows Explorer only accepts 250 characters. Some characters are not allowed in filenames. In DOS and Windows 3.x the brackets, colon, semicolon, plus sign, equal sign, backslash, forward slash, and comma ([ ] : ; + = \ / ,) are not allowed. In Windows 95 you can use the comma, plus sign, brackets, and equal sign. However, Windows 95 does not allow the use of the backslash, forward slash, colon, asterisk, question mark, quotation marks, greater than sign, less than sign, and pipe.

Here's a summary of the file naming rules by operation system:

	DOS	**Windows 3.x**	**Windows 95**
Filename limitation	8 characters long with a 3-character extension	8 characters long with a 3-character extension	supports long filenames of up to 255 characters
Invalid characters	[ ] : ; + = \ / , < > | * ? "	[ ] : ; + = \ / , < > | * ? "	\ / : * ? " < > |

♦ Command syntax in DOS, Windows 3.x, and Windows 95 is primarily the same. Spelling counts: If a command is spelled wrong, it will not be recognized. If you do not know the appropriate syntax, help is available by typing the command followed by /? (in DOS 6 or higher). For most commands, this is a valid switch that will display the proper syntax.

♦ System, Hidden, Read-Only, and Archive attributes are the common attributes that can be assigned to a file. The System attribute designates a system file. Setting the Hidden file attribute hides the file from default views. The Read-Only attribute makes a file read-only; users cannot modify it. The Archive attribute denotes the file's backup status.

♦ Backing up your computer requires a floppy drive, tape drive, or available network storage. DOS 6.x, Windows 3.x, and Windows 95 all have built-in backup software. Note, however, that the backup sets from any built-in software are not compatible with any other backup software.

♦ To format a disk, you designate a drive and use the DOS FORMAT command. You cannot format the drive that is executing the FORMAT command.

- To partition a disk, you use the FDISK utility. A disk must be partitioned before it can be formatted.

- Defragmenting a drive on a regular basis helps to ensure peak computer performance. Use the DEFRAG program in DOS/Windows3.x and in Windows 95.

- The ScanDisk utility verifies that the file system and physical disk are in proper working order. Run ScanDisk if you suspect that the hard drive may be failing, and it will locate bad blocks.

- FAT32 is an alternate file system available only in Windows 95 version OSR2. FAT32 uses 4KB blocks to maximize disk performance for the operating system. FAT32-formatted drives are recognizable only to Windows 95 OSR2 and Windows 95 OSR2-created boot disks. All operating systems can recognize a FAT32 formatted drive that is shared across a network. This works because Windows 95 OSR2 controls the sharing. FAT32 recognizes and is able to format drives greater than 2GB in size. FAT32 FDISK can create a partition larger than 2GB.

- FAT (file allocation tables) is the default file system of DOS and Windows 95 version A. FAT is recognizable to all operating systems both locally and from the network. FAT recognizes only partitions less than 2GB in size. FAT FDISK allows only a maximum 2GB partition. FAT block sizes depend on the partition size, but the minimum is 16KB blocks, which makes the block size four times that of FAT32.

- VFAT is the 32-bit Virtual File Allocation Table file system used by Windows 95's Virtual Memory Manager. It is created, placed in RAM, and utilized by Windows 95 and is not actually a file system with which a drive can be formatted.

OBJECTIVES

▶ Know the types of memory used by DOS, Windows 3.x, and Windows 95.

▶ Recognize the potential for memory address conflicts.

▶ Understand why a memory conflict happens.

▶ Describe a general protection fault and an illegal operation.

▶ Identify and use the appropriate memory management utilities for a given situation.

CHAPTER 15

Memory Management

TYPES OF MEMORY

This chapter discusses the different types of memory available to DOS and Windows environments and how each system uses memory. First, let's learn about the different types of memory.

In the original microcomputer design, it was thought that everything that people would ever need to do could be accomplished using 1MB of memory. The first 640KB of memory were reserved for use by DOS, while kilobytes 641 to 1024 were reserved for use by the system's BIOS and peripheral devices. This allowed the 8088 processor to utilize the full 1MB of RAM. As microprocessors became more powerful, they gained the ability to address more than a single megabyte. DOS, however, retained the original limitation of 1MB to maintain backward compatibility.

The following paragraphs discuss the different types of memory.

Conventional Memory

Conventional memory consists of two areas. The first 640KB is referred to as base memory, and the remaining 384KB is referred to as the Upper Memory Area. Base memory is the common operating area for PC-compatible systems and usually contains DOS, relocated ROM BIOS tables, and Interrupt Vector Tables. DOS programs utilize the remaining base memory space. The upper memory area, hexadecimal addresses A0000h to FFFFFH, is divided into 64KB blocks called Upper Memory Blocks (UMBs). Upper memory was originally used for video display memory and ROM-based functions.

Shadow RAM

Shadow RAM is when ROM BIOS or Video BIOS is written (shadowed) to the Upper Memory Blocks. This increases system performance by having programs access the shadow RAM rather than the slower actual BIOS.

Extended Memory

Once the 80286 processor was developed, computers could address more than a single megabyte of RAM. This new memory area, megabytes 2 through 16, is referred to as extended memory. 80386 and 80486 processors can address up to 4GB of extended memory. The 286 PC's ability to address RAM up to 16MB presented a dilemma for programmers. DOS-based programs were capable of addressing this new memory, but DOS was not. This problem lead to DOS 4.0, which had a new memory manager called HIMEM.SYS.

HIMEM.SYS was designed according to Microsoft's Extended Memory Specification (XMS). When HIMEM.SYS is launched, it allows the operating system to utilize the extended memory area known as the High Memory Area (HMA). Statements such as DOS=UMB and DOS=HIGH in CONFIG.SYS make the space usable. Windows 95 does not require these statements.

HIMEM.SYS takes control of the system's A20 interrupt handler (which is loaded at INT15) and manages the transfer of 64KB data blocks between the system and extended memory. INT15 also handles entries for microprocessor tables required for protected virtual addressing mode.

Expanded Memory

In 1985, Lotus, Intel, and Microsoft joined forces to address the issue of the 1MB limit. This summit lead to the development of what is today known as expanded memory specification or LIM (because of its creators) EMS. LIM EMS utilized memory areas that were outside the DOS memory area (by switching banks) but that were still addressable by the 8088 processor. EMM386 utilizes LIM.

Virtual Memory

Virtual memory refers to the use of hard drive space to trick the computer into using more memory than it really has. This is achieved through the use of what is called a swap file (sometimes referred to as a page file). The computer caches information into memory as it is needed, filling RAM with frequently used information.

Calling upon that information in RAM helps system performance, because retrieving from RAM is faster than retrieving from the hard disk. When RAM gets full, it writes or "swaps" the least-used information currently in RAM to a special area on the hard drive, thus freeing up RAM real estate. If the information that has been written to the swap file is then accessed, the virtual memory manager then retrieves the data from the swap file and enters it back into RAM. The virtual memory manager does this swapping without the program's knowing that the data was ever absent from RAM. Although utilizing virtual memory is slower than RAM, it is quicker than accessing data from the hard drive, because the virtual memory manager always knows where the data is in the swap file, reducing disk seek time.

At A Glance: Types of Memory

Memory Type	Where It Is
Conventional or "base" memory	From 0 to 640KB of the first megabyte
Extended memory from 2 to 16MB RAM	The addressable area above the first megabyte
Expanded memory	The addressable memory above 1MB gained by switching between two banks of memory chips
Upper memory	Memory above 640KB. Also called high memory
Virtual memory	Using disk space as memory

Other important memory factors are memory configuration options that are defined in CONFIG.SYS. The first of these options is the FILES= line. The FILES= line determines how many files can be open at any given time. The minimum number of files needed to run Windows is 30.

The next line that affects system memory is the BUFFERS= line. The buffers set aside memory to be used for disk buffers and are directly accessible by the processor.

Finally, the stacks command sets this special RAM storage area to be 64 memory stacks that are 500 bytes long—for example, Stacks=9264.

IDENTIFYING MEMORY CONFLICTS

Memory conflicts can be a very detrimental problem when dealing with programs. This section explores the causes of common memory problems.

What Is a Memory Conflict?

A memory conflict occurs when one device or process accesses memory that is being used by another device or process.

For example, suppose a user replaces an old video card with a new one from a different manufacturer. The new card uses a different memory address than the old one. When the PC boots, the system fails to load Windows, because the address space that the new card expects to have access to is being occupied by another device. Symptoms of a memory conflict include system lock-up, error messages, and the "blue screen" error message (also known as the "blue screen of death," or BSOD).

The General Protection Fault or GPF first became a problem when Windows 3.0 was released. It occurs when Windows attempts to access an unallocated memory area. The GPF corrupts the data in the violated memory space, and Windows usually has to be restarted. In Windows 3.1, a GPF generated an error message containing information about the fault and what program it involved. This helped you troubleshoot the problem. Not all GPFs are fatal ones (which force you to reboot). Minor faults let you ignore the error and continue or save your work. Applications are rarely fully functional following a fault.

Windows 95 greatly reduces the occurrences of general protection faults because of its unique manner of allocating resources to the system. Windows 95 avoids memory conflicts by assigning resources to Plug and Play devices every time a system boots. In addition to dynamic resource allocation, Windows 95's 32-bit system architecture gives applications their own area of memory in which to operate, known as the *virtual machine*. The virtual machine actually stops a program that tries to damage system integrity by causing a fault. If the (32-bit) application succeeds in creating a GPF, it is shut down without affecting other applications. 16-bit applications all run within the same virtual machine (shared memory space). Because of this, if one 16-bit application fails, it can affect the other 16-bit applications that are running.

Occasionally, an error will occur that locks up the system or does not display an error message. This is an optimal time to employ system utilities to aid in diagnosing the problem. We will discuss the utilities used to troubleshoot DOS and Windows in Chapter 17, "Diagnosing and Troubleshooting." Right now, let's focus on programs that help optimize memory and system performance.

With DOS and Windows 3.x programs depending on that initial first megabyte of memory, a wide range of products became available for memory management. A common user complaint is "I get a memory error saying that I am out of memory, but I have 16MB of RAM. How can that be?" Well, because DOS is concerned with only the first megabyte, it's easy to fathom how this happens, but a 486 PC with 16MB of RAM running out of memory is very difficult for users to understand. Although more than 1MB is installed, the DOS/Windows 3.x system is still bound by the constraint of conventional memory. Therefore, Windows 3.x has 16 mirror images of that first megabyte that it tricks programs into using. Since this is the case, it is very important to manage conventional memory to its fullest potential.

Optimizing DOS requires the use of a memory manager such as HIMEM.SYS to manage the use of extended memory in the system. HIMEM.SYS must be loaded before any other memory manager or device driver in CONFIG.SYS.

To access expanded memory, an additional memory manager is required. Usually this is EMM386.EXE, but it can also be a third-party utility such as Quarterdeck's QMEM memory manager. These memory managers work together to free as much conventional memory as possible by loading device drivers and portions of DOS into the High Memory Area. If you add the line DOS=HIGH, UMB to CONFIG.SYS, the portions of DOS that can be moved to HMA will be moved. EMM386.EXE allows for the utilization of expanded memory blocks and upper memory.

As you have seen thus far, optimizing conventional memory requires a reorganization of where device drivers and programs are placed. When you deal with this type of memory management, you need to know what a program's load size is versus its run size. A driver's load size is the amount of memory it takes to start and load into memory. The run size is the amount of memory the driver occupies after having started.

You can use the DIR command at the C:\WINDOWS> prompt to see a driver's physical size and its load size:

```
dir Himem.sys
```

Here's the output from this command:

```
Volume in drive C is PAVILION
Volume Serial Number is 3B1E-1D03
Directory of C:\WINDOWS
HIMEM.SYS      33,191  05-11-98  8:01p HIMEM.SYS
1 file(s)      33,191 bytes
0 dir(s)    4,381.61 MB free
```

Once the program is running, you can use the mem /c command to see the program's run size, as shown here:

```
Modules using memory below 1 MB:
Name          Total          Conventional     Upper Memory
........       .............  .............    .............
 SYSTEM       39,744  (39K)    10,608  (10K)    29,136  (28K)
 HIMEM         1,168   (1K)     1,168   (1K)         0   (0K)
 EMM386        4,320   (4K)     4,320   (4K)         0   (0K)
 DBLBUFF       2,976   (3K)     2,976   (3K)         0   (0K)
 WIN           3,712   (4K)     3,712   (4K)         0   (0K)
 vmm32        29,824  (29K)     1,840   (2K)    27,984  (27K)
 COMMAND       8,496   (8K)     8,496   (8K)         0   (0K)
 IFSHLP        2,864   (3K)         0   (0K)     2,864   (3K)
 Free        621,984 (607K)   621,984 (607K)         0   (0K)
```

Knowing the load and run sizes when manually managing memory is important because of what is called the *load window*. The load window is the amount of free upper memory that is available. (You use the MEM command to find this out as well.) Assume that you have three programs to load into upper memory:

- FIRST.EXE has a load size of 8KB and a run size of 4KB.

- SECOND.EXE has a load size of 10KB and a run size of 4KB.

- THIRD.EXE has a load size of 11KB and a run size of 5KB.

You have a load window of 13KB. You can load any of these three programs through the window, because all the load sizes are smaller than 13KB. If you load the 11KB program first, the 5KB run size is subtracted from your load window, making your new load window 8K. Now the only program you can load is the 8KB program, because you don't have enough space free to load the 10KB program, even though you have enough space to run it.

If you had loaded the 8KB program first, you would have reduced the load window to only 9KB, preventing you from loading either of the remaining programs. This example proves that when you're managing memory, load order is very important.

DOS 6 and higher shipped with a simple memory management utility called MEMMAKER.EXE. It analyzed what drivers were loading, compared that to the available upper memory, and made recommendations on optimizing memory. This was a great way to optimize your PC memory and make more conventional memory available to DOS and

Windows. Because MEMMAKER.EXE didn't analyze load order, it wasn't a replacement for tedious manual memory optimization, but it did make more conventional memory available.

Another system optimization utility is Smart Drive. It's available to MS-DOS 5.0 and higher and is integrated into Windows 95. Smart Drive (SMRTDRV.SYS) is not so much a utility as a device driver that uses extended memory as a disk cache for data read from the hard drive. Because RAM is faster than disk speeds, Smart Drive greatly increases performance. Smart Drive redirects requests aimed at the disk drive to the cache area. If the information needed is in cache, it is used. If not, Smart Drive redirects the request to the hard drive. Smart Drive copies all cached information back to disk when the system shuts down so that no data is lost. The available switches are listed in Table 15.1.

TABLE 15.1

SWITCHES FOR SMART DRIVE

Switch	Its Function
/X	Disables write-behind caching for all drives.
drive	Sets caching options on specific drive(s). The specified drive(s) will have write-behind caching disabled unless you add +.
+	Enables write-behind caching for the specified drive.
-	Disables all caching for the specified drive.
/U	Doesn't load the CD-ROM caching module.
/C	Writes all the information currently in the write cache to the hard disk.
/R	Clears the cache and restarts Smart Drive.
/F	Writes cached data before the command prompt returns (default).
/N	Doesn't write cached data before the command prompt returns.
/L	Prevents Smart Drive from loading itself into upper memory.
/V	Displays Smart Drive status messages when loading.
/Q	Doesn't display status information.
/S	Displays additional information about Smart Drive's status.
InitCacheSize	Specifies XMS memory (in kilobytes) for the cache.
WinCacheSize	Specifies XMS memory (in kilobytes) for the cache with Windows.
/E:ElementSize	Specifies how many bytes of information to move at one time.
/B:BufferSize	Specifies the size of the read-ahead buffer.

A device driver similar to SMRTDRV.SYS, RAMDRIVE.SYS actually lets you create a logical disk drive from available system RAM and assign it a drive letter. A RAM drive doesn't copy its contents to the real drive upon shut-down. Anything in the RAM drive is lost when the system is powered down. Both Smart Drive and RAM drive are governed by HIMEM.SYS.

In Windows 95, the system's architecture and the virtual memory manager handle all memory management and disk caching. Microsoft doesn't recommend adjusting the virtual memory manually. Windows 95 does a very good job of managing the system resources. However, if you suspect a problem with the way Windows 95 is passing out system resources, you should run the Windows 95 System Monitor. System Monitor doesn't get installed if you choose the Typical installation of Windows 95. You can add it using the Add/Remove Programs icon in the Windows 95 Control Panel. System Monitor is located in the System Tools program group. It is used to check performance related to disk activity, processor activity, and memory utilization. Figure 15.1 shows the Windows 95 System Monitor menu.

Although System Monitor cannot optimize the system, it is a great source of information about memory, disk, and processor usage. Note that a large amount of disk activity in Windows 95 does not necessarily indicate a disk problem.

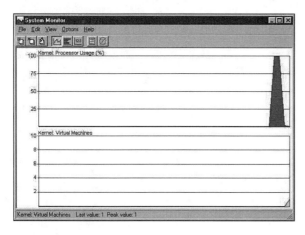

FIGURE 15.1
The Windows 95 System Monitor.

Remember that virtual memory uses disk space to trick the system into thinking it has more RAM than it actually does. Thus, a lot of disk activity in Windows 95 might indicate that you need to add RAM. (More RAM equals less swapping data to disk.)

NOTE Although Windows 95 can address up to 4GB of physical RAM in a computer, it can access and use only up to 2GB.

NOTE The 2GB limitation is theoretical. If you encounter any problems using more than 1GB of RAM, see the following article in the Microsoft Knowledge Base:

ARTICLE-ID: Q184447

TITLE: Insufficient Memory to Initialize Windows

WHAT IS IMPORTANT TO KNOW

- Conventional memory is the first 640KB of the first megabyte of memory.

- Upper memory is the remaining 360KB of the first megabyte of memory.

- Extended memory is the memory from 2–16MB that can be addressed by 286 or faster processors.

- High memory is the memory area that is enabled by HIMEM.SYS that is usable by DOS. High memory is memory above 640KB.

- Expanded memory is memory that is not used by DOS but can still be addressed by 8088 processors. This is defined by the LIM EMS standard.

- Virtual memory makes use of a swap file. A swap file is managed by Windows and cheats the system into using hard disk space as memory.

- A memory conflict occurs when one device or process accesses memory that is being used by another device or process. General protection faults and invalid page faults are common memory conflicts.

- Conflicts happen because the operating system is unaware of the memory addressing requirements of one or more programs or devices. This increases the potential for a memory overlap.

- Use utilities as a means of troubleshooting and diagnosis. The DOS MEM command and MSD are good memory troubleshooting utilities.

- General protection faults (GPFs) occur when Windows attempts to access an unallocated memory area. The GPF corrupts the data in the violated memory space, and Windows usually has to be restarted. In Windows 3.1, GPFs generated an error message giving information about the fault and what program it involved. This greatly aided troubleshooting the problem. Not all GPFs are fatal (force you to reboot); minor faults will let you ignore the error and continue or save your work. Applications are rarely fully functional following a fault.

- You can optimize memory by running DOS MemMaker to move as many programs as possible out of conventional memory. A more efficient means of optimizing memory is to do it manually. MemMaker is not able to reorganize programs into a different load order, which means that some programs that could fit into upper memory cannot be put there in the current load order. Manually rearranging the load order will help guarantee the best use of upper memory.

- System Monitor is a Windows 95 utility that allows you to monitor memory, processor, and disk utilization.

- HIMEM.SYS is the driver loaded in CONFIG.SYS that enables the use of upper memory blocks or UMB.

- SMARTDRV is a disk caching utility/device driver available in DOS and Windows 95 that uses extended memory as a disk cache for data read from the hard drive. This increases disk performance because accessing RAM is faster than accessing the hard disk controller.

- EMM386.EXE (expanded memory blocks) is a device driver that is loaded from CONFIG.SYS that enables the use of expanded and extended memory.

OBJECTIVES

▶ Identify procedures for installing, configuring, and upgrading DOS, Windows 3.x, and Windows 95.

▶ Identify the boot sequence of DOS, Windows 3.x, and Windows 95.

▶ Bring DOS, Windows 3.x, and Windows 95 to a basic operational level.

▶ Select and run the appropriate setup utility for a given situation.

▶ Know the steps to perform before upgrading.

▶ Upgrade from DOS to Windows 95.

▶ Upgrade Windows 3.x to Windows 95.

▶ Identify the boot sequences.

▶ Identify different ways to boot the systems.

▶ Identify the files that are required to boot.

▶ Create emergency boot disks.

▶ Create a Windows 95 startup disk.

▶ Understand what Safe Mode is.

▶ Understand what DOS mode is.

▶ continues...

CHAPTER 16

Installation, Configuration, and Upgrading

OBJECTIVES continued

▶ Identify procedures for loading/adding/removing device drivers for

 ◆ Windows 3.x.

 ◆ Windows 95.

 ◆ Plug and Play.

▶ Identify procedures for changing options and for configuring and using the Windows printing subsystem.

▶ Identify procedures for installing and launching applications in

 ◆ DOS.

 ◆ Windows 3.x.

 ◆ Windows 95.

INSTALLATION

As you learned in Chapter 14, "Function, Structure, Operation, and File Management," in order to install the operating system, you must have a hard disk that has been partitioned and formatted with a file system that the new OS will recognize. For example, if a drive is formatted with FAT32, the only OS that can be installed is Windows 95 OSR2 because OSR2 is the only OS that recognizes FAT32 as a valid partition.

Let's discuss installation procedures.

DOS

Although DOS has evolved throughout the years, in terms of media, there are still relatively few options. The original version of DOS was available only on 360KB 5 1/4-inch floppy disks, and the final release is available only on 3 1/2-inch floppy disks.

For the latest version of MS-DOS (6.22), the installation is fairly straight-forward. With a newly partitioned (with FAT16) and formatted disk, you simply boot the system with the first disk of the installation set in the floppy disk drive. This invokes DOS Setup, which will create the DOS directory, copy the DOS files to the DOS directory, and copy COMMAND.COM, IO.SYS, MSDOS.SYS, and DRVSPACE.BIN (MSDOS 6.0 uses DBLSPACE.BIN; all versions since use DRV-SPACE.BIN) to track one of the hard drives to make it bootable. The Setup routine prompts you to change disks when needed; and at the end, it prompts you to boot your computer using the newly installed DOS operating system.

Upgrading from an older version of DOS is slightly different in the sense that you run Setup (SETUP.EXE) from the command prompt instead of having to boot the PC from the first floppy disk. Once the upgrade begins, it does not differ from the fresh installation.

Windows 3.x

Unlike Windows 95, Windows 3.x must operate in conjunction with DOS and is not capable of operating on its own. Because of this, all of the installation requirements of DOS (except hardware) affect Windows

3.x. Windows (all versions) runs best when a swap file is used. Therefore, it runs best on a 386 PC with 2MB RAM or more. Windows will run on a 286 PC, but it will not use virtual memory due to limitations of the computer.

When you have a partitioned hard disk and DOS is installed, you can install Windows 3.x. Like DOS, Windows 3.x is primarily available on 3 1/2-inch or 5 1/4-inch floppy disks (when Windows was released, CD-ROM was not a widely used medium). On a system on which Windows is not already installed, you run the setup.exe command on the first floppy to start the Setup program. The Setup routine then guides you through changing floppies when needed; choosing what directory to install Windows in (usually c:\Windows); specifying what kind of video, keyboard, and mouse the system has; and modifying CONFIG.SYS and AUTOEXEC.BAT to support Windows 3.x. Near the end of Setup, the Windows Program Manager starts, and program groups are created. When Setup is finished, you are prompted to remove all floppies and reboot under the new combined power of DOS and Windows.

Windows upgrades run much the same as the fresh installation, simply overwriting files that already exist.

Windows 95

Windows 95 was released in 1995 and was a new innovation as far as operating systems are concerned. It offered vast differences from the DOS and Windows 3.x worlds. Windows 95 offers users 32-bit disk and file access while eliminating calls from DOS and BIOS, thus greatly improving performance over its predecessors. Plug and Play hardware detection was also a new feature Windows 95 brought to the OS world. All these improvements come at the price of higher minimum hardware requirements.

At A Glance: Windows 95 System Requirements

Processor	Memory	Hard Disk Space	OS for Upgrade Path	Video	Install Media Options
80386 DX20	4MB minimum; 8MB recommended; 24MB optimal	35–55MB free	DOS 3.21 or greater; MS-DOS 5.0 recommended	VGA or better	Floppy or CD-ROM

Although a mouse is not required, it is highly recommended because without one, the user would have to learn many complicated keyboard commands.

Hardware requirements aside, the Windows 95 installation functions in much the same way as a DOS installation. The first option is like that of DOS and a new hard disk. When you have a partitioned and formatted hard drive, you can install Windows 95. The installation media for Windows 95 is available on both floppy disk and CD-ROM. The better installation choice is CD-ROM because of the speed and ease it brings to the installation process.

To install from DOS, follow these steps:

1. Place the first floppy disk in drive A: or insert the CD-ROM in the CD drive.

2. Change to the drive where the setup files reside.

3. Type **SETUP.EXE** at the command prompt.

4. Answer the Setup screens.

To install from Windows 3.x, follow these steps:

1. From the Windows Program Manager, pull down the File menu, select Run, and type the path to SETUP.EXE on the Windows 95 media.

2. Answer the Setup screens.

> **NOTE**
>
> This is the recommended way of upgrading from Windows 3.x to Windows 95 because all Windows drivers are loaded. This makes the Windows 95 device detection phase more effective.

Three distinct stages of Setup ensue after the setup process has begun.

- *Phase One is the gathering of system information.* The user is prompted to provide this information or to at least verify it.

- *Phase Two is the copying of Windows 95 files.* These files are determined by the PC's hardware configuration and the information gathered in Phase One.

♦ *Phase Three is the final installation phase.* The computer is rebooted under the control of the new operating system and makes final adjustments to complete the installation process.

Gathering Information Phase

At the beginning of the gathering information phase, Windows 95 prompts you for your CD key or OEM license number, some basic information about your PC, and the location of where you want to install Windows 95. Setup also gives you some other options about the type of setup you would like. The choices include Typical, Portable, Compact, and Custom.

Typical setup is the default option and is recommended for most users. Most steps in the Typical setup are performed automatically. The only interaction required is to provide user and PC information, the installation directory, and whether or not you want to create a startup disk.

Portable setup installs the optimum set of files for use with a laptop computer, including the Windows 95 Briefcase and direct cable connection files.

Compact setup is just that: compact. This option installs only the files needed to run Windows 95—no accessories.

Custom setup allows the user the most freedom of choice. Selecting Custom setup allows you to make decisions regarding everything from application settings to network options. Custom setup is for experienced users that want more control of the way in which Windows 95 is loaded.

At A Glance: Overview of Installation Types

Typical	Little user intervention. Installs the most popular components.
Portable	Optimized for the laptop computer. Installs Briefcase and direct cable connection.
Compact	Installs the bare minimum required to run Windows 95.
Custom	Allows the user almost total control over what is installed.

The last stage of the gathering information phase is that of hardware detection. Windows 95 uses several methods for determining what hardware and drivers the system has and will use. Windows 95 checks the CONFIG.SYS, AUTOEXEC.BAT, WIN.INI, SYSTEM.INI, and

PROTOCOL.INI to determine what devices the previous version of Windows loaded. Next, it checks for Plug and Play devices by using programs called *bus enumerators*. Bus enumerators are designed to search for devices on specific system buses. (Examples include the PCI bus enumerator, ISA bus enumerator, and VESA bus enumerator.) The bus enumerator polls its bus looking for devices. If a device responds to the enumerator, that information is passed to Setup. The information found during hardware detection eventually ends up in the device list.

Copying Files Phase

The file-copying phase is the portion of Setup where old DOS/Windows 3.x files are upgraded to their newer 32-bit Windows 95 counterparts. A power failure during this phase of Setup could leave the system in an unbootable state. The type of setup chosen during Phase One dictates what files are copied during this phase. If this installation is an upgrade from Windows 3.x, you will be given the option of saving your old DOS/Windows 3.x files in case you want to uninstall Windows 95 and restore your system to its previous state. If you do not save these files, you cannot uninstall Windows 95.

Restarting the PC and Final Installation

The final phase of Setup occurs after the file copying phase is complete and the user is prompted to reboot. When the PC restarts, it is operating under the Windows 95 versions of COMMAND.COM, IO.SYS, and MSDOS.SYS. When Windows 95 starts for the first time, it assigns system resources to the devices it found during hardware detection and makes those devices available to the user. Finally, the Start menu is created, as are program groups and the default user interface settings.

Steps to Be Performed Before an Upgrade

You can take several steps to avoid trouble during an installation:

1. Scan the system for viruses before you begin the upgrade, and then shut down the virus program. If the PC has a CMOS-based antivirus program, it must be disabled as well. The reason is that when Windows 95 upgrades the boot sector, the antivirus software sees this as a potential virus attack, and Setup will stop.

2. Run ScanDisk (or Chkdsk) to ensure that the hard disk is in good order.

3. Make sure that there is enough free disk space to do the upgrade. (100–110MB is recommended; you'll need 110–120MB if you are saving the DOS/Windows 3.x information.)

4. Make sure that all your hardware and software is functioning correctly.

5. Shut down running programs, including TSRs and screen savers.

6. Make a backup of all your system files (CONFIG.SYS, AUTOEXEC.BAT, WIN.INI, and SYSTEM.INI).

7. Remove unnecessary lines in CONFIG.SYS and AUTOEXEC.BAT.

8. Remark out LOAD= and RUN= lines in the WINI.INI by placing a semicolon (;) in front of the lines.

9. Remove programs from the startup group. If they are needed, they can be added after the upgrade.

10. If at all possible, run Setup from within Windows 3.x.

Other issues of which to be aware during upgrade include dual-booting and migrating user environment settings or profiles. Dual-booting is covered in greater detail in this chapter in the section on different ways to boot the system. Both of these situations require some thought because one affects the other.

At A Glance: Dual-Booting and Migrating

Feature	Install Windows 95 in a new folder	Upgrade Windows 3.x to Windows 95
Dual-boot	Yes	No
Maintain current user profiles	No	Yes

If you choose to install Windows 95 in a new folder, existing user preferences will not migrate into Windows 95. Therefore, you will have to reinstall all of your applications into the Windows 95 directory, duplicating the application on your hard drive. This does create a dual-boot situation, however. So in essence, you will have two operating systems and two full sets of apps.

If you choose to install Windows 95 in the current Windows folder, all user and application information is migrated. In this situation, you will have one operating system and one set of apps.

THE BOOT SEQUENCE

When you're preparing for this exam, it is important that you understand the different events related to the system's boot process. The following section covers the boot sequence for DOS, Windows 3.x, and Windows 95.

DOS

When power is applied to the computer system, the PC begins its power on self-test (or POST) routine. Once the system passes the POST, control is passed to the system BIOS, which searches for the master boot record, or MBR, on the active partition. If the hard disk has DOS installed, control is passed to COMMAND.COM to continue processing DOS startup.

Windows 3.x

If Windows 3.x is installed, when COMMAND.COM executes CONFIG.SYS and AUTOEXEC.BAT, WIN.COM takes over and initializes KRNL386.EXE, USER.EXE, and GDI.EXE to load Program Manager.

Windows 95

The Windows 95 boot process is broken down into five stages.

Stage 1 is the BIOS bootstrap. In stage 1, the POST is performed (just like in DOS), Plug and Play devices are identified and assigned resources, and the MBR is located.

Stage 2 deals with the MBR and boot sector. In this stage, the MBR locates the bootable partition and passes control to the boot sector on that partition. The disk boot program locates the root directory and copies IO.SYS into memory.

Stage 3 is the real-mode boot. Windows 95 begins booting, and IO.SYS starts performing the following functions:

1. Loads a minimal FAT system to handle additional OS components.

2. Reads MSDOS.SYS for boot parameters.

3. Displays the message Loading Windows 95 and pauses in order to give the user time to select a function key. (This is covered in greater detail in the section about optional ways to boot the system.)

4. Displays the splash screen (LOGO.SYS).

5. Loads DRVSPACE.BIN for compressed drive support.

6. Scans the integrity of SYSTEM.DAT.

7. Loads SYSTEM.DAT and creates SYSTEM.DA0. (The backup SYSTEM.DAT file.)

8. Initializes double buffering for SCSI controllers if necessary.

9. Selects a hardware profile from the Registry.

10. Reads and processes CONFIG.SYS and AUTOEXEC.BAT.

Stage 4 is real-mode configuration. This stage loads the system configuration from CONFIG.SYS and AUTOEXEC.BAT. These files are used in Windows 95 only if you want to override the default settings.

Stage 5 is the protected-mode load. This is when WIN.COM loads VMM32.VXD and other device drivers. WIN.COM then switches the processor into protected mode and initializes the virtual device drivers. The core Windows kernel is loaded (KERNEL32.VXD) as are USER and GDI, and the Explorer interface is built. The programs referenced in the Run Once Registry (HKEY_LOCAL_MACHINE\SOFTWARE\ Microsoft\WINDOWS\CURRENTVERSION\RUNONCE) key are run, and the key is then cleared. An example of a run once program might be an antivirus update.

Note that as Windows 95 evolved from DOS, the process became considerably more complex.

Different Ways to Boot the Systems

While troubleshooting operating systems, there may come a time when you need to stop the system from going through the complete boot process. A few "tricks" that are built into DOS and Windows 95 allow you to do just this.

In both DOS and Windows 95, the F5 function key can be pressed when the MBR passes control to the operating system—when the screen displays the message Starting MSDOS (in DOS 6.0 or higher) or Starting Windows 95—causing the OS to bypass CONFIG.SYS and AUTOEXEC.BAT.

Likewise, if you do not want to bypass the configuration files, you can press the F8 function key, which will allow you to approve or "step through" each step of the CONFIG.SYS and AUTOEXEC.BAT. By using the F8 key, you can selectively load or not load the various lines of each file. Other Windows 95 considerations are a dual-boot and Safe Mode, which you access through a menu by pressing F8 at the Starting Windows 95 message.

You enable a dual-boot by installing Windows 95 into its own directory and setting the bootmulti= setting in MSDOS.SYS to 1. When these two requirements are met, the F4 function key is enabled. If you select F4 during the pause in Stage 3 of the Windows 95 boot process, the system will boot to the previous configuration. Note that MS-DOS 5.0 or later must be on the system for dual-boot to work.

Safe Mode offers a diagnostic way to start Windows 95. If the system does not shut down properly, or if something interrupts Windows operation and the machine reboots, Safe Mode becomes the default start option. Safe Mode bypasses the configuration files and loads only system default drivers so that the system can boot. After you boot to Safe Mode, you can remove drivers that are causing problems and then reboot to Normal mode Windows 95. In Windows 95, pressing the F5 function key brings up the MSDOS.SYS menu, which allows you to select from the boot menu. The Windows 95 boot menu for a system configured to dual-boot looks like the following:

```
Microsoft Windows 95 Startup Menu
=====================================

       1. Normal
       2. Logged (\BOOTLOG.TXT)
       3. Safe mode
       4. Safe Mode with Network Support
       5. Step by Step Confirmation
       6. Command Prompt Only
       7. Safe Mode Command Prompt
       8. previous Version of MS-DOS


     Enter a Choice:__


   F5=Safe mode Shift+F5=Command prompt Shift+F8=Step-by-step
   ➥confirmation [N]
```

Windows 95 DOS mode is one option you can select from the boot menu. DOS mode can also be accessed from inside the Windows 95 Explorer interface if you configure a DOS shortcut to reboot the system in DOS mode. This is also known as *modifying the PIF.* (PIF stands for Program Information File.) PIFs are files that tell Windows how to run a DOS application inside of Windows. PIFs are key in making Windows 95 backward-compatible with DOS programs. Figure 16.1 shows the Properties page of a DOS program, and Figure 16.2 shows the Advanced Properties of the same DOS program. The Advanced Properties sheet is where the PIF is modified for this application.

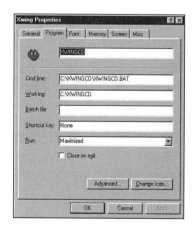

FIGURE 16.1
The Program tab of a DOS program's properties sheet.

FIGURE 16.2
The advanced properties of the program shown in Figure 16.1.

FILES REQUIRED FOR BOOTUP

At A Glance: File Requirements by OS

OS	Files Required for Booting	Files Required for Running Windows
DOS	IO.SYS, MSDOS.SYS, COMMAND.COM	N/A
Windows 3.x	IO.SYS, MSDOS.SYS, COMMAND.COM	WIN.COM, USER.EXE, GDI.EXE, PROGMAN.EXE, PROGMAN.INI, KRNL386.EXE
Windows 95	IO.SYS, MSDOS.SYS, COMMAND.COM	WIN.COM, USER.EXE, GDI.EXE, KERNEL32.DLL, USER.DAT, SYSTEM.DAT

Creating an Emergency Boot Disk

During the life of a computer system, it is safe to expect a problem with the system at some point in time. It is a good idea to keep a bootable floppy disk on hand to aid in recovering from this situation. To create an emergency boot disk, follow these steps:

1. Format a floppy disk with the /s switch (format a: /s). This copies COMMAND.COM, IO.SYS, MSDOS.SYS, and DRVSPACE.BIN (in DOS 6.1 and higher) to the floppy disk, making it bootable.

2. Copy CONFIG.SYS and AUTOEXEC.BAT to the floppy disk. For troubleshooting the system, it is a good idea to have a basic version of each file that excludes non-essential drivers (like a scanner) in case one of the drivers loading in CONFIG.SYS or one of the settings in AUTOEXEC.BAT causes a problem.

3. Copy any other utilities to the disk that you might use to recover or diagnose an error. (For example, you might include EDIT.COM so you can edit text, SCANDISK.EXE for checking the disk, or FORMAT, SYS, or FDISK.)

After you have created the disk, test it to see if it works by booting the system with it. If it's successful, save it in a safe place.

Creating a Windows 95 Startup Disk

Windows 95 comes with its own version of an emergency boot disk called a *startup disk* that you have the option of creating during installation. If you want to create the startup disk after installation, select Add/Remove Programs from Control Panel and click on the Startup Disk tab (see Figure 16.3).

The startup disk contains files used for diagnosing and recovering Windows 95. When the startup disk is created, the following files are copied to it (as outlined by the Microsoft Windows 95 Training manual):

ATTRIB.EXE	File attribute utility
CHKDSK.EXE	Disk status and repair utility
COMMAND.COM	Core operating system file
DEBUG.EXE	Debugging utility
DRVSPACE.BIN	Disk compression utility
EDB.SYS	Utility for the startup disk
EDIT.COM	Text editor
FDISK.EXE	Disk partition utility

FORMAT.COM	Disk format utility
IO.SYS	Core operating system file
MSDOS.SYS	Core operating system file
REGEDIT.EXE	Real-mode Registry editor
SCANDISK.EXE	Disk repair utility
SCANDISK.INI	ScanDisk configuration file
SYS.COM	System transfer utility
UNINSTAL.EXE	Utility for uninstalling Windows 95

Microsoft also recommends that you copy the following files to the startup disk as an extra recovery precaution: SYSTEM.DAT, AUTOEXEC.BAT, CONFIG.SYS, WIN.INI, and SYSTEM.INI, as well as CD-ROM and other device drivers.

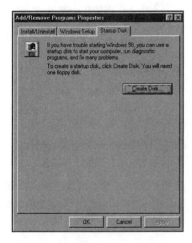

FIGURE 16.3
The Startup Disk tab from the Add/Remove Programs icon in Control Panel.

> **NOTE**
>
> The Registry files are sometimes too big to fit on a floppy disk. If this is the case, other options are to make a backup on the local hard drive using a larger capacity drive (like an IOMEGA ZIP disk), back up to tape, or use a compression utility on standard floppy disks.

Loading, Adding, and Removing Device Drivers

Being able to manage the many devices used by computers is a must for successfully tackling this exam. The following section covers device management as it relates to the A+ exam.

Windows 3.x Procedures

Loading device drivers by adding a device line in CONFIG.SYS makes the device available to Windows 3.x as well as DOS, but a few devices have Windows drivers that do not have to be loaded in DOS because DOS will not use them. Either these drivers are loaded via Windows Setup (these include mouse, keyboard, video, and network drivers), or they are loaded from the Control Panel as shown in Figure 16.4 (these include printers and sound card drivers that do not work in DOS). Unwanted devices are removed from the same locations through which they were added.

Windows 95 Procedures

Loading a device in CONFIG.SYS still works for Windows 95, but it limits the device to real mode. To avoid this, you should always load Windows 95 drivers when possible. Drivers that are not Plug and Play are loaded through the Add New Hardware Wizard in the Windows 95 Control Panel. Figure 16.5 shows the Add New Hardware Wizard.

To start the Add Hardware Wizard, you double-click its icon in the Control Panel. This gives you the choice of letting Plug and Play detect the new device or selecting it manually from a list (see Figure 16.6).

FIGURE 16.4
The Windows 3.x Control Panel.

FIGURE 16.5
The Windows 95 Add New Hardware Wizard accessible through the Control Panel.

FIGURE 16.6
Screen 2 of the Add/Remove Hardware Wizard.

If you select Let Windows Search for New Hardware, Plug and Play will find and configure the device. If you choose to add the device manually, you will be prompted to select the device type from a list. Alternately, you can click the Have Disk button and point Windows to another location such as a floppy disk or CD-ROM to find the necessary driver file.

To remove a device from the system, you must use the Device Manager shown in Figure 16.7. You access the Device Manager by selecting the System icon in Control Panel or by clicking on the My Computer icon on the desktop. From Device Manager, you can remove devices, modify resource assignments, and update drivers. It is also possible to disable a device from here.

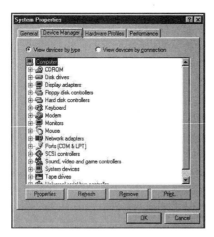

FIGURE 16.7
The Windows 95 Device Manager.

NOTE

If the device you are removing is a Plug and Play device, simply removing it from Device Manager will not work. If the device is not physically removed from the computer or disabled, Windows 95 will keep finding the device during the boot process and will try to assign it resources.

Changing Options, Configuring, and Using the Windows Printing Subsystem

Windows printers are among the most common devices a user will utilize. Being able to change options to optimize printing is a valuable skill.

Windows 3.x

To install a printer in Windows 3.x, you use the Printers section of the Control Panel. Double-click on the Printers icon to open the Print Manager. From inside the Print Manager, you can add a printer by selecting the Printer, New command or by clicking the New Printer icon on the toolbar. This brings up a dialog box in which you must either provide the path to the new driver or select it from a list. If you select a new driver, you will be prompted for the floppy disk containing the driver files. If you select a printer from the list, you are prompted to insert one of the Windows 3.x installation disks.

Windows 95

Like many things, installing a printer in Windows 95 is quite easy. Printer installation is wizard driven. To launch the Add Printer Wizard, open the Control Panel, click Printers, and select the Add New Printer icon. The wizard prompts you for the settings it needs to properly set up the printer. Figures 16.8–16.14 show the Add Printer Wizard dialog boxes.

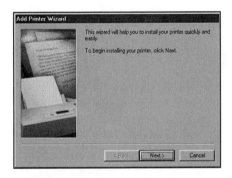

FIGURE 16.8
Step 1 of the Add Printer Wizard.

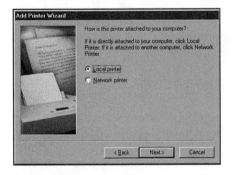

FIGURE 16.9
Step 2 of the Add Printer Wizard.

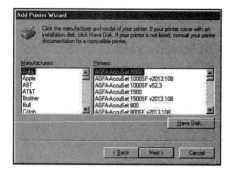

FIGURE 16.10
Step 3 asks you to select a printer model.

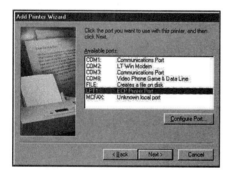

FIGURE 16.11
Step 4 asks you to assign the printer to a port.

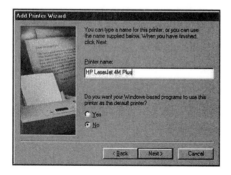

FIGURE 16.12
Step 5 asks you to name the printer and to indicate if you will be printing from DOS.

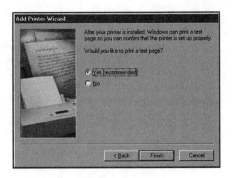

FIGURE 16.13
Step 6 asks if you want to print a test page.

FIGURE 16.14
The confirmation dialog box that is displayed if you select to print a test page.

After the printer is installed, some circumstances may arise that merit changing settings. For network printers, the most common change is the network port. Another example is changing the default paper orientation. If you need to change printer settings, open the Printers folder, right-click the icon for the printer you need to adjust, and select Properties. You will be presented with the printer's configuration tabs (see Figure 16.15). Different printers have different tabs that are specific to their model, but all printers have a General tab and a Details tab.

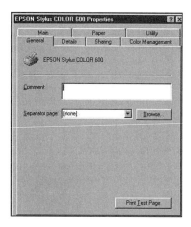

FIGURE 16.15
The General tab for the Epson Stylus 600 printer.

The settings on the General tab enable you to change whether the printer will have a separator page, add comments about the printer, or print a test page to verify printer communications and driver setup. For the separator page option, you can select None, Simple (a blank page) or Full (a page with job information). The information in the Comment section is displayed to a remote user's computer when he connects to this printer across a network, if this printer is being shared. The Print Test Page option enables you to print the same test page as when the printer was installed. The test page shows the port that the printer is using, the driver information, and all the files that are in use by the printer driver. The Windows 95 logo will print in color if you're testing a color printer.

The Details tab (available to all printers using drivers based on the Microsoft Mini driver model) displays the port and driver in use by this printer (see Figure 16.16). This is where you add ports, remove ports, or update the driver. Other options on the Details tab enable you to capture or release network printer ports and set printer communication timeout options. The Not Selected option enables you to tell Windows 95 how long to wait for a printer to come back online before reporting error messages; increase this setting for slow printers. The Transmission retry setting enables you to specify how many times Windows 95 will re-send data to the printer before displaying an error message; increase this option if your printer is slow.

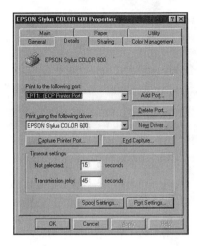

FIGURE 16.16
The Details tab for the Epson Stylus 600 printer.

The Port Settings button allows you to do two things. First, it allows you to spool MS-DOS print jobs. DOS programs often just dump data to an LPT port without formatting it. Windows 95 EMF printing does not format print jobs the same way; therefore, if the port is not configured to print DOS jobs, it will not do so. If you did not select to print MS-DOS print jobs during installation of this printer and you find that you have a DOS program that requires this function, this is where you turn it on (see Figure 16.17). The Port Settings button also allows you to check the port state before printing. Many graphics programs require bidirectional printing capability so that the printer can send information back to the program. Checking the port state before printing helps avoid corruption of graphics files by ensuring proper communication before sending the signal to the printer.

FIGURE 16.17
The Configure LPT Port dialog box. If the Spool DOS print jobs box is not checked, you may have difficulty printing from DOS programs.

The Spool Setting option is one of the most important options on the Details tab. This option gives you control of how Windows 95 passes print jobs to the printer. Windows 95 default print format is the enhanced metafile format or EMF. EMF reduces the time it takes for the printing subsystem to return control back to the application. Also known as background printing, EMF uses a background spooler to render the print job so that the application does not have to wait to do it. "RAW" print format is also supported under Windows 95. A RAW spool file is formatted for a specific printer and is ready to be sent directly to the printer.

With either format, you have the option of printing either after the first page is spooled or after the last page is spooled. Both options would be used for a shared printer. Beginning printing after the first page is spooled is the default. However, this option might block other users from getting their print jobs in a timely manner because this option occupies a lot of printer time. If you are sharing a printer and frequently print large jobs, you might consider printing after the last page is spooled because this occupies less printer time.

The last spool option is to print directly to the printer. This will slow down your application because it removes background printing, but on the other hand, it uses no disk space. Both EMF and RAW require disk space because they spool. If your computer is low on disk space and you are printing a large document, it may stall because there is no space to spool. If you select Print Directly to the Printer, you will be able to print anyway. Figure 16.18 shows the Windows 95 spool settings.

FIGURE 16.18
The spooling options for most printers.

The final option for spool settings is to enable or disable bidirectional support. Early PCs could not receive feedback from the printer like today's computers can. Some printers and computers cannot use bidirectional printing. For those devices, you'll want to disable this setting.

INSTALLING AND LAUNCHING APPLICATIONS

Understanding the process of adding programs to a PC and making them run is the key concept in the following section. Once again, this is a key topic in exam success.

DOS

Installing applications in DOS is a fairly simple process that involves running the installation program and selecting locations and settings. After the application is installed, you launch it by typing its executable command at the command line. Take into consideration whether or not the executable is in the DOS path (for information on the DOS path, see the section on AUTOEXEC.BAT in Chapter 14) and whether the system is configured correctly to run the program. Usually, both of these considerations are addressed during installation.

Windows 3.x

Installing applications in Windows 3.x differs slightly from installing in DOS. To install an application in Windows 3.x, you have to put in the floppy disk or CD-ROM and either double-click the setup program or select File, Run and type the path to the setup executable. After the program is installed, it usually creates its own program group and its own icons. Double-clicking on the icon launches the program.

Windows 95

Like most other functions from DOS/Windows environments, installing applications in Windows 95 adds several options. You can install programs in Windows 95 using the same procedure as Windows 3.x, but Windows 95 also offers other ways.

The recommended way of adding applications is to use the Add/Remove Programs icon in the Control Panel. This launches a wizard that searches floppy disk and CD-ROM drives for setup programs and installs them (see Figure 16.19). One benefit of using this utility to add programs is that it maintains a record of installed components and allows for a full uninstallation if necessary. Windows 95 keeps track of files installed by 32-bit applications by default; but to keep track of 16-bit installation files, you must use the Add/Remove Programs Wizard.

Another possibility for adding applications is the Autorun feature available for CD-ROMs. Autorun causes the setup application to launch automatically when the CD-ROM is inserted, and then the application prompts the user to run setup.

Again, after an application is loaded, it usually creates a group on the Windows 95 Start menu and adds icons for launching the program. By selecting the appropriate icon, you start the application. You can also launch a program in Windows 95 by selecting Run from the Start menu and typing the executable filename (just like the Run line in Windows 3.x) if it is in the path. If the filename is not in the path, you can type the full path to the executable. Another option is to double-click the executable file from Explorer.

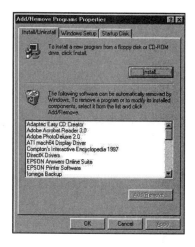

FIGURE 16.19
The Add/Remove Programs utility in the Windows 95 Control Panel.

WHAT IS IMPORTANT TO KNOW

- DOS is available on floppy disk and can be installed by booting the PC to the first disk of the installation set or simply by running Setup from the first disk. Setup prompts you to change disks when needed. When Setup is complete, you are prompted to remove the Setup floppy disk and reboot. The new installation and the upgrade are similar. Specific DOS configurations are made by modifying the CONFIG.SYS and AUTOEXEC.BAT files.

- Installing Windows 3.x is virtually the same as installing DOS. Invoke Setup and follow the prompts throughout the process. When the process is complete, you need to reboot. Aside from CONFIG.SYS and AUTOEXEC.BAT, configuration changes can be made from the Windows Control Panel.

- Windows 95 can be installed from floppy disk or CD-ROM. Type **Setup** from the command line or select the Windows File, Run command (this is the recommended way for upgrading from Windows 3.x) to start the process. Windows 95 Setup occurs in three phases. Phase one is the gathering of system information. Phase two is the copying of Windows 95 files. Phase three is the final installation. The computer is rebooted under the control of the new operating system and makes final adjustments that finish the installation process.

- The DOS boot sequence begins when power is applied to the computer system. The PC begins its power on self-test or POST routine. After the system passes the POST, control is passed to the system BIOS, which searches for the master boot record (or MBR) on one of the system's drives. If the hard disk has DOS installed (if it contains IO.SYS, MSDOS.SYS, COMMAND.COM, and the DOS program files), control is passed to COMMAND.COM to continue processing DOS startup by processing the CONFIG.SYS and AUTOEXEC.BAT files.

- The Windows 3.x boot sequence picks up where the DOS boot sequence ends. After COMMAND.COM executes CONFIG.SYS and AUTOEXEC.BAT, WIN.COM takes over, and if WIN.COM is in the AUTOEXEC.BAT, it initializes KERNL386.EXE, USER.EXE, and GDI.EXE to load Program Manager.

- The Windows 95 boot process is broken down into five stages. Stage 1 entails the BIOS Bootstrap and the POST process, which was also performed in DOS. In stage 2, the MBR and boot sector are located and given control. In stage 3, Windows 95 begins booting, and IO.SYS loads a minimal FAT system to handle additional OS components, reads MSDOS.SYS for boot parameters, displays the message Loading Windows 95, displays the splash screen (LOGO.SYS), loads, and then backs up the Registry. In stage 4, the system configuration is loaded from CONFIG.SYS and AUTOEXEC.BAT if it's present. In stage 5, WIN.COM loads VMM32.VXD and other device drivers. WIN.COM then initializes the Windows kernel, and Windows starts.

◆ If the partition holding the OS is not marked as active, the system will not boot. To correct this problem, boot to a floppy disk, run FDISK, and mark the appropriate partition as active. If the partition is FAT32, only a Windows 95 OSR2 boot disk will be able to see the partition. If the partition is larger than 2GB it must be a FAT32 partition; therefore, only a Windows 95 OSR2 boot disk can recognize it.

◆ A partition must be formatted to install an OS.

◆ If you format or delete a partition, all data that was on that partition is destroyed.

◆ If the partition is larger than 2GB, you must format it with Windows 95 OSR2.

◆ If you format a partition with FAT32, you must install Windows 95 OSR2.

◆ You can compile a custom installation of Windows 95 by customizing the MSBATCH.INF file. If MSBATCH.INF is used, however, you must use the appropriate switches when running Setup or the MSBATCH.INF modifications will be ignored.

◆ Plug and Play primarily handles the loading of drivers in Windows 95. You can load a device manually from the Control Panel's Add/Remove Hardware Wizard. If you manually add a device, you should let Windows 95 assign it resources. Manually assigning resources bypasses Plug and Play and leaves it unaware of your choices. If Plug and Play is unaware of resources you have assigned, it is likely to have Windows 95 assign the same resource to another device.

◆ You can take several steps to avoid trouble during an installation:

  ◆ Scan the system for viruses before you begin the upgrade, and then shut down the virus program. If the PC has a CMOS-based antivirus program, it must be disabled as well. The reason is that when Windows 95 upgrades the boot sector, the antivirus software sees this as a problem and stops Setup.

  ◆ Run ScanDisk (or CHKDSK) to ensure the hard disk is in good working order.

  ◆ Make sure there is enough free disk space for the upgrade. 100–110MB is recommended. (110–120MB is needed if you are saving the DOS/Windows 3.x information.)

- Verify that all your hardware and software is functioning correctly.

- Shut down running programs, including TSRs and screen savers.

- Back up all your system files (CONFIG.SYS, AUTOEXEC.BAT, WIN.INI, SYSTEM.INI).

- Remove unnecessary lines in CONFIG.SYS and AUTOEXEC.BAT.

- Remark out Load= and Run= lines in the WIN.INI.

- Remove programs from the startup group. If they are needed, they can be added after the upgrade.

- If at all possible, run Setup from within Windows 3.x.

- An upgrade from DOS to Windows 95 is really a DOS upgrade. Because there is no existing Windows directory, DOS programs are not added to the Windows 95 Start menu. For all effective purposes, this is a new installation of Windows 95. Existing DOS programs will have to be added manually, and DOS files are upgraded to Windows 95 versions.

- The upgrade from Windows 3.x to Windows 95 should be started from Program Manager. This helps the Windows 95 installation process identify any devices or programs that may be present in memory. During the upgrade, you will be asked what directory to install to. If you select the current Windows directory, all Windows 3.x program groups will be migrated to Windows 95 program groups. If you choose a different directory, programs and groups will not be migrated but you will be able to boot the system to either Windows 3.x or Windows 95. You will have to reinstall all applications for them to work in Windows 95.

- In both DOS and Windows 95, you can press the F5 function key when the screen displays the message Starting MSDOS or Starting Windows 95 if you want to bypass CONFIG.SYS and AUTOEXEC.BAT.

  If you do not want to bypass the configuration files, you can press the F8 function key to approve or "step through" each line of the CONFIG.SYS and AUTOEXEC.BAT files. (In Windows 95, F8 activates the boot menu, where you can select Step Through as an option.) By using the F8 key, you can selectively load or not load various commands. The F8 key is a highly effective troubleshooting tool.

- Other Windows 95 options are dual booting and Safe Mode. You enable dual booting by installing Windows 95 into its own directory and setting the bootmulti= setting in MSDOS.SYS to 1. When these two requirements are met, the F4 function key is enabled. Then you can press F4 during the pause in stage 3 of the Windows 95 boot process, and the system will boot to the previous configuration. Note that MS-DOS 5.0 or later must be on the system before Windows 95 is installed for dual booting to work.

Safe Mode is a diagnostic way to start Windows 95. If the system does not shut down properly or Windows operation is interrupted and the machine reboots, Safe Mode becomes the default start option. Safe Mode bypasses the configuration files and loads only the system default drivers so the system can boot. Once you've booted to Safe Mode, you can remove the offending drivers and reboot to Normal mode of Windows 95. In Windows 95, pressing the F8 function key brings up the MSDOS.SYS menu, which allows you to select a start option from the boot menu.

▶ Windows 95 DOS mode is another option you can select from the boot menu. You can also access DOS mode from inside the Windows 95 Explorer interface by configuring a DOS shortcut to reboot the system in DOS mode.

▶ With both DOS and Windows 95, MSDOS.SYS, IO.SYS, and COM-MAND.COM are required to boot the system. For the system to boot to Windows 95, it also needs WIN.COM, USER.EXE, GDI.EXE, SYSTEM.DAT, and USER.DAT.

▶ It is a good idea to create an emergency boot disk in case the hard drive becomes unable to boot the system. To create the emergency disk, format a floppy disk with the /s switch. This makes the floppy disk bootable. You should then copy the files that you will need to use for repairing the hard drive. Common files that may be needed are AUTOEXEC.BAT, CONFIG.SYS, EDIT.COM (EDIT requires QBASIC.EXE in DOS 6.x), SCANDISK.EXE, FDISK.EXE, XCOPY.EXE, and certain device drivers (like CD-ROM). If you think you might need other items, you should create other versions of boot disks for specific functions.

Most of the difficulty in creating an Emergency Boot Disk has been eliminated by Windows 95. From the Windows 95 Control Panel you can create what is called a Windows 95 Startup Disk. The Startup Disk is a bootable disk that has most of the needed recovery utilities already copied to it. (Note: CD-ROM drivers are not automatically added. You must do this yourself.)

▶ Devices in Windows 3.x and DOS are loaded in CONFIG.SYS and AUTOEXEC.BAT. Some devices are Windows 3.x-specific and can be loaded from Control Panel or Windows Setup. Devices are removed from the same applets with which they were added.

▶ Windows 95 loads drivers primarily by Plug and Play. You can manually add devices from the Add/Remove Hardware Wizard in Control Panel. You can remove devices from the Windows 95 Device Manager.

▶ Plug and Play is a term used to describe hardware that identifies itself to the operating system and configures itself. Plug and Play in Windows 95 is achieved via software programs called *bus enumerators*. The bus enumerators are specific to a type of bus architecture (PCI, VESA, MCA, and ISA). Each enumerator polls its bus looking for a response from hardware. If hardware responds to the polling, it is added to the Device Manager, and you are prompted to load software. Plug and Play does not remove hardware.

▶ The Windows 95 printing subsystem is configured from the Printers folder in Control Panel. Here you can add printers by using the Add Printer Wizard. Follow the wizard and answer the questions to install a printer. If a printer driver changes or you want to change other options about the printer (such as the port to which it's connected), you can select the printer's icon, right-click, and select Properties. The printer's properties sheet will contain at least the General tab and the Details tab. Most printers have more tabs, but they are specific to the driver. All options for a printer can be modified from its properties sheet.

▶ Windows 95 offers several new options for installing applications. Programs can be installed in Windows 95 just as they were in Windows 3.x, but Windows 95 offers some other means. The recommended way of adding applications is to use the Add/Remove Programs icon in Control Panel. This launches a wizard that searches floppy disk and CD-ROM drives for setup programs and installs them. One benefit of using this utility to add programs is that it maintains a record of installed components and allows for a full uninstallation if necessary. Windows 95 keeps track of files installed by 32-bit applications by default, but to keep track of 16-bit installation files, you must use the Add/Remove Programs Wizard.

▶ Another possibility for adding applications is the AutoRun feature used by CD-ROMs. AutoRun causes the setup application to launch when the CD-ROM drive reads the CD, prompting the user to run setup.

▶ After an application is loaded, it usually creates a group on the Windows 95 Start menu and adds icons for launching the program. You run the application by selecting the appropriate icon. You can also launch a program in Windows 95 by selecting Run from the Start menu and typing the executable (just like the Run line in Windows 3.x) if it is in the path. If it is not in the path, you can type the full path to the executable. Another option is to double-click the executable from Explorer.

▶ Installing applications in DOS is a fairly simple process that involves running the installation program and selecting locations and settings. Once the application is installed, you launch it by typing its executable command at the command prompt. Some points to consider are whether the executable is in the DOS path and whether the system is configured correctly to run the program. Usually both of these considerations are addressed during installation.

▶ Recognize and decipher common error codes and messages from the boot sequence and know how to correct them.

▶ Understand the concept of temporary and permanent swap files.

▶ Identify and correct common Windows-specific printing problems.

▶ Select the appropriate course of action to correct common errors in a Windows environment.

▶ Select and use DOS and Windows-based utilities to diagnose specific Windows/DOS behavior.

CHAPTER 17

Diagnosing and Troubleshooting

COMMON ERROR CODES AND STARTUP MESSAGES AND THE STEPS TO CORRECT THEM

A large part of being able to troubleshoot PCs is knowing as much as possible about how they operate. With as many computers as there are in the world today, it only makes sense that most of the problems faced by users are not unique. By knowing what causes common problems and how to correct them, you eliminate wasting time researching an issue someone else has already solved. This chapter discusses the most common error messages, identifies possible causes, and helps you determine how to resolve these problems.

Using Safe Mode to Diagnose Problems

As discussed in Chapter 16, "Installation, Configuration, and Upgrading," Safe Mode is the Windows 95 diagnostic mode that loads the minimum drivers required for loading Windows 95. If the system loses power or is shut down improperly, Safe Mode is automatically entered upon reboot. If a device driver issue is causing the failure, or an application error is to blame, Safe Mode gives you a chance to correct the problem by removing the offending driver or program in an environment that doesn't present the problem.

> NOTE
>
> Because only required drivers are loaded in Safe Mode, you will not have access to devices such as scanners.

Incorrect DOS version

The message Incorrect DOS version can occur for different reasons. One reason is that some applications check which version of MS-DOS is running when they start. These applications might not run if you are using a version of DOS that the application was not designed to use. For example, an application designed for DOS version 3.30 might not start if you are running DOS 6.22. Instead, the program displays Incorrect DOS version. This means that either the application isn't compatible with your version of DOS, or the application can't run because it interprets the DOS version as incompatible. The program manufacturer should have information on whether the application is compatible or not. If the application isn't compatible, check to see if there is an updated version that is. If the application is compatible, you must use the SETVER command to add your version of DOS to the version table.

An example of an incompatibility would be the use of a program that was compiled to run using MS-DOS on a PC that is running IBM DOS or Novell DOS.

The version table is a list of applications that need DOS to report a version number other than the current version. DOS maintains the version table in a file called SETVER.EXE, which is in your DOS directory. (In Windows 95, it is in the Windows directory.)

To use SETVER, you must have the device driver loaded in CONFIG.SYS (DEVICE=C:\DOS\SETVER.EXE). This installs SETVER.EXE, which contains the version table.

> **NOTE**
>
> Make sure you have only one SETVER.EXE file on your hard disk drive. Each copy has a unique version table. If you have more than one version table, SETVER might not report the correct version number to your programs.

To display the complete list of applications in the version table, type **SETVER** at the command prompt. Note that the DOS upgrade installation for versions 5.0 and up—as well as Windows 95—updates the version table. Add the application to the version table to correct the problem. Table 17.1 lists valid switches used to modify SETVER.EXE and the version table.

TABLE 17.1

SWITCHES USED TO MODIFY **SETVER.EXE** AND THE VERSION
TABLE

Modification	*Switch*	
Display current version table	SETVER [*drive:path*]	
Add entry	SETVER [*drive:path*] *filename n.nn*	
Delete entry	SETVER [*drive:path*] *filename* /DELETE [/QUIET]	
	[*drive:path*]	Specifies the location of the SETVER.EXE file.
	filename	Specifies the program's filename
	n.nn	Specifies the MS-DOS version to be reported to the program.
	/DELETE or /D	Deletes the version-table entry for the specified program.
	/QUIET or /Q	Hides the message typically displayed during the deletion of the version-table entry.

Another reason for the Incorrect DOS version message could be that IO.SYS, MSDOS.SYS, and COMMAND.COM might be different versions. To correct this problem, either reinstall or boot to a floppy disk and use the SYS command to transfer the system files to the hard disk again.

No Operating System found

The message No Operating System found is not a message you like to see, especially if you just installed the OS. There are a number of reasons that this error can appear, and some are not too bad. One of the simplest reasons for getting this message is that when the partition was created, it was inadvertently not marked as active. For an operating system to boot, BIOS must locate a bootable partition on one of the hard disks in the system. If the partition is not marked as active, BIOS will not pass control to the OS, even if the boot files exist there. To correct this problem, boot to a floppy disk, run FDISK, and mark the correct partition as active.

Another reason that this message is displayed is that the drive is being misrepresented in CMOS. On occasion, the system CMOS battery might need to be replaced. A bad CMOS battery can cause CMOS settings to be lost or changed. The No Operating System found message can be a result of this condition. To correct this problem, replace the CMOS battery and reset your CMOS drive settings. If the CMOS settings have been lost, you will need to either contact the manufacturer and get the drive specifications for your drive, or physically inspect the drive. Most drive specs are printed on the drive. If your system BIOS does not autodetect hard drive parameters, you will need the following parameters: number of heads, number of sectors, and number of sectors per track. Once you manually add your drive settings, you will have eliminated drive misrepresentation as a possible error. It's a good idea to write these parameters down for future reference in case you lose CMOS again.

Probably the worst scenario in which to see this message is a hard drive failure. In this instance, replace the drive and restore from a full backup, or begin again.

Error in CONFIG.SYS line *xx*

An error in a line of CONFIG.SYS isn't as bad as it sounds. In most cases, this is a syntax issue. If you see this message or notice that a device isn't working upon boot, restart the system, press the F8 function key when you see the message Now starting MS-DOS or Starting Windows 95, and step through each line of CONFIG.SYS to identify where the error is. Path, syntax, and spelling all count. (In Windows 95, the F8 key activates the MSDOS.SYS menu, where step through is an option.) If any of these are wrong, the line will not process as intended.

Bad or missing command interpreter

The message Bad or missing command interpreter tells you that something has corrupted or deleted the command interpreter, COMMAND.COM. To correct this issue, reformat the command interpreter with the /s switch, or boot to a floppy disk and use the sys command to transfer the system back to the drive.

HIMEM.SYS not loaded

The message HIMEM.SYS not loaded indicates that for some reason the device driver enabling high memory did not load. This presents a problem, because Windows won't load unless high memory is available. First, check to see if HIMEM.SYS exists in the location specified in CONFIG.SYS. If this is correct, check the file date on HIMEM.SYS to see if it is the most current version. If this is correct, boot from a floppy disk containing a minimum version of CONFIG.SYS and AUTOEXEC.BAT to see if you can start Windows. If this works, the problem exists within CONFIG.SYS or AUTOEXEC.BAT. If this doesn't work, there is probably a problem with the memory manager. To correct this problem, copy HIMEM.SYS again from CD, or install floppies.

You might have to use a diagnostic utility such as Microsoft Diagnostics (MSD) to determine if there is a conflict in upper memory. If there is an upper memory conflict, you should resolve it by unloading all drivers and TSRs (Terminate-and-Stay Resident programs, such as anti-virus programs) from upper memory.

Swap File

On Windows 3.x, users could enhance performance by changing virtual memory settings from temporary to permanent. The temporary swap file is created when Windows starts, slowing the start process. Running out of disk space will affect Windows' performance, because there won't be room for the swap file. The use of a permanent swap file allows for greater performance, because it always reserves disk space and is always available for use. Not having plenty of hard drive space available is the only reason not to use a permanent swap file in Windows 3.x. Sometimes, when you start Windows, you will receive a Swap file is corrupt message. Upon acknowledgment of this error, Windows starts and prompts you to create a new swap file. This usually occurs after you use a disk-cloning utility such as a PKZIP image or Symantec's Ghost.

The Windows 95 swap file is dynamic, so it can shrink or grow as needed. The Windows 95 swap file can occupy a fragmented region of the hard disk with no noticeable performance loss. Making sure that the disk containing the swap file has plenty of free space for expanding and contracting is the best way to optimize the Windows 95 dynamic swap file. Running out of disk space will reduce performance greatly.

Device referenced in `SYSTEM.INI`/`WIN.INI` could not be found

The absence of a device specified in one of the configuration files is very common following a program's uninstallation or deletion. Some uninstall programs don't remove referenced devices—either because they are poorly designed or because something interrupted the uninstall process. In any event, these absent devices can either stop the loading of Windows or simply slow it down. It is important to take notes and make a list of the files that the system lists as missing. Once you quit receiving messages stating that devices are missing, you should run SYSEDIT. SYSEDIT is a utility that opens all the common text-based system configuration files and allows you to edit them. Search WIN.INI and SYSTEM.INI for instances of the files you copied down as missing, and comment them out by adding a semicolon (;) to the beginning of the line. Once all missing files have been completely commented out, restart the system and watch for errors. If the system gives you more errors, repeat the process until Windows starts error-free. If the system boots correctly, double-check that all programs operate correctly, verifying that the items you commented out are not necessary. If not all the programs check out, reinstall the application to replace any files that were accidentally removed.

WINDOWS-SPECIFIC PRINTING PROBLEMS

Printing from Windows in general is the focus of this section. More specifically, it's important that you know the problems you might encounter when printing from Windows. This section discusses the common issues you might face when printing with Windows.

Stalled Print Spooler

A stalled print spooler is a common occurrence when you're printing from Windows. You can tell you have a stalled print spooler when you send print jobs to the printer, but nothing prints. If this occurs, double-click the printer's icon to see if jobs are listed. Sometimes, deleting the job at the top of the queue will start the print process again.

Make sure that there is enough disk space available to spool. If disk space is available, storage space is not the problem. If you are low on disk space, free up some space by backing up some data to other media, delete that data, and then try printing again. It's a good idea to have about twice as much disk space available as the size of the file you are trying to print.

If you still can't print, right-click the printer icon and select Properties. On the Details tab, select Spool Options. Change the spool settings to print directly to the printer. If this produces positive printer output, the problem is a stalled print spooler. Simply rebooting the machine can clear the spooler and restart printing. In the event that rebooting doesn't work, change the output from EMF to RAW. If you still can't print, check the Windows\system\spool\printers directory for *.SPL and *.TMP files and delete them if they exist. These could be the corrupt spool jobs. If none of these tasks restarts printing, the print spooler probably isn't the problem.

NOTE A reboot of the system and printer can clear up many printing issues.

Incorrect or Incompatible Printer Driver

Corrupt or incorrect drivers are probably the most common cause of Windows printing errors. If print jobs are coming out of the printer garbled or off-format, the printer driver is a likely culprit. Simply reinstalling the driver or updating the driver from the Printer Properties Details tab works most of the time, but some drivers are known to cause problems with different versions of Windows. For example, older HP LaserJet models such as the LaserJet III have been known to have difficulty printing in Windows 95 OSR2. The driver supplied on the Windows 95 CD-ROM can corrupt LPT.VXD, preventing print output. Updated drivers that can fix this problem are available for download from HP's Internet site at http://www.hp.com. If the LPT.VXD file is already corrupt, you might have to copy it from the CD-ROM to the Windows\System folder and restart the computer. This should cause printing to resume.

RECOGNIZING AND CORRECTING COMMON PROBLEMS

This section focuses on your ability to recognize problems and know corrective actions to take to combat common operating system errors.

General Protection Faults (GPFs)

General Protection Faults are not hard to identify. When one occurs, the system displays a message stating that a GPF has occurred and tells you which application caused it. GPFs that occur in 16-bit applications display a blue screen, while 32-bit applications display a Windows dialog box. 32-bit applications in Windows 95 aren't prone to GPFs because of the way Windows 95 assigns resources. Since the OS knows what device and program uses which memory areas, the occurrence of faults is greatly reduced. It is possible for a 32-bit application to have a General Protection Fault. Correcting this problem requires good note-taking when the error happens. Knowing what caused the problem greatly helps eliminate it. Use the Device Manager to see if any system hardware is using the memory area that the offending program tried to use. If there is an overlap, correct it by using Device Manager to reassign a memory area to the hardware.

> **NOTE**
> If you manually assign resources in Device Manager, the operating system no longer keeps track of that device. This can lead to more overlap of resources. It is usually best to let Windows 95 handle this allocation.

If hardware isn't causing the conflict, there is probably a corrupt file in the problematic application, or a version conflict with a system library. It is possible that a bad installation is the reason for the fault. A complete uninstall with a reinstall can correct the issue. If no devices are conflicting, or it appears to be a version conflict, contact the application's manufacturer for further information. The manufacturer might require your troubleshooting notes to help correct the problem.

Illegal Operation

An illegal operation is, in essence, a program flaw. The program expects the operating system to act a particular way, and the program stops when it does not. An example would be a DOS application that uses DOS extenders that do not recognize the Windows 95 extender. The fix is to get an updated version of the offending program. The unfortunate fact about illegal operations is that more often than not, a service pack or application update of some sort must be applied. Technical support sites and packages such as Microsoft TechNet have hundreds of articles pertaining to illegal operations with hundreds of different fixes.

Invalid working directory

The `Invalid working directory` error occurs when you're trying to launch a program in Windows 3.x and the working directory is set incorrectly. When a program installs in Windows 3.x and its program group is created, the properties of the icons in the program group give the path to the executable file and its directory location. This directory is known as the working directory. If a drive letter changes (such as when you add another hard drive or change the CD-ROM drive letter) and an icon still points to the previous drive letter, the `Invalid working directory` message is displayed. To correct this, select the icon, select File, Properties, and modify the path to the working directory to point to the correct location.

System Lockup

A system lockup occurs because the processor gets conflicting information or becomes unaware of what the operating system is doing. In DOS, the usual cause is a memory problem or a poorly written program.

In Windows 3.x, Microsoft introduced multitasking, which allowed users to carry out more than one task at a time. The type of multitasking that Windows 3.x used was called cooperative multitasking. This involves all the programs operating in the same memory space and cooperatively sharing resources. This means that the program is in control of the processor at all times. When the program finishes with the current task, it is supposed to relinquish control to the next program, and so on. If a program stalls while controlling the processor, the system stops. In Windows 3.x, this usually meant you had to reboot.

Windows 95's 32-bit architecture introduced a new kind of multitasking called preemptive multitasking. Preemptive multitasking gives the processor control over the applications. When the time that an application has allotted for processor functions expires, the processor takes control from the application and gives time to the next application in line. This is why you can press Ctrl+Alt+Delete and shut down a troubled program in Windows 95. However, to maintain backward compatibility with 16-bit applications that depend on cooperative multitasking, Windows 95 has an area of non-reentrant code known as the Win 16 Mutex. The Win 16 Mutex flag simulates the processor's being under the control of the 16-bit application. When the Win 16 Mutex flag is set (albeit only for a fraction of a second), if a 16-bit program hangs, it locks up the system. This usually means rebooting. To avoid hang-ups in Windows 95 that halt the entire system, use only 32-bit programs whenever possible. This is the one instance in Windows 95 where pressing Ctrl+Alt+Delete will reboot Windows 95.

Option Will Not Function

An option that does not function usually indicates that an installation did not complete appropriately, or has since become corrupt. A common example in Windows 95 is when Start menu shortcuts don't run the associated programs. One example is a damaged MS-DOS prompt on the Start menu that opens a DOS window and immediately closes it. In this instance, the PIF associated with the DOS prompt is set to close after executing, or it's simply pointing to the wrong program. There might not be an error message, which makes this kind of error difficult to troubleshoot. Correcting this issue requires patience. First, to eliminate the possibility that the shortcut has become damaged, launch the application from its home directory using Windows Explorer. If this doesn't work, rule out memory conflicts by checking the Device Manager for warnings. Also ensure that other applications aren't affected. This rules out a system problem. Last, back up the data, uninstall the application, reinstall the application, and restore the data. If the misbehaving function is part of the OS (such as the DOS PIF), the OS might have to be reinstalled. Another example of this is when the Modem option in the Windows 95 Control Panel never loads the modem settings. There are limitless reasons for an option not to function. The only way to correct the problem is good troubleshooting skills and good note-taking.

Application Will Not Start or Load

An option that does not work (such as a menu option that does nothing when selected) can be indicative of a bad install and/or damaged application files. An instance that comes to mind is older versions of Lotus applications that depend on temporary files in the \Windows\Temp directory. Some disk cleanup utilities delete *.TMP files from the disk. With the temporary files removed, the programs don't run properly. In Windows 3.x and DOS, you can undelete these files to correct the problem. In Windows 95, you need to reinstall.

Again, an application that does not start can have a multitude of factors that contribute to the problem. Good troubleshooting and note-taking skills are the quickest way to fix the problem.

First, eliminate the possibility that the problem is the PC or the OS by checking to see that there are no conflicts during start-up. Check to see that all other applications are unaffected. Check the Windows 95 Device Manager for warnings. After you've checked these things, it is likely to be an application issue.

Troubleshooting the application involves starting it and trying to notice system behavior or error messages. If you don't see any error messages, change the system video to basic VGA and try again. Some applications are written so that they will display messages in VGA mode. Fancier video cards might not be able to display the error, or will show only a black screen. (This works in Windows 3.x and DOS. For Windows 95, use Safe Mode.) If this application uses VGA for error messages, setting the system to basic VGA will show the message. If no messages are given, try booting the system in Windows 95 Safe Mode to see if it runs. If this is successful, the application has a conflict with a device driver that isn't loaded in Safe Mode (such as a video or network card). If the application still doesn't run, try booting with clean CONFIG.SYS and AUTOEXEC.BAT files. (In DOS/Windows 3.x environments, use a boot disk. In Windows 95, boot to the Startup Disk, or simply rename CONFIG.SYS and AUTOEXEC.BAT and boot.) If this proves unsuccessful, uninstall and then reinstall the application. Note that reinstalling corrects the problem only if there has been file corruption or an incomplete install.

Cannot log on to network

The Cannot log on to network error can be categorized into three areas, assuming that all hardware and software are functioning correctly: client issues, protocol issues, and permission issues. These are the three requirements to gain access to the network. (Again, note that we are assuming that all hardware and OS software is functioning as intended with no conflicts.)

Client issues arise when the client software is configured incorrectly. The majority of networks today are either Microsoft Windows-based or Novell NetWare-based, but there are many other possible network clients. Figure 17.1 shows the Microsoft client properties page. Figure 17.2 shows the NetWare client properties page. The most common problems with client configuration are caused by misspelling login domain names or preferred server names, or by simply not having the client installed.

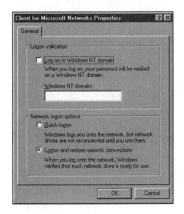

FIGURE 17.1
The properties page of the Microsoft network client.

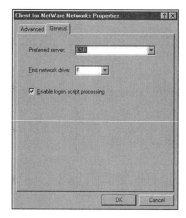

FIGURE 17.2
The properties page of the Microsoft Client for NetWare Networks.

Figure 17.3 shows the Identification tab from Network properties in the Windows 95 Control Panel. In Microsoft networking, computer names must be unique. Having two computers with the same name will deny network access to the computer that has been on for the least amount of time.

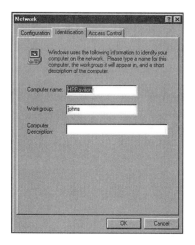

FIGURE 17.3
The computer Identification tab from the Windows 95 Network Control Panel.

The next issue with accessing the network is protocols. Simply installing a client in Windows installs the default protocol. Once a network client is installed, you can actually locate shared resources on a network. Actually accessing those resources requires that the requesting workstation and the computer with the shared resource have a common protocol. In essence, the two computers must speak the same language. A common issue with protocols is binding. Binding means that the protocol is associated with the client software. An example of binding occurs when the Microsoft Client for NetWare Networks adds and binds to the IPX/SPX-compatible protocol, or NWLink. Each protocol also has its own quirks that you must address before obtaining network access. Figure 17.4 shows the Advanced properties for the IPX/SPX-compatible protocol. The three most commonly used protocols are TCP/IP, IPX/SPX, and NetBEUI.

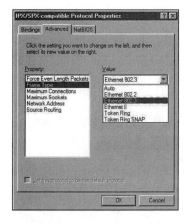

FIGURE 17.4
The Advanced properties of the IPX/SPX-compatible protocol, as shown in the properties sheet from the Network Control Panel.

Frame Types

If the protocol is the language that computers speak, the frame type is the dialect. IPX/SPX is a protocol that uses frame types. IPX/SPX frame types are automatically detected by default in Windows 95. Refer to Figure 17.4 to see the frame type settings available in Windows 95.

Auto-detect works most of the time. However, in NetWare environments that have more than one frame type running on the network, Windows 95 clients detect and bind to only the first frame type they find. If a client detects a different frame type than the one running on another computer, the client won't be able to access that computer. (Usually, the client can't even see PCs running other frame types.) You can correct this by manually selecting the frame type. Changing frame types requires you to reboot your system.

Configuring TCP/IP

The TCP/IP protocol can be configured two ways. The first and easiest way is through the Dynamic Host Configuration Protocol, or DHCP. DHCP is set up from a network server and automatically assigns IP addresses to workstations configured to use DHCP.

The next TCP/IP configuration possibility is to manually assign an address. The two required pieces for TCP/IP configuration are the actual IP address and the subnet mask. The IP address, which must be unique to the network, acts as the computer's "street address." At a fundamental level, the subnet mask must be common to all computers on your network, because it defines which network your computer is on. If the computer is in a routed network, it also requires a default gateway. The default gateway is where all IP requests to unknown addresses are forwarded. Figure 17.5 shows the IP Address tab of the Windows 95 TCP/IP properties page.

FIGURE 17.5
The IP Address tab of the TCP/IP settings from the Network Control Panel.

An incorrect IP address or subnet mask will prevent access to the network. To correct this problem, double-check the IP settings. The PING (Packet Internet Groper) utility is part of the TCP/IP protocol suite and is used to verify connectivity. Here is an example of PING syntax (from the command line):

```
Ping 127.0.0.1
```

This command will return the following information:

```
Pinging 127.0.0.1 with 32 bytes of data:
```

If it's successful, a reply will be received:

```
Reply from 127.0.0.1: bytes=32 time<10ms TTL=128
Reply from 127.0.0.1: bytes=32 time<10ms TTL=128
Reply from 127.0.0.1: bytes=32 time<10ms TTL=128
Reply from 127.0.0.1: bytes=32 time<10ms TTL=128
Ping statistics for 127.0.0.1:
    Packets: Sent = 4, Received = 4, Lost = 0 (0% loss),
Approximate round trip times in milliseconds:
    Minimum = 0ms, Maximum =   0ms, Average =   0ms
```

> **NOTE**
>
> Pinging the 127.0.0.1 ensures that TCP/IP is loaded correctly and bound to the network card. This is referred to as the loopback address. An unsuccessful PING attempt returns a message. Request timed out, Network host unreachable, and Bad IP address for *XXX* are common IP configuration error messages.

NetBEUI is another common protocol. It requires no configuration but is not routable. If your protocol is NetBEUI and you are in a routed network, you won't be able to access network hosts in remote networks.

The last network issue that can prevent logging on to the network is access permissions. If the computer holding the shared resources doesn't grant you access to the resource, you won't gain access. Figure 17.6 shows the Access Control tab on the Network properties in Control Panel.

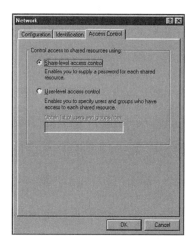

FIGURE 17.6
The Access Control tab of the Network Control Panel.

Share-level access is the default level of permissions in a peer-to-peer network. Share-level access can grant full access or read-only access, depending on passwords. User-level access can be used in a network environment where there is a server with user accounts. User-level access allows you to select which users have access and the type of access.

DOS- AND WINDOWS-BASED UTILITIES

Troubleshooting can be made easier by using tools supplied with the operating system. Some have already been discussed but have a specific purpose in troubleshooting. Let's take a closer look at a few.

ScanDisk

The ScanDisk utility shipped with MS-DOS 6.x, Windows 3.x, and Windows 95. It is widely used and well known among PC users. ScanDisk is not only a repair utility; it can be used as a diagnostic utility as well. For instance, if you notice that ScanDisk is finding bad disk sectors on a regular basis, this is probably a good indication that the hard drive might be going bad. ScanDisk can also be configured to keep a log of events when it runs. As always, utility logs can give you great insight into diagnosing a problem. Figure 17.7 shows the ScanDisk Advanced Options dialog box.

The ScanDisk log is maintained at the root of drive C:. The following is an example of what is contained in the SCANDISK.LOG file as it appears in Windows Notepad:

```
Microsoft ScanDisk for Windows
Log file generated at 15:44 on 10/13/1998.
ScanDisk used the following options:
      Thorough test
      No write-testing
      Check dates and times
      Don't check host drive first
Drive Pavilion (C:) contained the following errors:
      ScanDisk was canceled.
```

> **NOTE**
>
> If you use an MS-DOS program to view this file, some of the characters might appear incorrectly. Use a Windows program such as Notepad instead.

FIGURE 17.7
ScanDisk's advanced properties.

This SCANDISK.LOG shows the options that were used in scanning and the actions that were taken. This log indicates that the scan was canceled.

Device Manager

The Device Manager utility, shown in Figure 17.8, was a new addition to troubleshooting tools with the release of Windows 95. As part of Windows 95's Plug and Play subsystem, Device Manager keeps track of what resources are assigned to what devices. You can access Device Manager by right-clicking the My Computer icon on the Windows 95 desktop and selecting Properties, or through the System icon in Control Panel. Device Manager shows system devices by list or by connection. You can select either method, depending on your needs.

As you can see in Figure 17.8, Device Manager is showing the device Iomega Zip with a yellow warning sign (exclamation point). This indicates that there is a problem with this device. Figure 17.9 shows the properties page for the Zip and explains the warning. In this case, the Zip drive is not attached.

FIGURE 17.8
Device Manager shows a list of devices.

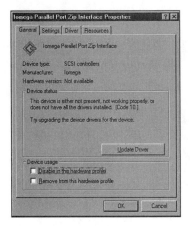

FIGURE 17.9
Properties of a device in Device Manager.

Figure 17.10 shows the Driver File Details dialog box for the Zip device. Notice that Device Manager keeps track of the driver files this device uses, as well as the resources.

Figure 17.11 shows theResources tab for the network adapter listed in the Device Manager. This device has had Plug and Play assigned system resources. By using the options on the Resource tab in Device Manager, you can manually set resource assignments. Plug and Play is not a perfect science and can sometimes cause a conflict. This is where the situation can be resolved.

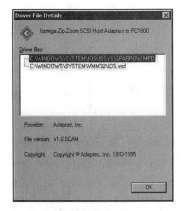

FIGURE 17.10
The Driver File Details dialog box.

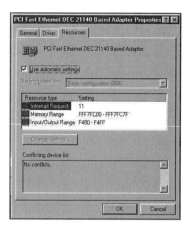

FIGURE 17.11
The Resources tab for the network adapter's properties sheet.

NOTE

Device Manager does not keep track of manually assigned resources. Therefore, Device Manager might try to assign a resource that it doesn't know is taken.

Also note that Plug and Play is great at finding devices, but doesn't automatically remove them from the device list when a device is uninstalled. To remove a nonexistent device from Device Manager, simply select it in the list and click Remove.

ATTRIB.EXE

ATTRIB.EXE is a useful utility for troubleshooting troublesome files. ATTRIB.EXE allows you to view or modify file attributes. As discussed in Chapter 14, "Function, Structure, Operation, and File Management," a file can have the following attributes: system, hidden, read-only, or archive. On occasion, you might need to use the ATTRIB utility to change file attributes while troubleshooting a system. In the event that Windows 95 becomes unable to start, and you can only obtain a DOS prompt, you would use ATTRIB to change the c:\Windows\system.da0 and c:\Windows\user.da0 (these are the Registry backup files) attributes from system, hidden, and read-only so that you can back them up to a floppy disk. You would not want to copy USER.DAT and SYSTEM.DAT, because those are the current system Registry, and Windows will not start. You must change the hidden attribute, or you won't be able to copy the files from a DOS prompt without getting a File not Found error message.

EXTRACT.EXE

Files sometimes become damaged and need to be replaced. The EXTRACT.EXE command resides in the Windows\command directory and can be used to extract a single file from the original install media without reinstalling the entire application or OS. Windows stores all install files in compressed files called cabinet files, or CABs. If you want to extract a file and you don't know in which CAB it is located, use the following command to search all the cabinet files in order and extract the file once it is found:

```
extract /a <cabinet> <filename> /l <destination>
```

For example, to extract GDI.EXE from disks in the A: drive and put them into the Windows\System directory, use the following command:

```
extract /a a:\win95_02.cab gdi.exe /l C:\Windows\system
```

The /a switch tells parameter. For example

```
extract /a a:\win95_02.cab *.txt /l c:\Windows
```

will extract all text files from the CABs and place them in the Windows directory.

Note that if you are extracting from a CD-ROM, you must modify the drive letter and <cabinet> parameter accordingly.

DEFRAG.EXE

The Defrag program normally isn't considered a diagnostic tool. However, it is a good practice to defragment a drive prior to troubleshooting to rule out fragmentation as a possible contributor. Also, a defragmented drive will perform better.

EDIT.COM

Diagnosing problematic programs often leads to inspecting configuration files such as INI files. From a command prompt you can use EDIT.COM to open, explore, and modify any text file. A common use is to edit CONFIG.SYS and comment out device drivers that might be causing trouble. Always make notes of what you change so that you can undo a change if necessary.

FDISK.EXE

FDISK.EXE is a program used to view, create, and delete partitions on hard disk drives. FDISK versions that ship with Windows 95 OSR2 are capable of reading FAT16 and FAT32 file systems. This is a good utility to include on your Emergency Boot Disk (it is already on the Windows 95 Startup Disk). Viewing partition information lets you know if the appropriate partition is marked as active, and with which file system it is formatted.

MSD.EXE

DOS and Windows 3.x both shipped with MSD.EXE as part of the operating system. MSD, or Microsoft Diagnostics, is not included with Windows 95, and not all versions recognize newer processors. Another limitation of MSD is that it doesn't report correct information about memory or system resources if it's running from inside Windows. Limitations aside, MSD can be a great diagnostic tool in a DOS/Windows 3.x environment. MSD will print system reports containing information on memory, drive configuration, video, operating system, and virtually everything else about a computer. MSD shows the memory map of the system and shows what occupies the different areas of memory. Most OEM versions of Windows 95 include a utility called MSINFO32.EXE that is a graphical adaptation of MSD. Although neither program can modify system settings, they still provide a great deal of information.

MEM.EXE

Troubleshooting often means finding out what is in memory. MEM.EXE is available in DOS, Windows 3.x, and Windows 95. Executed from the command prompt, MEM.EXE offers the following options:

- Mem /CLASSIFY or /C classifies programs by memory usage. It lists the size of the programs, provides a summary of memory in use, and lists the largest memory block available.

- Mem /DEBUG or /D displays the status of all the modules in memory, internal drivers, and other information.

- Mem /FREE or /F displays information about the amount of free memory left in both conventional and upper memory.

- Mem /MODULE or /M displays a detailed listing of a module's memory use. This option must be followed by the name of a module, optionally separated from /M by a colon.

- Mem /PAGE or /P pauses after each screen of information.

All these switches can be displayed by issuing the MEM /? command at the command prompt.

SYSEDIT.EXE

Windows-based systems have the SysEdit program, a cousin to EDIT.COM, available for quick access and editing of major Windows configuration files. Unlike EDIT.COM, which allows editing of one file at a time, running SysEdit brings up a window containing the CONFIG.SYS, AUTOEXEC.BAT, SYSTEM.INI, WIN.INI, and sometimes PROTOCOL.INI and MSMAIL.INI files in an editable state. If a quick look at Windows system files is what you need, SysEdit is a utility to remember. These files can be edited and closed one at a time.

VIRUSES

Since the beginning of computer software development, there have been individuals who have manufactured programs that are destructive in nature. These programs are called computer viruses. A computer virus is designed to damage normal computer operation in some way. It infects your computer, stays undetected, and makes itself available to spread to other systems by attaching itself to floppy disks, programs, and email. Originally, most viruses were DOS-based. These DOS viruses can still affect Windows 3.x and Windows 95 environments. As programs and operating systems advance, so do viruses, making the need for virus protection and removal mandatory for computer technicians.

Types of Viruses

Virus types have evolved with the progression of technology. Originally there were only three known virus types: the boot sector, file infector, and Trojan horse. Today there are many virus types that affect virtually every facet of computer environments. Let's discuss the original types and some of the more prevalent new viruses.

The boot sector virus copies itself to the boot tracks of hard drives and floppies, replacing the original boot sector instructions with its own. Because of this, it is loaded into memory before anything else, allowing its instruction set to execute and spread. An example is the Monkey-B virus.

The file infector is a virus that adds its own program code to other program executables. Once the infected program is executed, the virus is activated and spreads itself to other programs. An example is the Anti-exe virus.

The Trojan horse virus hides itself by seeming to actually belong on the disk. By being stealthy, this virus can cause very serious damage by destroying data and disk sectors. An example is the Readme virus.

A more recent addition to the virus family is the polymorphic virus. The polymorphic virus is dangerous because it is designed to find out what virus-scanning program you're using and emulate or avoid it. Most polymorphic viruses can be detected with a new update to your program's virus signature file. The polymorph must be cleaned immediately upon detection, because once it is detected, it learns to hide from the program that detected it.

Also, a recent virus addition is the macro virus. Macro viruses take advantage of word processor macro programming languages and cause problems with the application. Most macro viruses are only mischievous, doing things such as preventing you from saving a document; but some can damage data. A macro virus attaches itself to every document that is opened within the infected program by making itself a part of the normal layout template. An example would be the WAZU macro virus, which attaches itself to the Microsoft Word file NORMAL.DOT.

Virus Dangers

Virus dangers consist of anything from a minor irritant to major program and hardware damage. Boot sector viruses can destroy hard drives. File infectors can damage programs and data. Trojan horse variations can damage computers and programs. Variations of all these virus types can damage virtually anything.

Virus Symptoms and Sources

Major sources of viruses have been shareware programs obtained from bulletin boards or the Internet. Once a computer is infected, floppy disks, network storage, and email can transmit viruses. Symptoms of infection can include (but are not limited to) the following:

- Your hard disk stops booting.
- You frequently find corrupt files.
- Programs start behaving funny or slowly.
- Program options quit working.
- Floppies claim to be full when all files have been deleted.
- You experience hard drive controller failures.
- Your hard drive disappears (it isn't present or is unreadable from a boot floppy disk).
- CMOS reverts to default settings, even with a new battery.

- Files change size for no reason.

- You see a blank screen with a flashing cursor on boot-up, and the computer stops booting.

- Windows crashes.

- Your system slows down noticeably.

How to Identify, Avoid, and Remove Viruses

One way to avoid virus infection is to avoid activities that can expose your system to infection. However, by avoiding email, word processing packages, and corporate networks, you eliminate most of the activities that make a computer a productive tool. With this in mind, it is more reasonable to choose a virus-protection package that can identify virus activity, remove the virus, and protect your computer from further infection.

MS-DOS 6.x contains a virus-protection utility called VSafe that provides minimal protection. Because VSafe hasn't been updated since the last release of DOS, the virus definition files that the program uses to identify viruses are greatly out of date. VSafe monitors for virus activity while a program called MSAV removes them. Windows 3.1 offers updated versions of VSafe and MSAV. Windows 95 has no built-in virus-protection programs.

Many third-party companies offer scanning, detection, and removal programs. In most cases, these programs scan memory during installation to make sure that virus activity isn't present before the installation is completed. If the program notes suspicious activity, your best course of action is to boot the system to a known clean boot disk with a command-line scanning program and clean the system. Once you are sure the system is clean, you can resume the installation.

Once installed, a virus scan runs at system boot-up, and virus monitoring is constant when the system is on. If a virus is detected, you are prompted to clean the virus from the system.

WHAT IS IMPORTANT TO KNOW

- Safe Mode is the Windows 95 diagnostic mode that loads only the minimum drivers required for loading Windows 95. If the system loses power or is shut down improperly, it automatically enters Safe Mode when it's rebooted. If a corrupt or missing device driver is causing the failure, or an application error is to blame, Safe Mode gives you a chance to correct the problem by removing the offending driver or program in an environment that does not present the problem.

- The message `Incorrect DOS version` appears when an application checks the DOS version when it starts and finds a different version number than it expected. To correct this situation, use the `SETVER` command to add your DOS version to the version table. `SETVER` is a TSR utility that maintains a list of programs and the version of DOS each one is expected to use. Therefore, `SETVER` enables you to trick an old program into thinking it is operating in a DOS 3.3 environment even if it is actually running in a DOS 6.22 environment. Another reason for the `Incorrect DOS version` message could be that IO.SYS, MSDOS.SYS, and COMMAND.COM are of different versions. To correct this problem, either reinstall or boot to a floppy disk and use the `SYS` command to transfer the system files to the hard disk again.

- The `No operating system found` error is displayed when there is a problem locating the MBR (master boot record) on the active partition. To investigate this situation, boot to your emergency boot disk and check the active partition using the FDISK utility. The primary partition on the first hard drive must be marked as active in order for the system to boot. If the correct partition is active, transfer the system to the active partition using the SYS.COM utility. Verify that you are copying the same DOS/Windows 95 version that the hard drive is supposed to be using.

- The `Error in CONFIG.SYS line` xx message is usually a result of bad syntax or an incorrect path statement. CONFIG.SYS cannot load a driver it does not recognize or find. To correct this, check the path to the file to see if it is correct, check your spelling, and (as a last resort) reinstall the software affecting the line.

- The Command Interpreter is COMMAND.COM, and something has corrupted or deleted that file if you receive the message `Bad or missing Command Interpreter`. To correct this issue, reformat the drive if it is empty. If it has data on it, boot to a floppy and use the `SYS` command to transfer the system back to the drive.

- If you receive the message HIMEM.SYS not loaded, check to see if HIMEM.SYS exists in the location specified in CONFIG.SYS. If this is correct, check the file date on HIMEM.SYS to see if it is the most current version.

  If the date is correct, boot from a floppy containing a minimum version of CONFIG.SYS and AUTOEXEC.BAT to see if you are able to start Windows. If this works, the problem exists within CONFIG.SYS or AUTOEXEC.BAT. If this does not work, there is probably a problem with the memory manager. To correct this problem, copy HIMEM.SYS from CD again or install floppies.

- You may have to use a diagnostic utility like Microsoft Diagnostics (MSD) to determine if there is a conflict in upper memory. If you discover an upper memory conflict, you can resolve it by unloading all drivers and TSRs from upper memory.

- On Windows 3.x, users can enhance performance by changing virtual memory settings from temporary to permanent. When Windows starts, the temporary swap file is created, slowing down the start process. Running out of disk space will affect Windows performance because there will be no room for the swap file. The use of a permanent swap file allows for better performance because it always reserves disk space and is always available for use. Not having enough hard drive space available is the only reason not to use a permanent swap file in Windows 3.x. On occasion, when you start Windows, you will receive the message Swap file is corrupt. Upon acknowledgment of this error, Windows starts and prompts you to create a new swap file. This usually occurs after you've used a disk cloning utility such as PKZIP Image or Symantec's Ghost.

- The Windows 95 swap file is dynamic, so it can shrink or grow as needed. The Windows 95 swap file can occupy a fragmented region of the hard disk with no noticeable performance loss. Making sure that the disk containing the swap file has plenty of free space for expanding and contracting is the best way to optimize the Windows 95 dynamic swap file. Running out of disk space will impact performance greatly.

- The absence of a device specified in one of the configuration files is very common after a program has been uninstalled or deleted. Some uninstall programs do not remove referenced devices because they are poorly designed, or because something interrupts the uninstall process. In any event, these absent devices can either prevent Windows from loading or simply slow it down. It is important to take notes and make a list of the files that the system list as missing. When you quit receiving messages stating that devices are missing, you should run SysEdit.

Search the WIN.INI and SYSTEM.INI files for instances of the files you copied down as being missing, and mark them out. When all missing files have been completely commented out, restart the system and watch for errors. If the system gives you more errors, repeat the process until Windows starts error free. If the system boots correctly, double-check to make sure all programs operate correctly, verifying that the items you marked out are not necessary. If any program does not check out, run that program's setup routine again to replace any files that were accidentally removed.

- Symptoms of a stalled print spooler include print jobs being sent to the printer but not printing. If this occurs, double-click the printer's icon and see if any jobs are listed. Sometimes deleting the job at the top of the queue will start the print process again. Make sure there is enough disk space available to spool. If disk space is available, this is not the problem. If you are low on disk space, free up some space by backing up some data to other media, and then try printing again. It is recommended that you have about twice as much disk space available as the size of the file you are trying to print.

  If you still cannot print, right-click the printer icon and select Properties. On the Details tab, click the Spool Options button. Change the spool settings to print directly to the printer. If this produces positive printer output, the problem is a stalled print spooler. Rebooting the machine can clear the spooler and restart printing. If rebooting does not work, however, change the output from EMF to RAW. If you still cannot print, check the Windows\system\spool\printers directory for *.SPL and *.TMP files and delete any that exist. These could be the corrupt spool jobs. If none of these tasks restarts printing, the print spooler is probably not the problem.

- A corrupt or incorrect driver is probably the most common Windows printing error. If print jobs are coming out of the printer garbled or off-format, the printer driver is the likely culprit. Reinstalling the driver or updating the driver from the Printer Properties Details tab works most of the time, but some drivers are known to have problems with different versions of Windows. Updated drivers can fix this problem, and most are available for download. For instance, if you had an HP printer, you would point your browser to your printer manufacturer's Web site for the most up-to-date driver.

  When a GPF occurs, the system displays a message stating that a GPF has occurred and in what application. GPFs that occur in 16-bit applications display a blue screen, whereas 32-bit applications display a Windows dialog box. 32-bit applications in Windows 95 are not prone to

GPFs because of the way Windows 95 assigns resources. Since the OS is aware of what device and program is using which memory areas, the occurrence of faults is greatly reduced. It is possible, however, for a 32-bit application to have a General Protection Fault. Correcting this problem requires good note-taking when the error happens. Knowing what caused the problem helps eliminate it. Use the Device Manager to see if any system hardware is using the memory area that the offending program tried to use. If there is an overlap, correct it by using Device Manager to reassign a different memory area to the hardware. If hardware is not causing the conflict, it is probably the result of either a file in the problematic application or a version conflict with a system library. Contact the application manufacturer for further information.

◆ An `Illegal operation` message indicates that the program expected the operating system to act a particular way, and the program stopped because the system did not act in that way. For example, suppose a DOS application that uses DOS Extenders does not recognize the Windows 95 Extender. The fix is to get an updated version of the offending program. The unfortunate fact about illegal operations is that usually you must apply a service pack or an application update of some sort. Technical support Web sites and packages like Microsoft TechNet have hundreds of articles pertaining to illegal operations with hundreds of different fixes.

◆ The `Invalid working directory` message occurs when you try to launch a program in Windows 3.x and the working directory is wrong. When a program is installed in Windows 3.x and its program group is created, the properties of the icons in the program group give the path to the executable file and the directory where it is located. This directory is known as the *working directory*. If a drive letter changes (if, for example, another hard drive is added or you change the CD-ROM drive letter) and an icon still points to the previous drive letter, the `Invalid working directory` message appears. To correct this, select the icon, select File, Properties, and modify the path to the working directory to point to the correct location.

◆ A system lockup occurs when the processor gets conflicting information or becomes unaware of what the operating system is doing. In DOS, the usual cause is a memory problem or a poorly written program.

◆ Windows 3.x uses cooperative multitasking. In cooperative multitasking, all programs operate in the same memory space and cooperatively share resources. This means the programs are in control of the processor at all times. When the program finishes with the current task, it is supposed to relinquish control to the next program and so on. If a program stalls while controlling the processor, the system stops. In Windows 3.x, this usually forces you to reboot.

◆ Windows 95's 32-bit architecture takes advantage of preemptive multitasking. Preemptive multitasking gives the processor control over the applications. When the time that an application has been allotted for processor functions expires, the processor takes control from that application and gives time to the next application in line. This is why you can press Ctrl+Alt+Del to shut down a troubled program in Windows 95. However, to maintain backward compatibility with 16-bit applications that depend on cooperative multitasking, Windows 95 has an area of non-reentrant code known as the WIN16 Mutex. The WIN16 Mutex flag simulates the processor being under control of the 16-bit application. When the WIN16 Mutex flag is set (albeit only for a fraction of a second), if a 16-bit program hangs, it locks the system. This usually means rebooting. To avoid hang-ups in Windows 95, use only 32-bit programs whenever possible. Although this is not specifically testable material, you can find more information on the Win16 Mutex and the non-reentrant code in the Windows 95 Resource Kit.

◆ An option that does not function usually indicates that an installation was not completed appropriately or has since become corrupt. A common example occurs in Windows 95 when Start menu shortcuts do not run the associated programs. However, an error message might not be displayed, which makes this kind of error difficult to troubleshoot. Correcting this issue will require patience. First, launch the application from its home directory to eliminate the possibility that the shortcut has become damaged. If this does not work, rule out memory conflicts by checking the Device Manager for warnings. Also verify that other applications are not affected. This rules out a system problem. Last, back up data, uninstall the application, and then reinstall. If the misbehaving function is part of the operating system (such as the DOS PIF), the OS may have to be reinstalled.

◆ An application problem can indicate a bad installation and/or that an application file has become damaged. Good troubleshooting and note taking skills are the quickest way to fix the problem.

First, eliminate the possibility that the problem is the PC or the OS by verifying that there are no conflicts during start up. Check to see that all other applications are unaffected, and check the Windows 95 Device Manager for warnings. After performing these tasks, you can assume the problem is an application issue.

◆ Troubleshooting an application that won't start or load involves starting the application and trying to note system behavior or error messages. If you do not see any error messages, change the system video to basic VGA and try again. Some applications are written to display messages in VGA mode. Fancier video cards may not be able to display the error or might show only a black screen. (This works in Windows 3.x and DOS. For

Windows 95, use Safe Mode.) If no messages are given, try booting the system in Windows 95 Safe Mode to see if it runs. If this is successful, the application has a conflict with a device driver (such as a video or network card) that is not loaded in Safe Mode. If the application still does not run, try booting with clean CONFIG.SYS and AUTOEXEC.BAT files. (In DOS/Windows 3.x environments, use a boot disk. In Windows 95, boot to the startup disk or simply rename CONFIG.SYS and AUTOEXEC.BAT files and boot.) If this proves unsuccessful, uninstall and reinstall the application. Note that reinstalling only corrects the problem in the case of file corruption or an incomplete installation.

◆ To begin diagnosing the error message `Cannot log on to network`, make sure that all hardware is functioning properly and all software is installed correctly.

◆ Client problems are common culprits of logon problems. When the client software is configured incorrectly, logon will most likely fail. The most common problems with client configuration are misspelling the login domain or preferred server name, or simply not having the client installed.

◆ In Microsoft networking, computer names must be unique. If two users have the same computer name, network access will be denied to the computer that has been on for the least amount of time.

◆ Installing a client in Windows installs the default protocol. Once a network client is installed, you have the ability to locate shared resources on a network. Actually accessing those resources requires that the requesting workstation and the computer with the shared resource use a common protocol. A common problem with protocols is binding. Binding means that the protocol is associated with the client software.

◆ The protocol is the language that computers speak, and frame type is the dialect. IPX/SPX is a protocol that uses frame types. IPX/SPX frame types are automatically detected by default in Windows 95. Auto detect works most of the time; however, in NetWare environments that have more than one frame type running on the network, a Windows 95 client detects and binds only the first frame type it finds. If a client detects a different frame type on another computer, the client will not be able to access that computer. (Usually, the client cannot even see PCs running other frame types.) This can be corrected by manually selecting the frame type. Changing frame types requires you to reboot your system.

◆ The TCP/IP protocol can be configured manually or dynamically. The easiest way to configure it is through Dynamic Host Configuration Protocol, or DHCP. DHCP is set up from a network server and automatically assigns IP addresses to workstations configured to use DHCP.

Manual TCP/IP configuration requires you to add the IP address and the subnet mask. The IP address must be unique to the network and acts as the computer's street address. At a fundamental level, the subnet mask must be common to all computers in your network because it defines what network your computer is on. If the computer is in a routed network, it also requires a default gateway. All IP requests to unknown addresses are forwarded to the default gateway. You can verify IP settings by using the WINIPCFG utility and the PING utility.

- NetBEUI is another common protocol. It requires no configuration but is not routable. If your protocol is NetBEUI and you are in a routed network, you will not be able to access network hosts on the other side of the router from you.

- Access permissions can also prevent a user from logging on to the network. If the computer holding the shared resources does not grant you access to the resource, you will not gain access.

- ScanDisk is a utility that checks your system's FAT for inconsistencies, and corrects them. ScanDisk will also check and repair disk integrity and directory structure.

- The Device Manager utility was a new addition to troubleshooting tools with the release of Windows 95. As part of the Plug and Play subsystem of Windows 95, Device Manager keeps track of which resources are assigned to which devices. You can also manually configure resources in Device Manager.

- ATTRIB.EXE is the command prompt utility that allows you to view and modify file attributes.

- The EXTRACT.EXE command resides in the Windows\command directory and can be used to extract a single file from the original installation media without reinstalling the entire application or OS. Windows stores all installation files in compressed files called cabinet files, or CABS.

- The DEFRAG program is not normally considered a diagnostic tool. However, it is a good practice to defragment a drive before you begin troubleshooting in order to rule out fragmentation as a possible contributor. Also, a defragmented drive will perform better.

- Edit is the DOS/Windows text editor. You can use Edit as a diagnostic tool by using it to view and modify text-based configuration files such as CONFIG.SYS, AUTOEXEC.BAT, and all INI files.

- FDISK is the DOS/Windows disk partition tool. FDISK is a great utility to have on your boot floppy in case a partition becomes inactive or needs to be recreated.

- MSD.EXE is the Microsoft diagnostics program that comes with DOS and Windows 3.x. MSD has a detailed memory map that is great for troubleshooting upper memory issues and device memory conflicts. MSD shows most system information, such as information on installed drivers, video, memory, and the operating system. MSD is not a good diagnostic tool for Windows 95 (it is also not included with Windows 95). The Windows 95 memory model misrepresents information to MSD.

◆ MEM.EXE is available to DOS, Windows 3.x, and Windows 95. When executed from the command prompt, MEM.EXE displays what type of memory the system is using and what devices are using it. MEM.EXE is the correct utility to use when manually managing memory. You can display all MEM.EXE switches by issuing the `mem /?` command at the command prompt.

◆ Windows-based systems offer the SysEdit program for quick access and editing of major Windows configuration files. Unlike EDIT.COM, which allows you to edit only one file at a time, running SysEdit brings up a window containing the CONFIG.SYS, AUTOEXEC.BAT, SYSTEM.INI, WIN.INI, PROTOCOL.INI, and MSMAIL.INI files in an editable state. If a quick look at Windows system files is what you need, SysEdit is a utility to remember. You can edit and close these files one at a time.

◆ Originally, there were only three known virus types: the boot sector, the file infector, and the Trojan horse. Today multiple virus types affect virtually every facet of computer environments.

The boot sector virus copies itself to the boot tracks of hard drives and floppies, replacing the original boot sector instructions with its own. Because of this, it is loaded into memory before anything else, allowing its instruction set to execute and spread when a computer boots or attempts to boot from the disk. An example is the Monkey-B virus.

The file infector is a virus that adds its own program code to other program executables. When the infected program is executed, the virus is activated and spreads itself to other programs. An example is the Anti-exe virus.

The Trojan horse type virus hides itself by appearing to belong on the disk. By being stealthy, this virus can cause very serious damage, even destroying data and disk sectors. An example is the Readme virus.

◆ A more recent addition to the virus family is the polymorphic virus. The polymorphic virus is dangerous because it is designed to find out what virus-scanning program you are using and emulate it or avoid it. Most polymorphic viruses can be detected with a new update to your program's virus signature file. The polymorph must be cleaned immediately upon detection because once it is detected, it learns to hide from the program that detected it.

◆ Another recent virus addition is the Macro virus. Macro viruses take advantage of word processor macro programming languages and cause problems with the application. Most macro viruses are mischievous only in that they cause an irritant such as the inability to save a document; however, some can damage data. A macro virus attaches itself to every document that is opened with the infected program by making itself a part of the normal layout template. An example would be the WAZU macro virus that attaches itself to the Microsoft Word NORMAL.DOT template.

♦ Virus dangers range from a minor irritant to major program and hardware damage. Boot sector viruses can destroy hard drives. File infectors can damage programs and data. Trojan horse variations can damage computers and programs. Variations of all these virus types can damage virtually anything. The macro virus usually destroys only data.

♦ Major sources of viruses have been shareware programs obtained from bulletin boards or the Internet. Once a computer is infected, floppy disks, network storage, and email can transmit viruses. Symptoms of infection can include (but are not limited to) the following: the hard disk stops booting, frequent corrupt files, programs start behaving funny or slowly, and program options quit working. Other symptoms are floppies that claim to be full when all files have been deleted, hard drive controller failures, and hard drive disappearance (it is not present or is unreadable from a boot floppy). Other possibilities are the CMOS reverting to default settings even with a new battery, files changing size for no reason, a blank screen with a flashing cursor on boot up that does not go away, Windows crashes, and noticeable system slowdowns.

♦ You can prevent virus infection by avoiding those activities that can expose your system to infection. Realistically, you should choose a virus protection package that can identify virus activity, remove the virus, and protect from further infection.

♦ MS-DOS 6.x contains a virus protection utility called VSafe that provides minimal protection. Because VSafe has not been updated since the last release of DOS, the virus definition files the program uses to identify viruses are terribly outdated. Windows 3.x offered updated versions of VSafe and MSAV. Windows 95 has no built-in virus protection programs.

♦ Many companies offer scanning, detection, and removal programs. In most cases, these programs scan memory during installation to make sure that virus activity is not present before completing the installation. If the program notes suspicious activity, your best course of action is to boot the system to a known clean boot disk with a command line scanning program, and clean the system. When you are sure the system is clean, you can resume the installation.

♦ Once installed, virus software runs at system boot-up and monitors constantly when the system is on. If a virus is detected, you should be prompted to clean the virus from the system.

OBJECTIVES

▶ Discuss the network capabilities of MS-DOS/Windows.

▶ Connect a DOS workstation to a network.

▶ Connect a Windows 3.x workstation to a network.

▶ Connect a Windows 95 workstation to a network.

▶ Contrast different types of network designs.

▶ Distinguish between different types of network interface cards (NICs).

▶ Connect a DOS/Windows or Windows 95 workstation to the Internet.

CHAPTER 18

Networking

When sharing data between two or more computers became a necessity, the need for a networked environment was born. Networks enable users to access other computers' disk drives and printers as if they were actually attached to the users' PCs. Computer networks are categorized into two types. In a *peer-to-peer network*, two or more users share their computers' resources. In a client/server network, one or more users' computers can access resources on a computer dedicated for file and print sharing.

DOS NETWORKING CAPABILITIES

Inherently, DOS has no networking capabilities. Networking in DOS requires third-party software such as Microsoft LAN Manager or Novell NetWare. Both of these products use real-mode drivers to enable DOS network cards and bind protocols for network access.

WINDOWS NETWORKING CAPABILITIES

Windows networking comes as a result of Windows 3.11 or Windows for Workgroups (WFW). WFW was designed as a peer-to-peer networking solution that allowed computer users to share their local printers and disk space. Windows 3.1 computers can be networked with third-party add–on software. Windows 95, like WFW, is capable of peer-to-peer networking out of the box. Both Windows 95 and WFW are capable of participating in a client/server environment as well.

SHARING DISK DRIVES

Sharing resources is the reason for networking. Sharing files across a large building becomes difficult if the file size is larger than floppy disk capacity. Early Macintosh computers came with the capability to share their disk space using a network. PCs were soon to follow. Sharing in Windows is a service that is added via the Network Control Panel. Figure 18.1 shows the sharing services available to Windows 95 OSR2.

NOTE

Types of security are covered in Chapter 17, "Diagnosing and Troubleshooting," in the section on file and print sharing. The following text assumes you know the security types discussed in Chapter 17.

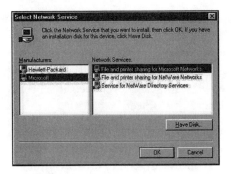

FIGURE 18.1
The Windows 95 file sharing services.

After it's installed, the File and Print Sharing service adds a Sharing menu option to Windows Explorer and the right-click context menu (shown in Figure 18.2). Windows for Workgroups shares resources in a similar way. When you allow file and print sharing, sharing becomes an option in File Manager. You must select the directory to be shared and share it by turning on the Sharing menu item. (The context menu is not available to Windows 3.x.)

Selecting the Sharing option displays the Sharing properties sheet for that object. The properties sheet looks different depending on which kind of access your computer is configured for. The two types of security available to the Windows 95 network user are user-level and share-level.

FIGURE 18.2
Sharing is added to the context menu when the File and Print Sharing service is installed.

Share-level security is controlled from the share itself. (Share-level is the only security available in peer-to-peer networks. Client/server environments can use either.) User-level security, on the other hand, depends on a network file server for security. Figure 18.3 shows the Sharing properties sheet for a computer configured to use share-level security. From here, you can choose to share or unshare this object.

Each share must have a unique name. The Comment field is optional. This dialog box also contains options with which you can control the type of share access. Full Control access allows anyone to create or delete items on your share. Read-Only access allows users accessing this share to read and copy objects only; they cannot add to or delete from the share. You also have the option of assigning access depending on a password. Figure 18.4 shows the properties sheet for a PC configured for user-level security. Figure 18.5 shows the Access Control tab from the Network Control Panel, where you choose between user-level and share-level access.

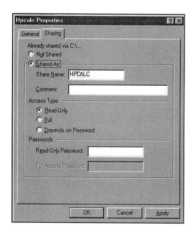

FIGURE 18.3
You enable share-level security from the Sharing properties sheet.

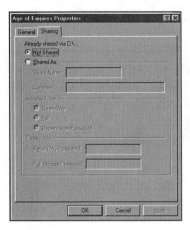

FIGURE 18.4
This PC is configured for user-level security.

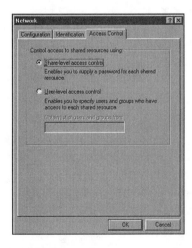

FIGURE 18.5
You choose which type of security you want to use in the Network Control Panel's
Access Control tab.

When you implement user-level access, you can still choose Full or Read-Only access, but you do not have the option of setting a password. A network file server that you select as a security provider manages the passwords. Custom access is now an option as well. To give access to users, you select their user IDs from the User list (maintained by the server) and add them to the appropriate access groups. You can give rights to a specific individual; however, in a large network with many users, it is better to assign users to groups and control access by group. This limits administrative tasks to only a few groups instead of every user.

When viewed in Windows Explorer from across the network, shared objects show up under the computer on which they reside as shown in Figure 18.6. When viewed from the computer on which it is shared, a share shows up as a regular folder icon with a hand under it (see Figure 18.7).

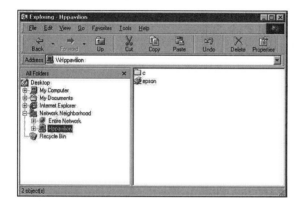

FIGURE 18.6
Shares as they appear in Explorer when viewed from across the network.

FIGURE 18.7
A share from the local PC is displayed with a hand icon under it.

SHARING FILE AND PRINT SERVICES

Sharing a Windows printer is very similar to sharing a folder. After the file sharing service is installed, you can share the printer by right-clicking its icon and selecting Sharing from the context menu. You can also enable printer sharing by selecting the File and Print Sharing button from the Network Control Panel and checking the appropriate box (see Figure 18.8).

As with a shared file, you can tell a printer is shared because a hand appears under the icon (see Figure 18.9).

Figure 18.10 shows the Print Sharing properties sheet. Notice that the controls for sharing a printer are not as extensive as those for sharing a file. From this dialog box, you can share the printer, give it a share name, and enter a password if desired.

FIGURE 18.8
Activating File and Print Sharing from the Network Control Panel.

FIGURE 18.9
The hand icon appears under a shared printer when it's viewed locally.

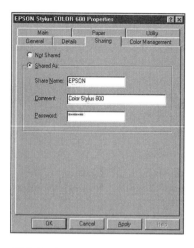

FIGURE 18.10
The Print Sharing properties sheet.

NOTE

When you name a shared object, you can make the last character a dollar sign ($) to hide the share from the view of users browsing the network. To access a hidden share, you must know its name and must connect by entering the complete path according to the Universal Naming Convention (UNC). For example, a UNC path would be \\*computername**sharename*$. This is a great way to give your network support staff access to all utilities in a share, yet make those utilities invisible to users accessing through Network Neighborhood.

At A Glance: Overview of Network Share Options

Type of Sharing	Security Provider	Types of Access
Share-level	Your computer	Read-Only Full Control Depends on password
User-level	Network server	Read-Only Full Control Custom Access can be granted or denied to users or groups of users.

NETWORK TYPE AND NETWORK CARD

As the need for networks arose, more than one technology was created to meet that need. These technologies came into being as network configurations that we now call *topologies*. A network topology defines the way in which a network is connected. There are three common network topologies.

Common Network Topologies

The first topology is called *bus* topology. In this design, each node has a unique address and connects to a central communication trunk. Any node can put information onto the network. Information put on the network must contain destination address information to ensure that the data arrives at its intended location. All network nodes ignore data that is not intended for their unique addresses.

The second type of configuration is called *ring* topology. A ring is just that: a closed ring of communication. Each network card in the ring network has a signal repeater built into it so that data not intended for that station can be repeated to the next node in the chain. Data is passed from node to node in this manner until it reaches its intended destination. If there is no intended destination for the signal, it will eventually return to the originating node, which will remove it from the ring.

The third topology is *star* topology. The star topology layout resembles a star or a snowflake in which all nodes are linked to a central unit. All nodes communicate with one another through the central unit. The central unit organizes all network communication by polling nodes to see if they have data to transmit. If a node responds that it has data to transfer, the central communication unit gives that node a specific time slice in which to transmit. Large messages that would take longer than the allotted amount of time are broken into smaller packets and sent through several polling cycles until transmission is complete.

In addition to network design, certain specifications govern network access. If all communication on the network occurred simultaneously, there would be, in essence, a "traffic jam." These traffic jams are called *collisions*. To prevent collisions, networks use *network access methods*. The most popular of these are Ethernet, token-ring, and ARCnet.

Ethernet networks use the bus network topology and operate on a media access method called Carrier Sense Multiple Access with Collision Detection (CSMA/CD). This means that an Ethernet node checks the LAN for traffic before sending data. If there is no traffic, the node transmits its data. A data collision occurs when more than one node transmits at the same time. All nodes that sent data or are waiting to send data detect the collision and then generate a random wait time before attempting to retransmit. This allows for all nodes to be able to gain exclusive access to the LAN.

ARCnet networks are ring networks by design, but they closely resemble a tree/star structure. In ARCnet, media access is governed by a data token. The token passes from node to node constantly. Only the node that possesses the token can transmit data to the LAN, and each node keeps the token for a set amount of time. If a node needs to transfer more data than it can in the allotted time, the data is segmented, and some is sent during the next token possession. A computer that joins or leaves the network must be added or removed using ARCnet management software. Because the token passing sequence is determined when the network starts, nodes that are not added via management software will be ignored. ARCnet cards are usually configured to announce themselves when they start up. The other nodes then poll the new node for identification and add it to the token-passing sequence automatically.

Token-ring networks use a ring design and a token-passing media access method similar to ARCnet. As in an ARCnet network, when a node possesses the token, it can transmit to the network. A token-ring node does this by turning the token into a start data packet and then appending its data. When the token reaches its intended destination, the data is copied to the receiver. Upon return to the transmitting station, the token is reconstructed and placed back on the ring.

At A Glance: Network Topologies

Network Design	How Nodes Are Connected	How Nodes Communicate with One Another
Bus	Central communication link	Directly to other nodes
Ring	Logical closed ring	Data is put on the ring and picked up by the destination node
Star	All nodes are connected to a central communication link	Through the central communication unit

At A Glance: Common Network Access Methods

Network Protocol Design	Type of Network Design	Media Access
Ethernet	Bus	CMSA/CD
ARCnet	Ring	Via token
Token-ring	Ring	Via token

SETTING UP A SYSTEM FOR INTERNET ACCESS

To set up a system for Internet access, you extend the computer onto the Internet by redirecting to the Internet all requests that are not intended for the local computer. The redirector can be either a network card or a modem. Accessing the Internet via a network card usually means that the network is connected to the Internet by means of a *proxy server*. A proxy server is a server that has a connection to the Internet and caches frequently used Internet sites. All clients on the network are configured to access the Internet through the proxy. Figure 18.11 shows the Proxy Server section of the Connections configuration page for Microsoft Internet Explorer 4.

For most Internet access setups, the computer must use an IP address. As you will learn later in this chapter, TCP/IP is the language the Internet speaks. Therefore, a client must be configured to use TCP/IP. An Internet client will need a unique IP address, a subnet mask, and a default gateway. If you are using a modem to access the Internet, the Internet service provider (ISP) is most likely going to assign an IP address through DHCP.

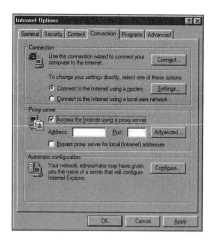

FIGURE 18.11
Proxy connection setup for Microsoft Internet Explorer.

Dial-Up Access

Setting up a computer for Internet access via modem is very similar to configuring a computer for network access. The modem takes the place of the network card and, while connected, acts like one. To set up a modem connection in Windows 95, perform the following steps:

1. Open the My Computer icon.

2. Open the Dial-Up Networking (DUN) folder.

3. Select the Make New Connection icon. This starts the Connection Wizard shown in Figure 18.12.

FIGURE 18.12
Clicking the Make New Connection icon starts the Internet Connection Wizard.

4. Give the connection a name and select a modem (see Figure 18.13).

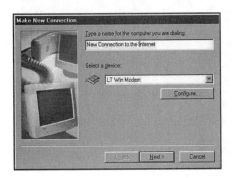

FIGURE 18.13
Step 1 of the Internet Connection Wizard or ICW.

5. Type in the area code, phone number, and country code, as shown in Figure 18.14.

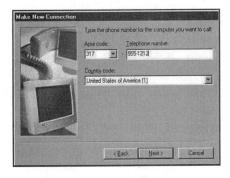

FIGURE 18.14
ICW step 2.

6. Select Finish to complete the process (see Figure 18.15).

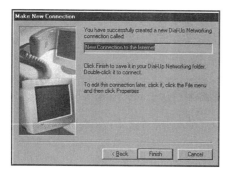

FIGURE 18.15
ICW's final step.

That completes the dial-up settings. Most dial-up connections will need to be configured to use the same protocol as the Internet service provider. To choose a protocol, right-click the newly created connection icon to access the properties sheet for this connection. Choose the Server Types tab to see a list of protocols (see Figure 18.16).

If you select the TCP/IP Settings button from this page, you can configure TCP/IP further with the options shown in Figure 18.17. Most Internet service providers will require a DNS server setting. DNS is short for Domain Name Service, and it is the means by which the Internet matches a specific IP address to a computer name. It would be extremely difficult to find resources on the Internet by IP address alone. DNS puts logical names to IP addresses.

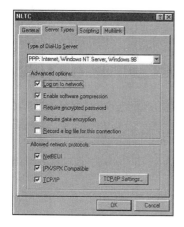

FIGURE 18.16
Protocol settings for dial-up accounts.

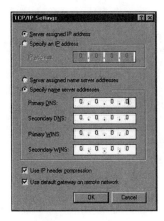

FIGURE 18.17
Dial-up TCP/IP settings.

Setup instructions specific to your ISP are provided by the ISP.

TCP/IP

TCP/IP is the protocol that is used by the Internet. To access the Internet, you must use TCP/IP. An IP address is a specific "street" address on the Internet and consists of a 32-bit, four-octet binary number. Most people recognize an IP address in its decimal format such as 45.222.202.7. Routers on the Internet interpret this decimal format in binary. For example, 45.222.202.7 in binary would be 00101101.11011110.11001010.00000111.

Valid IP addresses are those addresses that have been assigned by Stanford Research Institute (also known as InterNIC and SRINIC), the governing body of Internet addresses.

EMAIL

Probably the most widely used Internet resource available is electronic mail, or *email*. Email today has a wide range of collaboration tools including those that enable the user to attach files and graphics to a message and send it to another mail recipient. Originally, email content was little more than ASCII text files. Email uses the Internet and DNS to locate the intended recipient of a message.

A message is composed and sent to the user's address, such as *whoever@whatever.com*. Such a message leaves the local mail server in route to the domain whatever.com. If there is a mail server handling incoming Internet mail at whatever.com, the message will be routed to it. The whatever.com mail server then passes the message to the user called whoever. When the user checks his or her messages, the new message appears. If DNS servers are unable to resolve the name whatever.com, or if the whatever mail server does not recognize the user, a Non-Delivery Report (NDR) is returned to the message originator.

HTML

HTML, or Hypertext Markup Language, is a means of publishing information in a format common to Internet browsers and Web servers. HTML uses coded text to give the browser instructions on how text or pictures are to be displayed to the user. One such coded display is the *hyperlink*. A hyperlink appears to the user as underlined text that has a link to another Universal Resource Locator (URL) embedded into it. When the mouse arrow moves over a hyperlink, it changes to a pointing hand. Moving the pointing-hand pointer to the hyperlink and clicking will take you to the embedded link.

HYPERTEXT TRANSFER PROTOCOL (HTTP)

HTTP is the Hypertext Transfer Protocol. Most browser software uses this protocol for their normal navigation. The HTTP:// at the beginning of the address line designates that you are using HTTP to navigate. For example, you might enter the address `HTTP://www.basement.john-shouse.com` to indicate that you want to use HTTP to travel the World Wide Web to find the subdomain basement of the top-level domain johnshouse.com.

FILE TRANSFER PROTOCOL (FTP)

FTP is the File Transfer Protocol. FTP does not require the use of a browser; it is integrated into the TCP/IP protocol suite. FTP is used through an FTP–aware operating system such as Windows 95 (HyperTerminal and Command Prompt if TCP/IP is installed), a browser, or a third-party program written to use FTP. Users can copy files to or from a computer that's acting as an FTP host.

DOMAIN NAMES (WEB SITES)

Domain names are names assigned to top-level servers that are registered on the Internet. Several possible domain names can be assigned, depending on the role of the organization that owns the server. The most common and recognizable domain is the COM domain. The most common domains are listed here:

.COM	Commercial businesses, such as Microsoft.com
.ORG	Non-profit organizations, such as CompTIA.org
.EDU	Educational institutions, such as BSU.edu (Ball State University)
.GOV	Government organizations, such as white-house.gov
.MIL	Military installations, such as norfolknaval.mil
.INT	International organizations, such as amnesty.int
.NET	Large network providers or ISPs, such as worldcom.net

All these abbreviations are the domains. An example of a top-level domain would be johnshouse.com. Johnshouse is the highest level server in this domain. An example of a second-level domain would be basement.johnshouse.com, where basement is a division of johnshouse.

Domains are registered with DNS (Domain Name Service) servers across the Internet. DNS entries enable Internet clients to know that 192.102.198.160 is intel.com. DNS name resolution enables users to access different domains through their browsers by name, instead of having to know the IP addresses.

ISP

Internet service providers are companies that sell access to the Internet. Companies like these usually own blocks of registered IP address ranges, which they assign to individual modems when users dial in.

At A Glance: Common Internet Terms

Term	Definition
TCP/IP	Transmission Control Protocol, Internet Protocol. TCP/IP is the protocol suite used by the Internet.
Email	Means of transferring ASCII text and attachments from one Internet mail server to another.
HTML	Hypertext Markup Language. The publishing format for Web pages.
HTTP	Hypertext Transfer Protocol. Means of browsing the World Wide Web via hypertext.
FTP	File Transfer Protocol. Means of transferring files between two computers running the FTP service.
Domain names	DNS names associated with Web sites and servers.
ISP	Internet service provider. A company that sells access (usually by dial-up) to the Internet.
WWW	The World Wide Web. A collection of HTML pages from around the world.

WHAT IS IMPORTANT TO KNOW

♦ DOS has no networking capabilities out of the box. Networking in DOS requires use of a third-party product such as Microsoft LAN Manager or personal NetWare. (These products are no longer available, but both NetWare and Windows NT have DOS client software.)

♦ Windows for Workgroups (WFW) was designed as a peer-to-peer networking solution that allowed computer users to share their local printers and disk space. Windows 3.1 can be networked with a third-party add-on. Windows 95, like WFW, is capable of networking out of the box. Both Windows 95 and WFW are capable of participating in a client/server environment as well.

♦ Disk Drive sharing is installed as a service in Network Control Panel. Once installed, the File and Print Sharing service adds a Sharing menu option to Explorer and the context menu. Selecting the Sharing option invokes the Sharing properties sheet for that object. The properties sheets for various objects look different, depending on the kind of access your computer is configured for. The two types of security are user-level and share-level. Share-level security is controlled from the share itself, whereas user-level security depends on a network file server for security. Each share requires a unique name. From across the network, shared objects viewed from Windows Explorer appear under the computer where they reside. When viewed from the computer where it is shared, the share appears as a regular folder icon with a hand under it.

♦ Sharing Windows printers is very similar to sharing folders. After the File and Print Sharing service is installed, you can share a printer by selecting the printer, right-clicking, and selecting the Sharing option. Alternatively, you can open Control Panel, choose Networks, and click the File and Print Sharing button to activate print sharing. As with a shared file, you can tell when a printer is shared because a hand appears under the icon.

♦ A network topology describes the way in which a network is connected. There are three common network topologies. The first topology is called *bus* topology. In this design, all nodes have a unique address and connect to a central trunk. Any node can put information onto the network. Information put onto the network must contain destination address information to ensure the data can be delivered to its intended location. Each network node ignores data that is not intended for its unique address.

The second type of configuration is called *ring* topology. A ring is just that: a closed ring of communication. Each network card in the ring network has a signal repeater built into it so that data not intended for that station can be repeated to the next node in the chain. Data is passed from node to node in this way until it reaches its intended destination. If there is no intended destination for the signal, it will eventually return to the originating node, which will remove it.

The third topology is *star* topology. The star topology layout resembles a star or a snowflake: All nodes are linked to a central unit. The nodes communicate with one another through the central unit. The central unit organizes all network communication by polling nodes to see if they have data to transmit. If a node responds that it has data to transfer, the central communication unit gives that node a specific time slice in which to transmit. Large messages that would take longer than the allotted amount of time are broken into smaller packets and sent through several polling cycles until the transfer is complete.

♦ You set up a system for Internet access by extending the computer onto the Internet by way of an access point, which might be either a network card or a modem. When you access the Internet via a network card, the network is connected to the Internet by means of a proxy server or direct connection and some kind of WAN link. In this instance, Internet access is obtained by setting the computer's browser to point to the proxy server. When a router is used, the gateway address must be specified to direct Internet traffic outside the local network.

♦ Setting up a computer for Internet access via modem is very similar to configuring a computer for network access. The modem takes the place of the network card and, while connected, acts like one. To set up a modem connection, you must have a modem installed and configured. From the Dial-Up Networking folder located in the Windows 95 My Computer folder, double-click the Make New Connection icon to start the Make New Connection Wizard. Follow the wizard screens to create a new dial-up connection. Most dial-up connections will need to be configured to use the same protocol as the Internet service provider (ISP). To configure the protocol, right-click the newly created connection icon and select the Server Types tab. Most Internet service providers will require a DNS server setting. Setup instructions specific to your ISP are provided by the ISP.

♦ TCP/IP is the protocol used by the Internet. In order to access the Internet, your system must use TCP/IP. An IP address is a specific street address on the Internet and consists of a 32-bit 4-octet binary number. Most people recognize an IP address in its decimal format, such as 45.222.202.7. Routers on the Internet interpret this decimal format in binary. For example, in binary, 45.222.202.7 would be 00101101.11011110.11001010.00000111.

- Valid IP addresses are addresses that have been assigned by Stanford Research Institute (also known as InterNIC and SRINIC), the governing body of Internet addressing.

- One of the most widely utilized Internet resources available is electronic mail, or email. Today's email programs offer a wide range of collaboration tools, which enable you to perform such tasks as attaching files and graphics to a message and sending it to another mail recipient. Originally, email was little more than an ASCII text file. Email uses the Internet and DNS (Domain Name Service) to locate the intended recipient of a message.

- HTML, or Hypertext Markup Language, is a means of publishing information in a format common to Internet browsers and Web servers. HTML uses coded text to give the browser instructions on how text or pictures are to be displayed to the user. One such coded display is the *hyperlink*. A hyperlink appears to the user as underlined text that has a link to another Universal Resource Locator (URL) embedded into it. When you place the mouse arrow over a hyperlink, the arrow changes to a pointing hand. If you click while the pointing-hand cursor is over a hyperlink, you go straight to the embedded link.

- HTTP is the Hypertext Transfer Protocol. Most browser software uses this protocol for its normal navigation. The HTTP:// at the beginning of the Address line designates that you are using HTTP to navigate.

- FTP is the File Transfer Protocol. FTP does not require the use of a browser; it is integrated into the TCP/IP protocol suite. FTP is used through an FTP–aware operating system like Windows 95 (HyperTerminal and command prompt if TCP/IP is installed), a browser, or a third-party program written to utilize FTP. Users can copy files to or from a computer acting as an FTP host.

- Domain names are names assigned to top-level servers that are registered on the Internet. One of several possible domain names can be assigned, depending on the role of the organization that owns the server. The most common and recognizable domain is the .COM domain. Others are .ORG for non-profit organizations, .EDU for educational institutions, .GOV for government organizations, .MIL for military installations, .INT for international organizations, and .NET for large network providers or ISPs. All these abbreviations are the domains. Domains are registered with DNS servers throughout the Internet. DNS entries enable Internet clients to know that 192.102.198.160 is intel.com. DNS resolution enables users to use their browsers to access different domains by name so they don't have to remember the IP addresses.

◆ Internet service providers are companies that sell access to the Internet. Companies like these usually own blocks of registered IP address ranges, which they assign to individual modems when users dial in.

Think of this as your personal study diary—your documentation of how you beat this exam.

The following section of Objective Review Notes is provided so you can personalize this book for maximum effect. This is your workbook, study sheet, notes section, whatever you want to call it. *You* will ultimately decide exactly what information you'll need, but there's no reason this information should be written down somewhere else. As the author has learned from his teaching experiences, there's absolutely no substitute for taking copious notes and using them *throughout* the study process.

This section lists all the A+ DOS/Windows exam objectives. Each objective section falls under the main exam category, just as you'd expect to find it. It is strongly suggested that you review each objective and immediately make note of your knowledge level. Then flip to the Objective Review Notes section repeatedly and document your progress. Your ultimate goal should be to be able to review this section alone and know if you are ready for the exam.

OBJECTIVE REVIEW NOTES

Suggested use:

1. Read the objective. Refer to the part of the book where it's covered. Then ask yourself the following questions and act accordingly:

   - *Do you already know this material?* Then check "Got it" and make a note of the date.

   - *Do you need to brush up on this objective area?* Check "Review it" and make a note of the date. While you're at it, write down the page numbers you just looked at because you'll need to return to that section soon.

   - *Is this material something you're largely unfamiliar with?* Check the "Help!" box and write down the date. Now you can get to work.

2. You get the idea. Keep working through the material in this book and in the other study material you probably have. The better you understand the material, the quicker you can update and upgrade each objective notes section from "Help!" to "Review it" to "Got it."

3. Cross reference to the stuff *you* are using. Most people who take certification exams use more than one resource at a time. Write down the page numbers where this material is covered in other books you're using, which software program and file this material is covered on, which video tape (and counter number) it's on, or whatever you need that works for you.

Function, Structure, Operation, and File Management

► Objective: Identify the major components of DOS, Windows 3.x, and Windows 95.

☐ Got it
Date:_____

☐ Review it
Date:_____

☐ Help!
Date:_____

Notes:
_____
_____
_____
_____
_____

Fast Track cross reference, see pages:
_____
_____

Other resources cross reference, see pages:
_____
_____
_____

► Objective: Describe the differences between DOS, Windows 3.x and Windows 95 architecture.

☐ Got it
Date:_____

☐ Review it
Date:_____

☐ Help!
Date:_____

Notes:
_____
_____
_____
_____
_____

Fast Track cross reference, see pages:
_____
_____

Other resources cross reference, see pages:
_____
_____
_____

OBJECTIVE REVIEW NOTES

► Objective: Name the major system files in each operating system.

☐ Got it   ☐ Review it   ☐ Help!
   Date:_____   Date:_____   Date:_____

Notes:
_____
_____
_____
_____
_____

Fast Track cross reference, see pages:
_____
_____

Other resources cross reference, see pages:
_____
_____
_____
_____

► Objective: Recognize what files are needed to boot the system.

☐ Got it   ☐ Review it   ☐ Help!
   Date:_____   Date:_____   Date:_____

Notes:
_____
_____
_____
_____
_____

Fast Track cross reference, see pages:
_____
_____

Other resources cross reference, see pages:
_____
_____
_____
_____

► Objective: Identify the correct locations of important system files.

☐ Got it   ☐ Review it   ☐ Help!
   *Date:*_____   *Date:*_____   *Date:*_____

Notes:
_____
_____
_____
_____
_____

Fast Track cross reference, see pages:
_____
_____

Other resources cross reference, see pages:
_____
_____
_____
_____

Objective: Differentiate between a system file, a configuration file,
► and a user interface file.

☐ Got it   ☐ Review it   ☐ Help!
   *Date:*_____   *Date:*_____   *Date:*_____

Notes:
_____
_____
_____
_____
_____

Fast Track cross reference, see pages:
_____
_____

Other resources cross reference, see pages:
_____
_____
_____
_____

OBJECTIVE REVIEW NOTES

►Objective: Navigate the operating systems.

☐ **Got it**	☐ **Review it**	☐ **Help!**
*Date:*_____	*Date:*_____	*Date:*_____

Notes:

_____

_____

_____

_____

Fast Track cross reference, see pages:

_____

_____

Other resources cross reference, see pages:

_____

_____

_____

►Objective: Retrieve data from the operating systems using system utilities.

☐ **Got it**	☐ **Review it**	☐ **Help!**
*Date:*_____	*Date:*_____	*Date:*_____

Notes:

_____

_____

_____

_____

Fast Track cross reference, see pages:

_____

_____

Other resources cross reference, see pages:

_____

_____

_____

OBJECTIVE REVIEW NOTES

► Objective: Know how to create, view, and manage files and directories.

☐ Got it   ☐ Review it   ☐ Help!
   Date:_____   Date:_____   Date:_____

Notes:

_____
_____
_____
_____

Fast Track cross reference, see pages:

_____
_____

Other resources cross reference, see pages:

_____
_____
_____
_____

► Objective: Understand the concepts of disk management.

☐ Got it   ☐ Review it   ☐ Help!
   Date:_____   Date:_____   Date:_____

Notes:

_____
_____
_____
_____

Fast Track cross reference, see pages:

_____
_____

Other resources cross reference, see pages:

_____
_____
_____
_____

OBJECTIVE REVIEW NOTES

Memory Management

▶Objective: Know the types of memory used by DOS, Windows 3.x, and Windows 95.

☐ Got it   ☐ Review it   ☐ Help!
   Date:_____   Date:_____   Date:_____

Notes:
_____
_____
_____
_____
_____

Fast Track cross reference, see pages:
_____
_____

Other resources cross reference, see pages:
_____
_____
_____
_____

▶Objective: Recognize the potential for memory address conflicts.

☐ Got it   ☐ Review it   ☐ Help!
   Date:_____   Date:_____   Date:_____

Notes:
_____
_____
_____
_____
_____

Fast Track cross reference, see pages:
_____
_____

Other resources cross reference, see pages:
_____
_____
_____
_____

OBJECTIVE REVIEW NOTES

► Objective: Understand how a memory conflict happens.

☐ Got it   ☐ Review it   ☐ Help!
  Date:_____   Date:_____   Date:_____

Notes:
_____
_____
_____
_____
_____

Fast Track cross reference, see pages:
_____
_____

Other resources cross reference, see pages:
_____
_____
_____
_____

► Objective: Describe a general protection fault and an illegal operation.

☐ Got it   ☐ Review it   ☐ Help!
  Date:_____   Date:_____   Date:_____

Notes:
_____
_____
_____
_____
_____

Fast Track cross reference, see pages:
_____
_____

Other resources cross reference, see pages:
_____
_____
_____
_____

OBJECTIVE REVIEW NOTES

OBJECTIVE REVIEW NOTES

►Objective: Identify and use the appropriate memory troubleshooting utilities for a given situation.

☐ **Got it**　　　☐ **Review it**　　　☐ **Help!**
　　Date:　　　　　*Date:*　　　　　　*Date:*

Notes:

_____
_____
_____
_____
_____

Fast Track cross reference, see pages:

_____
_____

Other resources cross reference, see pages:

_____
_____
_____
_____

►Objective: Discuss memory management and optimization.

☐ **Got it**　　　☐ **Review it**　　　☐ **Help!**
　　Date:　　　　　*Date:*　　　　　　*Date:*

Notes:

_____
_____
_____
_____
_____

Fast Track cross reference, see pages:

_____
_____

Other resources cross reference, see pages:

_____
_____
_____
_____

Installation, Configuration, and Upgrading

► Objective: Identify procedures for installing, configuring, and upgrading DOS, Windows 3.x, and Windows 95.

☐ Got it   ☐ Review it   ☐ Help!
   *Date:*____   *Date:*____   *Date:*____

Notes:

_____

_____

_____

_____

Fast Track cross reference, see pages:

_____

_____

Other resources cross reference, see pages:

_____

_____

_____

_____

► Objective: Identify the boot sequence of DOS, Windows 3.x, and Windows 95.

☐ Got it   ☐ Review it   ☐ Help!
   *Date:*____   *Date:*____   *Date:*____

Notes:

_____

_____

_____

_____

_____

Fast Track cross reference, see pages:

_____

_____

Other resources cross reference, see pages:

_____

_____

_____

_____

OBJECTIVE REVIEW NOTES

► Objective: Bring DOS, Windows 3.x, and Windows 95 to a basic operational level.

☐ **Got it**   ☐ **Review it**   ☐ **Help!**
Date:_____   Date:_____   Date:_____

Notes:

_____

_____

_____

_____

_____

Fast Track cross reference, see pages:

_____

_____

Other resources cross reference, see pages:

_____

_____

_____

_____

► Objective: Select and run the appropriate setup utility for a given situation.

☐ **Got it**   ☐ **Review it**   ☐ **Help!**
Date:_____   Date:_____   Date:_____

Notes:

_____

_____

_____

_____

_____

Fast Track cross reference, see pages:

_____

_____

Other resources cross reference, see pages:

_____

_____

_____

_____

OBJECTIVE REVIEW NOTES

► Objective: Know the steps to perform before upgrading.

☐ Got it   ☐ Review it   ☐ Help!
   Date: Date: Date:

Notes:

_____
_____
_____
_____
_____

Fast Track cross reference, see pages:

_____
_____

Other resources cross reference, see pages:

_____
_____
_____
_____

► Objective: Upgrade from DOS to Windows 95.

☐ Got it   ☐ Review it   ☐ Help!
   Date: Date: Date:

Notes:

_____
_____
_____
_____
_____

Fast Track cross reference, see pages:

_____
_____

Other resources cross reference, see pages:

_____
_____
_____
_____

OBJECTIVE REVIEW NOTES

▶Objective: Upgrade Windows 3.x to Windows 95.

☐ Got it	☐ Review it	☐ Help!
Date:	Date:	Date:

Notes:

_____
_____
_____
_____
_____

Fast Track cross reference, see pages:

_____
_____

Other resources cross reference, see pages:

_____
_____
_____
_____

▶Objective: Identify the boot sequences.

☐ Got it	☐ Review it	☐ Help!
Date:	Date:	Date:

Notes:

_____
_____
_____
_____

Fast Track cross reference, see pages:

_____
_____

Other resources cross reference, see pages:

_____
_____
_____
_____

OBJECTIVE REVIEW NOTES

► Objective: Identify different ways to boot the systems.

☐ Got it
Date:_____

☐ Review it
Date:_____

☐ Help!
Date:_____

Notes:

_____
_____
_____
_____
_____

Fast Track cross reference, see pages:

_____
_____

Other resources cross reference, see pages:

_____
_____
_____
_____

► Objective: Identify the files that are required to boot.

☐ Got it
Date:_____

☐ Review it
Date:_____

☐ Help!
Date:_____

Notes:

_____
_____
_____
_____
_____

Fast Track cross reference, see pages:

_____
_____

Other resources cross reference, see pages:

_____
_____
_____
_____

OBJECTIVE REVIEW NOTES

►Objective: Create emergency boot disks.

☐ **Got it** ☐ **Review it** ☐ **Help!**
*Date:*_____ *Date:*_____ *Date:*_____

Notes:
_____
_____
_____
_____
_____
_____

Fast Track cross reference, see pages:
_____
_____

Other resources cross reference, see pages:
_____
_____
_____
_____

►Objective: Create a Windows 95 startup disk.

☐ **Got it** ☐ **Review it** ☐ **Help!**
*Date:*_____ *Date:*_____ *Date:*_____

Notes:
_____
_____
_____
_____
_____
_____

Fast Track cross reference, see pages:
_____
_____

Other resources cross reference, see pages:
_____
_____
_____
_____

OBJECTIVE REVIEW NOTES

► Objective: Understand what Safe Mode is.

☐ Got it
  Date:_____
☐ Review it
  Date:_____
☐ Help!
  Date:_____

Notes:

_____
_____
_____
_____
_____

Fast Track cross reference, see pages:

_____
_____

Other resources cross reference, see pages:

_____
_____
_____
_____

► Objective: Understand what DOS mode is.

☐ Got it
  Date:_____
☐ Review it
  Date:_____
☐ Help!
  Date:_____

Notes:

_____
_____
_____
_____
_____

Fast Track cross reference, see pages:

_____
_____

Other resources cross reference, see pages:

_____
_____
_____
_____

OBJECTIVE REVIEW NOTES

► Objective: Identify procedures for loading/adding/removing device drivers for

♦ Windows 3.x.

♦ Windows 95.

♦ Plug and Play.

☐ **Got it** / ☐ **Review it** / ☐ **Help!**
*Date:*_____ *Date:*_____ *Date:*_____

Notes:

_____
_____
_____
_____

Fast Track cross reference, see pages:

_____
_____

Other resources cross reference, see pages:

_____
_____
_____

► Objective: Identify procedures for changing options and for configuring and using the Windows printing subsystem.

☐ **Got it** / ☐ **Review it** / ☐ **Help!**
*Date:*_____ *Date:*_____ *Date:*_____

Notes:

_____
_____
_____
_____

Fast Track cross reference, see pages:

_____
_____

Other resources cross reference, see pages:

_____
_____
_____

OBJECTIVE REVIEW NOTES

► Objective: Identify procedures for installing and launching applications in

- ◆ DOS.

- ◆ Windows 3.x.

- ◆ Windows 95.

☐ Got it	☐ Review it	☐ Help!
Date:	Date:	Date:

Notes:

_____

_____

_____

_____

_____

_____

Fast Track cross reference, see pages:

_____

_____

Other resources cross reference, see pages:

_____

_____

_____

_____

OBJECTIVE REVIEW NOTES

Diagnosing and Troubleshooting

► Objective: Recognize and decipher common error codes and messages from the boot sequence and know how to correct them.

☐ Got it	☐ Review it	☐ Help!
Date:____	Date:_____	Date:____

Notes:

_____
_____
_____
_____
_____

Fast Track cross reference, see pages:

_____
_____

Other resources cross reference, see pages:

_____
_____
_____
_____

► Objective: Understand the concepts of temporary and permanent swap files.

☐ Got it	☐ Review it	☐ Help!
Date:____	Date:_____	Date:____

Notes:

_____
_____
_____
_____
_____

Fast Track cross reference, see pages:

_____
_____

Other resources cross reference, see pages:

_____
_____
_____
_____

OBJECTIVE REVIEW NOTES

► Objective: Identify and correct common Windows-specific printing problems.

☐ Got it	☐ Review it	☐ Help!
*Date:*_____	*Date:*_____	*Date:*_____

Notes:

_____

_____

_____

_____

_____

Fast Track cross reference, see pages:

_____

_____

Other resources cross reference, see pages:

_____

_____

_____

_____

► Determine the appropriate course of action to correct common errors in a Windows environment.

☐ Got it	☐ Review it	☐ Help!
*Date:*_____	*Date:*_____	*Date:*_____

Notes:

_____

_____

_____

_____

_____

Fast Track cross reference, see pages:

_____

_____

Other resources cross reference, see pages:

_____

_____

_____

_____

OBJECTIVE REVIEW NOTES

►Identify and use DOS and Windows-based utilities to diagnose specific Windows/DOS behavior.

☐ Got it   ☐ Review it   ☐ Help!
   Date: Date: Date:

Notes:

_____
_____
_____
_____
_____
_____

Fast Track cross reference, see pages:

_____
_____

Other resources cross reference, see pages:

_____
_____
_____
_____

OBJECTIVE REVIEW NOTES

Networking

► Objective: Discuss the network capabilities of MS-DOS and Windows

☐ Got it   ☐ Review it   ☐ Help!
   *Date:*_____   *Date:*_____   *Date:*_____

Notes:

_____
_____
_____
_____
_____

Fast Track cross reference, see pages:

_____
_____

Other resources cross reference, see pages:

_____
_____
_____
_____

► Objective: Connect a DOS workstation to a network.

☐ Got it   ☐ Review it   ☐ Help!
   *Date:*_____   *Date:*_____   *Date:*_____

Notes:

_____
_____
_____
_____
_____

Fast Track cross reference, see pages:

_____
_____

Other resources cross reference, see pages:

_____
_____
_____
_____

OBJECTIVE REVIEW NOTES

►Objective: Connect a Windows 3.x workstation to a network.

☐ Got it
Date:_____

☐ Review it
Date:_____

☐ Help!
Date:_____

Notes:

_____
_____
_____
_____
_____
_____

Fast Track cross reference, see pages:

_____
_____

Other resources cross reference, see pages:

_____
_____
_____
_____

►Objective: Connect a Windows 95 workstation to a network.

☐ Got it
Date:_____

☐ Review it
Date:_____

☐ Help!
Date:_____

Notes:

_____
_____
_____
_____
_____
_____

Fast Track cross reference, see pages:

_____
_____

Other resources cross reference, see pages:

_____
_____
_____
_____

OBJECTIVE REVIEW NOTES

► Objective: Contrast different types of network designs.

□ Got it
Date:_____
□ Review it
Date:_____
□ Help!
Date:_____

Notes:

_____
_____
_____
_____

Fast Track cross reference, see pages:

_____
_____

Other resources cross reference, see pages:

_____
_____
_____
_____

► Distinguish between different types of Network Interface Cards (NICs).

□ Got it
Date:_____
□ Review it
Date:_____
□ Help!
Date:_____

Notes:

_____
_____
_____
_____
_____

Fast Track cross reference, see pages:

_____
_____

Other resources cross reference, see pages:

_____
_____
_____
_____

OBJECTIVE REVIEW NOTES

➤ Connect a DOS/Windows or Windows 95 workstation to the Internet.

☐ Got it   ☐ Review it   ☐ Help!
Date:_____   Date:_____   Date:_____

Notes:

_____
_____
_____
_____
_____
_____

Fast Track cross reference, see pages:

_____
_____

Other resources cross reference, see pages:

_____
_____
_____
_____

OBJECTIVE REVIEW NOTES

PART IV

INSIDE THE A+ DOS/WINDOWS EXAM

Part IV of this book is designed to round out your exam preparation by providing you with the following chapters:

The exam is divided into five objective categories:

▶ Function, Structure, Operation, and File Management

▶ Memory Management

▶ Installation, Configuration, and Upgrading

▶ Diagnosing and Troubleshooting

▶ Networking

CHAPTER 19

Fast Facts Review

WHAT TO STUDY

This chapter highlights the concepts needed for each section of the A+ DOS/Windows exam. Use it as a review on the day of the exam.

FUNCTION, STRUCTURE, OPERATION, AND FILE MANAGEMENT

The function of DOS is to be the disk operating system. DOS is the interface between the computer hardware and the user.

Windows 3.x is a shell that runs on top of DOS. Its function is to provide a graphical user interface and to better manage program resource management.

Windows 95 is a combination of DOS and Windows 3.x. It functions as both the operating system and the graphical user interface. Windows 95 provides better program control and system stability.

The major components of DOS are IO.SYS, MSDOS.SYS, and COMMAND.COM. These files are required to boot the system. CONFIG.SYS and AUTOEXEC.BAT are system configuration files. EMM386.EXE and HIMEM.SYS are DOS memory configuration files. ANSI.SYS and KEYBOARD.SYS are user interface configuration files. Common internal commands that are part of COMMAND.COM are VER, CLS, DIR, CD, COPY, DEL, MD, MORE, PATH, PROMPT, REN, and TYPE.

Windows 3.x runs on top of DOS, so Windows 3.x also needs all files that are needed to run DOS. Some files, such as EMM386.EXE and HIMEM.SYS, have been updated since the initial DOS release and have Windows counterparts. Using the Windows counterparts makes the system more efficient. The major components of Windows 3.x are KRNLxxx.EXE, USER.EXE, GDI.EXE, WIN.COM, and PROG-MAN.EXE. These files are required to launch Windows. Windows needs WIN.INI, SYSTEM.INI, and PROGMAN.INI, which are the Windows configuration files.

Windows 95 requires its own version of MSDOS.SYS, IO.SYS, and COMMAND.COM. As in DOS, these files are required to boot the system. Windows 95 does not require CONFIG.SYS and AUTOEXEC.BAT, but it does use them for backward compatibility with older DOS/ Windows 3.x programs.

Windows 95 has its own versions of WIN.COM, USER.EXE, and GDI.EXE. The Windows 95 operating system uses the system Registry instead of INI files for configuration. You can access the Registry with the Regedit utility. USER.DAT and SYSTEM.DAT are the user- and system-specific Registry files.

Windows 3.x is a 16-bit shell that runs on top of DOS. Windows 3.x uses cooperative multitasking. The primary user interface is Program Manager. Windows 3.x uses the DOS memory management model based on conventional memory and a swap file. Pressing Ctrl+Alt+Del reboots the system.

Windows 95 is a 32-bit operating system. The primary user interface is Windows Explorer. Windows 95 utilizes preemptive multitasking for all programs but emulates cooperative multitasking for 16-bit programs. Windows 95 utilizes a more efficient swap file than its Windows 3.x predecessor. Pressing Ctrl+Alt+Del accesses the Task Manager and allows you to shut down non-responsive programs.

> **NOTE**
>
> For greater clarification of the use of Ctrl+Alt+Del, see the Fast Facts Review under system lockup.

IO.SYS is responsible for loading real-mode drivers and terminate-and-stay-resident programs (TSRs) specified in the CONFIG.SYS and AUTOEXEC.BAT files. (In other words, it loads input and output devices—thus the name IO.SYS.)

MSDOS.SYS is responsible for communication between internal computer components.

COMMAND.COM is the command interpreter that actually interprets commands from the keyboard and decides how they should be executed.

CONFIG.SYS is responsible for providing DOS with system hardware configuration information. CONFIG.SYS is where memory management begins as well.

AUTOEXEC.BAT contains commands and final configuration settings in a DOS system.

ANSI.SYS is a device driver in CONFIG.SYS that enables the system to recognize the ANSI character set.

EMM386.EXE enables the system to recognize memory above 640KB.

HIMEM.SYS is the device driver that enables DOS to use the high memory area (memory above 640KB).

KRNLxxx.EXE controls the PC's memory and I/O resources and loads Windows. It is also known as the Windows kernel.

WIN.COM launches Windows. It coordinates the efforts of KRNL386.EXE, USER.EXE, and GDI.EXE into the Windows interface familiar to most computer users.

WIN.INI is the initialization file containing the information on the appearance and behavior of Windows.

SYSTEM.INI contains configuration information about the available devices.

PROGMAN.INI contains configuration information about the appearance and behavior of Program Manager.

PROGMAN.EXE is the Windows 3.x Program Manager program.

USER.EXE controls the user interface in Windows. It is responsible for interpreting commands from the mouse, keyboard, and COM ports.

GDI.EXE controls all the graphics display functions of Windows.

IO.SYS is the same as IO.SYS for DOS, only for Windows 95.

MSDOS.SYS for Windows 95 is virtually the same as its DOS predecessor. In Windows 95, you can edit and manipulate MSDOS.SYS to allow for various menu options.

COMMAND.COM in Windows 95 is simply an updated version of the DOS COMMAND.COM. Issuing the VER command from a Windows 95 command prompt would return the version number of DOS as 7.0. Newer versions of Windows 95 return the version number as Windows 95. You can use REGEDIT.EXE to edit the Windows 95 Registry.

SYSTEM.DAT is the hidden system file that contains system information from the Registry.

USER.DAT is the hidden system file that contains user information from the Registry.

DOS navigation consists primarily of command line executables like CD, DIR, MD, COPY, and DEL.

In Windows 3.x, navigation is performed with Program Manager and File Manager. The File Manager interface offers all major DOS commands from the pull-down menus. File Manager is a graphical representation of the computer's file system hierarchy.

The main means of navigating Windows 95 is the Windows Explorer interface. Explorer is a blend of Windows 3.x Program Manager and File Manager. All DOS commands are available from both pull-down menus and context menus. For those users who are uncomfortable with the graphical interface, navigating through a DOS window is possible. Although this type of navigation was not covered in this book or on the exam, keyboard commands are available for navigating Windows 95 as well. For more information on using keyboard commands, refer to the Windows 95 user manual.

You can view file attributes of Windows 95 objects by selecting the object in Explorer, right-clicking, and selecting Properties (or by simply selecting Properties from the pull-down menu). This displays the file attributes and allows you to modify them if desired. Explorer allows you to create folders and populate them by selecting objects in Explorer and dragging them to the folders.

Filenames in DOS and Windows 3.x can be eight characters long with a three-character extension. Windows 95 supports long filenames of up to 255 characters, but Windows Explorer only accepts 250 characters. Some characters are not allowed in filenames. In DOS and Windows 3.x the brackets, colon, semicolon, plus sign, equal sign, backslash, forward slash, and comma ([ ] : ; + = \ / ,) are not allowed. In Windows 95 you can use the comma, plus sign, brackets, and equal sign. However, Windows 95 does not allow the use of the backslash, forward slash, colon, asterisk, question mark, quotation marks, greater than sign, less than sign, and pipe.

Here's a summary of the file naming rules by operation system:

	DOS	**Windows 3.x**	**Windows 95**
Filename limitation	8 characters long with a 3-character extension	8 characters long with a 3-character extension	supports long filenames of up to 255 characters
Invalid characters	[ ] : ; + = \ / ,	[ ] : ; + = \ / ,	\ / : * ? " < > |

Command syntax in DOS, Windows 3.x, and Windows 95 is primarily the same. Spelling counts: If a command is spelled wrong, it will not be recognized. If you do not know the appropriate syntax, help is available by typing the command followed by /? (in DOS 6 or higher). For most commands, this is a valid switch that will display the proper syntax.

System, Hidden, Read-Only, and Archive attributes are the common attributes that can be assigned to a file. The System attribute designates a system file. Setting the Hidden file attribute hides the file from default views. The Read-Only attribute makes a file read-only; users cannot modify it. The Archive attribute denotes the file's backup status.

Backing up of your computer requires a floppy drive, tape drive, or available network storage. DOS 6.x, Windows 3.x, and Windows 95 all have built-in backup software. Note, however, that the backup sets from any built-in software are not compatible with any other backup software.

To format a disk, you designate a drive and use the DOS FORMAT command. You cannot format the drive that is executing the FORMAT command.

To partition a disk, you use the FDISK utility. A disk must be partitioned before it can be formatted.

Defragmenting a drive on a regular basis helps to ensure peak computer performance. Use the DEFRAG program in DOS/Windows 3.x and in Windows 95.

The ScanDisk utility verifies that the file system and physical disk are in proper working order. Run ScanDisk if you suspect that the hard drive may be failing, and it will locate bad blocks.

FAT32 is an alternate file system available only in Windows 95 version OSR2. FAT32 uses 4KB blocks to maximize disk performance for the operating system. FAT32-formatted drives are recognizable only to Windows 95 OSR2 and Windows 95 OSR2-created boot disks. All operating systems can recognize a FAT32 formatted drive that is shared across a network. This works because Windows 95 OSR2 controls the sharing. FAT32 recognizes and is able to format drives greater than 2GB in size. FAT32 FDISK can create a partition larger than 2GB.

FAT (file allocation tables) is the default file system of DOS and Windows 95 version A. FAT is recognizable to all operating systems both locally and from the network. FAT recognizes only partitions less than 2GB in size. FAT FDISK allows only a maximum 2GB partition. FAT block sizes depend on the partition size, but the minimum is 16KB blocks, which makes the block size four times that of FAT32.

VFAT is the 32-bit Virtual File Allocation Table file system used by Windows 95's Virtual Memory Manager. It is created, placed in RAM, and utilized by Windows 95 and is not actually a file system with which a drive can be formatted.

MEMORY MANAGEMENT

Conventional memory is the first 640KB of the first megabyte of memory. Upper memory is the remaining 360KB of the first megabyte of memory. Extended memory is the memory from 2–16MB that can be addressed by 286 or faster processors. High memory is the memory area that is enabled by HIMEM.SYS and that is usable by DOS. High memory is memory from 640KB up to 1,024KB. Expanded memory is memory that is not used by DOS but can be addressed by 8088 processors. This is defined by the LIM EMS standard. EMS is enabled by the use of EMM386.EXE.

Virtual memory is the process of using a swap file. A swap file is managed by Windows and allows the system to use hard disk space as memory.

A memory conflict occurs when one device or process accesses memory that is being used by another device or process. General Protection Faults and Invalid Page Faults are common memory conflicts. Conflicts happen because the operating system is unaware of the memory addressing requirements of one or more programs or devices. This increases the potential for a memory overlap.

General Protection Faults (GPFs) occur when Windows attempts to access a memory area allocated to another program. The GPF corrupts the data in the violated memory space, and Windows usually has to be restarted. In Windows 3.1, GPFs generated an error message giving information about the fault and what program it involved. This greatly aids the person troubleshooting the problem. Not all GPFs are fatal (force you to reboot); minor faults will let you ignore the error and continue or save your work. Applications are rarely fully functional following a fault.

You can gain more conventional memory space by optimizing memory. You optimize memory by running DOS MemMaker to move as many programs as possible out of conventional memory. A more efficient means of optimizing memory is to do it manually. MemMaker is not able to re-order programs into a different load order efficiently; some programs that might fit into upper memory cannot do so in their current load order. Manually rearranging the load order will get you the best upper memory utilization. Having more free conventional memory gives DOS programs that utilize conventional memory better performance.

Use utilities as a troubleshooting and diagnosing means. The DOS MEM command and MSD are good memory troubleshooting utilities.

System Monitor is a Windows 95 utility that enables you to monitor memory, processor, and disk utilization.

HIMEM.SYS is the driver loaded in CONFIG.SYS that enables the use of Upper Memory Blocks or UMB.

SMARTDRV is a disk caching utility/device driver available in DOS and Windows 95 that uses extended memory as a disk cache for data read from the hard drive. (Windows 95 does not use this by default; it uses its own disk cache instead. SMARTDRV is available, however, for backward compatibility.) This increases disk performance because RAM is faster than the hard disk controller is.

EMM386.EXE (expanded memory blocks) is a device driver that is loaded from CONFIG.SYS enabling the use of expanded/extended memory. The syntax is

```
EMM386 [ON ¦ OFF ¦ AUTO] [W=ON ¦ W=OFF]
```

where the following switches are available:

ON ¦ OFF ¦ AUTO	Activates or suspends the EMM386.EXE device driver or places it in auto mode.
W=ON ¦ OFF	Turns on or off Weitek coprocessor support.

INSTALLATION, CONFIGURATION, AND UPGRADING

DOS is available on floppy disk and can be installed by booting the PC to the first disk of the installation set or simply by running Setup from the first disk. Setup prompts you to change disks when needed. When Setup is complete, you are prompted to remove the Setup disk and reboot. The new installation and the upgrade are pretty similar. Specific DOS configurations are made by modifying the CONFIG.SYS and AUTOEXEC.BAT files.

Installing Windows 3.x is virtually the same as installing DOS. Invoke Setup and follow the prompts throughout the process. When the process is complete, you need to reboot. Aside from CONFIG.SYS and AUTOEXEC.BAT, configuration changes can be made from the Windows Control Panel.

Windows 95 can be installed from a floppy disk or CD-ROM. Type **Setup** from the command line or select the Windows File, Run command (this is the recommended way for upgrading from Windows 3.x) to start the process. Windows 95 Setup occurs in three phases. Phase one is the gathering of system information. Phase two is the copying of Windows 95 files. Phase three is the final installation. The computer is rebooted under the control of the new operating system and makes final adjustments that finish the installation process.

The DOS boot sequence begins when power is applied to the computer system. The PC begins its power on self-test or POST routine. After the system passes the POST, control is passed to the system BIOS, which searches for the master boot record (or MBR) on one of the system's drives. If the hard disk has DOS installed (if it contains IO.SYS, MSDOS.SYS, COMMAND.COM, and the DOS program files), control is passed to COMMAND.COM to continue processing DOS startup by processing the CONFIG.SYS and AUTOEXEC.BAT files.

The Windows 3.x boot sequence picks up where the DOS boot sequence ends. After COMMAND.COM executes CONFIG.SYS and AUTOEXEC.BAT, WIN.COM takes over, and if WIN.COM is in the AUTOEXEC.BAT, it initializes KERNL386.EXE, USER.EXE, and GDI.EXE to load Program Manager.

The Windows 95 boot process is broken down into five stages. Stage 1 entails the BIOS Bootstrap and the POST process, which was also performed in DOS. In stage 2, the MBR and boot sector are located and given control. In stage 3, Windows 95 begins booting, and IO.SYS loads a minimal FAT system to handle additional OS components, reads MSDOS.SYS for boot parameters, displays the message `Loading Windows 95`, displays the splash screen (LOGO.SYS), loads, and then backs up the Registry. In stage 4, the system configuration is loaded from CONFIG.SYS and AUTOEXEC.BAT if it's present. In stage 5, WIN.COM loads VMM32.VXD and other device drivers. WIN.COM then initializes the Windows kernel, and Windows starts.

If the partition holding the OS is not marked as active, the system will not boot. To correct this problem, boot to a floppy disk, run FDISK, and mark the appropriate partition as active. If the partition is FAT32, only a Windows 95 OSR2 boot disk will be able to see the partition. If the partition is larger than 2GB it must be a FAT32 partition; therefore, only a Windows 95 OSR2 boot disk can recognize it.

A partition must be formatted to install an OS.

If you format or delete a partition, all data that was on that partition is destroyed.

If the partition is larger than 2GB, you must format it with Windows 95 OSR2.

If you format a partition with FAT32, you must install Windows 95 OSR2.

You can compile a custom installation of Windows 95 by customizing the MSBATCH.INF file. If MSBATCH.INF is used, however, you must use the appropriate switches when running Setup or the MSBATCH.INF modifications will be ignored.

Plug and Play primarily handles the loading of drivers in Windows 95. You can load a device manually from the Control Panel's Add/Remove Hardware Wizard. If you manually add a device, you should let Windows 95 assign it resources. Manually assigning resources bypasses Plug and Play and leaves it unaware of your choices. If Plug and Play is unaware of resources you have assigned, it is likely to have Windows 95 assign the same resource to another device.

You can take several steps to avoid trouble during an installation:

+ Scan the system for viruses before you begin the upgrade, and then shut down the virus program. If the PC has a CMOS-based antivirus program, that must be disabled as well. The reason is that when Windows 95 upgrades the boot sector, the antivirus software sees this as a problem and stops Setup.

+ Run ScanDisk (or CHKDSK) to ensure the hard disk is in good working order.

+ Make sure there is enough free disk space for the upgrade. 100–110MB is recommended. (110–120MB is needed if you are saving the DOS/Windows 3.x information.)

+ Verify that all your hardware and software is functioning correctly.

+ Shut down running programs, including TSRs and screen savers.

+ Back up all your system files (CONFIG.SYS, AUTOEXEC.BAT, WIN.INI, SYSTEM.INI).

+ Remove unnecessary lines in CONFIG.SYS and AUTOEXEC.BAT.

- Remark Load= and Run= lines in the WIN.INI.

- Remove programs from the startup group. If they are needed, they can be added after the upgrade.

- If at all possible, run Setup from within Windows 3.x.

Other issues to be aware of during upgrade include dual-booting and migrating user environment settings or profiles.

An upgrade from DOS to Windows 95 is really a DOS upgrade. Because there is no existing Windows directory, DOS programs are not added to the Windows 95 Start menu. For all effective purposes, this is a new installation of Windows 95. Existing DOS programs will have to be added manually, and DOS files are upgraded to Windows 95 versions.

The upgrade from Windows 3.x to Windows 95 should be started from Program Manager. This helps the Windows 95 installation process identify any devices or programs that may be present in memory. During the upgrade, you will be asked what directory to install to. If you select the current Windows directory, all Windows 3.x program groups will be migrated to Windows 95 program groups. If you choose a different directory, programs and groups will not be migrated but you will be able to boot the system to either Windows 3.x or Windows 95. You will have to reinstall all applications for them to work in Windows 95.

In both DOS and Windows 95, you can press the F5 function key when the screen displays the message Starting MSDOS or Starting Windows 95 if you want to bypass CONFIG.SYS and AUTOEXEC.BAT.

If you do not want to bypass the configuration files, you can press the F8 function key if you want to approve or "step through" each line of the CONFIG.SYS and AUTOEXEC.BAT files. (In Windows 95, F8 activates the boot menu, where you can select Step Through as an option.) By using the F8 key, you can selectively load or not load various commands. The F8 key is a highly effective troubleshooting tool.

Other Windows 95 options are dual booting and Safe Mode. You enable dual booting by installing Windows 95 into its own directory and setting the `bootmulti=` setting in MSDOS.SYS to 1. When these two requirements are met, the F4 function key is enabled. Then you can press F4 during the pause in stage 3 of the Windows 95 boot process, and the system will boot to the previous configuration. Note that MS-DOS 5.0 or later must be on the system before Windows 95 is installed for dual booting to work.

Safe Mode is a diagnostic way to start Windows 95. If the system does not shut down properly or Windows operation is interrupted and the machine reboots, Safe Mode becomes the default start option. Safe Mode bypasses the configuration files and loads only the system default drivers so the system can boot. Once you've booted to Safe Mode, you can remove the offending drivers and reboot to Normal mode of Windows 95. In Windows 95, pressing the F8 function key brings up the MSDOS.SYS menu, which enables you to select a start option from the boot menu.

Windows 95 DOS mode is another option you can select from the boot menu. You can also access DOS mode from inside the Windows 95 Explorer interface by configuring a DOS shortcut to reboot the system in DOS mode.

With both DOS and Windows 95, MSDOS.SYS, IO.SYS, and COM-MAND.COM are required to boot the system. For the system to boot to Windows 95, it also needs WIN.COM, USER.EXE, GDI.EXE, SYS-TEM.DAT, and USER.DAT.

It is a good idea to create an emergency boot disk in case the hard drive becomes unable to boot the system. To create the emergency disk, format a floppy disk with the /s switch. This makes the disk bootable. You should then copy the files that you will need to use for repairing the hard drive. Common files that may be needed are AUTOEXEC.BAT, CONFIG.SYS, EDIT.COM (EDIT requires QBASIC.EXE in DOS 6.x), SCANDISK.EXE, FDISK.EXE, XCOPY.EXE, and certain device drivers (like CD-ROM). If you think you might need other items, you should create other versions of boot disks for specific functions.

Most of the difficulty in creating an Emergency Boot Disk has been eliminated by Windows 95. From the Windows 95 Control Panel, you can create what is called a Windows 95 Startup Disk. The Startup Disk is a bootable disk that has most of the needed recovery utilities already copied to it. (Note, CD-ROM drivers are not automatically added. You must do this yourself.)

Devices in Windows 3.x and DOS are loaded in CONFIG.SYS and AUTOEXEC.BAT. Some devices are Windows 3.x-specific and can be loaded from Control Panel or Windows Setup. Devices are removed from the same applets with which they were added.

Windows 95 loads drivers primarily by Plug and Play. You can manually add devices from the Add/Remove Hardware Wizard in Control Panel. You can remove devices from the Windows 95 Device Manager.

Plug and Play is a term used to describe hardware that identifies itself to the operating system and configures itself. Plug and Play in Windows 95 is achieved via software programs called *bus enumerators*. The bus enumerators are specific to a type of bus architecture (PCI, VESA, MCA, and ISA). Each enumerator polls its bus looking for a response from hardware. If hardware responds to the polling, it is added to the Device Manager and you are prompted to load software. Plug and Play does not remove hardware.

The Windows 95 printing subsystem is configured from the Printers folder in Control Panel. Here you can add printers by using the Add Printer Wizard. Follow the wizard and answer the questions to install a printer. If a printer driver changes, or you want to change other options about the printer (such as the port to which it's connected), you can select the printer's icon, right-click, and select Properties. The printer's properties sheet will contain at least the General tab and the Details tab. Most printers have more tabs, but they are specific to the driver. All options for a printers can be modified from its properties sheet.

Windows 95 offers several new options for installing applications. Programs can be installed in Windows 95 just as they were in Windows 3.x, but Windows 95 offers some other means. The recommended way of adding applications is to use the Add/Remove Programs icon in Control Panel. This launches a wizard that searches floppy disks and CD-ROM drives for setup programs and installs them. One benefit of using this utility to add programs is that it maintains a record of installed components and allows for a full uninstallation if necessary. Windows 95 keeps track of files installed by 32-bit applications by default, but to keep track of 16-bit installation files, you must use the Add/Remove Programs Wizard.

Another possibility for adding applications is the AutoRun feature used by CD-ROMs. AutoRun causes the setup application to launch when the CD-ROM drive reads the CD, prompting the user to run Setup.

After an application is loaded, it usually creates a group on the Windows 95 Start menu and adds icons for launching the program. You run the application by selecting the appropriate icon. You can also launch a program in Windows 95 by selecting Run from the Start menu and typing the executable (just like the Run line in Windows 3.x) if it is in the path. If it is not in the path, you can type the full path to the executable. Another option is to double-click the executable from Explorer.

Installing applications in DOS is a fairly simple process that involves running the installation program and selecting locations and settings. Once the application is installed, you launch it by typing its executable command at the command prompt. Some points to consider are whether the executable is in the DOS path and whether the system is configured correctly to run the program. Usually both of these considerations are addressed during installation.

Diagnosing and Troubleshooting

Safe Mode is the Windows 95 diagnostic mode that loads only the minimum drivers required for loading Windows 95. If the system loses power or is shut down improperly, it automatically enters Safe Mode automatically when it's rebooted. If a corrupt or missing device driver is causing the failure or an application error is to blame, Safe Mode gives you a chance to correct the problem by removing the offending driver or program in an environment that does not present the problem.

The message Incorrect DOS version appears when an application checks the DOS version when it starts and finds a different version number than it expected. To correct this situation, use the SETVER command to add your DOS version to the version table. SETVER is a TSR utility that maintains a list of programs and the version of DOS each one is expected to use. Therefore, SETVER enables you to trick an old program into thinking it is operating in a DOS 3.3 environment even if it is actually running in a DOS 6.22 environment. Another reason for the Incorrect DOS version message could be that IO.SYS, MSDOS.SYS, and COMMAND.COM are of different versions. To correct this problem, either reinstall or boot to a floppy disk and use the SYS command to transfer the system files to the hard disk again.

The No operating system found **error is displayed** when there is a problem locating the MBR (master boot record) on the active partition. To investigate this situation, boot to your emergency boot disk and check the active partition using the FDISK utility. The primary partition on the first hard drive must be marked as active in order for the system to boot. If the correct partition is active, transfer the system to the active partition using the SYS.COM utility. Verify that you are copying the same DOS/Windows 95 version that the hard drive is supposed to be using.

The Error in CONFIG.SYS line xx **message is** usually a result of bad syntax or an incorrect path statement. CONFIG.SYS cannot load a driver it does not recognize or find. To correct this, check the path to the file to see if it is correct, check your spelling, and (as a last resort) reinstall the software affecting the line.

The Command Interpreter is COMMAND.COM, and something has corrupted or deleted that file if you receive the message Bad or missing Command Interpreter. To correct this issue, reformat the drive if it is empty. If it has data on it, boot to a floppy disk and use the SYS command to transfer the system back to the drive.

If you receive the message HIMEM.SYS not loaded, check to see if HIMEM.SYS exists in the location specified in CONFIG.SYS. If this is correct, check the file date on HIMEM.SYS to see if it is the most current version.

If the date is correct, boot from a floppy disk containing a minimum version of CONFIG.SYS and AUTOEXEC.BAT to see if you are able to start Windows. If this works, the problem exists within CONFIG.SYS or AUTOEXEC.BAT. If this does not work, there is probably a problem with the memory manager. To correct this problem, copy HIMEM.SYS from CD again or install disks.

You may have to use a diagnostic utility like Microsoft Diagnostics (MSD) to determine if there is a conflict in upper memory. If you discover an upper memory conflict, you can resolve it by unloading all drivers and TSRs from upper memory.

On Windows 3.x, users could enhance performance by changing virtual memory settings from temporary to permanent. When Windows starts, the temporary swap file is created, slowing down the start process. Running out of disk space will affect Windows performance because there will be no room for the swap file. The use of a permanent swap file allows for better performance because it always reserves disk space and is always available for use. Not having enough hard drive space available is the only reason not to use a permanent swap file in Windows 3.x. On occasion, when you start Windows, you will receive the message Swap file is corrupt. Upon acknowledgment of this error, Windows starts and prompts you to create a new swap file. This usually occurs after you've used a disk cloning utility such as PKZIP Image or Symantec's Ghost.

The Windows 95 swap file is dynamic, so it can shrink or grow as needed. The Windows 95 swap file can occupy a fragmented region of the hard disk with no noticeable performance loss. Making sure that the disk containing the swap file has plenty of free space for expanding and contracting is the best way to optimize the Windows 95 dynamic swap file. Running out of disk space will impact performance greatly.

The absence of a device specified in one of the configuration files is very common after a program has been uninstalled or deleted. Some uninstall programs do not remove referenced devices either because they are poorly designed or because something interrupts the uninstall process. In any event, these absent devices can either prevent Windows from loading or simply slow it down. It is important to take notes and make a list of the files that the system lists as missing. When you quit receiving messages stating that devices are missing, you should run SysEdit. Search the WIN.INI and SYSTEM.INI files for instances of the files you copied down as being missing and remark them out. When all missing files have been completely commented out, restart the system and watch for errors. If the system gives you more errors, repeat the process until Windows starts error free. If the system boots correctly, double-check to make sure all programs operate correctly, verifying that the items you remarked out are not necessary. If any program does not check out, run that program's setup routine again to replace any files that were accidentally removed.

Symptoms of a stalled print spooler include print jobs being sent to the printer but not printing. If this occurs, double-click the printer's icon and see if any jobs are listed. Sometimes deleting the job at the top of the queue will start the print process again. Make sure there is enough disk space available to spool. If disk space is available, this is not the problem. If you are low on disk space, free up some space by backing up some data to other media, and then try printing again. It is recommended that you have about twice as much disk space available as the size of the file you are trying to print.

If you still cannot print, right-click on the Printer icon and select Properties. On the Details tab, click the Spool Options button. Change the spool settings to print directly to the printer. If this produces positive printer output, the problem is a stalled print spooler. Rebooting the machine can clear the spooler and restart printing. If rebooting does not work, however, change the output from EMF to RAW. If you still cannot print, check the Windows\system\spool\printers directory for *.SPL and *.TMP files and delete any that exist. These could be the corrupt spool jobs. If none of these tasks restarts printing, the print spooler is probably not the problem.

A corrupt or incorrect driver is probably the most common Windows printing error. If print jobs are coming out of the printer garbled or off-format, the printer driver is the likely culprit. Reinstalling the driver or updating the driver from the Printer Properties Details tab works most of the time, but some drivers are known to have problems with different versions of Windows. Updated drivers can fix this problem, and most are available for download. For instance, if you had an HP printer, you would point your browser to your printer manufacturer's Web site for the most up-to-date driver.

When a GPF occurs, the system displays a message stating that a GPF has occurred and in what application. GPFs that occur in 16-bit applications display a blue screen, whereas 32-bit applications display a Windows dialog box. 32-bit applications in Windows 95 are not prone to GPFs because of the way Windows 95 assigns resources. Since the OS is aware of what device and program is using which memory areas, the occurrence of faults is greatly reduced. It is possible, however, for a 32-bit application to have a General Protection Fault. Correcting this problem requires good note-taking when the error happens. Knowing what caused the problem helps eliminate it. Use the Device Manager to see if any system hardware is using the memory area that the offending program tried to use. If there is an overlap, correct it by using Device Manager to reassign a different memory area to the hardware. If hardware is not causing the conflict, it is probably the result of either a file in the problematic application, or a version conflict with a system library. Contact the application manufacturer for further information.

An `Illegal operation` message indicates that the program expected the operating system to act a particular way, and the program stopped because the system did not act in that way. For example, suppose a DOS application that uses DOS Extenders does not recognize the Windows 95 Extender. The fix is to get an updated version of the offending program. The unfortunate fact about illegal operations is that usually you must apply a service pack or an application update of some sort.

Technical support Web sites and packages like Microsoft TechNet have hundreds of articles pertaining to illegal operations with hundreds of different fixes.

The `Invalid working directory` message occurs when you try to launch a program in Windows 3.x and the working directory is wrong. When a program is installed in Windows 3.x and its program group is created, the properties of the icons in the program group give the path to the executable file and the directory where it is located. This directory is known as the *working directory*. If a drive letter changes (if, for example, another hard drive is added or you change the CD-ROM drive letter) and an icon still points to the previous drive letter, the `Invalid working directory` message appears. To correct this, select the icon, select File, Properties, and modify the path to the working directory to point to the correct location.

A system lock up occurs when the processor gets conflicting information or becomes unaware of what the operating system is doing. In DOS, the usual cause is a memory problem or a poorly written program.

Windows 3.x uses cooperative multitasking. In cooperative multitasking, all programs operate in the same memory space and cooperatively share resources. This means the programs are in control of the processor at all times. When the program finishes with the current task, it is supposed to relinquish control to the next program and so on. If a program stalls while controlling the processor, the system stops. In Windows 3.x, this usually forces you to reboot.

Windows 95's 32-bit architecture takes advantage of preemptive multitasking. Preemptive multitasking gives the processor control over the applications. When the time that an application has been allotted for processor functions expires, the processor takes control from that application and gives time to the next application in line. This is why you can press Ctrl+Alt+Del to shut down a troubled program in Windows 95. However, to maintain backward compatibility with 16-bit applications that depend on cooperative multitasking, Windows 95 has an area of non-reentrant code known as the WIN16 Mutex. The WIN16 Mutex flag simulates the processor being under control of the 16-bit application. When the WIN16 Mutex flag is set (albeit only for a fraction of a second), if a 16-bit program hangs, it locks the system. This usually means rebooting. To avoid hang-ups in Windows 95, use only 32-bit programs whenever possible. Although this is not specifically testable material, you can find more information on the Win16 Mutex and the non-reentrant code in the Windows 95 Resource Kit.

An option that does not function usually indicates that an installation was not completed appropriately or has since become corrupt. A common example occurs in Windows 95 when Start menu shortcuts do not run the associated programs. However, an error message might not be displayed, which makes this kind of error difficult to troubleshoot. Correcting this issue will require patience. First, launch the application from its home directory to eliminate the possibility that the shortcut has become damaged. If this does not work, rule out memory conflicts by checking the Device Manager for warnings. Also verify that other applications are not affected. This rules out a system problem. Last, back up data, uninstall the application, and then reinstall. If the misbehaving function is part of the operating system (such as the DOS PIF), the OS may have to be reinstalled.

An application problem can indicate a bad installation and/or that an application file has become damaged. Good troubleshooting and note taking skills are the quickest way to fix the problem.

First, eliminate the possibility that the problem is the PC or the OS by verifying that there are no conflicts during startup. Check to see that all other applications are unaffected, and check the Windows 95 Device Manager for warnings. After performing these tasks, you can assume the problem is an application issue.

Troubleshooting an application that won't start or load involves starting the application and trying to note system behavior or error messages. If you do not see any error messages, change the system video to basic VGA and try again. Some applications are written to display messages in VGA mode. Fancier video cards may not be able to display the error or might show only a black screen. (This works in Windows 3.x and DOS. For Windows 95, use Safe Mode.) If no messages are given, try booting the system in Windows 95 Safe Mode to see if it runs. If this is successful, the application has a conflict with a device driver (such as a video or network card) that is not loaded in Safe Mode. If the application still does not run, try booting with clean CONFIG.SYS and AUTOEXEC.BAT files. (In DOS/Windows 3.x environments, use a boot disk. In Windows 95, boot to the startup disk or simply rename CONFIG.SYS and AUTOEXEC.BAT files and boot.) If this proves unsuccessful, uninstall and reinstall the application. Note that reinstalling only corrects the problem in the case of file corruption or an incomplete installation.

To begin diagnosing the error message `Cannot log on to network`, make sure that all hardware is functioning properly and all software is installed correctly.

Client problems are common culprits of logon problems. When the client software is configured incorrectly, logon will most likely fail. The most common problems with client configuration are misspelling the login domain or preferred server name, or simply not having the client installed.

In Microsoft networking, computer names must be unique. If two users have the same computer name, network access will be denied to the computer that has been on for the least amount of time.

Installing a client in Windows installs the default protocol. Once a network client is installed, you have the ability to locate shared resources on a network. Actually accessing those resources requires that the requesting workstation and the computer with the shared resource use a common protocol. A common problem with protocols is binding. Binding means that the protocol is associated with the client software.

The protocol is the language that computers speak, and frame type is the dialect. IPX/SPX is a protocol that uses frame types. IPX/SPX frame types are automatically detected by default in Windows 95. Auto detect works most of the time; however, in NetWare environments that have more than one frame type running on the network, a Windows 95 client detects and binds only the first frame type it finds. If a client detects a different frame type on another computer, the client will not be able to access that computer. (Usually, the client cannot even see PCs running other frame types.) This can be corrected by manually selecting the frame type. Changing frame types requires you to reboot your system.

The TCP/IP protocol can be configured manually or dynamically.
The easiest way to configure it is through Dynamic Host Configuration
Protocol, or DHCP. DHCP is set up from a network server and auto-
matically assigns IP addresses to workstations configured to use DHCP.

Manual TCP/IP configuration requires you to add the IP address and
the subnet mask. The IP address must be unique to the network and acts
as the computer's street address. At a fundamental level, the subnet mask
must be common to all computers in your network because it defines
what network your computer is on. If the computer is in a routed network, it also requires a default gateway. All IP requests to unknown
addresses are forwarded to the default gateway. You can verify IP settings
by using the WINIPCFG utility and the PING utility.

NetBEUI is another common protocol. It requires no configuration
but is not routable. If your protocol is NetBEUI and you are in a routed
network, you will not be able to access network hosts on the other side
of the router.

**Access permissions can also prevent a user from logging on to the
network.** If the computer holding the shared resources does not grant
you access to the resource, you will not gain access.

ScanDisk is a utility that checks your system's FAT for inconsistencies
and corrects them. ScanDisk will also check and repair disk integrity and
directory structure.

The Device Manager utility was a new addition to troubleshooting
tools with the release of Windows 95. As part of the Plug and Play subsystem of Windows 95, Device Manager keeps track of which resources
are assigned to which devices. You can also manually configure resources
in Device Manager.

ATTRIB.EXE is the command prompt utility that enables you to
view and modify file attributes.

The EXTRACT.EXE command resides in the Windows\command
directory and can be used to extract a single file from the original installation media without reinstalling the entire application or OS. Windows
stores all installation files in compressed files called cabinet files or CABS.

The DEFRAG program is not normally considered a diagnostic tool. However, it is a good practice to defragment a drive before you begin troubleshooting in order to rule out fragmentation as a possible contributor. Also, a defragmented drive will perform better.

Edit is the DOS/Windows text editor. You can use Edit as a diagnostic tool by using it to view and modify text-based configuration files such as CONFIG.SYS, AUTOEXEC.BAT, and all INI files.

FDISK is the DOS/Windows disk partition tool. FDISK is a great utility to have on your boot floppy disk in case a partition becomes inactive or needs to be recreated.

MSD.EXE is the Microsoft diagnostics program that comes with DOS and Windows 3.x. MSD has a detailed memory map that is great for troubleshooting upper memory issues and device memory conflicts. MSD shows most system information, such as information on installed drivers, video, memory, and the operating system. MSD is not a good diagnostic tool for Windows 95 (it is also not included with Windows 95). The Windows 95 memory model misrepresents information to MSD.

MEM.EXE is available to DOS, Windows 3.x, and Windows 95. When executed from the command prompt, MEM.EXE displays what type of memory the system is using and what devices are using it. MEM.EXE is the correct utility to use when manually managing memory. You can display all MEM.EXE switches by issuing the mem /? command at the command prompt.

Windows-based systems offer the SysEdit program for quick access and editing of major Windows configuration files. Unlike EDIT.COM, which allows you to edit only one file at a time, running SysEdit brings up a window containing the CONFIG.SYS, AUTOEXEC.BAT, SYSTEM.INI, WIN.INI, PROTOCOL.INI, and MSMAIL.INI files in an editable state. If a quick look at Windows system files is what you need, SysEdit is a utility to remember. You can edit and close these files one at a time.

Originally, there were only three known virus types: the boot sector, the file infector, and the Trojan horse. Today multiple virus types affect virtually every facet of computer environments.

The boot sector virus copies itself to the boot tracks of hard drives and disks, replacing the original boot sector instructions with its own. Because of this, it is loaded into memory before anything else, allowing its instruction set to execute and spread when a computer boots or attempts to boot from the disk. An example is the Monkey-B virus.

The file infector is a virus that adds its own program code to other program executables. When the infected program is executed, the virus is activated and spreads itself to other programs. An example is the Anti-exe virus.

The Trojan horse type virus hides itself by appearing to actually belong on the disk. By being stealthy, this virus can cause very serious damage, even destroying data and disk sectors. An example is the Readme virus.

A more recent addition to the virus family is the polymorphic virus. The polymorphic virus is dangerous because it is designed to find out what virus-scanning program you are using and emulate it or avoid it. Most polymorphic viruses can be detected with a new update to your program's virus signature file. The polymorph must be cleaned immediately upon detection because once it is detected, it learns to hide from the program that detected it.

Another recent virus addition is the Macro virus. Macro viruses take advantage of word processor macro programming languages and cause problems with the application. Most macro viruses are mischievous only in that they cause an irritant such as the inability to save a document; however, some can damage data. A macro virus attaches itself to every document that is opened with the infected program by making itself a part of the normal layout template. An example would be the WAZU macro virus that attaches itself to the Microsoft Word NORMAL.DOT template.

Virus dangers range from a minor irritant to major program and hardware damage. Boot sector viruses can destroy hard drives. File infectors can damage programs and data. Trojan horse variations can damage computers and programs. Variations of all these virus types can damage virtually anything. The macro virus usually destroys only data.

Major sources of viruses have been shareware programs obtained from bulletin boards or the Internet. Once a computer is infected, floppy disks, network storage, and email can transmit viruses. Symptoms of infection can include (but are not limited to) the following: the hard disk stops booting, frequent corrupt files, programs start behaving funny or slowly, and program options quit working. Other symptoms are floppy disks that claim to be full when all files have been deleted, hard drive controller failures, and hard drive disappearance (it is not present or is unreadable from a boot disk). Other possibilities are the CMOS reverting to default settings even with a new battery, files changing size for no reason, a blank screen with a flashing cursor on boot up that does not go away, Windows crashes, and noticeable system slowdowns.

You can prevent virus infection by avoiding those activities that can expose your system to infection. Realistically, you should choose a virus protection package that can identify virus activity, remove the virus, and protect from further infection.

MS-DOS 6.x contains a virus protection utility called VSafe that provides minimal protection. Because VSafe has not been updated since the last release of DOS, the virus definition files the program uses to identify viruses are terribly outdated. Windows 3.x offered updated versions of VSafe and MSAV. Windows 95 has no built-in virus protection programs.

Many companies offer scanning, detection, and removal programs. In most cases, these programs scan memory during installation to make sure that virus activity is not present before completing the installation. If the program notes suspicious activity, your best course of action is to boot the system to a known clean boot disk with a command line scanning program and clean the system. When you are sure the system is clean, you can resume the installation.

Once installed, virus software runs at system boot-up and monitors constantly when the system is on. If a virus is detected, you should be prompted to clean the virus from the system.

NETWORKING

DOS has no networking capabilities out of the box. Networking in DOS requires use of a third-party product like Microsoft LAN Manager or Personal NetWare. (These products are no longer available, but both NetWare and Windows NT have DOS client software.)

Windows for Workgroups (WFW) was designed as a peer-to-peer networking solution that enabled computer users to share their local printers and disk space. Windows 3.1 can be networked with a third-party add-on. Windows 95, like WFW, is capable of networking out of the box. Both Windows 95 and WFW are capable of participating in a client/server environment as well.

Disk Drive sharing is installed as a service in Network Control Panel. Once installed, the File and Print Sharing service adds a Sharing menu option to Explorer and the context menu. Selecting the Sharing option invokes the Sharing properties sheet for that object. The properties sheets for various objects look different depending on the kind of access your computer is configured for. The two types of security are user-level and share-level. Share-level security is controlled from the share itself, whereas user-level security depends on a network file server for security. Each share requires a unique name. From across the network, shared objects viewed from Windows Explorer appear under the computer where they reside. When viewed from the computer where it is shared, the share appears as a regular folder icon with a hand under it.

Sharing Windows printers is very similar to sharing folders. After the File and Print Sharing service is installed, you can share a printer by selecting the printer, right-clicking, and selecting the Sharing option. Alternatively, you can open Control Panel, choose Networks, and click the File and Print Sharing button to activate print sharing. As with a shared file, you can tell when a printer is shared because a hand appears under the icon.

A network topology describes the way in which a network is connected. There are three common network topologies.

The first topology is called *bus* topology. In this design, all nodes have a unique address and connect to a central trunk. Any node can put information onto the network. Information put onto the network must contain destination address information to ensure the data can be delivered to its intended location. Each network node ignores data that is not intended for its unique address.

The second type of configuration is called the *ring* topology. The ring is just that: a closed ring of communication. Each network card in the ring network has a signal repeater built into it so that data not intended for that station can be repeated to the next node in the chain. Data is passed from node to node in this way until it reaches its intended destination. If there is no intended destination for the signal, it will eventually return to the originating node, which will remove it.

The third topology is the *star* topology. The star topology layout resembles a star or a snowflake: All nodes are linked into a central unit. The nodes communicate with one another through the central unit. The central unit organizes all network communication by polling nodes to see if they have data to transmit. If a node responds that it has data to transfer, the central communication unit gives that node a specific time slice in which to transmit. Large messages that would take longer than the allotted amount of time are broken into smaller packets and sent through several polling cycles until the transfer is complete.

You set up a system for Internet access by extending the computer onto the Internet by way of an access point, which might be either a network card or a modem. When you access the Internet via a network card, the network is connected to the Internet by means of a proxy server or direct connection and some kind of WAN link. In this instance, Internet access is obtained by setting the computer's browser to point to the proxy server. When a router is used, the gateway address must be specified to direct Internet traffic outside the local network.

Setting up a computer for Internet access via modem is very similar to configuring a computer for network access. The modem takes the place of the network card and, while connected, acts like one. To set up a modem connection, you must have a modem installed and configured. From the Dial-Up Networking folder located in the Windows 95 My Computer folder, double-click the Make New Connection icon to start the Make New Connection Wizard. Follow the wizard screens to create a new dial-up connection. Most dial-up connections will need to be configured to use the same protocol as the Internet service provider (ISP). To configure the protocol, right-click the newly created connection icon and select the Server Types tab. Most Internet service providers will require a DNS server setting. Setup instructions specific to your ISP are provided by the ISP.

TCP/IP is the protocol used by the Internet. In order to access the Internet, your system must use TCP/IP. An IP address is a specific street address on the Internet and consists of a 32-bit 4-octet binary number. Most people recognize an IP address in its decimal format, such as 45.222.202.7. Routers on the Internet interpret this decimal format in binary. For example, in binary, 45.222.202.7 would be 00101101.11011110.11001010.00000111.

Valid IP addresses are addresses that have been assigned by Stanford Research Institute (also known as InterNIC and SRINIC), the governing body of Internet addressing.

One of the most widely utilized Internet resources is electronic mail or email. Today's email programs offer a wide range of collaboration tools, which enable you to perform such tasks as attaching files and graphics to a message and sending it to another mail recipient. Originally, email was little more than an ASCII text file. Email uses the Internet and DNS (Domain Name Service) to locate the intended recipient of a message.

HTML, or Hypertext Markup Language, is a means of publishing information in a format common to Internet browsers and Web servers. HTML uses coded text to give the browser instructions on how text or pictures are to be displayed to the user. One such coded display is the *hyperlink.* A hyperlink appears to the user as underlined text that has a link to another Universal Resource Locator (URL) embedded into it. When you place the mouse arrow over a hyperlink, the arrow changes to a pointing hand. If you click while the pointing-hand cursor is over a hyperlink, you go straight to the embedded link.

HTTP is the Hypertext Transfer Protocol. Most browser software uses this protocol for its normal navigation. The HTTP:// at the beginning of the Address line designates that you are using HTTP to navigate.

FTP is the File Transfer Protocol. FTP does not require the use of a browser; it is integrated into the TCP/IP protocol suite. FTP is used through an FTP-aware operating system like Windows 95 (HyperTerminal and command prompt if TCP/IP is installed), a browser, or a third-party program written to utilize FTP. Users can copy files to or from a computer acting as an FTP host.

Domain names are names assigned to top-level servers that are registered on the Internet. One of several possible domain names can be assigned, depending on the role of the organization that owns the server. The most common and recognizable domain is the .COM domain. Others are .ORG for non-profit organizations, .EDU for educational institutions, .GOV for government organizations, .MIL for military installations, .INT for international organizations, and .NET for large network providers or ISPs. All these abbreviations are the domains. Domains are registered with DNS (Domain Name System) servers throughout the Internet. DNS entries enable Internet clients to know that 192.102.198.160 is intel.com. DNS resolution enables users to use their browsers to access different domains by name so they don't have to remember the IP addresses.

Internet service providers are companies that sell access to the Internet. Companies like these usually own blocks of registered IP address ranges, which they assign to individual modems when users dial in.

CHAPTER 20

Insider's Spin on the DOS/Windows Exam

At A Glance: Exam Information

Exam number	220-102
Minutes to complete	75
Questions	70
Passing score	66
Single-answer questions	No
Multiple-answer with correct number given	Yes
Multiple-answer without correct number given	No
Ranking order	No
Choices of A–D	Yes
Choices of A–E	No
Objective categories	5

The A+ DOS/Windows Exam consists of 70 multiple choice questions aimed at determining the test taker's skill level with DOS and Microsoft Windows. CompTIA states that this exam is designed so that a technician with six months experience in working with these products should be able to pass the exam. The exam must be completed in 75 minutes. The multiple choice questions are not misleading questions and mostly ask for specifics that require little thought for the experienced candidate. Experience with all five testing categories prior to taking this exam greatly increases the odds of passing. Several possible exams can be given. When this exam was in its beta cycle, there were a couple hundred questions. Once CompTIA decided what questions were valid, a few different versions of the exam were created. Although there are different versions, all the major categories are tested in each version.

GET INTO THE COMPTIA MINDFRAME

Unlike many vendor-specific exams, the A+ exams are as vendor non-specific as possible. One example would be the following: In questions about File and Printer Sharing in the network section of the exam, the questions maintain a vague nature even though Microsoft distributes the only operating systems being tested. The questions already assume that you know you are talking about the Windows File and Print Sharing Service, and a question would sound similar to the following:

1. Which of the following is a reason that a user cannot gain access to your shared drive? Choose the best answer.

   A. They have a different operating system than you.

   B. They are using a different font than you.

   C. They do not have permission.

   D. They have the wrong color scheme loaded.

Answer: C. The user must have permission to access a share.

The moral of the story is to not get overly concerned with vendor specifics; the overall concept is what is being tested.

UNDERSTAND THE TIME FRAME OF THE EXAM

This exam has been live since July 31, 1998 and replaced the previous A+ exam that focused primarily on DOS/Windows 3.1. Even though the new exam is primarily based on testing Windows 95 experience, Windows 3.1 concepts are still tested (but no more than 20%). The more you know about the exam the better. Knowing what you will face is one of the most important factors in exam preparation. Many candidates fail exams because they are caught off guard by concepts being tested. This exam is only the second version of the A+ DOS/Windows test, and because it is very new, it will probably not be replaced very soon.

GET USED TO ANSWERING QUESTIONS QUICKLY

You have one hour and 15 minutes to complete this exam. That is a little more than one minute per question. This is no cause for concern; the nature of this exam is very short multiple-choice questions. Knowing the concept being tested and reading the question carefully will help you identify the correct answer quickly. Do not be rushed. One hour and 15 minutes is plenty of time for this test. However, if you are running out of time, note that all unanswered questions are automatically wrong. Make an effort to at least mark questions before time runs out.

BECOME ACQUAINTED WITH ALL THE RESOURCES AVAILABLE TO YOU

Begin by registering for the A+ Certification exam by calling 1-800-77-MICRO (1-800-776-4276). Tests are given at Sylvan Prometric™ Authorized Test Centers. The A+ test is available throughout the world in English.

When you call, please have the following information available:

- Social Security number or Sylvan Prometric™ ID number (provided by Sylvan Prometric™)

- Mailing address and telephone number

- Employer or organization

- Date you wish to take the test

- Method of payment (credit card, check, purchase order; call CompTIA Certification Department at 630-268-1818 extension 305 or 359 for further clarification)

The test is available to anyone who wants to take it. There are no prerequisites. Candidates may retake the test as often as they like, but both the Core/Hardware and the DOS/Windows exams must be passed within 90 calendar days of each other in order for the user to become certified.

Visit the CompTIA Web site at `http://www.comptia.org` and familiarize yourself with the exam process and the objectives. Read the objectives and try to identify any areas in which you may be weak. Once you have made yourself familiar with all aspects of the exam, you may opt to try a practice exam. Practice exams are available from a number of third-party software developers.

WHERE THE QUESTIONS COME FROM

As stated before, the more you know about the testing process, the better your odds of passing. Some of the items that you should try to master are the types of questions, how they are created, and from where they come.

When this exam went through its beta-testing phase, hundreds of questions were submitted by the exam writers. Up to the release of the beta exam, these writers reviewed the questions and removed the ones that were deemed too vague, too specific, too leading, and so forth. Once the beta pool was selected, it was released to the public. Hundreds of beta test takers attempted to pass the exam. The beta results were reviewed, and again, the questions determined to be bad questions were removed from the pool. From this point, the final exams were compiled into the various DOS/Windows exams that you will encounter at testing time.

DIFFERENT FLAVORS OF QUESTIONS

Unlike many vendor-specific exams, there are currently no variations of CompTIA A+ exam questions. Multiple choice with answers from A–D are all that you will see.

IN THE FUTURE

In the future, you may see more exam questions geared toward Windows NT Workstation and Windows 98 in addition to the current pool of Windows 95 questions. As the industry evolves, the A+ exams must follow suit.

Another popular testing innovation in use by other vendors is that of the adaptive exam. The adaptive exam asks weighted questions. A question is asked that is considered to be of medium difficulty. If the candidate answers correctly, a more-difficult question is asked. If the candidate answers incorrectly, a less-difficult question is asked. This type of test asks fewer questions and takes the difficulty level of each question into account when figuring the final score.

Exam writers see the adaptive exam as a better testing tool because performance-based questions actually ask the test taker to demonstrate a skill. The exams, being shorter in length, give the exam taker a smaller sample of the questions in the question pool, making it more difficult for memorization to occur. Less memorization equates to a more valid test because the candidate will not have had his peers tell him all the answers prior to the test.

CONCEPTS YOU MUST KNOW

This section outlines the concepts you must know for the various objective categories covered on the exam.

Function, Structure, Operation, and File Management

Absolute must-have concepts for this section:

1. Know beyond a shadow of a doubt how to navigate using DOS, Windows 3.x File Manager and Program Manager, and Windows 95 Explorer.

2. Know what files each system uses and why.

3. Know what each file contains.

4. Understand the Windows 95 Registry (not each key, just user and system).

5. Know the different file systems.

Memory Management

Absolute must-have concepts for this section:

1. Know the difference between upper, high, extended, expanded, and virtual memory.

2. Know what causes a memory conflict.

3. Know what tools are used for memory troubleshooting and how to use them.

Installation, Configuration, and Upgrading

Absolute must-have concepts for this section:

1. Know how to create a boot floppy disk.

2. Know the steps to perform before an upgrade to Windows 95.

3. Know DOS mode.

4. Know Safe Mode.

5. Know common Windows 95 configuration utilities (Device Manager, Control Panel, and so on).

6. Know how to configure and change Windows 95 printing.

7. Know how to install and launch applications from Windows 95.

Diagnosing and Troubleshooting

Absolute must-have concepts for this section:

1. There is no substitute for good troubleshooting skills.

2. Know all the common computer error codes and messages.

3. Know common Windows 95 printing problems.

4. Understand and correct common application problems.

5. Understand what a virus is and does.

6. Know the appropriate utility to use in a given situation.

Networks

Absolute must-have concepts for this section:

1. Understand resource access from across the network.

2. Know common problems specific to network type.

3. Know how to set up dial-up access to the Internet.

4. Know common Internet terminology.

Finally...

All in all, this is not a difficult test for those candidates that have a few months experience and know the objectives. The concepts are the testable portion of what you have studied. You do not have to have the memory map memorized; you simply have to know what it is and what problems are common with it.

CompTIA Web Site Frequently Asked Questions

The CompTIA Web site is located at http://www.comptia.org and has a great wealth of information. The following list of frequently asked questions can be obtained from the Web site. (I added them to this section to save you valuable preparation time.)

Retaking the Test

I took the old version of the A+ test, and my score report says I have 90 days to retake the test. Didn't the old test close on July 30, 1998?

On any score report dated on or before July 30, the 90-day stipulation is incorrect. You were right that you had to pass both tests by close of business day July 30. This message was given out when you called Sylvan Prometric to register as part of the forced message. Furthermore, this has been posted on our Web site. The old test was no longer available after close of day on July 30, 1998.

Who May Take the Test

What qualifications are needed to take the exams?

A+ Certification is open to anyone who wants to take the tests. The A+ exam is targeted for entry-level computer service technicians with at least 6 months on-the-job experience. No specific requirements are necessary, except payment of the fee.

How Many Questions?

How many questions are on the new A+ tests?

There are 69 questions on the Core/Hardware portion. There are 70 questions on the DOS/Windows portion.

Percentage Needed to Pass

To pass the Core/Hardware exam, a score of at least 65% is required. To pass the DOS/Windows exam, a score of at least 66% is required. Candidates are given one hour to complete the Core/Hardware portion, and candidates are given 1 hour and 15 minutes to complete the DOS/Windows.

Cost for the Test

$215 for both exams.

90 Calendar Days

What is the 90 calendar days rule?

The 90 calendar days rule states that a candidate must take the Core/Hardware and DOS/Windows portion within 90 calendar days of one another. If the two parts are taken outside of the 90 calendar day window, the candidate will re-take both sections in order to receive the A+ designation. It is the responsibility of the candidate to count the days and to take the portion of the exam that is needed by the 90th calendar day. It is for this reason that we strongly encourage candidates to take the Core/Hardware and DOS/Windows portions at the same time.

> **NOTE**
>
> If you took the Core/Hardware or DOS/Windows modules prior to July 31, 1998 and did not earn your A+ certification, you will need to retake both portions to become A+ certified. This is required because the new exam does not reflect any of the materials covered on the previous version.

Mixing and Matching Tests

Can I take part of the earlier version of the A+ exam and part of the exam released on July 31, 1998 to earn my certification?

The earlier version of the A+ exam is no longer available. If a candidate did not receive the A+ designation prior to July 31, 1998, both the Core/Hardware and DOS/Windows portions of the revised exam must be taken, regardless if one part of the A+ exam was previously passed.

Macintosh Questions

Are there going to be Macintosh questions on the Core/Hardware exam after July 31?

Due to the discontinuation of the Macintosh OS module, there will be no Macintosh questions on the A+ certification exam.

Customer Service Questions

Are customer service questions included?

There are customer service questions on the Core/Hardware exam. These questions are not included in the final score. The scores from this section are reported at the bottom of the score report so that employers and clients know how the candidate performed on this section.

Seeing the Answers

If I failed, may I see my answers?

As an internationally recognized entry-level professional certification for service technicians, the test must remain secure at all times. Thus, no test questions or answers are ever released. In order to maintain the high quality of the exam, no exceptions are made.

Failing Part of the Test

If I failed a portion of the test, will I have to pay to retake that portion?

Yes, each time you take the test, you must pay a fee. Call Sylvan Prometric at 1-800-776-4276 to re-register.

Unhappy with a Test Question

What if I am unhappy with a test question?

If you are unhappy with a test question, you may comment on this issue at the time you take the exam. Furthermore, we invite your comments in writing. Please fax them to 630-268-1384 to the attention of the Certifications Department.

Test Vouchers

How long is my test voucher good for?

The vouchers are valid for one calendar year and expire after that period.

Taking the Modules Separately

Can I take the Core/Hardware and the DOS/Windows exams at different times?

Although it is possible, we strongly recommend that you take both parts of the exam at the same time.

Lost Certificate or ID

What do I do if I lose my A+ certificate or ID card?

Please call Sylvan Prometric at 1-800-776-4276 and request a replacement.

How Long Is Certification Good For

How long is the A+ certification good for?

Once you are A+ certified, you are certified for life.

New Exam Codes

What are the new exam codes for the new A+ tests?

The new exam code for the Core/Hardware exam is 220-101. The new exam code for the DOS/Windows exam is 220-102.

Getting a Reprint of Certificate

If you need a new certificate within three months of the original printing, the first copy is free. Each subsequent printing carries a $15 charge. This charge is also instituted for any reprint requested after six months of certifying.

I took the Macintosh OS Module to earn my A+ certification, and I know that you are no longer offering this module. However, I lost my certificate. Can I get a reprint?

Yes, A+ certificates with the Macintosh OS Specialty will continue to be printed indefinitely. However, you will receive a certificate and logo sheets (with the new A+ logo) only. Pins and ID cards will not be provided. Please call Sylvan Prometric at 1-800-776-4276 to request a reprint.

I earned my certification under the previous version of the exam. All the other techs have been certified under the test version as of July 31, and our certificates do not look the same. Can I get my certificate reprinted on the new certificate paper?

Yes, this option is available to you. There will be a $15 charge for this printing because this is considered a request for a duplicate. Please call Sylvan Prometric at 1-800-776-4276 to request a copy.

Publisher's Note:

The hotlist is meant as a reference for you to use if you run across a term you do not know while studying for this exam. The terms themselves are not likely to appear on the A+ Certification exams. However, you need to know the terms and understand the concepts in order to answer questions that deal with them.

Chapter 12 contains a complete "Hotlist of Exam-Critical Concepts." That hotlist is applicable to material covered on both the Core/Hardware and DOS/Windows exams. In the interest of avoiding repetitive material, we direct you to Chapter 12, which appears in Part II, "Inside the A+ Core/Hardware Exam."

C H A P T E R 21

Hotlist of
Exam-Critical Concepts

CHAPTER 22

Sample Test Questions

QUESTIONS

1. From which file is EMM386.EXE executed?

   A. AUTOEXEC.BAT

   B. CONFIG.SYS

   C. WIN.INI

   D. SYSTEM.INI

2. SYSTEM.INI contains which of the following?

   A. Instructions on how to configure Control Panel

   B. Instructions on how to configure the computer system

   C. Program Manager settings

   D. DOS configuration variables

3. Which of the following is a real Windows 95 Registry key?

   A. HKEY_USERS_MACHINE

   B. HKEY_CONTROL_SET

   C. HKEY_DYN_DATA

   D. HKEY_FOREIGN_MACHINES

4. What is the Windows 95 equivalent of Windows 3.x File Manager?

   A. Explorer

   B. Internet Explorer

   C. Control Panel

   D. Start menu

5. Which of the following shows the appropriate syntax for the COPY *command?*

   A. `Copy  c:\<filename> to a:\`

   B. `Copy  c:\<filename> to c:\<filename>`

   C. `Copy c:\<filename>  c:\<new filename>`

   D. `<filename> copy a:\`

6. How do you find a file's attributes in Windows 95?

   A. Select the file, and then select Attributes from the File menu.

   B. Select the file, right-click, and select Attributes.

   C. Select the file, right-click, and select File Attributes.

   D. Select the file, right-click, select Properties, and view the attributes from the General tab.

7. *How do you view hidden files from Explorer?*
   A. From the File menu, select View Hidden Files.
   B. From the View menu, select View Hidden Files.
   C. From the File menu, select Options and select View Hidden Files.
   D. From the View menu, select Options and select View Hidden Files.

8. *What utility do you use to speed up programs and optimize disk space?*
   A. Defrag
   B. ScanDisk
   C. System Monitor
   D. MSD

9. *You boot to a floppy disk and try to view your 6.0GB partition. FDISK states that there are no logical drives defined. What is most likely the problem?*
   A. You have no logical drives defined.
   B. You have no physical drives defined.
   C. Your boot disk was not created with Windows 95 OSR2.
   D. Your boot floppy does not have large disk support enabled.

10. *You cannot read a DOS backup set in Windows 95 Backup. What is the problem?*
   A. You cannot read a DOS backup set from Windows 95 Backup.
   B. You have not imported the backup set.
   C. You have not recovered the backup database.
   D. You have not performed a merge of the backup databases.

11. *What must you do in Windows 95 to move the swap file to the D: drive?*
   A. Boot to DOS and copy the WIN386.SWP file to the D: drive.
   B. Disable virtual memory.
   C. Modify the swap file location from SYSTEM.INI.
   D. From the System icon in Control Panel, select the Virtual Memory tab and select Manual Memory Configuration. Change the path to the new swap file.

12. **What is memory above 640KB called?**
    A. High memory
    B. Virtual memory
    C. Conventional memory
    D. Shadow memory

13. **What utility uses buffer space to optimize disk I/O.**
    A. ScanDisk
    B. DRVSPACE
    C. SMARTDRV
    D. RAMDrive

14. **GPF stands for what?**
    A. General Program Failure
    B. Generic Protection Fault
    C. General Protection Fault
    D. General Processor Fault

15. **What command syntax will cause an unconditional format and transfer the system?**
    A. `Format /q/s`
    B. `Format /u/s`
    C. `Format /u/q`
    D. `Format /s`

16. **The DOS 6.22 SYS C:\ command transfers what files to C:\?**
    A. IO.SYS, MSDOS.SYS, COMMAND.COM
    B. IBMDOS.COM, IBMIO.COM, COMMAND.COM
    C. IO.SYS, CONFIG.SYS, COMMAND.COM
    D. IO.SYS, MSDOS.SYS, COMMAND.COM, DRVSPACE.BIN

17. **Where do you create a Windows 95 start disk?**
    A. Control Panel, Add/Remove Programs, Startup Disk tab
    B. Control Panel, System, Startup Disk tab
    C. Control Panel, Add/Remove Hardware, Startup Disk tab
    D. Start menu, Run, type **startdisk**

18. *You just upgraded Windows 3.x to Windows 95, and all your program groups are missing. What is the problem?*

    A. You overwrote the program groups in the upgrade.
    B. You did not select to migrate programs during setup.
    C. You did not save your previous installation.
    D. You installed into a different directory from that of the previous installation.

19. *You just upgraded Windows 3.x and DOS 6.22 to Windows 95, and you do not have the option to boot to your previous version of Windows. What is the problem?*

    A. You installed into the same directory as that of the previous installation.
    B. You did not select to migrate programs during setup.
    C. You did not save your previous installation.
    D. You installed into a different directory from that of the previous installation.

20. *From Windows 95 Device Manager, you select a plug-and-play device and select Remove. What is the result?*

    A. The device is removed from the system and cannot be added again.
    B. The device is removed but will be detected by Plug and Play when the system starts again.
    C. The device is disabled in this profile.
    D. The device must be added manually.

21. *What must you do to create a disk partition larger than 2GB?*

    A. Use DOS FDISK.
    B. Use a Windows 95 OSR2 startup disk.
    C. Use a Windows 95 OSR2 startup disk and enable large disk support.
    D. This cannot be done.

22. *What file launches Windows?*

    A. WIN.EXE
    B. WIN.COM
    C. WIN.INI
    D. PROGMAN.EXE

23. *What two tabs are common to all printers in Windows 95?*

    A. General and Paper
    B. Paper and Details
    C. Details and General
    D. General and Driver

24. *What is the default print spool format of Windows 95?*

    A. EMF
    B. RAW
    C. PCL
    D. PostScript

25. *What do you do to start Windows 95 with a minimal set of drivers?*

    A. Press F5 when booting.
    B. Press F8 when booting.
    C. Boot to DOS mode.
    D. Boot to Safe Mode.

26. *How can you fix* Incorrect DOS version *problems?*

    A. Use the DOS SETVER command.
    B. Use the DOS VER command.
    C. Use the DOS TIME command.
    D. Rerun Setup.

27. *What is the most likely cause of a printer printing gibberish?*

    A. Incorrect print priority
    B. Incorrect print spool settings
    C. Incorrect printer driver
    D. Incorrect share settings

28. *What will overcome a system lockup in Windows 95?*

    A. Pressing Alt+Tab.
    B. Pressing Ctrl+Alt+Del.
    C. Pressing Ctrl+Option+Apple.
    D. Pressing Ctrl+Esc.

29. *If Windows 95 cannot be unlocked from Task Manager, what is the problem?*

   A. You did not press Ctrl+Alt+Del hard enough.
   B. Hardware failure.
   C. Win16 Mutex Flag is set.
   D. Programming code error.

30. *What do you modify to configure a legacy DOS application to run under Windows?*

   A. CONFIG.SYS
   B. AUTOEXEC.BAT
   C. PROGRAM.INI
   D. The application's PIF

31. *A DOS PIF is automatically created when?*

   A. You run Windows 95 Setup.
   B. You run the DOS application for the first time in Windows 95.
   C. You run the DOS application for the second time in Windows 95.
   D. Never.

32. *What utility is used to retrieve a file from a compressed CAB file?*

   A. Extract
   B. Expand
   C. WinZip
   D. CABOpen

33. *Your virus detection software detected a virus the last time you booted, and you did not clean it. Now you boot but do not find a virus. What is the problem?*

   A. Faulty virus detection software.
   B. The virus disappeared by itself.
   C. The virus was a Trojan horse virus.
   D. The virus was a polymorphic virus.

34. *What type of networking was Windows for Workgroups designed to do out of the box?*

    A. Ethernet

    B. Peer-to-peer

    C. Client/server

    D. Token-ring

35. *A bus network is characteristic of what type of network?*

    A. ARCnet

    B. Token-ring

    C. Ethernet

    D. Fast ethernet

36. *What type of domain is www.microsoft.com?*

    A. Government

    B. Internet service provider

    C. Organization

    D. Commercial

37. *One of your network clients cannot access other computer shares in an IPX network. What is most likely the problem?*

    A. Incorrect TCP/IP settings

    B. Incorrect frame type

    C. Incorrect computer name

    D. Duplicate IPX network number

38. *Which of the following is the most likely reason why another user cannot gain access to your shared drive?*

    A. He has a different operating system than you.

    B. He is using a different font than you.

    C. His computer is configured with a different protocol than yours.

    D. He has the wrong color scheme loaded.

39. *A client configured for a routed TCP/IP network requires what three settings?*

    A. IP address, subnet mask, DNS server

    B. IP address, DNS server, default gateway

    C. IP address, default gateway, subnet mask

    D. Subnet mask, DNS server, default gateway

ANSWERS AND EXPLANATIONS

1. **B**   EMM386.EXE is the enhanced memory manager and is loaded in the CONFIG.SYS file.

2. **B**   SYSTEM.INI contains the instructions telling Windows how to configure the system.

3. **C**   HKEY_DYN_DATA is the only real Windows 95 Registry key in this list. The others are made up. The real Registry keys are HKEY_LOCAL_MACHINE, HKEY_USERS, HKEY_CURRENT_USER, HKEY_CURRENT_CONFIG, HKEY_CLASSES_ROOT, and HKEY_DYN_DATA.

4. **A**   The Windows Explorer interface replaced File Manager.

5. **C**   The syntax in answer C is correct. Although answers A and B look correct, the presence of the word "to" makes the copy fail. Answer D just doesn't work.

6. **D**   Selecting Properties from the context menu will display the file attributes.

7. **D**   To view hidden files from Explorer, you must select the View, Options command and choose the option to view hidden files.

8. **A**   Defrag optimizes disk space and speeds up programs.

9. **C**   To be able to view a partition that is larger than 2GB from FDISK, you must enable large disk support, which is available when using FDISK from Windows 95 OSR/2. The key to this question is the 6.0GB partition.

10. **A**   The different versions of Backup that ship with DOS and Windows 95 cannot read one another's backup sets.

11. **D**   To use a swap file on a disk other than the disk where Windows is installed, you must choose to manually manage the memory configuration.

12. **A**   High memory is the area *above* the first 640KB.

13. **C** Smart Drive utilizes disk buffers to improve disk I/O performance.

14. **C** GPF stands for General Protection Fault.

15. **B** The unconditional format is invoked by the /U switch; the system is transferred by using the /S switch.

16. **D** DOS 6.22 contained the first SYS.COM that transferred DRVSPACE.BIN in addition to COMMAND.COM, MSDOS.SYS, and IO.SYS.

17. **A** Start disks are created from the Control Panel, Add/Remove Programs applet, Startup Disk tab.

18. **D** If you install Windows 95 into a different directory, program groups are not migrated.

19. **A - C** If you install Windows 95 into the same directory as the previous version of Windows, dual-booting is not an option. Also, if you choose not to save the upgraded program files, the dual-boot feature is removed.

20. **B** Removing a plug-and-play device from Device Manager does not permanently remove it. It will be detected again when the system is rebooted. To permanently remove a device, you must disable it in Device Manager.

21. **C** The Windows 95 OSR/2 version of FDISK allows you to enable large disk support, after which FDISK will allow you to create partitions larger than 2GB.

22. **B** WIN.COM launches Windows.

23. **C** For all printers managed by Windows 95, the properties sheet contains a General tab and a Details tab.

24. **A** Enhanced Metafile or EMF is the default Windows 95 spool format.

25. **D** Safe Mode, by definition, loads Windows with a minimal set of drivers.

26. **A** Adding the SETVER command to CONFIG.SYS eliminates the Incorrect DOS version error.

27. **C** An incorrect printer driver is the most common reason a printer prints jibberish.

28. **B** The Ctrl+Alt+Del key sequence invokes Task Manager and enables you to overcome a system lock up. Ctrl+Alt+Del will not always recover a system lockup if a 16-bit program freezes when it has control of the processor.

29. **C** The Win16 Mutex Flag is set to indicate that a 16-bit program froze up when it had processor control.

30. **D** The PIF is the Windows program information file that tells Windows how to run the program.

31. **B** Running a DOS program (inside Windows) from its executable file creates a PIF file.

32. **A** The Windows 95 Extract command extracts files from cabinet files.

33. **D** A polymorphic virus can hide from a virus detection program that has previously detected it.

34. **B** Peer-to-peer was the network design that WFW supported without purchasing any further software.

35. **C - D** Ethernet networks use a bus topology.

36. **D** Commercial, designated by .COM.

37. **B** An incorrect or different frame type is the equivalent of two or more computers speaking the same language but not understanding the different dialects.

38. **C** Computers sharing information must be using a common protocol (speaking the same language).

39. **C** The IP address identifies this computer as a unique location; the default gateway is where the computer forwards requests that are addressed to computers on unknown networks; and the subnet masks distinguish which networks are local and which are remote.

CHAPTER 23

Did You Know?

Function, Structure, Operation, and File Management

- ◆ The original name for IO.SYS was IBMIO.COM.

- ◆ The original name for MSDOS.SYS was IBMDOS.COM.

- ◆ Windows 3.x used the system Registry as does Windows 95, but only for application registration.

- ◆ During an upgrade from Windows 3.x to Windows 95, the file that Windows 95 looks for to qualify the upgrade is GDI.EX_ (GDI.EXE compressed).

- ◆ Multiple products are available that can toggle the active partition upon start up so you can select an operating system from a menu. The two most popular are Partition Magic by PowerQuest and Norton Disk Commander.

- ◆ FAT32 uses disk space more efficiently than FAT because FAT32 uses a smaller cluster size.

Memory Management

- ◆ Disabling Windows 95 control of virtual memory can prevent a computer from booting.

- ◆ Plug-and-play hardware helps eliminate memory overlap errors.

Installation, Configuration, and Upgrading

- ◆ It is possible to trick the OSR2 installation into thinking that a Windows 95 Version A installation is actually a Windows 95 Version B installation, thus allowing an upgrade from Win 95 A to OSR2. To do this, run the installation from Windows 95. When you're asked to accept licensing terms, do nothing. Press Alt+Esc to open the Start menu, select Run, and then select Notepad. When Notepad opens, select SETUPPPP.TXT from the c:\winins40 directory. Go to the heading [data] and make the first line read OEMUP=1. Save and exit. Press Alt+Tab to return to the licensing screen and continue.

- A third release of Windows 95 labeled as Windows 95 C or OSR2.5 has shipped with OEM products since January 1998.

- The Windows 98 boot disk has CD-ROM drivers already installed. If you boot to a Windows 98 startup disk, you see a CONFIG.SYS menu that asks if you would like to boot with CD-ROM support. Selecting this option starts the search for an IDE or SCSI CD-ROM drive.

- Windows 98 has a system information utility that contains a tool called Version Conflict Manager. The Version Conflict Manager knows of potential problems with certain DLL files and will allow you to restore originals when there is a conflict.

- The Windows 98 Update Web site contains all the latest files for Windows 98. Simply visit the site and choose Update to install the latest versions to your computer.

- Windows NT uses a file system called NTFS that allows you to add security to local files and folders.

- NTFS formatted partitions are not recognizable from DOS boot floppies.

Diagnosing and Troubleshooting

- Numerous troubleshooting tools that are available on the market can make your life easier. Microsoft publishes *TechNet* on a monthly basis. *TechNet* lists common issues related to all Microsoft products and their appropriate fixes.

- Third-party utilities like Norton Utilities and Nuts and Bolts can perform deeper troubleshooting functions than the operating system utilities alone.

Networks

- CompTIA has plans to release a vendor in specific Networking Certification to accompany A+. It will be called Network+.

- A cable modem gives you Internet access that can match speeds of a 10Mbps (megabits per second) network and does not tie up your phone line or cable television. A cable modem does display your computer to all other users in your workgroup, though, so it is important that you *don't* share directories with the Full Control option. (Sharing to everyone with full access is always a bad idea!)

INDEX

MCSE Fast Track: Networking Essentials

1-56205-939-4,
$19.99, 9/98

 MCSE Fast Track: TCP/IP

1-56205-937-8,
$19.99, 9/98

 MCSE Fast Track: Windows 98

0-7357-0016-8,
$19.99, 12/98

 MCSE Fast Track: Internet Information Server 4

1-56205-936-X,
$19.99, 9/98

 MCSE Fast Track: Windows NT Server 4

1-56205-935-1,
$19.99, 9/98

 MCSD Fast Track: Solution Architectures

0-7357-0029-X,
$19.99, Q2/99

 MCSE Fast Track: Windows NT Server 4 Enterprise

1-56205-940-8,
$19.99, 9/98

 MCSD Fast Track: Visual Basic 6, Exam 70-175

0-7357-0018-4,
$19.99, 12/98

 MCSE Fast Track: Windows NT Workstation 4

1-56205-938-6,
$19.99, 9/98

 MCSD Fast Track: Visual Basic 6, Exam 70-176

0-7357-0019-2,
$19.99, 12/98

TRAINING GUIDES

*Complete, Innovative,
Accurate, Thorough*

Our next generation *Training Guides* have been developed to help you study and retain the essential knowledge needed to pass the MCSE exams. We know your study time is valuable, and we have made every effort to make the most of it by presenting clear, accurate, and thorough information.

In creating this series, our goal was to raise the bar on how MCSE content is written, developed, and presented. From the two-color design that gives you easy access to content, to the new software simulator that allows you to perform tasks in a simulated operating system environment, we are confident that you will be well-prepared for exam success.

Our New Riders Top Score Software Suite is a custom-developed set of fully functioning software applications that work in conjunction with the *Training Guide* by providing you with the following:

The Exam Simulator tests your hands-on knowledge with over 150 fact-based and situational-based questions.
Electronic Study Cards really test your knowledge with explanations that are linked to an electronic version of the *Training Guide.*
Electronic Flash Cards help you retain the facts in a time-tested method.
An Electronic Version of the Book provides quick searches and compact, mobile study.
Customizable Software adapts to the way you want to learn.

MCSE Training Guide: Networking Essentials, Second Edition

1-56205-919-X, $49.99, 9/98

MCSE Training Guide: Windows NT Server 4, Second Edition

1-56205-916-5, $49.99, 9/98

MCSE Training Guide: Windows NT Server 4 Enterprise, Second Edition

1-56205-917-3, $49.99, 9/98

MCSE Training Guide: Windows NT Workstation 4, Second Edition

1-56205-918-1, $49.99, 9/98

MCSE Training Guide: Windows 98

1-56205-890-8, $49.99, 2/99

MCSE Training Guide: TCP/IP, Second Edition

1-56205-920-3, $49.99, 11/98

MCSE Training Guide: SQL Server 7 Administration

0-7357-0003-6, $49.99, Q2/99

MCSE Training Guide: SQL Server 7 Design and Implementation

0-7357-0004-4, $49.99, Q2/99

MCSD Training Guide: Solution Architectures

0-7357-0026-5, $49.99, Q2/99

MCSD Training Guide: Visual Basic 6

0-7357-0002-8, $49.99, Q1/99

TRAINING GUIDES
First Editions

Your Quality Elective Solution

MCSE Training Guide: Systems Management Server 1.2, 1-56205-748-0

MCSE Training Guide: SQL Server 6.5 Administration, 1-56205-726-X

MCSE Training Guide: SQL Server 6.5 Design and Implementation, 1-56205-830-4

MCSE Training Guide: Windows 95, 70-064 Exam, 1-56205-880-0

MCSE Training Guide: Exchange Server 5, 1-56205-824-X

MCSE Training Guide: Internet Explorer 4, 1-56205-889-4

MCSE Training Guide: Microsoft Exchange Server 5.5, 1-56205-899-1

MCSE Training Guide: IIS 4, 1-56205-823-1

MCSD Training Guide: Visual Basic 5, 1-56205-850-9

MCSD Training Guide: Microsoft Access, 1-56205-771-5

TESTPREP SERIES

Practice and cram with the new, revised Second Edition TestPreps

Questions. Questions. And more questions. That's what you'll find in our New Riders *TestPreps*. They're great practice books when you reach the final stage of studying for the exam. We recommend them as supplements to our *Training Guides*.

What makes these study tools unique is that the questions are the primary focus of each book. All the text in these books supports and explains the answers to the questions.

Scenario-based questions challenge your experience.

Multiple-choice questions prep you for the exam.

Fact-based questions test your product knowledge.

Exam strategies assist you in test preparation.

Complete yet concise explanations of answers make for better retention.

Two practice exams prepare you for the real thing.

Fast Facts offer you everything you need to review in the testing center parking lot.

MCSE TestPrep: Networking Essentials, Second Edition

0-7357-0010-9, $19.99, 12/98

MCSE TestPrep: Windows 95, Second Edition

0-7357-0011-7, $19.99, 12/98

MCSE TestPrep: Windows NT Server 4, Second Edition

0-7357-0012-5, $19.99, 12/98

MCSE TestPrep: Windows NT Server 4 Enterprise, Second Edition

0-7357-0009-5, $19.99, 11/98

MCSE TestPrep: Windows NT Workstation 4, Second Edition

0-7357-0008-7, $19.99, 12/98

MCSE TestPrep: TCP/IP, Second Edition

0-7357-0025-7, $19.99, 12/98

MCSE TestPrep:
Windows 98

1-56205-922-X, $19.99, 11/98

TESTPREP SERIES
FIRST EDITIONS

MCSE TestPrep: SQL Server 6.5
Administration, 0-7897-1597-X

MCSE TestPrep: SQL Server 6.5 Design
and Implementation, 1-56205-915-7

MCSE TestPrep: Windows 95 70-64
Exam, 0-7897-1609-7

MCSE TestPrep: Internet Explorer 4,
0-7897-1654-2

MCSE TestPrep: Exchange Server 5.5,
0-7897-1611-9

MCSE TestPrep: IIS 4.0, 0-7897-1610-0

How to Contact Us

IF YOU NEED THE LATEST UPDATES ON A TITLE THAT YOU'VE PURCHASED:

1) Visit our Web site at www.newriders.com.

2) Click on the DOWNLOADS link, and enter your book's ISBN number, which is located on the back cover in the bottom right-hand corner.

3) In the DOWNLOADS section, you'll find available updates that are linked to the book page.

IF YOU ARE HAVING TECHNICAL PROBLEMS WITH THE BOOK OR THE CD THAT IS INCLUDED:

1) Check the book's information page on our Web site according to the instructions listed above, or

2) Email us at support@mcp.com, or

3) Fax us at (317) 817-7488 attn: Tech Support.

IF YOU HAVE COMMENTS ABOUT ANY OF OUR CERTIFICATION PRODUCTS THAT ARE NON-SUPPORT RELATED:

1) Email us at certification@mcp.com, or

2) Write to us at New Riders, 201 W. 103rd St., Indianapolis, IN 46290-1097, or

3) Fax us at (317) 581-4663.

IF YOU WISH TO PREVIEW A[N] OF OUR CERTIFICATION BOO[K] FOR CLASSROOM USE:

Email us at pr@mcp.com. Your message [?] include your name, title, training company school, department, address, phone numb[er] office days/hours, text in use, and enrollm[ent] Send these details along with your reques[t] desk/examination copies and/or additiona[l] information.

IF YOU ARE OUTSIDE THE UNITED STATES AND NEED TO FIND A DISTRIBUTOR IN YOUR AREA:

Please contact our international department at international@mcp.com.

WE WANT TO KNOW WHAT YOU THINK

To better serve you, we would like your opinion on the content and quality of this book.
Please complete this card and mail it to us or fax it to 317-581-4663.

Name _____

Address _____

City _____ State_____ Zip _____

Phone _____ Email Address _____

Occupation _____

Which certification exams have you already
passed? _____
_____
_____
_____

Which certification exams do you plan to take? __
_____
_____
_____

What influenced your purchase of this book?
❑ Recommendation   ❑ Cover Design
❑ Table of Contents   ❑ Index
❑ Magazine Review   ❑ Advertisement
❑ Publisher's reputation   ❑ Author Name

How would you rate the contents of this book?
❑ Excellent   ❑ Very Good
❑ Good   ❑ Fair
❑ Below Average   ❑ Poor

What other types of certification products will
you buy/have you bought to help you prepare for
the exam?
❑ Quick reference books   ❑ Testing software
❑ Study guides   ❑ Other

What do you like most about this book? Check
all that apply.
❑ Content   ❑ Writing Style
❑ Accuracy   ❑ Examples
❑ Listings   ❑ Design
❑ Index   ❑ Page Count
❑ Price   ❑ Illustrations

What do you like least about this book? Check all
that apply.
❑ Content   ❑ Writing Style
❑ Accuracy   ❑ Examples
❑ Listings   ❑ Design
❑ Index   ❑ Page Count
❑ Price   ❑ Illustrations

What would be a useful follow-up book to this one for you?_____

Where did you purchase this book?_____

Can you name a similar book that you like better than this one, or one that is as good? Why?_____

_____
_____

How many New Riders books do you own? _____

What are your favorite certification or general computer book titles? _____

_____

What other titles would you like to see us develop? _____

_____

Any comments for us? _____

_____

Fold here and tape to mail

Place
Stamp
Here

New Riders
201 W. 103rd St.
Indianapolis, IN 46290